MW01077639

Robert Gioielli → prof & author of Univ of
Cincinnati

America's First Black Socialist

def of pre-eminent

- Black Codes in Ohio

- what was our econ system
B4 capitalism

- Lane Seminary & Colonization
debates in 1820's

- Coloniza'n → white lead movemt

- Urban Roots podcast 9/24 sat 24 7p

- Producerism - mercantile
rob.gioielli@uc.edu libraries
OhmuseumO?

America's First
Black Socialist

The Radical Life
of Peter H. Clark

Nikki M. Taylor

UNIVERSITY PRESS OF KENTUCKY

Scholarly publisher for the Commonwealth, serving Bellarmine University, Berea College, Centre College of Kentucky, Eastern Kentucky University, The Filson Historical Society, Georgetown College, Kentucky Historical Society, Kentucky State University, Morehead State University, Murray State University, Northern Kentucky University, Transylvania University, University of Kentucky, University of Louisville, and Western Kentucky University.

Editorial and Sales Offices: The University Press of Kentucky
663 South Limestone Street, Lexington, Kentucky 40508-4008
www.kentuckypress.com

17 16 15 14 13   5 4 3 2 1

Library of Congress Cataloging-in-Publication Data

Taylor, Nikki Marie, 1972-
  America's first black socialist : the radical life of Peter H. Clark / Nikki M. Taylor.
    pages cm
  Includes bibliographical references and index.
  ISBN 978-0-8131-4077-3 (hardcover : alk. paper) — ISBN 978-0-8131-4078-0 (pdf) (print) — ISBN 978-0-8131-4099-5 (epub) (print)   1. Clark, Peter Humphries, 1829–1925.   2. Ohio—Politics and government—19th century.   3. African Americans—Ohio—Politics and government—19th century.   4. African Americans—Ohio—Social conditions—19th century.   5. Political activists—Ohio—Biography.   6. African American political activists—Ohio—Biography.   7. Educators—Ohio—Biography.   8. African American educators—Ohio—Biography.   9. Socialists—Ohio—Biography.   I. Title.
  F496.C53T39 2013
  977.1'03092—dc23
  [B]

                                                    2012041012

This book is printed on acid-free paper meeting
the requirements of the American National Standard
for Permanence in Paper for Printed Library Materials.

Manufactured in the United States of America.

Member of the Association of
American University Presses

To Kaia,
for being a pure beauty inside and out,
and to the memory of my friend and collaborator
Walter P. Herz

Contents

Illustrations

Introduction

I do not forget the prejudice of the American people; I could not if I
would. I am sore from sole to crown with its blows.

Peter Clark, 1873

Black Ohioans traveled to Dayton on September 22, 1873, to commemorate Emancipation Day—the day President Abraham Lincoln signed the
Emancipation Proclamation. The celebration began on the railcars carrying African Americans into the city. People dressed in their Sunday best
could hardly contain their excitement as the trains pulled into the station.
The revelry followed them from the trains into the depot, where arriving
travelers were greeted by two different bands blaring popular tunes. People
gaily danced in the station. The Sons of Protection and Lincoln Guards,
two black militia groups, wearing brightly colored regalia, marched with
muskets resting against one shoulder. The sky was remarkably clear; the
mood, exuberant and festive. The 1873 Emancipation Day celebration
drew a daunting three thousand people—the biggest Emancipation Day
celebration on record.

A Cincinnatian named Peter H. Clark, one of the most popular and
electrifying African American orators in the state, was scheduled to deliver
the keynote address. After his arrival on a special train, the Sons of Protection and Lincoln Guards, marching in step, led the procession toward
the county fairgrounds. There, African Americans enjoyed an entire day
of music, speeches, dancing, and food, and other activities in celebration
of Emancipation.[1] The keynote address—the centerpiece of such celebrations—bridged two aspects of African American public culture: black festive culture and public oratory.

No stranger to Emancipation Day celebrations or public orations,
Clark frequently had been called upon to deliver the keynote address at
these events. This time, his speech was about a broader type of freedom
than Emancipation: he articulated a vision of a fuller realization of black
freedom through political power. He told his enormous audience that

1

African Americans "do not demand one-eighth of the offices of the land, or . . . any of the offices, on the ground of color; but we do demand that color shall not be a bar to office; that the political rights of the colored man shall not be exhausted when he has cast his ballot. . . . The offices do not belong to the whites of this land, but to the *people* of this land [emphasis added]." Clark went on to criticize the Republican Party for taking black voters for granted: "We protest against the colored man being listed in the assets of the Republican party as a voting machine, which simply does the work of its master, and is then shelved until next election, as is the case in Ohio."[2] Such blunt critiques of the Republican Party, coupled with public demands for political opportunities for African Americans, were a constant throughout Clark's political life. In fact, he is one of a very small number of black nineteenth-century activists who identified political opportunities as a necessary condition of full freedom and equality.

Such powerfully incisive public lectures made Peter H. Clark (1829–1925) one of the foremost public intellectuals in nineteenth-century African American history. As an eloquent and persuasive public speaker, he was often called upon to deliver keynote addresses to a multiplicity of interracial and interethnic audiences. As a journalist, Clark penned editorials that captured America's attention and provoked debate in Cincinnati and beyond. He used the press and podium not only as forums for discussing African Americans' status, but as vehicles to lobby for their freedom. Of all his intellectual activities, Clark was most committed to education. For him, education was more than just a profession: he considered it essential for improving the African American condition and forging a path to full and equal citizenship. As a young man, he led the fight for African Americans' access to public schools—a fight that included the bold decision to sue the City of Cincinnati to release tax monies paid by African American taxpayers for schools. After a victory that literally thrust open the doors of local public schools in the 1850s, Clark became the first African American to teach in Ohio's Colored Schools, and later, the first principal of the first black high school (1866) in the state. In his more than fifty-year teaching career, he educated hundreds of African American children. Both his peers and students commended him as one of the finest educators in the nation. Moreover, Clark participated in some of the major intellectual conversations of his day, including whether African Americans should lead black colleges and universities. He debated the merits of industrial education with Frederick Douglass and Dr. James McCune Smith decades before W. E. B. Du Bois and Booker T. Washington.

Clark was not just an intellectual, but a *radical* intellectual. Historically, black radical intellectuals have strenuously confronted the hypocrisies of American democracy. Rejecting the master narrative and myths about American democracy, freedom, and equality, they are masters at truth telling. These thinkers confront the American conscience, critique the hypocrisies in the national discourse, and articulate a radical, more inclusive, democratic, and egalitarian vision of America. In other words, a black *radical* intellectualism criticizes America for what it is, while articulating a vision of what it ought to be. Because of the nature of their mission, black radical intellectuals like Clark stand diametrically opposed to those people, ideas, policies, and customs that preserve the status quo. They are the voice of the disempowered, disfranchised, illiterate, and inarticulate; as Edward W. Said asserts, "intellectuals belong on the same side with the weak and unrepresented."[3] Essentially, they become the de facto voice of their communities.

Clark's oratory is a crucial part of his identity and contributions as a radical intellectual. He rose to national fame because of his oratorical skills. Cedric J. Robinson notes that the words of radical intellectuals uttered in a public forum have particular power: "With words they [leaders] might and did construct new meanings, new alternatives, new realities for themselves and others." And that is precisely what Clark did with his words.[4] As a radical intellectual, he raised some of the most forward-looking and controversial ideas about racial uplift, civil rights, political power, and equality of his generation.

Many black intellectuals of his day comprised a racial vanguard. Clark performed dual roles as a "race man" and "representative colored man"—or "leading colored man."[5] As a race man, he belonged to the class of black elite that believed their free status, education, light skin, or white ancestry entitled them to be spokespersons for their community. A spokesperson, however, is not necessarily a leader: the person must also be anointed a leader by his or her own community. African Americans wanted leaders they could trust and who would courageously and unapologetically confront racism and inequality and consistently act in their best interests. Cincinnati's black community appointed Clark a leader because people knew and trusted him and his family. He had been raised in that community and had a sustained record of acting in its best interests. The community appreciated his intellectual prowess and skills with words. Most important, though, it designated Clark as a leader because African Americans believed he had political courage. As one black Cincinnatian observed,

"In his veins coursed no bootlicking blood."[6] In other words, he had the courage to speak squarely and forcibly to white elites about inequality.[7] In addition to being a race man with an obligation to his own community, Clark also functioned as a representative colored man, meaning local white elites like Levi Coffin, Salmon Portland Chase, George Hoadly, and Alphonso Taft considered him to be the leader of his people—largely because of his respectability and education, although white family lineage, free status, and eloquence also mattered. Hence, Clark was burdened by dual mandates as a race and representative man, and sometimes those interests conflicted. The local African American community ultimately reserved the right to discard those leaders who ceased to serve its interests.

As Joy James asserts, nineteenth-century black leaders like Clark "debated not *whether* they were obligated to serve the advancement of a besieged people, but how *best* to fulfill those obligations [emphasis added]."[8] He experimented with varied strategies across educational, legal, and political areas. Some met with measured success, while some failed altogether. He came to believe wholeheartedly that a political strategy would best solve the problems facing African Americans. Although a political strategy was not the only strategy Clark advocated throughout his lifetime, it is an *essential* feature in his activist career. Even during the brief time he advocated an economic solution as a socialist, he did not abandon the idea of a political one until 1882, when he became a Democrat. However, Clark did not always believe that those political solutions could be found in either of the two major parties.

His life clearly is a testament to the black political tradition. Although he never held a formal political position, Clark was a skilled politician in the broader sense of the word. He wielded a great deal of informal power: his alliances and friendships with white financial and political elites guaranteed that his influence reached all the way from Cincinnati to the state capital, to the nation's capital. He exerted influence on legislators, Ohio governors, presidents, and Supreme Court justices—all of whom knew Clark personally and sought his help in courting the African American vote, which held the balance of power in Ohio in the Reconstruction era and beyond. Moreover, leaders of both political parties sought his advice on civil rights issues. At the state level, Clark wielded so much political capital that he was able to insert an African American agenda into several Ohio gubernatorial elections. Not quite a partisan, he proved, instead, to be an astute independent who used both parties as tools to get what he wanted for African Americans and himself: political power. He employed every strategy imaginable to obtain collective political power, including critiquing his party from within, joining factional and third parties, playing machine politics, and advocating political realignment and political independence. In its entirety, his life offers many lessons about the political strategies northern blacks used to obtain power and position in the nineteenth century—in spite of how rarely they were elected or appointed to political offices.

For roughly the first half of his public career, Clark embodied the black *radical* tradition—meaning he refused to embrace dominant racist mores, values, history, or social hierarchies, and waged an unrelenting battle against oppression. Black radicals, after all, aim not just for the "absence of chains, but . . . a new society." In this vein, Clark constructed and pursued a revolutionary vision of America in which the highest ideals of freedom, democracy, and equality reigned. In that vein, Clark joined three radical political parties in his career—parties that wanted nothing short of a social or economic revolution. Moreover, his assertion of African Americans' humanity, their demands for equal rights as U.S. citizens, and their equality as human beings constitute the keystone of the black radical tradition.[9]

Clark's radical consciousness had been raised in his youth in a black family with a history of slavery, freedom, and resistance. The virulently and often violently racist and proscriptive world of nineteenth-century Cincinnati certainly played a role. Clark first actualized his radicalism through militant expressions of black nationalism—expressions that included advocating withdrawal from the United States, emigration to Africa, and establishing a black republic in Central America that would pressure the United States to emancipate African Americans. He also embraced Radical Abolitionism *and* revolutionary armed violence, threatening that those with hands bloodied by slavery would be sent to "hospitable graves."[10] The fact that Clark's initial step into radicalism would be through the lens of race, as a militant black nationalist, should not be surprising given the extremely hostile and racist climate in which he was raised.[11] The oppression he witnessed in that environment played more than a minor role in shaping his worldview, ideology, and approaches to activism.

Clark's radicalism was actualized most clearly through socialism. He was the first African American to publicly identify himself as a socialist in U.S. history.[12] Hence, long before Lucy Parsons, George Washington Woodbey, Frank Crosswaith, Hubert Harrison, W. E. B. Du Bois, Chandler Owen, and Asa Philip Randolph, Peter H. Clark blazed the path for the early black socialist tradition in Afro-America. With the exception of Winston James, few historians of twentieth-century black radicalism have acknowledged their nineteenth-century forebears.[13] Although Clark's lectures as a socialist constitute the foundation of African American socialist thinking, history has effectively erased this father of black socialism from a larger and much longer tradition dating back to the antebellum era.

Socialist ideas permeated Clark's worldview and colored his activism dating back to the 1840s, although he did not actualize those ideas until 1876, when he became the first African American to join a major socialist political party. Although he was just one of a few native-born American leaders in a movement dominated by German immigrants, Clark became one of the most influential American socialists—irrespective of race. Still, he adopted a German worldview as a socialist that made it difficult for him to make the movement respond to the needs of African Americans. He represents a small minority of African American leaders who expressed solidarity with European laborers and revolutionaries such as Gottfried Kinkle and Lajos Kossuth—critical figures in the 1848 German and Hungarian struggles for independence, respectively.[14] These struggles resonated with Clark more than black liberation struggles like the Haitian Revolution because he was immersed in an immigrant community with a living memory of German and Hungarian revolutionary struggle. He never learned how to make that history useful for African Americans.

Curiously, Clark's radical politics before 1882 are matched by an equally conservative sort from 1882 onward. He left the Republican Party for good that year, after it failed one too many times to award him a patronage post. Not only did he adopt a conservative politics as a Democrat, but a conservative *racial* politics. By the former, I mean his membership in the Democratic Party and his subsequent refusal to wage any real challenges to the status quo or received culture; by the latter, I mean that Clark stopped seeing his destiny as tied to that of American Americans as a whole, and began doggedly pursuing political power strictly for personal gain. On the whole, his conservatism is the product of dreams abandoned after years of disappointment and disillusionment as a Republican and third-party member. According to some, his politics grew increasingly antithetical to African Americans' best interests. Considered a political opportunist by then, Clark frequently demonstrated a willingness to pursue personal political power through any means necessary, including the mass disfranchisement of black voters, character assassination of other African American men, and bribery. By embracing such unsavory politics, he eventually lost all credibility as a local, state, and national leader of African Americans in the 1880s. The penalty for betraying African Americans' interest was heavy. The black press relentlessly abused Clark. The *Cleveland Gazette,* for example, identified him as an enemy of his people and leveled charges accusing him of being a "race traitor," "infidel Democrat," "wooden-headed," and an "offensive partisan," among other things.[15] This book chronicles the rise and fall of a race man who became corrupted by an unrelenting quest for political power.

The fact that Clark never secured a political post even after resorting to unprincipled tactics illustrates that, for northern African Americans, conservative politics that went against the will and interests of their people offered no guarantees of political patronage, as they often did in the South. His story sheds light on failed African American leadership and the elusiveness of political power in the largely un-Reconstructed North.

Peter H. Clark defies typification. He felt as much at ease in the Liberal Republican and socialist movements as in the black emigrationist and black convention movements. One would be as likely to find him in a pulpit speaking in front of an all-black audience at an Emancipation Day festival or black convention meeting as before an assembly of German immigrants expressing solidarity with John Brown. One might find him extolling Thomas Paine's principles of freedom or railing about how wage slavery had reduced wage workers to beggars. Clark easily moved between worship services in the African Methodist Episcopal (AME) church to those in the local Unitarian church. His activism included everything from participating in the Underground Railroad to editing his own journal; from protesting in the streets with German radicals during the Great Railroad Strike to addressing the state legislature. His political affiliations ran the spectrum from Radical Abolitionist to Republican to Liberal Republican to Socialist to Democrat. Clark made indelible imprints on the political culture and public life of America. His life proves that it is possible for activists to cross boundaries of race, class, religion, ethnicity, and partisanship, even at a moment in U.S. history when that seems most implausible: the nineteenth century. Although Clark never quite felt American, he embodies America in that era.

Moreover, his actions and beliefs are angular to those of the rest of the African American local, state, and national leadership. For example, he joined a Unitarian congregation when most African American Christians affiliated with the Baptist and AME churches. This peculiarity meant he routinely had to defend his faith and even suffered reprisals from his community and beyond. In the same vein, Clark advocated socialism when most African American leaders subscribed to free-market values and capitalism. He became an active and vocal member of the Democratic Party in 1882, when most African Americans were still wholly loyal to the Republican Party. Furthermore, Clark supported separate schools when most black Ohioans desired integrated education. At times, he seemed to have a fundamental faith in the American system and fought for inclusion within it; at others, he embraced radical ideas like emigration, Radical Abolitionism, and socialism. Moreover, it is hard to categorize him as either a socialist with black nationalist sentiments, or a black nationalist with socialist sentiments. Certainly, as historian Lawrence Grossman concludes, Clark "fits no ideological school."[16] For some, that might make him a less attractive figure to study, but his complexity is highly attractive and instructive.

There is no easy way to explain Clark's ideological contradictions and complexities without analyzing their roots. His intellectual, political, and activist roots borrowed heavily from several traditions. Very few African American intellectuals, then or now, have drawn *simultaneously* from so many schools of thought as he. First, Clark's belief in the efficacy of moral suasion, coupled with his use of oratory and the press as forms of protest, are firmly rooted in the abolitionist tradition. His formal education in abolitionist schools and informal education in abolitionist conventions are sources of that programming. The abolitionist movement taught him about third-party politics and to use them to press for social change. The German workingmen tradition tutored him in free-labor ideals, working-class consciousness, and labor activism. Moreover, German political philosophy is responsible for his socialist and revolutionary ideologies and his formal affiliation with socialist political parties. No other leading African American in this period was as influenced by German-speaking immigrants as he. Third, the freethinking tradition, shaped by people like Thomas Paine, governed another aspect of Clark's intellect. It can take credit for his philosophies on democracy, freedom, social equality, citizenship, religious freedom, and universal humanity. Moreover, this tradition led him to question received culture, traditional institutions, and values, and led him down the path to Unitarianism and, ultimately, black humanism.[17]

African American religious, intellectual, and activist traditions developed Clark's philosophy on manhood, self-help, self-respect, and leadership. Black manhood, for him, was inscribed with public—and less private—meaning. Nineteenth-century black activists like Clark believed manhood was synonymous with protest. They best expressed manhood through defiant resistance and aggressive demands for freedom and equality. Clark embodied what Darlene Clark Hine and Earnestine Jenkins calls a "Masculine Achiever" version of black manhood, which exuded self-respect, independence and self-sufficiency, respectability, political activism, race leadership, and bravery through military service. The African American religious tradition, through independent black churches, played an instrumental role in preparing Clark for leadership.[18] Specifically, the AME church introduced him to the power of oratory as a strategy for uplift, empowerment, and protest. It is no wonder, then, that oratory became central to his public identity. He also learned about the institutional side of black nationalism through his experience in the AME church, black private and public schools, black conventions, the Colored Orphanage, and Prince Hall Masons. Finally, the African American activist tradition developed Clark's race consciousness and cultivated the stinging critique of racism that became his signature.

The final tradition responsible for Clark's development is American nationalism. In the spirit of this tradition, he frequently invoked the ethos and spirit of the American Revolution and Declaration of Independence as a gauge to measure the nation's adherence to ideals of American freedom and democracy. This tradition, with its emphasis on military heroism and frontier exploration, may have moved him to falsify a kinship to both the explorer William Clark and War of 1812 veterans. It also inspired him to write a real history of a Cincinnati black regiment that preceded the birth of the United States Colored Troops. He wanted nothing more than for African Americans to be included in this tradition.

Clark gained more than ideology, strategy, and worldviews from these diverse ideological traditions; he also built close alliances with powerful people in these respective activist, religious, and "thought communities," alliances that factored prominently in his quest for political power. What makes him so exceptional is the ease with which he moved between these various communities in spite of the rigid racial, ethnic, religious, class, and ideological divides that typified the period.

Because Clark's intellectual, political, and activist philosophies drew on multiple traditions, it is not surprising that his actions appear "paradoxical and quixotic" or "bizarre and uninterpretable" to some historians, or devoid of "a consistent racial outlook," to others.[19] His actions *would* be difficult to interpret without a fuller appreciation of his entire life and the multiple traditions that *simultaneously* influenced him. These ideologies and traditions all overlapped and complemented one another in ways that led him to develop unconventional strategies to improve the social, political, and economic status of African Americans. Moreover, many of his strategies made him a trailblazer. For example, he was not only the first black socialist, but also one of the first African Americans to advocate independent politics and routinely use factional and third parties as a strategy to secure freedom and civil rights.

If we compare Clark's seemingly contradictory political affiliations and alliances to those of other leading African American intellectuals, though, his actions appear neither "bizarre" nor "uninterpretable." The truth is, as historian Wilson J. Moses posits, "most thinkers of any consequence" are full of contradictions, or worse, "permanent irreconcilables, both ideological and 'pragmatic.'"[20] As wide-ranging and contradictory as Clark's political paths seem to be, they certainly are not exceptional in African American history. Even Frederick Douglass at times advocated black institutions, and at other times denounced them; he also expressed contempt for emigration, but later flirted with the idea. Douglass was "elegantly inconsistent on the entire question of identity politics, which he supported or opposed as the spirit moved him." Booker T. Washington also exhibited stark contradictions between his public and private personas.[21]

Nor was Clark's voracious hunger for personal political power in the post-Emancipation era uncommon. At least a few other black politicians of his day were accused of using unprincipled tactics to obtain or maintain political position or patronage. James O'Hara of Halifax County, North Carolina, for example, who was at least as preoccupied as Clark with obtaining political position, was accused of voting to pay local officials exorbitant "ex officio allowances" once he finally was elected to serve on the county board of commissioners. He also was indicted fifteen times for corruption and tried for fraudulent appropriation of county funds. As August Meier contends, black politicians who were deeply committed to serving their communities often were also extremely personally ambitious people who doggedly pursued prestigious political posts and power.[22] Clark's life offers a case in point. Surprisingly, few scholars have explored the extent to which the desire for patronage positions governed the actions and deeds of black politicians in this era.

Nor are Clark's politics exceptional in the history of African American radicalism. Hubert Harrison took a "contradictory" journey from the Republican Party to socialism and political independence forty years later.

Even W. E. B. Du Bois supported the Republican Party, the Democratic candidate Woodrow Wilson in 1912, socialism, communism, third-party candidates, as well as a form of political independence that historian David Levering Lewis calls "flexible partisanship" in his equally long public career. George Edwin Taylor's political path included the Republican Party, the Democratic Party, and then the all-black National Liberty Party, when in 1904 he became the first African American to be nominated for president of the United States on that ticket.[23]   *[handwritten: 1st black of to run for pres]*

Clark fits into several historiographies. The literature on African American socialists in the nineteenth century is anemic, leading to the perception that no such people existed. Admittedly, very few African Americans joined the socialist ranks in the nineteenth century; among those who did, Peter Clark is the most prominent.[24] Most historians have mischaracterized his socialist career, an error this book corrects. First, Clark was introduced to socialist tenets much earlier than has been previously asserted—as early as the late 1840s. His political, intellectual, and religious associations with German workingmen, socialists, rationalists, and freethinkers in the late 1840s and 1850s provide incontrovertible evidence that he supported such ideas then. Second, socialism played a more significant role in shaping his early political consciousness and ideological development than has been otherwise asserted. Clark did not subscribe to socialism because of its potential to liberate African Americans, as some have argued. He never expected socialist political organizations to become vehicles to obtain racial equality exclusively, nor did he ever insist that they insert racial issues into their agenda. Moreover, Clark never criticized socialists for unresponsiveness to African Americans' plight. In fact, he hardly mentioned race or racism during the time he formally affiliated with socialist political organizations and actually grew more conservative on racial issues during that time.

Much of what has been written about Clark focuses on his socialist career—to the exclusion of his myriad other accomplishments and contributions. Clearly his life begs for a fuller treatment; this project does just that. His contributions to the socialist movement were neither the most nor the least significant acts of his political life. In fact, Clark enjoyed a long and distinguished career that was not limited to his affiliation with socialism.

Historians David Gerber, Lawrence Grossman, and Winston James go the furthest in providing an overview of Clark's entire *political* life. Gerber, in a brilliantly written overview of Clark's political life, illuminates all the complicated, and often contradictory, politics that he employed—from realist to idealist, integrationist to black nationalist. Gerber argues that the contradictions reflect a struggle between Clark's personal and private selves. His portrayal of Clark as a contradictory and unpredictable soul driven by divergent beliefs that "mingled in apparently unrationalized profusion" may be a tad unfair and does not fully explain his motivations or how he reconciled those contradictions. Lawrence Grossman and Winston James move beyond the Clark-as-socialist model, casting him as a pivotal figure in post-Emancipation racial politics. Both of these historians appreciate how his larger life story and experiences shaped his political views; and, ultimately, their chapter-length examinations depict him as a deliberate and thoughtful political actor. Still, their studies are not exhaustive biographies and thus leave us with other questions.[25]

Clark's political life demands a full treatment: condensed snapshots of certain moments of his career cannot provide a full narrative of his contributions across the nearly one hundred years he lived. We have yet to fully appreciate how central this man was to African American political strivings and intellectual life in the nineteenth century. Despite his best (and worst) efforts as a member of different parties, the fact that he never secured a political post teaches us much about the intersection of race and American politics. Moreover, his intellectual life also illuminates the manifold debates that have been central to nineteenth-century African American intellectual history, including the usefulness of "social mingling," emigration, separate schools, and industrial education.

Despite his colorful and varied contributions to the texture of American life, thought, and society, history has forgotten the man; this eloquent orator, intellectual, and teacher has receded into the historical shadows. Even in his hometown of Cincinnati, the memory of Clark faded long ago. In the nineteenth century, however, most people recognized the name Peter H. Clark. His contemporaries respected him as one of the most commanding orators, intellectuals, educators, and activists of his time. In 1890, the *Indianapolis Freeman* conducted a poll asking its readers to name the "ten greatest Negroes who ever lived." Clark's name is among the ten. Most of the other names on the list of ten are readily recognizable to us now—including Frederick Douglass, Blanche K. Bruce, Daniel A. Payne, George Washington Williams, and Toussaint L'Overture.[26] All of his equal contemporaries, including John Mercer Langston, Martin Delany, T. Thomas Fortune, George Washington Williams, and Booker T. Washington, are the subjects of published biographies. Clark, who is historically more significant than at least of few of them, is only now joining that club.

At least a small part of the reason history has forgotten this man is that he lived and *lives* in the shadow of Frederick Douglass. Douglass groomed and mentored the young Cincinnatian and pulled him into the two areas that became the center of Clark's public intellectualism: lecturing and using politics as an instrument for social change. But Clark stepped beyond his mentor's shadow, blazed his own ideological path, and established his own reputation, independent of his mentor. Both attended and commented publicly about many of the most historically significant meetings, events, and moments in mid- to late nineteenth-century African American history. Powerful orators *and* editors, both men wielded significant political influence in the African American community and beyond. With similar racial uplift goals, Clark and Douglass both desired to see an immediate end to slavery and the full extension of civil rights to freed people. Both believed in the efficacy of education and politics as a means to elevate the condition of African Americans. On the great issues of their day, the press called on Douglass and Clark alike for their views. At one point, the men appeared to be on the path to rivalry for leadership of their people. While much has been said about Douglass's competitive interactions with other African American men, he and Clark never considered each other adversaries and never had any public conflicts.[27] In fact, their private letters reveal that they maintained a father-son type of respect and fondness for one another throughout their lives.

The men did fall on the opposite sides of significant political issues, such as the merits of Republican partisanship, political independence, emigration, industrial education, and socialism. In fact, Clark is one of a handful of contemporary voices that dared to challenge Douglass's views publicly. He seemed to be the more radical and forward-thinking of the two, though: he often advocated ideas long before his mentor. For example, Clark understood long before Douglass the role labor would play in any revolution. At the very least, their competing political ideologies and Clark's willingness to voice his position illustrate that Douglass was neither the only nor the most authoritative or radical leader in Afro-America before Reconstruction. Moses is right when he asserts that historians have "gigantized" Douglass's image so much that his equally talented contemporaries like Clark have been eclipsed.[28]

By contrast, Clark met Booker T. Washington very late in his public career. Their relationship never came close to what he shared with Douglass. Nonetheless, Clark and Washington shared common ground. For one, both men assumed relatively conservative positions at times and embraced aspects of black nationalism. Neither saw social integration as central to the African American agenda, for example. Consequently, both were accused of accommodationism by some of their contemporaries. But Clark is no forerunner of Washington—at least not a clear one. After all, his primary goal before 1882 was securing full and equal citizenship for African Americans, using a political strategy. Washington believed in an economic solution, while postponing electoral politics. Moreover, Clark stood opposite both Washington and Douglass on industrial education. Clark and Washington, however, understood something that Douglass never did: that politics first had to be negotiated locally. Their respective local political climates in Cincinnati and Tuskegee dictated that they operate as Democrats at the local and state levels.

In the final analysis, Clark deserves a seat at the table with the giants: very few figures in American history can lay claim to having fought for African American freedom on all fronts: from abolition to access to public education, citizenship and voting rights to political power, access to trades to unionism to socialism, or across several periods in history—antebellum, Civil War, Reconstruction, and post-Reconstruction eras. In fact, there were few significant moments in African American history in this period that Clark did not witness, participate in, speak about, or protest. With such a record, it is no wonder that Clark once said, "I am sore from sole to crown" from the blows of racism.[29]

This book is an intellectual and political biography of a political figure who left behind no diary or significant central collection of letters or other personal papers. Clark's personal papers—if they ever existed—have disappeared. The only sign of them was at an estate sale in St. Louis two decades ago when a buyer happened upon boxes of them. Unfortunately, she sifted through them, took what looked interesting, and left the rest to an unknown fate. Clark's descendants also have deliberately disappeared across the other side of the Color Line.

I searched for primary-source evidence about Clark in dozens of newspapers, presidential and gubernatorial papers, and in the papers of prominent nineteenth-century figures, including Frederick Douglass, Booker T. Washington, Dr. James McCune Smith, Salmon Portland Chase, George Hoadly, Moncure Conway, and John Mercer Langston. The fact that Clark's name can be found in the papers of several presidents and governors underscores his significance in American political life. Fortunately, because he was such an exceptional educator and community leader, both mainstream and African American national presses widely reported his actions and speeches. Still, the records are few and far between, which may explain why no full-length biography of Clark has yet been published. Nevertheless, the body of his published speeches is the key to understanding the career of this historical actor. The only problem with relying on public records and speeches is that Clark's motivations are sometimes left to educated conjecture.

As the number of superb recent biographies demonstrates, this genre is becoming an increasingly common way to examine the lives and careers of African American radicals, politicians, and intellectuals. Through biography we can recover the lives, words, and ideas of important historical actors and better appreciate their motivations and influences. Moreover, biographies also bear witness to the disappointments that lead people to become radical or conservative.

Biography also illuminates how African Americans imagine and pursue political power across time. Particularly, they allow us to probe why political figures make the choices they do, how and why those choices change over time, the alliances people sometimes must make, and how they negotiate for more political leverage. Biographies of black political leaders illuminate how they functioned at the local and state levels, and how they tried to convert political capital to political power. Clark's life proves that nineteenth-century African Americans were astute political players who believed politics and racial uplift—broadly defined—to be a panacea for racial inequality and unfreedom. As his life demonstrates, African Americans saw political power before and after Emancipation and Reconstruction as central to their definition of freedom.[30]

Biography is not only the best way to remember and honor our heroes; it is also the best way to critique them. Like Moses, I believe that "African-American thinkers should be judged by the same criteria as anyone else—their ability to identify the problematic, to recognize paradox, to anticipate counterarguments, and to focus on contradiction."[31] And by those standards, Clark has been judged in the following pages. As a leader, he had plenty of moments that would make us cringe—and even more that would make us applaud. But through it all, he was impossibly *human.*

He could have remained buried for another century, but must be resurrected at this point because his life offers so many lessons for African American public intellectuals and politicians today. We have forgotten how radical our past leaders were and why they had to be. Consequently, we no longer remember that the black radical political and intellectual traditions helped democratize America.

Chapter One

Launching a Life

I do not forget the prejudice of the American people. . . . It stood by
the bedside of my mother and intensified her pains as she bore me.
It darkens with its shadow the grave of my father and mother. It has
hindered every step I have taken in life.

Peter Clark, 1873

A few months after Peter Humphries Clark's birth on March 29, 1829,
racial violence erupted in Cincinnati, Ohio. On several muggy nights
between August 15 and 22, mobs of two hundred to three hundred men
attacked the African American neighborhood near Columbia and Western Row Streets. Armed largely with huge stones, the mob destroyed
black-owned or occupied buildings, homes, and shops.[1] Terror reigned.
According to one source, "The houses of the Blacks were attacked and
demolished, and the inmates beat and driven through the streets till beyond
the limits of the corporation."[2] African Americans found neither protec-
tors nor friends in the city: appeals to police were met with indifference.[3]
When the smoke cleared, between 1,100 and 1,500 African Americans had
left Cincinnati during the week of violence.[4] It would be another ten years
before the community recovered.

The mob action of 1829 was a direct reaction to the rapid, heavy, and
seemingly incessant flow of African Americans into the city in a short period of time. Between 1820 and 1829, the city's black population swelled
over 400 percent—from 433 to 2,258.[5] Although the white population also
grew quickly in the same period, its rate of growth was not as fast. The
largest increase in the black population came in the three-year period between 1826 and 1829.[6] By 1829, blacks made up 9.4 percent of the entire
Cincinnati population of slightly more than 24,000.[7] "Gentlemen of property and standing"—or business owners, council members, colonizationists, and other elite whites—felt threatened by what they perceived as the

growing "Africanization" of Cincinnati. They believed it would stymie trade with the South and darken the city's reputation and image. The white laboring classes had different reasons for concern about the influx. They resented the competition posed by the new class of laborers. Hence, the 1829 mob action represents a marriage of mutual interests between the "gentlemen of property and standing" and the white working class.[8]

The 1829 mob also symbolizes the physical enactment of a racist and repressive social, legal, and economic apparatus directed at African Americans in Cincinnati—an apparatus designed to discourage them from settling in the city and relegating those who did to noncitizenship status. For example, the state's so-called "Black Laws" severely proscribed black immigration into the state and excluded them from several rights of citizenship. The 1804 Black Law required African Americans to register their freedom papers at the local clerk's office. The law also prohibited employers from hiring undocumented African Americans and subjected those who did to steep fines. Essentially, the law hoped to discourage fugitive slaves from settling in Ohio. The 1807 Black Law, designed to discourage African Americans from settling in the state, required them to produce two freehold sureties within twenty days of settlement in the penal sum of five hundred dollars should they become unemployed, indigent, or criminals. These two laws together treated African Americans as undocumented noncitizens. While the laws were only sporadically enforced in the rest of the state, Cincinnati officials invoked them several times to force African Americans from their jobs and even the city.[9] "Enforcement" in the Queen City usually meant mob violence, as it did in 1829. In the ensuing years, a series of additional legislative assaults denied African Americans the typical rights of citizens. They could not vote, testify in court against whites, or serve on juries or in the militia. Moreover, laws and customs denied African Americans access to common schools until an 1825 legislative act finally provided for universal public education.[10] For a brief, four-year period, they enjoyed that privilege. Sadly, that door of opportunity slammed shut when the legislature repealed the act in 1829—the year of Clark's birth.

In many ways, the setbacks African Americans experienced in 1829 proved to be harbingers of Clark's future life's work. The riot underscores the multiple ways African Americans had been denied citizenship in Cincinnati; the struggle for full equality and citizenship would become not only a centerpiece of Clark's work, but also the motivation for many of the choices he made in his political life. The year 1829 also witnessed African

Americans' exclusion from public school education. Ironically, that year also brought forth a person who would devote the better part of his life to educating them. It is not, however, the knowledge that Clark *gave* that would define him: it is the education he would *receive.*

Several things in Clark's childhood and early adulthood awakened his consciousness and developed his political, intellectual, and public selves. First, the racial violence and repression he witnessed and experienced as a youth taught him unspoken lessons about the racism and second-class citizenship status that made African Americans vulnerable to everything from petty social indignities to mob violence. More important, Clark learned that African Americans could never truly be free until they obtained civil rights, and he made that one of his life's missions. Hence, without Cincinnati and its unique brand of racism, repression, exclusion, and inequality, there might have been no Peter H. Clark. Second, his formal education sharpened his natural gifts and provided him with the bourgeois tools needed to deconstruct slavery, racism, and inequality. Clark's classical education gave him an expansive knowledge base, as well as the critical thinking, writing, and oratorical skills he used to launch abolitionist, teaching, and political careers. Finally, specific people in his inner circle also contributed to his political development in untold ways. From his paternal grandmother, uncle, father, and childhood friend he would learn how to summon the courage to demand equality and civil rights, and the resolve to lobby for them. His aunt, her husband, his principal, and his first employer would teach him the fundamentals of socialism, including intellectual examples of its practical application. All of these sources laid the foundation for his philosophies about work, commitment to community, civil rights activism, and racial uplift.

Contrary to popular belief, Peter H. Clark is not the grandson of William Clark, the explorer. In fact, his ancestry is far less distinguished. His lineage can be traced as far back as his grandmother Elizabeth "Betty" Clarke, who had been born into slavery in 1784 in Charlottesville, Virginia.[11] Betty, her parents, and siblings were owned by a William Clarke. Upon William Clarke's death in 1793, his son John was appointed executor of his estate, and assumed ownership of Betty and her other enslaved family members. In the early 1780s, John Clarke married Sarah (also known as Sallie) Smith, the daughter of a wealthy tobacco planter. The couple produced three children before her untimely death around 1794. Clarke, now a widower, moved to Kentucky with his three young children between

1796 and 1798, bringing his enslaved workforce with them, including the teenaged Betty; her mother, Lucy; and her siblings. After the more than 400-mile trip, Clarke temporarily settled in Lexington before purchasing 400 acres of land in Paddy's Run, Kentucky, located just south of Cynthiana in Harrison County (near the Bourbon County line). After building a home at Paddy's Run, Clarke, his children, and entire enslaved workforce settled into their new residence sometime after 1798.[12]

Unfortunately, Betty's owner, John Clarke, made sure she lost her innocence while yet a child. With the death of his wife, the thirty-seven-year-old Clarke turned to Betty to meet his sexual needs. He impregnated her for the first time when she was just fourteen years old. He subsequently fathered at least three—and possibly four—of her five children: Michael (b. 1798), Eliza (b. 1802), Evelina (b. 1806), and Elliott (b. 1806), and a daughter who died in infancy.[13] With the exception of her eldest, Michael, who was born in Lexington, the rest of Betty's children were born at the Paddy's Run residence. It is not certain whether the sexual relationship between her and Clarke was one of repeated rape or whether Betty reluctantly served as his concubine. Regardless, the stark age and power inequalities between them meant that she did not willfully choose her children's father. Clarke never remarried, nor did he have to: his bondswoman Betty satisfied his sexual needs and, along with her aging mother, filled the role of mother by raising Clarke's and Sarah's children—including William, who was just ten years her junior—alongside her own.

Although John Clarke never freed Betty or their children during his lifetime,[14] upon his death in 1814, his will provided not only for their manumission but also for their care.[15] Without explanation, though, he chose not to manumit eight-year-old Elliott along with his mother and three siblings. Instead, Clarke willed the child to his twenty-year-old son, William S. Clarke, along with other bondspeople, the family farm, and 200 acres of land. Betty remained with her children at Paddy's Run for two years after her manumission, presumably at the request of young William, who would have needed her help on the farm. She also wanted to remain close to her own son Elliott, who remained enslaved. Within one year of John Clarke's death, though, William, likely under pressure from Betty, filed a deed with the county clerk promising to immediately free Elliott upon his own death or when the boy turned twenty-one, granted that he "behaves himself and pleases me." The carefully worded document did not guarantee Elliott's manumission at age twenty-one; instead, it left a loophole that gave William the right to arbitrarily rescind his promise if Elliott did not "behave himself" or "please" his presumed half-brother turned slave owner.[16] The will and the manumission deed suggest that Elliott may not have been John Clarke's child, as were Betty's other three children, whom he did free.

In 1816, Betty and her daughters finally left Paddy's Run, heading for Cincinnati, the closest major city in the free North. Neither son left with her, though.[17] Michael, a free man and an adult by then, had no reason to remain in Kentucky but may have decided to stay behind to watch after his brother, Elliott, who remained in bondage. That decision proved to be a wise one—especially given how frequently enslaved people from Upper South states like Kentucky were sold farther down the river to supply bodies for the Cotton Kingdom. Such a prospect might have proved too tempting for William S. Clarke, who was, by then, in a great deal of debt. Nonetheless, in Cincinnati, Betty Clarke, a former bondswoman and possible concubine, charted a new destiny for herself and her children. Not only did the family drop the "e" from their surname, but Betty began going by her birth name, Elizabeth. On December 16, 1819, she married Isom Gaines, an African American man fourteen years her senior. At least this time, she exercised her own will in choosing her mate and the father of her children. Very little is known about Isom Gaines other than that he was legitimately free—like his wife—and owned his own home. The couple settled into his home on the south side of Sixth Street, between Broadway and Culvert, where they lived for years. Already responsible for Elizabeth and her two daughters, Isom Gaines worked hard to provide for his family, which continued to grow. Elizabeth would give birth to three more sons—including John Isom Gaines, born November 6, 1821, who would factor prominently in Peter Clark's political development.[18] The elder Gaines enrolled in evening school; by the time he turned forty-five, he had learned how to read.[19] Tragically, he succumbed to cholera in the 1832 epidemic, but his beloved Elizabeth would live another decade in their marital home.[20]

Before she left Kentucky for good, Elizabeth had negotiated with William S. Clarke to free her youngest child and had ensured that the transaction was filed in court, for her own protection. She also made him sign a promissory note dated August 28, 1816, for funds owed to her. That note read: "Due Betty a negro woman formerly owned by my father sixty five dollars for value received to be returned in interest from the date until paid." The debt appears to be for wages owed to Betty for her continued services at Paddy's Run after her legal manumission in 1814.[21] Regardless,

Clarke surely never expected that Betty/Elizabeth would ever try to collect that debt after she left Kentucky. He was wrong—terribly wrong. Elizabeth Gaines held onto that promissory note, counting the days until her son Elliott turned twenty-one. When the boy came of age in 1827, Clarke did honor his word and manumitted him. Michael and Elliott left Harrison County, Kentucky, and headed straight to Cincinnati to be with his family, from whom he had been separated for more than a decade. But the story did not end there. Elizabeth, perhaps still bitter that her son had remained enslaved so long, decided to make good on her promissory note. She waited until Elliott arrived safely in Cincinnati before filing a lawsuit in Harrison County Circuit Court against William S. Clarke on February 28, 1829, requesting payment for the debt. Elizabeth enlisted the help of Augustine Respass, Clarke's brother-in-law, who himself was in the process of suing him for unpaid debts. Respass, a wealthy slaveholder with both economic and political clout, proved to be a trusted sponsor. He not only provided her with an attorney, but signed the one-hundred-dollar bond required as a surety for her court costs. William S. Clarke, who had squandered his inheritance by then, failed to appear in court, so Elizabeth won her judgment in absentia for one hundred dollars, which included the sixty-five dollars plus thirteen years of interest, and $5.71 in court costs. The victory was more symbolic than anything since the ne'er-do-well owned no land and owed multiple people money.[22] Yet, Elizabeth Gaines should be commended for her tremendous fortitude and courage in bringing suit. Few African American women sued anyone in court in the 1820s; even fewer were successful. It helped that Elizabeth had been assisted and sponsored by a wealthy slaveholder. Nonetheless, her bold decision to sue in court created a legacy of empowerment and activism for her family. Although it is not clear exactly how much Peter Clark knew of her story, both he and his uncle John Isom Gaines would carry her legacy forward.

When Elizabeth's daughters, Evelina and Eliza Clark, came of age, they both married men from Cincinnati's African American elite. In 1833, Evelina married John P. Woodson, a master carpenter from Virginia. Not only was Woodson one of the few African American carpenters in Cincinnati at that time, but he employed ten men in the 1830s and 1840s—a remarkable marker of economic success for any entrepreneur, much less an African American carpenter. Moreover, Woodson also held interests in the Iron Chest Company, a joint-stock enterprise that purchased real estate properties for rental income. The profits from that company made Woodson relatively wealthy. In addition to his economic fortunes, Woodson also made significant contributions to the African American community. Described as "fairly educated," he actually had more education than most—which he put to good use teaching at Allen Chapel's (AME) Sabbath school and in other private schools for African Americans. Woodson served as an officer of the Moral Reform Society, which promoted values of respectability such as temperance, industry, and virtue, and would later help found the Colored Orphan Asylum in 1844 along with his brother-in-law Michael Clark. Deeply committed to racial elevation through a middle-class work ethic and morality, Woodson easily earned the distinction of being one of the most prominent and respected African Americans in Cincinnati before 1840. An abolitionist editor described him as "steady, industrious, and cherishing proper ideas of what is necessary for [African American] elevation."[23]

Elizabeth's other daughter, Eliza, married another carpenter, Peter Harbeson (alternatively spelled Harveson or Harrison in the record), who distinguished himself as the chief architect and carpenter for the first African American church in the city. Like his brother-in-law Woodson, Harbeson made lasting contributions to the community. He frequently served as a lay preacher and routinely advised the church leadership on its affairs. Beyond church activities, the Harbeson couple eventually would serve as the first steward and matron of the Colored Orphan Asylum in 1846, and he would serve as a trustee for the Colored Schools in 1855–1856.[24]

The Clark women's marriages to carpenters earned them a place among the African American elite—if for no other reason than that African Americans rarely held skilled positions in antebellum northern cities. In Cincinnati, white employers, journeymen, and masters collaborated to prevent and protest their entry into the trades. The Ohio Mechanical Institute vowed to make certain that "no colored boy could learn a trade or find employment." The membership censured its own president for teaching an African American a trade. Consequently, only a handful were employed as carpenters in Cincinnati in 1836 when the Clark women got married.[25] In antebellum African American communities, respectability also played a role in determining one's class status. Both Peter Harbeson and John P. Woodson were considered highly respectable men because of their morality, industry, temperance, and engagement in church and civic affairs.

Elizabeth Gaines's sons, Michael and Elliott Clark, both assumed respectable professions as barbers. Elliott worked at Dennison House—a local whites-only hotel—for years before opening his own shop on Fifth Street, between Main and Sycamore Streets. Michael owned and operated a successful barbershop and bathhouse on Broadway, between Front and Second Streets.[26] There is no record that either son received any formal education.

Michael Clark married three times. In 1825, he married his first wife, Riney Clark, who died three years later after giving birth to his first child, Ann. Within months of her death, the widower married Ann Humphries, a seventeen-year-old girl from Pennsylvania who was the mulatto daughter of an Irish woman and an African American man, Samuel Humphries. Ann's parents had met while apprenticing to the same family in Philadelphia.[27] A year after marrying Michael Clark, Ann gave birth to her only child, Peter Humphries Clark, on March 29, 1829. Tragically, the young wife and mother succumbed to cholera in 1833, when Peter was just four years old. Since men did not typically raise children alone then, Michael Clark quickly took yet another wife, Eliza Jane Morris, the following year. Although this woman raised Peter, he never expressed any special devotion to her as a mother in any of his writings of speeches, and remained emotionally detached from her. Eliza and Michael had three children together: Laura (b. 1836), John Alexander (b. 1838), and Elizabeth Augusta, or "Gussie" (b. 1845 or 1847).[28] The blended family settled into a nice home on S. Broadway.[29]

Although Michael Clark had neither an education nor a trade, he ascended to elite status based on his income as a barber. Moreover, his associations and civic engagements only bolstered his position in that class. He, along with elite whites and African Americans, established the Colored Orphan Asylum in 1844.[30] His leadership in that organization lasted several years and solidified his standing in the larger Cincinnati society. His son, his sisters, and their husbands all served in leadership roles in that orphanage for decades as matrons, stewards, and members of the board.

Born into such a family, Peter benefitted from the privileges afforded to him by his father's financial stability and independence and his own free status, color, and formal education. In fact, he represented the third generation of free people in his family—although his is the first generation born into freedom. Even as late as 1829, African American families rarely boasted three generations of free people. But legitimate free status is only one reason this family ranked among the elite; financial stability played an equally important part. As the child of a successful barbershop and bathhouse owner, Peter did not want for much during his childhood. Although not wealthy by any means, Michael Clark did provide his family with a comfortable home and lifestyle. Neither his wife nor children were compelled to work to supplement his income as were so many other

African American wives and children. In fact, as proof of his financial security, Michael could afford to send his children to private school at a time when only the smallest minority of African Americans in Cincinnati or beyond could do so. Skin color also solidified Peter Clark's elite status. As the child of two mulatto parents, he had enough white blood in his veins to afford him many advantages and privileges in antebellum Cincinnati. For example, as an adult he would exercise the franchise in Ohio years before other African Americans obtained that right through the Fourteenth Amendment to the Constitution. Also, whites did not raise as much resistance when mulattos and quadroons sought education. Many of them were even permitted to attend schools with whites.

Young Peter grew up in the compact world around Sixth and Broadway Streets in Cincinnati with his sister Ann, their father, stepmother, and younger siblings. Peter's grandmother Elizabeth Gaines and her children resided right around the corner, on the south side of Sixth Street, between Broadway and Culvert. His aunt Eliza; her husband, Peter Harbeson; and their children lived right next door to the matriarch Elizabeth. In addition to Clark being surrounded by his family, his neighborhood also lay at the epicenter of Cincinnati's African American community. Roughly one-half of the city's African American population resided in the First Ward neighborhood that ran north of Sixth Street, east of Sycamore. Because of the relatively high concentration of African Americans there, the area was pejoratively called "Bucktown" by whites. African Americans gravitated to this neighborhood for a number of reasons, including the availability of unskilled work, low rents, and the proximity of black institutions like churches and schools. The AME church was located right across the street from Peter's grandmother's home.[31]

As legitimate free persons, Elizabeth Gaines and her extended family enjoyed relative stability and security. Unlike many African Americans in northern cities in the antebellum era, Elizabeth's family would not have to endure a lifetime of moving from town to town to stay ahead of slave catchers. More important, they had the peace of mind of knowing that their freedom could not be challenged; they had the papers to prove it. Moreover, all of Elizabeth's kin had made good on the promise of freedom and enjoyed gainful employment as barbers or carpenters. Several members of her extended family had obtained respectability, wealth, and independence through entrepreneurship and ingenuity. The truth is that Peter H. Clark lived a relatively comfortable and privileged childhood with far more advantages than most African Americans, and many whites.

Elizabeth Gaines's descendents secured a permanent place for themselves among Cincinnati's African American elite—a status they maintained for generations. In fact, their names routinely appeared in the *Cincinnati Commercial Gazette*'s weekly column "Our Colored Citizens," which reported on the social doings of this class into the 1880s. Still, none of these social advantages would be enough to shelter Peter from the worst that Cincinnati had to offer its African American residents.

Harrowing racial violence book-ended Clark's early childhood in Cincinnati. At the tender age of seven, he would have witnessed the 1836 riot, which had been precipitated by the decision of editor, attorney, and former slave owner James G. Birney to move his antislavery journal, the *Philanthropist,* from Danville, Kentucky, to New Richmond, Ohio, a village outside of Cincinnati, in early 1836. Birney moved his journal to Ohio because he had been fearful of jeopardizing his safety by continuing to print antislavery materials in the proslavery South. The threats grew increasingly deadly: one group of Kentuckians issued a one-hundred-dollar reward for the delivery of Birney's body, "who in all his associations and feelings is black."[32] But Birney, ironically, received no warm welcome on the other side of the Ohio River, either. Anti-abolitionist meetings were called, and the press and its editor were openly threatened. The *Cincinnati Christian Journal* warned, "We have little doubt that his office will be torn down."[33]

Tensions continued to mount—especially after Birney moved his paper to Cincinnati that summer. On July 5, the day African Americans set aside to celebrate their own Independence Day, a belligerent and confrontational group of whites shouting epithets and insults approached them as they paraded through town. One African American, "whose spirit had not been subdued into full submission," answered with "a firmness and fierceness of tone and language." Caught off guard by that response, the group of whites left the place in embarrassment. Perhaps this exchange incited the events that followed.[34]

At midnight on the night of July 12, 1836, a mob of thirty to forty men broke into the office of Achilles Pugh, the printer of the *Philanthropist,* and proceeded to destroy the paper and ink and dismantled the type. So confident were they that their lawlessness would go unpunished that the next day anti-abolitionists posted placards along street corners warning abolitionists, "If an attempt is made to re-establish their press, it will be viewed as an act of defiance to an already outraged community, and on their own heads be the results which follow."[35]

Because Birney stood his ground and refused to cease publication, the mob reassembled on July 30. Rioters proceeded to break into the *Philanthropist* office, "scattered the type into the streets, tore down the presses," and ransacked the building. The rioters decided against burning the building, but after they left they moved to Achilles Pugh's home. Luckily, he was not there. Next, the band proceeded to Birney's home, intending to tar-and-feather him. Fortunately, they could not find him, either. Returning to the *Philanthropist* office, the mob broke the presses and threw the pieces into the Ohio River. The lawless band then turned its wrath toward the African American community in Church Alley, attacking homes, brothels, and grog shops. Homes and furnishings were ransacked and destroyed.[36] The violence spanned nearly the entire month of June and resulted in the widespread destruction of property. It would have been difficult for Clark not to have remembered the summer of 1836. But this would not be the last mob action to take place during his youth.

In late August 1841, Cincinnati's African American community endured the third major mob attack to occur during Clark's twelve-year life. The mob had been precipitated by increasing abolitionist activity, decreasing wages, and the incendiary rhetoric of the *Cincinnati Daily Enquirer,* a conservative, Democratic, proslavery journal. The journal manipulated existing seeds of antipathy toward African Americans, planted new ones, articulated the resentment for this community, and subtly encouraged citizens to enforce the Black Laws and literally drive African Americans from the city. In a city where mob violence had been ingrained into the political, social, and economic culture, the signs of an impending attack had become all too familiar to African Americans after an entire summer of mounting antiblack editorials and racial skirmishes on the streets. Rather than sit and wait to be victimized again, African Americans organized their own self-defense. Women and children were forwarded to safety, arms were distributed, and the men were assigned to posts throughout the neighborhood. On Friday, September 3, fifty armed African American men waited on rooftops, in alleys, and behind buildings for their attackers to descend on their neighborhood, determined not to allow mob violence run them from their homes, terrorize their families, and destroy property.[37]

At the same time, a preparation of a different sort unfolded at the Fifth Street Market. At about eight o'clock that same evening, a mob comprised of Kentuckians, other "strangers . . . connected with the river navigation," and "boat hands of the lowest and most violent order," and probably joined by elements of the Irish community, assembled. Armed with clubs, sticks,

and stones, the mob proceeded toward Sixth and Broadway, attracting re-
cruits as it went. The mob moved toward Clark's First Ward neighborhood, which was at the heart of Cincinnati's black community. Forty-three
percent of the city's 2,240 African Americans resided there, and many
black institutions were located there as well. Eyewitnesses reported that
the mob numbered upward of seven hundred or eight hundred people.[38]
As it descended onto the neighborhood at Sixth and Broadway, African
American men, garrisoned at different points in the neighborhood, fired
into the crowd. The mob dispersed several times, regrouped, and advanced
again. Several casualties and injuries later, the rioters retrieved an "iron
six-pounder from near the river, loaded [it] with broiler punchings, &c.
and hauled" it to Clark's neighborhood.[39] The mob discharged the cannon
multiple times into black homes and buildings as officials stood idly by.
In spite of the cannon fire, these African American men held their ground
most of the night. But as the night grew old, they could no longer sustain
an effort against cannon fire and a mob of hundreds of lawless whites.

African Americans may have hoped that the militia's arrival would
offer a reprieve from the attacks, but much to their dismay, it declared
martial law against their community.[40] The militia cordoned off several
blocks of the black neighborhood at Sixth and Broadway Streets and held
those within captive. African Americans from other parts of the city were
rounded up, arrested, marched to the area in the First Ward, and detained
until they paid bond. Clark's own uncle, John P. Woodson, barely escaped
these mass arrests, hiding in his chimney to avoid detection.[41]

Clark must have witnessed most of this violence in 1841, especially
given the fact that the focus of the attack was his family's own neighborhood at Sixth and Broadway Streets. Such a violently racist scene surely
left an indelible scar on him. It is no wonder that, looking back at his
childhood in Cincinnati some time later, Clark once bemoaned that racism "stood by the bedside of my mother and intensified her pains as she
bore me. It darkens with its shadow the grave of my father and mother. It
has hindered every step I have taken in life."[42] But if Clark witnessed the
violence, he also must have seen the organized self-defense. The sight of
African American armed men standing to defend their homes and property
must have radicalized the bright twelve-year-old.

Another young witness to those harrowing events was John Mercer Langston, the free-born child of Ralph Quarles, a wealthy Virginia
slaveholder, and his free West Indian lover, Lucy Langston. Born in 1829,
the same year as Peter Clark, Langston was orphaned in 1834, when his

parents had died within months of each other, although Quarles did leave a sizeable fortune for his children's education. John's older brothers initially took him to Chillicothe, Ohio; in 1840, his eldest brother, Gideon Quarles Langston, called him to Cincinnati to receive an education in the city's private schools for African Americans. For the first six months after settling in the Queen City, Langston boarded with Peter Clark's aunt Evelina and her husband, John P. Woodson.[43] The two boys met and became playmates and friends, and when Clark's older sister, Ann, married Langston's older brother Gideon in 1844, the two boys became family.

What began as an innocent childhood friendship evolved into a common racial awakening precipitated by the shared trauma of that 1841 mob action. Although John Mercer Langston spent fewer than two years in the city before moving on to attend Oberlin College, the relationship between him and Clark would span a lifetime.[44] Although the two came into their radical consciousness around the same time, Langston's political star would shine brighter than Clark's. Langston stormed onto the state's African American political scene in 1849 with his blunt remarks at the Convention of the Colored Citizens of Ohio. Perhaps it seems trite to say that he was destined for greatness and exceptionalism, but that reality proved itself. Among the first of Oberlin's African American graduates, Langston would later become the first African American in the state not only to pass the Bar exam, but to become an attorney. He emerged as the leading voice in the state black convention movement in the 1850s. Although Langston often took the unpopular position there, he vociferously stated his opinions and effectively convinced others to assume his position. He would later establish Howard University's Law Department and even serve as its head for some time. Langston's political destiny would include the distinctions of serving as the U.S. minister to Haiti and as the first African American elected to Congress in Virginia. An exceptional orator, Langston would routinely be called upon to deliver addresses throughout his life. Langston was, without a doubt, one of the foremost activists in his time. His superior education, higher socioeconomic background, accomplished political career, stirring oratory, and good looks gave him a palpable air of superiority over Clark and most of their other peers. It is not clear whether Langston held Clark in the same regard that Clark held him; in his autobiography, Langston failed to mention him even once.

At the very least, theirs remained an unequal and one-sided "friendship" to death. Clark emulated Langston for decades and, until the 1860s, even echoed Langston's political views. Even as an elderly man, Clark thought highly of his childhood friend. He even acknowledged Langston's superior qualities: "We entered upon our manhood's career, he filling the high sphere which his talents permitted. I on an humbler plane. In all his career, so distinguished, so honorable, he found in me at all times an earnest admirer and that admiration was given warmth by the existence of a personal regard which I held, because he was my friend." An 1897 condolence letter to Langston's widow, Carrie, illuminates the depth of his respect for his childhood friend: "The American Negro loses its most eminent man, a man fitted by his virtues to adorn and honor the race, and by wisdom to guide it, and by his genius to defend it."[45] Only at Langston's death was Clark freed from walking in his friend's shadow.

Although uneducated himself, Michael Clark encouraged his son's early interest in reading. Although African Americans were not allowed to attend public schools in the state until 1849, several private schools—wholly funded by philanthropy and tuition—operated for their benefit in the city. Determined to secure an education for his children, Michael sent his son to school regularly starting in 1836. As the child of one of only a handful of African American entrepreneurs in the city, Peter enjoyed a childhood of privilege, and nowhere is that privilege more evident than in his educational opportunities. Most Americans in the early nineteenth century considered education to be a luxury. Most African American children of his day could not attend school even if the laws had allowed it: either they were compelled to work to contribute to the family's income, or their families simply could not afford the exorbitant private-school tuition. Emeline Bishop, an antislavery activist and young Peter's first teacher, taught him rudimentary skills, or "the elements of a plain English education."[46] It is not inconsequential that Clark's first teacher was an antislavery activist. If nothing else, as he learned to recognize his letters and how to read, he also got a lesson in abolitionism.

Clark not only attended elementary school throughout his childhood, but also belonged to an even smaller number of African Americans with the added privilege of attending high school. He attended Cincinnati High School, the first high school for African Americans in the state, established in 1844 through the beneficence of Hiram S. Gilmore, a wealthy New England Methodist Episcopal minister and antislavery advocate.[47] At the time, most African American schools amounted to little more than classes held in converted pork shops, rooms in abandoned buildings, or parlors in people's homes. Sparing no expense, Gilmore erected a large, three-room schoolhouse on Harrison Street, complete with a chapel, a playground, and gym equipment.[48] Here, African American children learned with dignity, without the stain of inferiority. Cincinnati High School's classical curriculum included Greek, Latin, philosophy, rhetoric, elocution, composition, geography, and music; it was designed to prepare its pupils for college. The school even published its own monthly paper, the *Reformer and Cincinnati High School Messenger,* edited by Gilmore, the principal.[49] There is no doubt that young Peter gained his oratorical and writing skills in the rhetoric, elocution, and composition classes; perhaps the school's journal even roused his desire to go into printing, editing, and journalism later.

Not only was Cincinnati High School one of only a few high schools for African Americans in the nation, it was, arguably, the most renowned.[50] Only the best teachers, educated at the finest colleges, taught at the school. The school earned such an excellent reputation that southern slave owners sent their mulatto children to the city to attend this exceptional school, as did prominent free African American families from other states.[51] Among the most noteworthy of Cincinnati High graduates were several who went on to have illustrious careers as adults, including P. B. S. Pinchback, as the lieutenant governor of Louisiana; Thomas Ball, as a renowned daguerreotypist; and James Monroe Trotter, as the U.S. recorder of deeds.[52] Even among such notable pupils, Clark distinguished himself at the top of the class. He so impressed school officials at the school that, two years into his education there, they asked him to be an assistant teacher while still a student himself. He finished his studies in 1848.[53]

Clark graduated from Cincinnati High School with much more than a classical education; he also received an education in socialism. During his formative years, he had several role models and mentors who undoubtedly introduced him to socialist concepts, including Gilmore, the founder and principal of the school, who subscribed to the communitarian socialist ideas of people like Robert Owen and Charles Fourier.[54] Owen's ideas were based on communalism, while Fourier's built upon the joint-stock principle.[55] Although these two socialist intellectuals differed about the vehicle for union—home or business—their philosophies shared many commonalities. Both proposed to redesign society so that households combined their resources for the good of the whole. They both imagined that people would live and work together and the profits from work would benefit not just themselves and their families, but the entire community. Together, the philosophies of Owen and Fourier laid the foundation of early socialist thought and practice. Cincinnatians were particularly receptive

joint-stock?

to socialist ideas; in fact, the city was well-known as an Owenite and Fourierist stronghold in the mid-nineteenth century. Socialist organizers who conceived of and planted several communitarian experiments, including the Prairie Home Community, the Clermont Phalanx, the Integral Phalanx, Utopia, and the Universal Brotherhood community, had Cincinnati roots.[56]

Gilmore, along with John O. Wattles and John P. Cornell—two men who frequently joined him in Fourierist projects—formed an organization called the Universal Brotherhood, which hosted weekly Spiritual meetings and lectures at either the Kemble Street Chapel or the Unitarian Church. The Universal Brotherhood consisted of Spiritualists who believed they had the ability to communicate with spirits "by observing and obeying certain mental and physiological laws" and maintaining purity of mind. Members of the church sought the spirit world's help for "knowledge of spiritual, philosophical and religious truth." Hence, the spirit world would direct them how to improve their own souls and how to achieve "universal brotherhood." Church members received their inspiration through a faith in the concept of universal brotherhood—or absolute legal, moral, economic, and social equality—of the human race.[57] It is that vision of universal brotherhood that led these people to ascribe to socialism.

The Universal Brotherhood also subscribed to a concept called "Associative Unity," which they defined as a "union of such individuals as can harmonize with each other . . . with a true devotion to God." Embracing Fourierist principles, they also vowed to "act unitedly and advisedly for a common end, guaranteeing to each other mutual support, and pledging the profits of their several occupations to the extension of the field of operation." Universal Brotherhood members believed that all personal wealth should be dedicated and sacrificed for the good of improving the human condition. These Spiritualists—some of them quite wealthy—turned their personal wealth and property over to the association for the "regeneration of the race."[58]

In the fall of 1847, Gilmore and his associates decided to move beyond merely holding spiritual meetings, and conceived and planned a self-contained Spiritualist community based on Fourier's principles—essentially a faith-based Fourierist community. Fourierist communities—known as "phalanxes"—were cooperative democratic communities whereby members would cohabitate and produce for the good of the whole. The products of their labor would then be sold and divided among members according to their talents and efforts—what was called a joint-stock enterprise.[59] Fourierist phalanxes offer a practical example of what Karl

Marx labeled "utopian socialism," and what others have defined as "communitarian socialism," or more simply, "communitarianism." Phalanxes were part of a worldwide social movement aimed at eliminating competition and its accompanying evils—inequality, greed, and corruption—by reshaping and reordering society.[60] Gilmore and his associates recruited an estimated one hundred people to their religious communitarian scheme in Clermont County, just east of Cincinnati. The settlers included some families from a previously failed Fourierist community on the same site, as well as Cincinnatians, including Clark's aunt Evelina, and her husband, John P. Woodson.[61] Woodson left a thriving carpentry business in Cincinnati to be part of the Universal Brotherhood's phalanx. As a highly skilled master carpenter, his expertise would have been quite an asset in the joint-stock enterprise. He likely helped to build its main communal residential structure—known as the phalanstery—designed to be the heart of every Fourierist community. The community built its phalanstery close to the Ohio River's banks, a location that would play a role in an ensuing tragedy.

Although the record is silent about why this experiment in communitarian socialism appealed to Peter's relatives, they were not the only African Americans to join the Universal Brotherhood's phalanx. The little evidence that can be gleaned from the extant sources indicates that the community was racially inclusive.[62] Even more significant is the fact that the Woodsons' presence here proves that African Americans embraced socialism much earlier than previously believed. The Woodsons' decision to move to such a community, plus Gilmore's role in organizing it, introduced Clark to socialist principles. The teenaged Clark probably had conversations with the couple about the merits of the philosophy and lifestyle. He may have even visited them during the construction of the community. Regardless, the birth of the Universal Brotherhood phalanx marks the moment socialism first piqued Clark's interest.

Sadly, the Universal Brotherhood's Spiritualist communitarian community would never reach its potential. A winter storm set in motion a series of events that led to tragedy and its premature demise. In early December 1847, several days of heavy snow and rain sent waters over the boundaries of the riverbanks. Floodwaters threatened the very lives and property of Universal Brotherhood's phalanx located on the edge of the Ohio River. As the river swelled to threatening levels, the families made the fateful decision to move from temporary, fragile residential structures into what they *believed* to be a more sturdy structure—the community's three-story phalanstery.[63] Certainly they must have debated the wisdom of moving closer to the raging river, but they decided that the structure was safer than where they had been. On December 15, as people slept, the walls of the hastily and poorly constructed phalanstery collapsed around them. Those who did not perish under the weight of the falling debris drowned in the swollen, icy waters of the Ohio River. Seventeen people lost their lives that night. Among the dead was John P. Woodson.[64] According to nineteenth-century sources, the tragedy "struck terror to the hearts of the people," sounding the death knell for this communitarian experiment.[65] Members subsequently scattered, while the Universal Brotherhood founders allowed the strains from the tragedy, resentment, and suspicion to divide them. Although the founders eventually reconciled publicly in late 1848, the Brotherhood would not survive.[66] Its principal organizer, Gilmore, quit his organization, closed his high school, and left the area in 1849.[67] Notwithstanding the fate of the community, Gilmore's socialist beliefs surely had a long-term impact on the young Peter, who held his principal in high esteem.

Although many of Cincinnati High School's graduates went on to continue their education at Oberlin College, Clark never attended that or any other college, although Wilberforce University later granted him an honorary master's degree.[68] While pursuing his high school education, Peter had vowed never to pursue any profession that would make him "subservient to white men," regardless of how profitable it might be.[69] Since sons generally were expected to follow their father's trade, Michael did teach his son how to barber. Undoubtedly though, a combination of Clark's classical education, teaching experience, and observing his father at work made him loathe servile and subservient occupations like barbering. Clark had a mixture of pride in and contempt for his father's chosen profession. There is no doubt that he loved and respected his father, but watching him interact with his white clients must have been deeply humiliating. Michael Clark's success in the profession meant that he must have been particularly adept at wearing a mask of servility and pretending to accept the racial status quo. Many black Cincinnatians of his generation were less inclined to openly resist or confront racism for fear of physical and economic reprisals. Some hid their real feelings behind smiles of feigned complacency. For their part, white men in antebellum Cincinnati not only expected African American men to serve them, but most would never have patronized a barber who openly advocated racial equality or abolition. Peter surely witnessed his father performing the role of a servile and docile barber in order to appease his clientele, which may explain why Peter vehemently rejected the profession for himself.

Despite his assumptions, though, barbering was not quite as subservient as he believed. To the contrary, barbering and barbershop entrepreneurship provided African American men in the antebellum era with a great deal more financial independence, social autonomy, and political freedom than most. Less dependent on whites for their wages, barbers possessed a great deal more political self-respect than other laborers—a self-respect that led to higher rates of activism. Cincinnati's history is littered with example after example of African American barbers involved in politics, acting as agents on the Underground Railroad, and educating their children.

Moreover, cutting and styling hair for white clientele proved to be remarkably lucrative. Many of the city's wealthiest African American men were barbers.[70] Barbering, in fact, provided the surest and easiest path to the African American middle class. Clark's father had a thriving barbering and bathhouse business, which provided nicely for his family and enabled him to send his children to private schools.[71] Moreover, he belonged to the churches and civic associations that were representative of that class. His family, along with many of the city's African American elite, belonged to the Allen Chapel AME church. Hence, his legitimate free status, respectability, income, independence, children's education, and membership in the AME church and on the Colored Orphan Asylum's board firmly cemented Michael Clark's standing as part of the African American elite in his community.

Peter Clark's refusal to work in any subservient position left him few options in a city where African Americans not only endured severe economic repression and oppression but were *expected* to fill these positions. Despite the obstacles, Clark decided to pursue printing. His father paid Thomas Varney, a local white stereotypist, two hundred dollars to teach him the trade.[72]

In all likelihood, Gilmore introduced Clark to Varney. After all, Gilmore associated with a community of freethinkers and radicals like the Owenites Thomas Varney and his wife, Maria, who experimented with ideas as far-reaching as communism, land reform, feminism, and anarchism. The Varneys, like many early American socialists, actually supported a number of socialist projects, sometimes even simultaneously. For example, the couple had been involved in the land-reform movement in the 1840s—which advocated a radical and socialist vision of land redistribution in America—and the free-soil movement.[73] Moreover, the couple

Meeting in the Cincinnati AME Church (Allen Temple), April 30, 1853. (Courtesy of the Cincinnati Museum Center.)

associated with some of the biggest names in radical reform circles, including the prominent former Owenites Josiah Warren and Lewis Masquerier. Josiah Warren, a Cincinnatian, had participated in Owen's communist colony at New Harmony, Indiana, before rejecting that version of communitarian socialism. Instead, Warren espoused "individual sovereignty," a concept that earned him the distinction of being the first American anarchist. He opened his Times Store in Cincinnati in 1827, which practically applied the concept of cooperation—specifically, equal labor exchanges, or "Equitable Commerce." Warren later tested that idea in his own community, "Utopia," which was situated less than a mile from Gilmore's failed phalanx. The Varneys knew Warren and even used his stereotyping technique in their printing business.[74] The couple also communicated with Lewis Masquerier, the founder of the National Reform Association, a socialist land-reform organization. Moreover, Maria L. Varney wrote for at least two radical journals, including the *Herald of Truth*, whose articles on

Portrait of Thomas Varney, ca. 1860s. (Photograph by
Jacob Shew. Carte de visite. Courtesy of the California
Historical Society, CHS2012.842.tif.)

socialism, Fourierism, Universal Brotherhood, and Spiritualism appealed
to Cincinnati's social and religious radicals. She also wrote for Horace
Greeley's *New York Tribune* in the 1840s, a paper that propagated the ideas
of Fourierist socialism. Some of the world's most radical intellectuals also
wrote for the paper: its European correspondents included Karl Marx and
Friedrich Engels. But beyond knowing key people and traveling in socialist circles, the Varneys published socialist literature, including John
Pickering's *Working Man's Political Economy,* which offered one of the
harshest critiques of capitalism in its day.[75]

When Thomas Varney gave him an opportunity to become his stereotyping apprentice after he finished Cincinnati High School, Clark fell into
the direct tutelage of the most radical couple in antebellum Cincinnati.[76]
The young apprentice likely overheard conversations between the Varneys

Portrait of Maria Varney, ca. 1860s. (Photograph by Bradley & Rulofson. Carte de visite. Courtesy of the California Historical Society, CHS2012.843.tif.)

and their associates about cooperation and socialism; he would have read the writings of Maria L. Varney and other radicals published by their press. An added benefit was the fact that Stanley Matthews—destined to become a congressman, Ohio state senator, and associate Supreme Court justice— printed his Free-Soil paper, the *Cincinnati Herald,* in the same building as the Varneys' press. Clark claimed that he frequently ran errands between the Varneys and Matthews's office.[77]

But the relationship between the master and his young apprentice did not last long: less than a year later, the Varneys sold their business and headed to California in February 1849 to seek fortunes in the Gold Rush, leaving Clark without his mentors or his job.[78] Unfortunately for him, the next owner of the printing business had no interest in training African Americans.[79] Clark would use the few things he learned from Varney when he started his own paper a few years later. Still, the brief time he spent with the couple was more than enough to have made an indelible and lifelong impact on Clark. These associations should not be dismissed or minimized. They planted seeds of socialism in his mind, although it would be another two decades before that tree bore tangible fruits.

Michael Clark's extended illness in 1849 and his subsequent death found Peter managing his barbershop, much to his chagrin. Although his father's will stipulated that his stepmother would have use of the business for six months, Peter inherited it and all the tools thereafter.[80] He dutifully, albeit ambivalently, assumed the mantle of barbershop owner to honor his father's memory. But parental obligation only went so far. As proprietor, Clark made a conscientious decision to defy the color line by serving clients of all races at his shop. One of his contemporaries observed that he ran the business as a "civil rights barber shop."[81] This open defiance of the color line is significant. African American and white men simply did not get shaved in the same spaces. Whites generally refused to patronize barbers who also served African Americans; consequently, African American barbers were forced to—in the name of financial solvency—refuse to serve members of their own race. Hence, a barber shop that serviced clientele of all races as Clark's did was rare. It quickly became abundantly clear that this line of work would not suit him when an incident with a client precipitated Clark's hasty departure from the profession. One day, as Clark shaved him, a white client asked him to introduce him to some African American women. Suspecting the man wanted to use him to gain sexual access to these women, Clark refused to honor his request, telling the client that he knew he did not regard black women as his equals and, therefore, would not treat them with any respect. In what was his only public feminist act, Clark refused to facilitate black women's sexual exploitation by white men. The two men then had a heated exchange, and the enraged customer swore never to return to the shop. Clark vowed never to return himself: he allegedly threw his shaving cup to the floor and swore never to shave another white man; if he did, he said, he would "cut his throat."[82] Perhaps this issue hit a nerve, considering that his own grandmother had been victimized sexually by a white man. Nonetheless, this outburst would be the only time Clark ever lost control of himself publicly.

After this dramatic and sudden exit from barbering, Clark briefly worked as a clerk at his uncle's grocery on the Cincinnati levee, where he sold chickens, fruits, and vegetables to steamboat workers.[83] Peter killed and dressed chickens and carried them, along with heavy bushels of potatoes and cabbage, to the waterfront daily. The load was heavy, the work labor-intensive, the weather hot, and the pay low—similar to the work of other levee workers. Yet, Clark found some dignity in it: despite the work being menial, backbreaking labor, at least he did not have to be subservient to whites.[84] At this point in his life, manhood, dignity, and being treated as an equal were more important to him than either wealth or status.

Clark gained something even more priceless at that grocery: the chance to work with his uncle, John Isom Gaines. Forced to provide for his mother and siblings after his father's untimely death in 1832, Gaines learned the principles of temperance, self-reliance, and industry at an early age. He received neither a high school nor a college education, although he did attend an abolitionist school early in his childhood. Regardless, he still was highly regarded as one of his community's foremost intellectuals. Described in William Wells Brown's *The Rising Son* as of "pure African descent, small in stature, of genteel figure, countenance beaming with intelligence, eloquent in speech and able in debate," Gaines attended his first black convention in 1838, at just sixteen years of age. His contemporaries commented on how well he represented himself at that meeting that was dominated by men superior to him in age and wisdom.[85] Nonetheless, that 1838 convention galvanized the young man to political action.

A few years later, a young Gaines courageously spoke out against the 1841 mob violence that had terrorized African Americans in their homes, burned their businesses, beaten them in the streets, shot cannons into their neighborhoods, and tried to drive many of them from the city. He consequently made his mark as one of black Cincinnati's most gifted orators, frequently being invited to speak at functions in his community and beyond. In 1849, Gaines served as a delegate to the state black convention, a body that aggressively petitioned the legislature for the repeal of the Black Laws—specifically the provision that denied African Americans the right to a public education. Bowing to such political pressure, the Ohio legislature repealed those laws just one month after that 1849 convention, opening the doors of public schools for African Americans for good. Gaines, a vocal and influential delegate in the black state conventions, would lead the African American community's struggle for educational self-determination and autonomy in the 1850s. Clark's relationship with his uncle stands as one of the most defining of his life. Only eight years his nephew's senior, Gaines assumed the roles of employer, mentor, role model, and friend and had a profound impact on Peter's personal and political development. The two young men undoubtedly had many conversations about racial justice, civil rights, education, and political activism inside that grocery—conversations that surely had a profound effect on Clark. Gaines introduced him to one of the most powerful movements for change of their time—the black convention movement—and to other power brokers in the state's racial politics. Gaines also likely inspired his nephew to develop his skill as a charismatic orator. More than anything else, Gaines led his young protégé into the field of education and educational activism.

In many ways, Clark lived a charmed childhood as a member of Cincinnati's African American elite. His free status, color, education, networks, and his father's financial security positioned him to come into adulthood having enjoyed comparatively more benefits and advantages than most African Americans, and even many whites. Yet, Clark's privileged background never led to complacency; if anything, it only made him more aware of the limited opportunities and elusive nature of racial equality. Besides that, his class background did not shield him from the racial violence that was so endemic in Cincinnati's culture and terrorized him during his childhood. Coming of age in one of the most racially violent cities in nineteenth-century America made him keenly aware of how white supremacy circumscribed opportunities for African Americans—even upper-class ones. But rather than use his class privileges to mitigate the sting of racism personally, Clark would employ the very advantages he had been given to launch his struggle for racial equality.

Learning—both inside the classroom and in the streets of Cincinnati—defined his first twenty years. From white Cincinnatians, he learned about the depravity of racial violence, legal inequalities, and stunted economic and educational opportunities that dogged the African American experience there. That core education about black inferiority was directly challenged by what Clark learned from his own grandmother and community about resistance. Added to those layers of education is a classical education that equipped him to transcend the practical stigmas of his race. That classical education itself served as a canvas onto which abolitionist and socialist thought would be painted. Certainly, as Clark marched into his manhood, he held a wealth of radical ideas that would shape his worldview. Specifically, black nationalism, socialism, and abolitionism, in one form or another, would undergird much of his radical thinking and politics for the next decade of his life.

Chapter Two

Voice of Emigration

We can effect no good by remaining here. We ought to occupy some territory in America. . . . We seem determined to remain slaves. We want the Spirit of men, and therefore we had better leave.

Charles Langston, 1852

In Columbus on January 11, 1849, the Convention of the Colored Citizens of Ohio debated the advantages of leaving the United States through a colonization scheme to Liberia, when twenty-year-old John Mercer Langston took the floor. Taking exception to a proposed resolution that opposed emigration, Langston proclaimed: "I . . . am willing, dearly as I love my native land, (a land which will not protect me however,) to leave it, and go wherever I can be free. We have already drank too long the cup of bitterness and wo [*sic*], do gentlemen want to drink it any longer? The spirit of the people must be aroused, they must feel and act as men." Doubtful that the racism and discrimination against African Americans could ever be abated, Langston told his audience, "We must have a nationality, before we can become anybody." Furthermore, he asserted that remaining in the United States not only was "humiliating," but conceded "inferiority to the white man." Another convention delegate stated in no uncertain terms that he did not want to depend on whites for anything—even rights. He continued: "We must have a nationality. I am for going anywhere, so we can be an independent people."[1]

Benedict Anderson argues that nations are imagined into existence. In short, when people think of themselves as a nation, they are a nation. Patrick Rael extends that theory by asserting that nations are imagined into existence through public debate and discourse. In essence, before a group can imagine that it is a nation, a concept of nationhood must be articulated and debated—as it was in that 1849 Ohio convention.[2] Langston and other delegates not only saw themselves as one people who suffered a common oppression, but they also believed they needed to act as a collective in order to solve their problems. The discourse of nation and "nationality" that ensued among the Ohio conventioneers shaped and defined a collective vision of a black nation based on manhood notions of freedom, independence, equality, and dignity.

Peter H. Clark certainly accompanied his uncle to that convention—which would have been his first—and heard the fiery words of his childhood friend Langston and other advocates of emigration and black nationalism debate with those who believed their struggle and destiny rested in the United States. The arguments would have made a great deal of sense to him. At the very least, listening to the discourse of nation at the 1849 convention politicized and radicalized the impressionable nineteen-year-old Clark.

Historian Wilson Jeremiah Moses, the leading scholar of nineteenth-century black nationalism, contends that most blacks were not serious about leaving the United States, and even fewer were serious about establishing a nation. Moreover, he asserts that even those who supported emigration often approached it as a civilizing or Christianizing mission to "uplift" Africans from their "degraded" condition.[3] Put another way, black nationalists who *talk* about leaving, yet never make any real concerted efforts to emigrate, are just disgruntled integrationists. Another historian concludes that many of this kind were "merely assimilationists disguised as emigrationists" because they never intended to quit America.[4] Unlike most of his peers, though, Clark actually took real steps to emigrate, and that is what separates him from the rest. Moreover, his ideology about black nationalism in general, and emigration in particular, was not steeped in presumptions of Africans' inferiority or driven by a need to Christianize, civilize, or otherwise uplift Africans. His black nationalism did not privilege European society and culture—especially Protestant Christianity—nor did it aim to assimilate African Americans. Clark pursued a vision of nationhood outside of U.S. soil that would be politically, economically, and socially independent and equal to that of the United States. He also envisioned strategic alliances with other black nations, and military power that could be mobilized to fight to free enslaved African Americans, if need be. In short, Clark advocated a radical black nationalism.

News of the 1829 racial violence in Cincinnati spread through free black communities around the country and inspired the birth of the black convention movement in the United States. Not only did free African Americans living in northern cities feel increasingly defenseless and vulnerable, but they realized the precariousness of that freedom. Fearful that another attempt to force an exodus would crop up elsewhere, African American leaders desired to unite on a national level to prevent that. In the spring of 1830, Baltimorean Hezekiah Grace sent an invitation to African American leaders throughout the North and West to convene in Philadelphia to discuss their concerns. Many heeded that initial call. From September 20 to September 24, 1830, twenty-six delegates representing several communities across the nation met in Bethel Church in Philadelphia primarily to discuss the events in Cincinnati but also to consider whether to migrate to Upper Canada.[5] The group formed an organization, the American Society of Free Persons of Colour, that hosted conventions for African Americans.

The following summer, on June 6, 1831, the First Annual Convention of Free People of Colour convened in Philadelphia. The convention gave birth to a black convention movement that would span several decades. Some African Americans traveled from as far as Rhode Island. At the convention, leaders not only discussed problems confronting African Americans, but also explored solutions. The body decided that the best means of elevating the race were education, temperance, and economy. They made plans to establish a manual labor college for African Americans in New Haven, Connecticut.[6] Subsequent conventions were held annually until 1835, after which they became less regular.[7] Held under various names, including the Convention of Colored Citizens, the Convention of Colored Men, the Convention of Colored People and Their Friends, and the Colored National Convention, the meetings forged a collective political identity for African Americans.

Important vehicles of mobilization and civil rights activism in the antebellum era, black conventions provided a forum for African Americans across the nation to discuss the obstacles in their respective communities. African Americans learned that although they faced a different type of oppression than enslaved people, they were hardly free themselves. The black convention movement provided a political forum whereby free African Americans openly condemned slavery, inequality, and their second-class citizenship. Moreover, these conventions provided the opportunity to explore and debate mutually beneficial solutions and the best means of racial uplift, including moral reform, temperance, and education. Most importantly, delegates also outlined strategies to agitate for emancipation, civil rights, suffrage, and equality. In the 1830s, convention leaders advocated moral suasion as the strategy for racial uplift; by the 1840s, it was political action; by the 1850s, these conventions emphasized black nationalist strategies of self-help, racial solidarity, economic advancement, and emigration.[8] Those conventions collectively laid the cornerstone of a nineteenth-century civil rights struggle.

Black conventions also proved to be a central component of African American abolitionist efforts. Although not typically considered part of mainstream abolitionist activism, black conventions are a critical aspect of *African American* abolitionism. African American abolitionists had a double agenda: they were concerned not only with ending slavery, but with securing civil rights for free African Americans as well. Black conventions allowed them to address both issues simultaneously.

Inasmuch as the black conventions collectivized the efforts, nationalized the identity and concerns of the free African American community, and shaped its political agenda, they made a more significant impact at the local level. Ohio held its first convention in Columbus in 1835 and held one every couple of years thereafter. Ohio had the most active of the black state conventions; no other state matched it in the frequency of its conventions or the longevity of its movement. Reflecting back years later, Clark remarked that Ohio's conventions were in a class by themselves. The conventions of other states, he believed, were "simply anti-slavery conventions," and their resolutions largely aimed at ending slavery; by contrast, Ohio conventions focused on improving the status of free African Americans living there.[9] He is correct. Ohio's conventions focused just as much on improving the status of African Americans as on ending slavery. Black Ohioans strategized about how to obtain civil rights, equality under the law, and access to public schools. Moreover, Ohio's conventioneers also lobbied to repeal the Black Laws, to secure the right to a trial by jury, and for laws to protect fugitive slaves. They discussed strategies of uplift that mirrored the national black convention movement, including moral reform, temperance, and education. Because of black Ohioans' aggressive campaign to secure freedom, equality, and civil rights, one historian concluded that theirs was the most "militant" of the state conventions.[10]

As the racial lines hardened in the late 1840s and 1850s, free African Americans moved from a strategy of self-help and reform to one of increasing militancy. That evolution is apparent in the shifting strategies of the Ohio black conventions. In the 1830s and 1840s, the conventions focused on reforming legislation to allow African Americans to enjoy full equality under the law, access to public schools, and the vote. By the late 1840s, delegates adopted a more urgent, if not militant posture. The

1849 Convention of the Colored Citizens of Ohio marked a watershed in the spirit and tone of these conventions. The convention's radicalism and sense of urgency were rather pronounced; in resolution after resolution, this convention demanded militant abolitionism from all African Americans—enslaved and free—and promised to humiliate and ostracize those who failed to comply. Not only did the body encourage enslaved African Americans to escape bondage, but it also recommended distributing David Walker's *Appeal* and Henry Highland Garnet's *Address to the Slaves*, two pamphlets that made the most radical calls for armed revolution of their day. In addition, the resolutions specifically outlined how free African Americans should pursue militant abolitionism. One warned all would-be kidnappers and slave catchers that "no person claimed to be a slave shall be taken from our midst without trouble," insinuating that the African American communities of Ohio would resort to armed resistance, if necessary, to prevent anyone from kidnapping or capturing so-called fugitive slaves. Moreover, the 1849 convention also called upon all African Americans in the state to actively assist fugitive slaves as they pursued freedom from bondage. Those who refused to help them, the body cautioned, would be publicly denounced as a "bitter enemy to the cause of justice and humanity." Another resolution mandated that all African American organizations must speak out against slavery whenever the opportunity arose; those that failed to do so were judged "undeserving of our confidence, but deserving of our deepest reprobation." The body had no sympathy for anyone who failed to act in the best interest of black freedom. In fact, the body even took issue with those who treated other African Americans poorly in favor of whites—even in the interests of economic gain. Such practices, the convention warned, would no longer be tolerated. Violators of that covenant would be considered "outcasts."[11]

Even if Clark had not been completely radicalized by the increasing militant black nationalism of Ohio's African American leaders who attended that convention, the 1850 Fugitive Slave Law certainly finished the job. The Fugitive Slave Law—part of the Compromise of 1850—was intended to cool mounting sectional tensions that had been brewing between antislavery and proslavery elements. To appease antislavery elements, the Compromise admitted California to the Union and ended the slave trade in the nation's capital. The concessions designed to placate southern states ultimately destabilized northern free black communities, however. The provisions granted slaveholders greater authority to retrieve fugitives from free states. The burden of proof for them was very low: the only requirement was to appear before a federal commissioner with an affidavit from someone in the home state attesting to the fugitive's identity. Moreover, the law also compelled federal officers to actively assist in seizing fugitives. Federal commissioners could be fined for failing to return a fugitive to his or her owners. But the law provided commissioners with a healthy incentive to rule in favor of the claimant: commissioners who remanded an African American to slavery were paid ten dollars and those who ruled in favor of the alleged slave received only five dollars. Furthermore, the Fugitive Slave Law of 1850 gave federal marshals the power to compel "all good citizens" to assist in capturing runaway slaves. Those who interfered with the return of a fugitive slave could be fined one thousand dollars or subjected to a six-month jail sentence.[12] The law's provisions aimed to halt the flow of runaways out of the South and cripple the Underground Railroad by punishing its northern sympathizers and operators.

The 1850 Fugitive Slave Law threatened fugitive slaves, free African Americans, and abolitionists alike. Those African Americans living in free states no longer benefitted from the presumption of freedom. Those fugitives who had been living as free people for decades now had to look over their shoulders at every turn. Even legitimately free people now worried about false claims against that freedom. The threat to African American freedom was especially potent in border cities like Cincinnati where proslavery sentiment made it easier to seize African Americans without just cause or due process, or kidnap them with impunity. Suspected fugitive slaves reserved no rights to contest the claim, to a jury trial, or to testify in court on their own behalf. Moreover, the law made no provision for the writ of habeas corpus.[13] African Americans' freedom and security hung in the balance. Although some free African Americans vowed open defiance of the law by continuing to harbor fugitive slaves, others responded by fleeing the country—mostly to Canada. Most would have never considered quitting the United States before 1850, but the passage of the Fugitive Slave Law accelerated a massive out-migration.[14] The odious legislation led Clark to conclude that emigration was the only sensible option. For him, disillusionment about the federal legislation may have been compounded by the failure to secure suffrage for African Americans at the 1851 Ohio Constitutional Convention. Free, educated, urban African Americans like Clark had internalized enough of the mainstream political and social values to believe in the promise of America. Their exclusion from society, legal, educational, and political disabilities, and denial of opportunities proved the promise did not exist and never would for African

Americans. This class found that reality particularly unbearable because they had wanted it so much. They resented their noncitizen status and were prepared to act on it.[15]

African Americans who had opposed colonization and emigration one year earlier found themselves seriously considering it after the passage of the Fugitive Slave Law of 1850.[16] Even black Cincinnati—a community with a serious commitment to emigration dating back to 1829, when half the African American population left and settled in a colony it planted in Wilberforce, Ontario—considered this option again in July 1850. This time, though, a segment of the community organized to explore settlement in an African colony established by the Ohio chapter of the American Colonization Society (ACS), rather than one it planted itself.[17] Clark quite possibly attended that July meeting. Regardless, a few months later he, along with 1850 Oberlin graduate Lawrence M. Minor and William R. Casey, organized an emigration society and named it the Liberia League. In September 1850, Clark wrote to the ACS requesting information about its Liberian colony. Specifically, he asked whether African Americans might obtain jobs as bookkeepers there. The letter also indicates that he and some others in the league planned to take courses in penmanship and bookkeeping so that they might secure jobs in Africa. After inquiring about bookkeepers' and teachers' salaries, Clark next asked about the conditions in Liberia and what emigrants needed to take with them.[18]

Within two months, the Liberia League's founders moved from inquiring about Liberia to actively taking steps to leave the United States. In November 1850, the three men appealed to the Cincinnati chapter of the ACS for financial assistance for their organization. The men spoke before the ACS body, detailing key successes of the Liberia League, particularly in recruiting African Americans. Satisfied with the report, the ACS promised its "energetic co-operation" and agreed to fund the organization's printing and correspondence costs.[19]

Clark and Liberia League members planned to relocate to a colony dubbed "Ohio in Africa," that had been established by the Ohio chapter of the ACS. Charles McMicken, a wealthy slaveholder, influential member of the Cincinnati business elite, and founder of the Cincinnati College (now University of Cincinnati), had purchased a tract of land northwest of Monrovia, Liberia, for five thousand dollars, on which "Ohio in Africa" would be planted. Not merely a passive financier, but an opponent to black freedom on United States soil, McMicken had taken an active role in planning the colony, purchasing land, and recruiting settlers—including his own bondspeople. Although the Ohio ACS told the Ohio legislature that the colony would be part of a larger scheme designed to break up the slave trade in that region by strategically placing African Americans along trade routes, relocating them there also served the more sinister goal of ridding the state of its African American population. The ACS organ, the *African Repository*, ensured its readers that colonization was "of great and over-powering necessity." Colonization, it continued, was a "high and exalted obligation, enforced by all the duties of self-preservation to both races."[20] Driven by an almost singular wish to expel African Americans from the state, the Ohio ACS petitioned the state legislature to appropriate money to help them emigrate to "Ohio in Africa."[21]

Given the history of the ACS, it is a bit perplexing that Clark would ever participate in any of its schemes. After all, no one could forget the long history of animosity between the ACS and African Americans dating back to its founding in 1816.[22] Most African Americans saw no redemption in the ACS; most were suspicious of its motives and considered it to be nothing more than a racist deportation society. African American communities all over the nation vehemently opposed the organization and colonization, in general.[23] Black Cincinnati even had joined the chorus of condemnation once.[24]

Not surprisingly, because of such widespread resistance, early ACS efforts proved less successful than members had hoped. Throughout the nation, only 1,670 African Americans migrated to Liberia between 1820 and 1830.[25] The organization foundered until its resurgence in the late 1840s. By then, white slaveholders returned to a familiar solution for the "problem" of the increasing number of free African Americans in their midst. Many were alarmed by the increased threat of slave insurrections and troubled by the frequency of enslaved people escaping into northern cities. Some of these slaveholders believed that free African Americans created problems by inducing bondspeople to escape. They reasoned that if they could eliminate that "problem," bondspeople would readily accept their status. Consequently, southern legislators pursued colonization again. The revival of colonization schemes in the 1850s ushered in a "golden age" for the ACS. Remarkably, the organization managed to gain the support and endorsements of leading politicians and legislators. For example, in 1851, Daniel Webster requested federal funding for colonization. Later that same year, Maryland, Kentucky, Missouri, Virginia, and Tennessee revived colonization programs and appropriated state funds toward that end. Slaveholders redoubled their efforts to free bondsmen and women and immediately send them to Liberia. Even Charles McMicken freed a few of his bondspeople this way. Slaveholders sent more freed bondspeople to Liberia between 1848 and 1860 than in the previous thirty years combined. More than 1,500 southern free blacks left for Liberia between 1848 and 1860.[26]

Most nineteenth-century black nationalists who advocated emigration believed that emigration and colonization were different. For them, emigration consisted of the voluntary exodus of African Americans who desired freedom, autonomy, citizenship, and self-determination. Emigrants chose their own destination and ran the new colony themselves. Whites initiated colonization schemes—determining *where* African Americans would settle as well as *when* and *how*. Whites not only organized the resulting colonies but managed them. African American emigrationists condemned the ACS colonization scheme and dismissed its Liberia colony. Martin Delany, one of the most prominent advocates for emigration and Pan-Africanism in the nineteenth century, considered Liberia "but a poor miserable mockery—a burlesque on a government—[that resulted in] a pitiful dependency on the American Colonizationists."[27]

Emigrationists consciously and conscientiously rejected America's definition of freedom, citizenship, and equality. Many had grown disillusioned and dejected by the failure of the American promise, the slow journey to emancipation, and the denial of citizenship and equality, and decided to pursue these ideals elsewhere. A fundamental lack of faith that the social, political, or economic conditions facing African Americans in this country could, or *would,* improve in the future, fueled emigrationist movements. In short, emigration is black nationalism in protest mode.[28] Clark's emigrationist desires certainly were born of protest about, and discontentment with, the African American condition.

Many black nationalists hoped to relocate to Africa not just because it was the land of their ancestors and the basis of African American culture and identity, but because its rich history had the potential to redeem oppressed African Americans by instilling them with pride. Africa also offered a sense of belonging and rootedness. Clark never avowed any emotional, racial, or cultural connection to Africa, or even a desire for an African identity. Nor was he an African civilizationist: he felt no obligation to uplift Africans or Africa. Moreover, he did not have a Christianizing or civilizing mission like Martin R. Delany and other emigrationists. In short, Clark did not imagine that he could liberate Africa or Africans; on the contrary, he hoped the continent would liberate *him* from second-class status and inequality. For him, the continent promised a rare opportunity for black self-governance, self-determination, and freedom from racism.[29] Therein lies the reason Clark differed from so many of his peers.

By seeking financial assistance from the local chapter of the ACS—an organization that had been reviled in many African American communities—Clark and the two other Liberia League leaders negotiated a paradoxical conflict of interests between colonization and emigration, whereby they accepted paternalistic assistance in order to leave.[30] It is difficult to determine whether Clark's Liberia League officially operated under the auspices of Ohio's chapter of the ACS because a prominent ACS member, Charles McMicken, personally sponsored the league, communicated with its founders, and funded Clark's journey to Africa. He even met him in New Orleans in late January 1851 and personally escorted him and four of his New Orleans bondspeople to a vessel bound for Liberia.[31] Clark had no problem requesting and receiving assistance from the ACS, or relocating to and settling in its colony. The question that emerges is whether that makes him any less a black nationalist.

By accepting paternalistic assistance from the Ohio chapter of the ACS, he made a practical decision to obtain the financial resources needed to carry out his plans, at all costs. He temporarily surrendered self-determination and autonomy to achieve his ultimate goal of leaving the United States. Clark is not alone; history is littered with other examples of black nationalists who, for practical reasons, accepted help from whites and even the ACS to carry out emigration schemes. Martin Delany sought and accepted assistance from the ACS in Philadelphia in 1859 for his Niger Valley Exploring Party, yet, no one would ever question Delany's commitment to black nationalism.[32] Certainly the line between emigration and colonization is sharp on ideology and blurred on practical execution.

In January 1851, Clark traveled all the way to New Orleans, the port for embarking to Africa. Intending to board an Africa-bound vessel upon his arrival there, he cheerfully reported back to his ACS sponsors that he had arrived safely and eagerly awaited his departure.[33] Clark never boarded the vessel headed to Liberia and abandoned his emigration plans there in New Orleans. Later, when recounting why he never left for Africa, he said that when he first laid eyes on the vessel chartered for his voyage, the image horrified him. The *Peytona,* he wrote, was nothing more than a "dirty, little lumber schooner." Clark decided not to board the vessel after seeing its poor condition. As a free man, he had a choice; McMicken's bondspeople, who could only enjoy freedom in Africa, were not as fortunate. When the *Peytona* left New Orleans on February 12, 1851, it held 139 emigrants, and McMicken's bondspeople numbered among them.[34] Although Clark claimed that he simply decided to wait for a better vessel, the truth is that several "better" vessels left New Orleans bound for Liberia in the ensuing months, yet he was aboard none of them. Instead, he took a job as a clerk, remaining in New Orleans for a year. His nationalist-emigrationist impulse did not die then, but shifted to other places.[35]

Upon his return to Cincinnati in late 1851 or the first few weeks of 1852, Clark rejoined the Ohio black convention movement. He had been absent at the 1851 meeting in Columbus that issued a damning and daring critique of the Fugitive Slave Law of 1850 and the government.[36] He did attend the 1852 Convention of the Colored Freemen of Ohio—held at Cincinnati's Baker Street Church on January 14–18, and served on its Committee on Emigration. His service on that committee would throw him to the center of a national debate on emigration, two months before the publication of Martin Delany's *Condition, Elevation, Emigration, and Destiny of the Colored People of the United States*. By the early 1850s, emigration had moved from the margins to the center of African American political discourse. Specifically, it moved from being a radical and remote possibility among disaffected African Americans to a sensible and feasible option for a significant minority of that community. Clark spearheaded a committee at the 1852 convention to investigate the feasibility of emigration to Canada. A few weeks before the convention, Clark wrote to Henry Bibb, editor of the *Voice of the Fugitive,* an Afro-Canadian journal, inquiring about the "moral, mental, and pecuniary condition, and the legal obstacles" facing black people in Canada. Bibb responded that their condition compared "favorably" with the white population, although he admitted that there was "room for improvement."[37] Clark shared his findings with the convention's Committee on Emigration, which had been commissioned to decide whether emigration was in African Americans' best interest.

The five-person committee divided on the question, and that division is representative of divisions in the larger community on the issue. Emigrationism blossomed as a movement in the early 1850s—precipitated by the 1850 Fugitive Slave Law—and so, too, did the discourse about it. Hence, the African American leadership split about whether emigration should be pursued as a solution to the racial inequality; so, too, did the 1852 Convention of the Colored Freemen of Ohio's Committee on Emigration. The committee voted 3 to 2 in favor of emigration. Peter Clark, Charles H. Langston, and H. Ford Douglass all supported emigration. These three drafted a majority report that proclaimed that voluntary emigration to another place in North America offered "the only relief from the oppressions of the American [white] people." The report also condemned the ACS because it supported colonization, rather than emigration. The two dissenting members of the Committee on Emigration, Lewis D. Taylor and L. C. Flewellen, drafted a minority report indicating their opposition to emigration. The first and third resolutions capture the substance of that position. The first resolution reads: "That it is not expedient for the free people of color . . . to emigrate to any place out of these States while one slave is in chains." That resolution makes it clear that the destinies of enslaved and free people were linked. The third declares, "That this is our native land—the land of our birth and inasmuch as birth gives citizenship according to the . . . Supreme Court, it is our duty to contend for our rights as American citizens."[38] In no uncertain terms, the minority report concludes that free African Americans had a duty to remain in the United States and fight for their rights.

The minority report reflects the integrationist views expressed by Frederick Douglass and other African American leaders who opposed emigration and urged free African Americans to fight for inclusion in American society, instead. Integrationists also believed African Americans had few better alternatives than remaining in the United States, where they could lobby to change the laws. They refused to distinguish between colonization and emigration: in their minds, they were the same—both antithetical to the abolitionist struggle. Their chief priority, as the first resolution shows, was making a commitment not to abandon enslaved people.[39] Committee members could not agree, so both reports were brought before the entire convention for consideration.

In a letter to the *Voice of the Fugitive* summarizing this particular debate, Clark reported that the emigration question elicited the most spirited and engaging debate of the convention. He recounted how the discussion started one evening and did not conclude until the following afternoon. Convention president John Mercer Langston delivered a stirring two-hour address in which he contended that race relations were irreparable because slavery created a "natural repellency between the two races" based on whites' "consciousness . . . that they were the oppressors, and among blacks that they were oppressed." Langston concluded that the resulting antagonism ensured that the races "could never live together on terms of equality." Moreover, he also warned that if African Americans remained in the United States, they "tamely and meanly assented to the absorption and extinction of their race." According to the *Cincinnati Gazette,* Langston denounced everyone who supported amalgamation, or race mixing. He is reported to have said that interracial relationships threatened African Americans' survival—an ironic position, considering he was a product of such a union himself. His opposition to interracial relationships was driven by a desire to preserve the black nation, and not necessarily racial chauvinism or assumptions that other races were inferior. Still, it is a dangerous concept either way. Clark agreed with Langston's position: fondly recalling the speech five decades later, he asserted it was "the best [speech] of his life" and concluded "time has vindicated [Langston's] position."[40]

Members of the 1852 Convention's Committee on Emigration, including Clark, Charles H. Langston, and H. Ford Douglass, followed Langston's speech with their own endorsing emigration. Although Clark's speech was not recorded, H. Ford Douglass's speech emphasized that since African Americans had experienced "no real progress in human intelligence, civilization, or freedom" in the United States, their situation was hopeless. Charles H. Langston proclaimed that African Americans could "effect no good by remaining here." He dismissed integrationist arguments that an exodus would make the institution of slavery more secure: "If going away would tend to perpetuate slavery, we ought to die here," he defiantly declared. He reasoned that free African Americans had a better chance of effecting the end of slavery by leaving and forming their own nation. Invoking nineteenth-century notions of black manhood to appeal to the audience's conscience, Charles Langston argued that if African Americans desired dignity and self-respect, leaving was their only option: "We seem determined to remain slaves. We want the spirit of men, and therefore we had better leave." Langston's final admonishment: "If [you are] willing to die [fighting] for freedom, then remain." The Langston brothers clearly articulated the most militant and forceful arguments in favor of emigration at the convention. For them, remaining in America would lead to certain race suicide either through race mixing or a loss of dignity as humans. Other emigrationists at the convention justified their position in less radical terms. One person, for example, argued that citizenship was "essential to the development of a manly and independent character" in the race.[41] The reasoning here is that without citizenship rights, African Americans would remain vulnerable, weak, and dependent on others to protect them.

Black nationalist-emigrationists present at the convention articulated a desire to see a mass migration to another location in the Americas and the subsequent rise of an independent black nation. Although their first priority was their own liberation from oppression, these black nationalist-emigrationists also believed they could best help enslaved people through a separate, sovereign black nation. They imagined that their nation would unite with another government to exert pressure on the United States to end slavery. If diplomacy failed and enslaved people had no options left but to "appeal to arms," they planned to provide "material aid" to their insurrection.[42]

Clark participated in a discourse that imagined "an aggregation of the Negro population around the gulf regions of the continent and that in time the entire gulf would be surrounded by a circle of Negro Commonwealths, beginning at the keys of Florida and ending at the Orinoco [River]." While most other nationalist-emigrationists proposed Haiti, Africa, or other symbols of black freedom as sites for their nation, their imagined nation encompassed the Mississippi gulf region, the West Indies, Central America, and the northern region of South America. What is interesting is that they imagined a black *region*—not just a nation. Those locations were selected as potential sites for the new black nation because of the high concentration of people of African descent. Martin R. Delany would echo the choice of Central and South America as the best sites for planting this new nation in his *Condition, Elevation, Emigration, and Destiny of the Colored People of the United States* published two months later. In that work, Delany contends that Central and South America are desirable sites because the region has a high number of people of color, a favorable climate, a wealth of natural resources, and its geographic location is close enough for fugitive slaves to reach. Moreover, it was unlikely that this region would be annexed by the United States. Clark and the emigrationists envisioned a sovereign black nation in Central and South America that would form alliances with other nations and put economic and political pressure on the United States to free enslaved people. In short, this black region would approach diplomacy with the United States as equals. They indicated that in the event that a "black Kossuth" started a slave revolt, their nation would offer military assistance.[43]

One has to wonder to what extent Clark internalized the discourse and imaginations of black nationhood at this convention. To what extent did he believe this black nation-region might materialize; to what extent did he believe it a mere fantasy? His views about the feasibility of establishing such a nation were not recorded then, but reflecting back to that moment thirty years later, he readily admitted that although he believed the United

States to be African Americans' home, he did not consider it their ultimate destiny.[44]

Peter's own uncle emerged as the leading voice of opposition to emigration at the 1852 Ohio convention. Gaines's vehement opposition to emigration, though, was legendary. A contemporary considered him the "most ultra anti-emigrationist in the West . . . and the most talented one."[45] When he took the convention floor, Gaines told the body that he would remain in the country, "survive or perish." For him, emigration and colonization were one and the same. He roared that emigration amounted to nothing more or less than "'old coon' colonization." Despite his opposition, Gaines remained fully confident that the majority of African Americans were disinclined to leave anyway, rendering the whole debate futile.[46]

Clark and other emigrationists failed to garner popular support; convention delegates voted overwhelmingly to oppose emigration 36 to 9.[47] Although the 1852 convention decided to stand against emigration, emigrationists played a critical role in shaping the discourse. The final resolutions bear the stamp of both sides of the debate, with at least a few of them reflecting black nationalist values like self-respect, mutual responsibility, and self-sufficiency, while others emphasize integration, assimilation, and acculturation.[48]

Resolutions 17 through 19 reveal that the 1852 convention delegates also embraced internationalism and solidarity with European freedom fighters. Referring to the 1848 revolutions in Europe, Resolution 17 reads: "We sympathize with the oppressed Hungarians and German Socialists in their efforts to throw off the yoke of despotism and re-establish their liberty." Resolution 19 draws parallels between American slavery and Russian serfdom: "Tyranny in Russia, Austria, and America, is the same and that tyrants throughout the world are united against the oppressed, and therefore the Russian Serf, the Hungarian Peasant, [and] the American Slave and all other oppressed people, should unite against tyrants and despotism." Going beyond mere intellectual parallels between the conditions of enslaved African Americans, Hungarian peasants, and Russian serfs, this body resolved to forge alliances with these revolutionaries by providing tangible assistance to Gottfried Kinkle and Lajos Kossuth, critical figures in the 1848 German and Hungarian revolutions, respectively. Delegates promised financial aid and offered military assistance. The body resolved to provide "the same aid which our fathers gave in the American revolution at the battle of New Orleans, and to Bolivar in the contest for Columbian independence."[49] It is sheer irony that this body of free African Americans, which had earlier debated emigration, looked not to the U.S. South, Haiti, Africa, or Jamaica for revolutionary role models, but to Europe. Certainly they cannot be considered Pan-Africanists—who believed in the global struggle for black freedom—but *internationalists*. They aligned themselves with European others oppressed by despotic repression throughout the world. Although these delegates understood the importance of linking their struggles to international revolutions and found much in common with these European revolutionaries, neither Kinkle nor Kossuth ever acknowledged the black freedom struggle in their tours of the United States. Kossuth, in fact, vowed not to "meddle with any domestic concerns," including slavery, and was noticeably and uncomfortably silent on the issue during his tour of the United States—to the disappointment of African Americans and abolitionists.[50]

This 1852 convention, an important watershed in the history of the state black convention movement in general, provided an impetus for Clark's development as a leader. Some of the men who supported emigration at the 1852 convention went on to build national reputations for themselves. Langston's address earned him such regard among emigrationists that Delany invited him to address the National Emigration Convention in Cleveland two years later, although by then Langston—two weeks from being admitted to the Ohio Bar—had retreated from his position. Langston took the podium then and proclaimed—to everyone's surprise—that he would "work out my destiny in Lorain County, Ohio." H. Ford Douglass, who also attended that convention, expressed his disappointment that Langston appeared to be "wiring in and wiring out," in reference to his apparent wavering from advocating emigration and black nationhood two years earlier, to embracing his American nationality now. H. Ford Douglass, for his part, had become increasingly militant in the intervening two years. He made it clear then that he was prepared to seek freedom elsewhere; and he eventually followed his conscience and moved to Canada. He returned by the Civil War, when he fought in the United States Colored Troops.[51] The last of the three, Clark, also retreated from his emigrationist position in 1853—ironically, around the same time that it became a viable movement in the mainstream African American community.

Clark attended his first *national* black convention in Corinthians Hall in Rochester, New York, in July 1853—an experience that may have led him to jettison his position on emigration. Never before had the nation witnessed such an assembly of the nation's foremost African American intellectuals, activists, and race leaders. Those in attendance included John

I. Gaines, William H. Day, John Mercer Langston, Charles H. Langston, James C. Pennington, James McCune Smith, George B. Vashon, George T. Downing, Robert Purvis, David Ruggles, Charles L. Redmond, and Frederick Douglass. Clark, acting as secretary of the meeting, met many of them for the first time, and some became his lifelong friends and confidantes. The impressive agenda and resolutions of the 1853 Colored National Convention insisted on an American nationality and outlined a strategy to secure it. Convention delegates believed that African Americans' future lay in the United States. Indirectly dismissive of the discourse of emigration, the body instead invoked the language of the Constitution and Declaration of Independence to assert their heritage as Americans. In the convention's written address to the American public, it asserted that African Americans were Americans—culturally, politically, birth, and because of their oppression and contribution to American struggles for independence: "By birth, we are American citizens; by the principles of the Declaration of Independence, we are American citizens; within the meaning of the United States Constitution, we are American citizens; by the facts of history, and the admissions of American statesmen, we are American citizens; by the hardships and trials endured; by the courage and fidelity displayed by our ancestors in defending the liberties and independence of our land, we are American citizens." Using the discourse of American nationalism, this address lays claim to the promises of citizenship, freedom, and equality articulated in the Founding documents. It buttresses that claim by invoking the memory of African American contributions to the American Revolution. Convention proceedings illustrate that these conventioneers possessed a faith that political rights and social equality would be secured in America one day, so they committed themselves to work within the system to obtain this vision. For them, emigration was not an option.[52]

These convention leaders refused to acknowledge emigration as a viable competing racial agenda. The proceedings suggest that delegates considered emigration to be little more than a misguided idea that was inconsequential to their agenda. In an address to the convention, Frederick Douglass asserted: "We are here, and here we are likely to remain. Individuals emigrate—nations never." His reference to African Americans as a nation suggests that he embraced elements of black nationalism himself. Still, Douglass opposed the other chief black nationalist tenet—emigrationism. Illuminating his integrationist views, he continued, "We have grown up with this Republic; and I see nothing in our character, or even the character of the American people, as yet, which compels the belief that we must leave the United States."[53] The convention's Committee on Colonization seconded this position. The committee gave a report that outlined the myriad problems in the Liberian colony—chief among them was dependence on the ACS.[54]

Clark, who served as the convention secretary, must have been profoundly influenced by the addresses, sessions, and committee deliberations, because from that point forward, he never again publicly advocated emigration.[55] In fact, he became an ardent opponent of both emigration and colonization thereafter.[56] Ironically, the same man who had recently seriously considered and attempted emigration not only absented himself from the National Emigration Convention held in Cleveland in August the following year, but became one of its principal critics in Ohio.[57] In October 1854, just months after that convention, Clark and Cincinnati's other African American leaders organized a meeting at the Union Baptist Church to protest what they called "African Colonization"—a broad category that included emigration. As chairman of the meeting's resolutions committee, Clark played a critical role in drafting them. Hence, the resolutions provide insight into where he stood on emigration in 1854. In no uncertain terms, the resolutions proclaim: "We are native born Americans. . . . [W]e are entitled to the elective franchise and all other rights that are common to American citizens, and we intend to struggle and wait for the 'good time coming,' in the language of the Rochester Convention." The body denounced the ACS as a "foul libeler, bitter persecutor, and steady enemy of the elevation of the colored man." Moreover, the resolutions also denounce all recent colonization and emigration efforts, including the Methodist church's organization of a state colonization society and the National Emigration Convention. Cincinnati's African Americans rejected the Emigration Convention's assertion that the only remedy to the "disease" of political inequality was emigration. Although it reserved its sharpest reproach for the ACS, and not the National Emigration Convention, Cincinnati's African American community, like Clark, no longer cared to differentiate between colonization and emigration.[58]

Peter Clark began the 1850s with little faith in the promise of America, but by 1854 he could not imagine any solution outside of it. Never again would he take any concrete steps to emigrate to Africa. In fact, by 1853, he abandoned the idea of a black nationality altogether, deciding, instead, to work for inclusion into American society. Although he abandoned the most radical forms of black nationalism, he would cling even more tightly to the institutional form of it—through the black church, a black Masonic organization, the black press, black conventions, and finally, black schools. Arguably, that side of his black nationalism had the most staying power in his political career.

Chapter Three

Voice of Purpose

Away with religious proscription, say we. We are living in the
Nineteenth Century—not the middle ages!
Cincinnati Daily Times, August 11, 1853

The most enduring legacy of Ohio's private schools is that they succeeded
in educating and grooming a generation of leaders, teachers, and activists, including Peter H. Clark. By the early 1840s, a core group of African
American men and women had been educated in these private schools
and were, in turn, educating others. This generation of educated African
Americans also led the struggle for access to common schools. Beginning in the early 1840s, local activists shifted their focus from opening
private schools to gaining access to public ones. After all, private school
education had not been wholly successful: philanthropy could not meet all
of the operating expenses; increasing tuition costs was not feasible given
most parents' inability to pay even a small fee. Consequently, many of
these schools were extremely short-lived. Even when benevolent whites
completely funded these private schools, as Hiram Gilmore had done with
Cincinnati High School, they still failed. Moreover, private schools could
not meet the needs of the rapidly growing, largely unschooled black population. African American leaders realized that the only hope for their full
education would be by gaining access to public schools.

African American leaders attacked their exclusion from public schools
from at least two angles. First, the 1844 state convention of black men
resolved to fight for common school privileges by "testing the validity and
constitutionality of those statute laws" that excluded African Americans.[1]
There is no evidence that they ever put this plan into action, however.
Instead, black Ohioans constructed their strongest argument for access to
public education on the unjust tax system. An 1829 Ohio act mandated that
black property holders pay a school tax, and that their monies would be

appropriated by township trustees for their education in separate schools.[2] In practice, however, African Americans paid taxes for more than a decade, and no separate school fund or schools for their benefit ever materialized. Although subsequent state legislation exempted them from paying school taxes altogether, they continued to be taxed.[3] In essence, their tax dollars supported the very same public schools that excluded them. Although African Americans in some Ohio communities requested that their share of the local school funds be refunded so they could start their own schools, such requests were typically ignored.[4]

A power struggle between Ohio Whigs and Democrats in the 1848–1849 state legislature provided the conditions that would dismantle the laws that codified African Americans' noncitizenship status. Free Soil legislators first proposed to repeal the Black Laws, including legislation that denied African Americans access to public schools. In a deal that would swing the balance of power to the Whigs or Democrats, two Free Soil representatives offered their votes to the party that would support, among other things, the establishment of a public school system for African American children. Democrats accepted the offer and moved forward with honoring the terms of the deal. On February 10, 1849, the bill that overturned the state's Black Laws passed, effectively removing from Ohio's law books almost all laws that allowed for the denial of civil rights on the grounds of race.[5] After a battle of more than twenty years, no more barriers remained. The legislature, careful not to authorize integration in the schools, provided for separate public school systems for African American children. These schools were supposed to receive a proportionate share of the township's public funds allocated for common schools.[6] The Ohio legislature also made provisions for African Americans to manage and control their own schools through a Colored School Board. Classes would be taught by black teachers, and the school systems would be managed by a black school board, to be elected by black male property owners from each district.[7] Hence, this community would have autonomy and self-determination from the classroom to the school board, pedagogy to policy.

Cincinnati's black community wasted no time getting schools up and running. It quickly elected six trustees to manage the schools, including John I. Gaines as the president of the board. The newly elected trustees commenced organizing schools and hiring teachers: Clark was hired as the first teacher. Unfortunately, the Cincinnati city government frustrated these efforts to educate black children. When the African American school board tried to withdraw monies from the school fund to meet expenses and pay salaries for the first time, the city treasurer, William Disney, refused to release the funds, claiming no law had authorized him to withdraw funds from the treasury. He also contended that he could not be compelled to release the funds to educate people who were not citizens: he did not consider African Americans to be citizens of any state or country.[8] Hence, years before the Supreme Court declared in the *Dred Scott* decision that African Americans were not citizens, Disney had asserted the same in Cincinnati. Although the laws that delineated white skin and male sex as the criteria for citizenship in Ohio had been erased, the mentality remained. Still, no local, state, or federal laws explicitly conferred citizenship on African Americans. The Cincinnati City Council disregarded the fact that African American taxpayers had paid into the school fund, and, without access to those funds, the Colored School system closed.[9] The closing of those school doors marks the beginning of Peter Clark's journey.

African Americans refused to concede defeat after having waited so long for the right to attend public schools. Invigorated by their gains, John Isom Gaines and Clark accepted the challenge of organizing the community to action and raised money to file a lawsuit challenging the city's refusal to hand over funds.[10] In 1851, the state Supreme Court resolved, in *State ex. Rel. Directors of the Eastern and Western School Districts of Cincinnati v. the City of Cincinnati,* that city tax receipts would be appropriated for the benefit of the Colored School system. The decision stipulated that a school board elected by African Americans would manage the money. With this monumental victory, African Americans reopened their schools in 1852, and Clark resumed his teaching position.

African American educational autonomy in Cincinnati would not last long. Beginning in 1853, a series of legislative decisions stripped Cincinnatians of the right of school governance, including the right to manage the budget for their schools. Adding further insult, the community also lost the power to elect its own school trustees; that power transferred to the white Board of Trustees and Visitors of Common Schools.[11] The Colored School Board elected by the African American community was thereby dismantled. Cincinnati's Board of Trustees and Visitors of Common Schools— the "White Board," as African Americans called it—handpicked African American men to serve on the White Board.[12] Generally, the politics of these representatives concurred with the desires of the White Board. These developments prompted the African American community to mobilize for action. One faction, likely led by Gaines and Clark, asserted that these "selected" trustees "had no power to act . . . [except] at the nod of the Board of

Trustees for the white schools." Furthermore, this faction feared that these selected trustees were "merely the *machines* in the hands of the 'White Board'" and therefore could not, or would not, act in the best interest of their community (emphasis in original).[13] The community felt it had been stripped of its autonomy on every level—from the classroom to the board-room. Not only was the board elected by African Americans replaced with one selected by the White Board, but a white man, Stephen Massey, was appointed superintendent of the Colored Schools. Under Massey's watch, white teachers systematically began to replace black teachers. Massey boasted that such a move ushered in "a higher order of talent,"[14] but the racist implications did not escape the African Americans. These moves seemed to be deliberate and direct attempts to thwart their desires for self-education, self-governance, and self-determination.

Ever since his days in Cincinnati High, Clark had aligned himself with lo-cal German-born radicals, many of whom had migrated to the city in 1848. "Forty-Eighters," as they were called, left Germany in response to the Rev-olution of 1848, coming to America as refugees. Cincinnati, which already had a high population of German immigrants, attracted a lion's share of these refugees—nearly five thousand more settled in the city, swelling the number of Germans to nearly one-third of the total population. The major-ity of the Forty-Eighters settled in the area north of the Miami Canal, east of Plum Street, and just south of the Hills. The Miami Canal reminded them of their beloved Rhine River, so they called this area "Over-the-Rhine," and it became the center of German community, language, and culture almost overnight. Unlike earlier German immigrants to the city, the Forty-Eighters resisted assimilation at all costs. First, they made a con-certed effort to live in the same neighborhood. They were slow to give up their native tongue: the German language could be heard on the streets in Over-the-Rhine and beyond, as well as in schools and churches. Old World beer gardens, saloons, bratwurst stands, and "wienerwurst men" were rep-licated on the streets of Over-the-Rhine. Moreover, this wave of German immigrants conscientiously retained their cultural heritage by establishing civic associations, clubs, newspapers, debating clubs, and schools. Radi-calized by revolution at home, the Forty-Eighters scorned any semblance of aristocracy, class privilege, or inequality; instead, they brought with them radical definitions of freedom, democracy, and equality, which they tried to apply to their new milieu. But German culture is not the only thing the Forty-Eighters retained.

German radicals successfully preserved the Old World revolutionary spirit through the radical organizations they established in Cincinnati. The nation's first radically German political organization, the Turnverein, was founded in the city in 1848 to pursue a more egalitarian and democratic society. In fact, Turnverein members—or, Turners, as they were called—numbered among the first Cincinnatians to organize against the Kansas-Nebraska Act. German workers also established a Workingmen's Club to protest unfair wages, while the more intellectual radicals organized freethinking clubs to sponsor discussions on Marxism, socialism, and abolitionism.[15]

While not all Forty-Eighters can be defined as radicals—some were quite racist and conservative—the radicals embraced some of the most controversial concepts in nineteenth century America, including immediate abolition, natural rights for all, racial integration, interracial solidarity, and socialism. A March 1854 state convention of German radicals, freethinkers, and workingmen held at Cincinnati's Freeman Hall in Over-the-Rhine, condemned both political parties for supporting "slaveholding, manhunting, and the Nebraska betrayal" and demanded an immediate end to slavery. The body insisted that free homesteads also be granted to African Americans.[16] Never before had any ethnic immigrant group in America advocated land redistribution in favor of African Americans. It is no wonder, then, that Clark later concluded that German radicals were truly "the only freedom-loving people of this city."[17]

Constituting the most exploited class of all, German wage earners—or workingmen—also embraced radical ideas. But unlike the intellectuals, German workingmen had practical reasons to embrace radicalism.[18] German workingmen fiercely opposed the Kansas-Nebraska Act because they feared the growth of slavery in western lands would give rise to a slave aristocracy that would be deeply hostile to free labor there. They also imagined that the existence of such an aristocracy would make it impossible for wage earners to compete with slave labor, leading to a depression of their wages and living standards.[19] Hence, German workingmen had practical reasons to support abolition, advocate for free soil, and oppose the expansion of slavery.

Although Clark did not join any German labor, intellectual, or political society in the 1850s, it is easy to understand why he would have been attracted to the intellectual dynamism of this community of German-born radicals.[20] His interactions and conversations with them pushed him to think beyond America's very narrow definitions of equality and democracy.

Moreover, the fact that they possessed a stronger abolitionism and greater sympathy for African Americans than *American* abolitionists certainly proved quite appealing. Last, Clark surely found a common ground with them because of their shared socialist proclivities.[21]

In many ways, his affiliation with the German radicals is part of a natural progression: Clark had been introduced to multiple socialist influences in his childhood. By the early 1850s, he began to openly associate in socialist and freethinking circles and experiment with practical applications of socialism. For example, in 1852, he presented a petition to the Convention of the Colored Freemen of Ohio encouraging African Americans to form labor unions. At that same convention, he served on the Committee on Education, which recommended the formation of an African American teachers' association. Although the historical record leaves many unanswered questions about both the petition and the specific nature of the teachers' association, it is a crucial step in a long journey that would lead Peter H. Clark to trade unionism and, eventually, socialism.[22] Clark even began to apply freethinking to religion and began attending Unitarian services at the First Congregational Church.

That same 1852 Convention of the Colored Freemen of Ohio passed resolutions that, in their language and substance, bear the mark of Clark's influence. Resolution 17, for example, expresses sympathy for "the oppressed Hungarian and German Socialists in their efforts to throw off the yoke of despotism and re-establish their liberty."[23] Clark was the only African American present at that 1852 convention with significant ties to German revolutionaries and socialists. Because of his experience and relationships in Cincinnati's Forty-Eighter community, he was also the only one sympathetic enough to Socialists to introduce such a resolution at the convention.

In 1853, Cincinnati's German-born freethinkers, intellectuals, and labor radicals invited Clark to deliver an address at a celebration commemorating the life and writings of Thomas Paine, a Founding Father. The freethinking community had been publicly celebrating Paine's life and work since the late 1830s. The 1853 celebration drew attention because for the first time in its history, it featured a young African American speaker, who happened to be the first black teacher in Cincinnati's Colored Schools. The press descended on Greenwood Hall to hear what this young teacher had to say. Clark would not disappoint. His lecture highlighted Paine's most memorable arguments in *The Age of Reason* (1794).[24] In that controversial text, Paine—or Tom Paine, as he is commonly called—

condemns organized religion and priests and accuses the Christian church of having created several myths and then passing them off as bona fide historical accounts. These "myths" included Bible stories about Adam's sin in the Garden of Eden, the Immaculate Conception and virgin birth, the Crucifixion and Resurrection, and the afterlife. Paine contends that the works of the prophets mixed "poetry, anecdote, and devotion."[25] According to him, the only miracles that mattered were those of creation and self-existence.

In the eighteenth and nineteenth centuries, any critical interrogation of the Bible or Christianity was considered sacrilegious in the United States. Those who did were deemed heretics at worst, and atheists at best. Paine's seemingly irreverent critiques of the Bible and Christianity and his rejection of Jesus as savior led most nineteenth-century Americans to brand him an infidel. Although Paine is accused of atheism, he actually practiced a faith called deism. Deists believe that the only way to know the true nature of God is through science and reason—not the Bible. They believe in a single, supreme God who created the universe but remains removed from its daily affairs.[26] Paine encouraged people to use reason to reveal what he considered to be contradictions, myths, and unfounded assertions in the Bible. Clark's admiration of Paine had a lot to do with the fact that he recently had begun attending Unitarian services at the First Congregational Church and associating with several of its key members.

The Unitarian movement can be traced back to the First Great Awakening, when some liberal Christians began to question the Christian theory that people are inherently sinful. They also shunned the emotionalism of the revivals. Rather than use emotion to get closer to God, this group of liberals believed that morality and ethical conduct was the best path to get closer to the Divine. They established the Unitarian Church, which emphasizes rational thought, morality, and harmony. Central to their ideology is a faith in the *unity* of God and a rejection of the Trinity. For Unitarians, the Holy Spirit is not a separate and distinct force, but a manifestation of God sent to reassure believers about His Divine Will. Christ, for them, was simply a very moral man with a divinely inspired mission to bear witness to God's word.[27] In that vein, Unitarianism bears great similarity to Paine's deism because both reject the standard doctrine of Christianity, particularly the Trinity. Like Paine, Clark's faith played a significant role in his own political thinking.

Like his hero, Clark also embraced humanism, which is based on the idea that humanity, not God, is responsible for social ills and suffering.

He arrived at this belief system through free thinking, rationalism, and Unitarianism. Clark embraced a black humanism, which is defined as "a canon of philosophical, historical, and religious knowledge by, for, and about people of African descent with the ultimate goal of achieving social justice for all people." In short, black humanism helped him understand racial injustice because it attributes African Americans' condition and suffering to society—not to the will of God; black humanism looks to humanity to correct those injustices.[28]

Beyond faith, Clark had countless secular reasons to admire Paine's writings and legacy. Paine was among the first to advocate for the abolition of slavery in his essay "African Slavery in America" (1775). In that work, he expressed deep sympathy for Africans and strenuously asserted their humanity. He also condemned the institution of slavery as "savage," "inhuman," "unnatural," and "monstrous." Paine also pointed out the hypocrisy of American colonists—for railing against their own "enslavement" while enslaving countless Africans—and of Christians, for setting a bad example to those they claimed to want to enlighten. Certainly Paine's abolitionism, assertion of Africans' humanity, and seething denunciation of slavery would have created a fervent disciple in Clark.

But there were more reasons Clark admired Paine. Staunchly championing republican democracy throughout his life, Paine promoted radical ideas in his collective writing such as political equality, natural rights, natural equality between men, and religious tolerance. In what arguably may be his most democratic publication, Paine's *Rights of Man* (1791) advocated the unity and equality of man. He insisted that God made no natural or racial distinctions when he created humans; so, he did not support political distinctions between them.[29] Hence, it is easy to see why Paine's political and religious philosophies appealed to Clark even fifty years after his death. Considered seditious in his own lifetime in late eighteenth-century Europe, Thomas Paine's writings were no less threatening to the status quo in 1850s Cincinnati.

Drunk on Paine's writings and brazen enough to celebrate them publicly, Clark underestimated the depth of Protestantism in Cincinnati. Antebellum Cincinnatians harbored deep biases against people they considered "infidels"—in other words, those who did not practice Christianity. Although religious freedom had been enshrined in the U.S. Constitution, religious tolerance in Cincinnati was another matter altogether. Despite the fact that the city boasted robust religious diversity in 1853, nativism and Protestantism dominated the tone and climate in the city, where Catholics,

Jews, Unitarians, and others who did not practice Protestant Christianity often met with a great deal of hostility and derision. In fact, Protestant anxieties bubbled to the surface during the 1853 local spring elections, which centered on school issues.[30] By then, public sentiment against hiring "infidels" as teachers or for any position in which they might have the opportunity to influence children became particularly strong. After learning about Clark's Paine lecture, the Cincinnati School Board expressed its misgivings about approving his teaching job for the following year.

Sometime that summer, the School Board's Committee on Colored Schools called Clark in to question him about his religious views. The board asked him whether he had ever tried to impose his faith on his students, about the content of his January Paine lecture, and whether he avoided using New Testament scriptures in his morning lessons. Cincinnati school teachers were expected to use the New Testament scriptures in morning lessons—a clear Christian bias. Clark chose not to do so; his failure to use scriptures was tantamount to a rejection of the Christian faith—which went against school policy. Clark informed the Committee on Colored Schools that he did not realize he had violated any school policy by lecturing about Paine since he did so outside of school hours. Mindful of the School Board's concerns, though, he promised never to impose his religious views upon his pupils, directly or indirectly. He offered no explanation about why he chose not to use scriptures in his morning lessons, though. The committee decided not to recommend censure or termination.[31] Regardless of that decision, the larger school board upheld its reservations about his suitability to teach and debated that well into early August 1853.[32]

Members of the smaller Committee on Colored Schools defended Clark's integrity as a teacher. They assured other board members that he was a man of unquestionable honesty and unimpeachable moral character. One member even reminded the larger board that Clark had been a model teacher who had earned the respect of his entire community. Another expressed confidence that there was not the "least shadow of proof" that he ever had tried to promote his religious views to his students: he had been wholly compliant with the board's mandate that forbade teaching religion in schools. The committee then denounced religious proscription and reaffirmed the constitutional right to freedom of religion. When the question went to a vote, the majority of the Cincinnati School Board members thought otherwise and rejected Clark's nomination to be a teacher in the schools for the 1853–1854 school year, effectively terminating him. Every member of the three-person Committee on Colored Schools resigned in protest of the decision, although their resignations were rejected.[33]

Clark's termination sparked a debate in Ohio newspapers about censorship, religious tolerance, religious freedom, and the separation of church and state. The *Cleveland Plaindealer* implored the Cincinnati School Board to "retract their narrow tyrannizing sentiments" and to keep sectarianism out of schools. That paper cautioned against allowing the faith of any one majority to dominate the schools because it could lead parents of minority religious faiths to withdraw their children. A *Cincinnati Daily Times* editorial insisted that the majority faith had no right to force its religious doctrines upon the minority.[34] Several other local newspapers supported the Cincinnati School Board's decision, including two religious papers, the *Catholic Telegraph* and the *Western Christian Advocate,* a Protestant journal. The *Western Christian Advocate* applauded Clark's termination, editorializing that the School Board must "keep a look out [so] that no Paine or Robespierre should control the hearts and minds of our youth."[35] Even the papers that defended Clark could not shake their Christian bias. An editorial in the *Cincinnati Daily Times* pointed out that while the School Board had terminated Peter Clark based on the fact that he did not believe in Christ's divinity, it had not terminated any Jewish teachers for the same reason.[36] By mentioning Jews in the same context, the editorial aimed to illuminate the hypocrisy and double standard behind Clark's termination as an African American "infidel," while others who rejected Jesus' divinity escaped such persecution. Yet, the paper's insinuation that Jews were infidels, coupled with its anti-Catholic rhetoric, illuminates the Christian *and* Protestant bias rampant in the city's culture in the antebellum era.

Clark's staunchest supporters included German workingmen and African Americans. Although the African American community had relatively little power to influence the Cincinnati School Board's decisions, a group of sixty-four made a strong show of support for Clark at one of its meetings before his termination.[37] Despite the fact that the community had no power to weigh in on his termination, the sheer show of force sent a message to the School Board. Shortly after Clark's termination, a group of African Americans placed a notice of support in the *Cincinnati Daily Commercial* that outlined reasons the School Board should reconsider its position. Although acknowledging that Clark had lectured about Tom Paine, the first resolution insisted that he was neither a "propagandist of infidelity, nor is he an Atheist." The second resolution underscored the fact that Clark had always been loyal and dutiful to his job. The notice ended by reaffirming his "invaluable service to aid in improving the condition of our race," and admitted that few dedicated themselves to that line of work.[38]

After months of controversy, Clark conceded defeat. Dejected and weary, he penned a final letter to the Committee on Colored Schools asking to withdraw his name for consideration, noting, "I am sick of the notoriety which my name has gained." No longer interested in pursuing a position mired in so much controversy, Peter Clark promised he would "cease to be an obstacle in the way of schools."[39]

Despite his own decision to end his fight for the position, the African American community continued to protest on his behalf. In late August 1853, it held a meeting to organize its protest of Clark's termination and to refute the common misperception that he was an atheist. Charles and John Mercer Langston had traveled from northeast Ohio to support their friend; both brothers addressed the assembly, and Charles H. Langston spoke against using religious tests as a basis for employment.

This community's support for Clark is remarkable because African Americans in that era tended to be antagonistic to liberal religious beliefs—especially those that contradicted Protestantism. Even Frederick Douglass endured sharp criticism from the African American community in Philadelphia two decades later for espousing the same, freethinking principles of religious liberty.[40] But the show of support for Clark illustrates that the community understood the importance of religious freedom and the danger of using religion as a barrier to employment. If nothing else, African Americans could see that religious discrimination and intolerance were closely aligned with racial discrimination.

When Clark addressed the assembly gathered on his behalf, he indicated that he did not wish the issue to be made personal. Nor did he think his religious views were the real issue; he believed the matter centered on whether African American taxpayers had the right to select their own teachers. It was that simple for him. The body ended the meeting by unanimously passing a resolution demanding Clark's reappointment.[41] It would be several years, however, before that would happen. In the meantime, Clark went on with his life.

On July 26, 1854, Peter H. Clark married Frances Ann Williams (1830–1902), the daughter of Pleasant Ann and Charles Francis Williams. Her father, employed as a steamboat steward, had a net worth of ten thousand dollars in 1853. Her grandfather, William Anderson, had served as a soldier in the Sixth Maryland Regiment during the American Revolution. His captain, Jeremiah Collins, knew Anderson to be a soldier of "undoubted courage" who served both American and French forces. Anderson fought at the Battle of Brandywine in 1777 and the Siege of Yorktown—a battle that witnessed the surrender of Major General Lord Charles Cornwallis on October 1781. Although severe injuries to his left thigh left Anderson disabled, forcing him to depend on charity thereafter, his military service was a source of great pride to Frances and her family.[42]

By all indications, Frances Williams's family belonged to the black elite, as evidenced by her opportunity to attend college. She enrolled in the Ladies' Course at Oberlin College, graduating in 1853. She was only the second African American woman and the eighth African American of either sex to graduate from that institution. Williams graduated with only a diploma, though, because bachelor's degrees were not then being offered to women. Nevertheless, she is part of a very small, but highly distinguished group of African Americans who attended Oberlin in those days, including George B. Vashon—the first black to earn a bachelor's degree from Oberlin—William H. Day, and all three Langston brothers. Most of the African American women who graduated from Oberlin before the end of the Civil War went on to build teaching careers for themselves.[43] In fact, college-educated African American women had few other occupational options besides teaching. Frances, though, opted to devote herself to housekeeping and supporting her husband in his community endeavors, particularly the Colored Orphan Asylum. She only occasionally taught in Cincinnati's Colored Schools.

Peter's activist career took off shortly after they exchanged their vows; he frequently absented himself from home to attend various antislavery and black conventions and to speak on the antislavery lecture circuit, leaving Frances alone. In addition to his extended absences, the Clarks' early years of marriage were plagued by financial troubles and instability. After losing his teaching position, Clark returned to what he knew: he took a position as a clerk at Wilcox and Roxborough, a local grocery owned by African Americans. Having clerked twice before, he had a fair amount of experience. Clark's desire to be self-sufficient and provide for his new bride prompted him to open his own grocery in 1854, a move that brought him in direct competition with his own uncle. But he was not destined to be a grocer; he left the business soon thereafter for unknown reasons. For the next three years, Clark edited antislavery journals.[44] This occupation provided little economic security, though, since the papers—particularly the African

Peter and Frances Clark, ca. 1895–1900. (Courtesy of Clark N. Jones.)

American ones—languished for a scarcity of subscribers. The period of economic hardship and instability undoubtedly strained the Clarks' new marriage. Only after the Colored School System rehired Clark in 1857 did the couple's financial problems disappear for good. Regardless, their lives were still marked by a level of residential instability: between 1858 and 1869, the Clarks lived at eight different residences. Not until 1869 did the family finally settle down at 104 Barr Street, where they remained for six years—the longest they ever lived in any home in Cincinnati. Then, in 1875, the yearly moving commenced again—this time, probably more as a result of the nature of rental homes in late nineteenth-century Cincinnati than of finances.

Clark spent little quality time with his three children, Ernestine (1855–1928), Herbert (1859–192?), and Consuelo (1861–1910). Regardless, the role he played in setting a high standard of achievement is evident in their accomplishments. All three Clark children attended Gaines High, where he worked, but Herbert failed to graduate—surely a source of deep disappointment for his father. The eldest child, Ernestine, had musical gifts, and she managed to craft a career as an accomplished pianist and vocalist. After graduating from the Cincinnati Music Academy, she took a job teaching music in the Colored Schools. Ernestine later married John Nesbitt, Cincinnati's first African American mail carrier, and the couple produced four daughters. The Nesbitt girls were Peter Clark's only grandchildren; neither Consuelo nor Herbert ever had children. In spite of not graduating from high school, Herbert became an educator and taught at an African American school in Alabama. After returning to Cincinnati, he would benefit from several patronage positions in the 1880s, including deputy sheriff, two appointments to the U.S. Treasury Department as a gauger, and a job in the office of the Ohio legislature. He also edited a Democratic paper. Herbert eventually moved to Oklahoma with his wife, Leanna, and lived out the remainder of his days estranged from his father. The youngest of Clark's children, Consuelo, inherited her father's intellectual gifts and would earn distinction for her intelligence. She attended the Art Academy and then graduated from Boston University's Medical School. She would become the first African American woman licensed to practice medicine in Ohio. After practicing in Cincinnati for some years, Consuelo married William R. Stewart, an attorney, and the young couple relocated to Youngstown, Ohio. Tragically though, her life would prove to be no fairy tale: As a young woman, Consuelo contracted an unspecified wasting disease that plagued her her entire life and may have prevented her from having children. Regardless, the Stewarts established successful practices in their respective fields and enjoyed a life of leisure until Consuelo's untimely death at age forty-nine.

Clark never developed close bonds with any of his siblings or other members of his family. His widowed stepmother, Eliza Clark, remarried the same year he wed Frances. She married Daniel Payne, a prominent AME minister who also held a doctorate degree. In July 1856, the Paynes took Michael Clark's youngest two children and moved to Tawawa Springs, Ohio—later renamed Wilberforce.[45] When Eliza Clark married Payne—a man at least eight years her senior—she owned property valued at fifteen thousand dollars, which she had inherited from Peter's father, Michael.[46] Her wealth brought added financial security to the newlyweds. Payne did not need her money, however, since he himself was graced with education, respectability, and high social standing. He would later become president of Wilberforce University and bishop of the AME church. Owing to Eliza's money and Bishop Payne's power and position, the Paynes were the leading African American family in Wilberforce, and among the

Dr. Consuelo Clark Stewart, Peter Clark's daughter. (Courtesy of Vince Shivers.)

most influential African American families in the state and nation. Clark only occasionally visited his family in Wilberforce, although the town is only fifty miles from Cincinnati. Ironically, just as his ties to the AME church grew tighter through his stepmother's marriage to Payne, Clark began hitching his faith to another wagon: Unitarianism.

Clark began attending Unitarian church services in the early 1850s at Cincinnati's First Congregational Church—one of a few local churches that did not exclude African Americans. A negligible number of Cincinnati's

Four generations of Clarks, 1918. Clockwise: Peter H. Clark; Dorothea (Nesbit) Jones holding Dorothy Rachel Jones; and Ernestine (Clark) Nesbit. (Courtesy of Clark N. Jones.)

African Americans attended Unitarian services there without incident in the antebellum era. Clearly conflicted about his deep roots in the Allen Chapel AME church, Clark did not immediately leave the church of his youth. Undoubtedly, he had had strong reservations about walking away. Not only had his entire family attended the AME church, but he even helped organize another, Brown Chapel, and held services in his home in the 1860s.[47] Clark clove to the AME church not merely because he had been raised in its theology and rituals, but because it had cultural resonance for him. African American Christianity shaped a distinct worldview rooted in African Americans' peculiar experiences in America. Arguably, the AME church served as the most potent symbol of freedom and progress African Americans had. As the only independent black church in America at the time, it could afford to be vocal, overtly political, and uncompromising in its agitation for social change. Moreover, local AME congregations committed themselves to many levels of freedom—from harboring fugitives in the basement of the church to serving as a launch pad for community protests.[48] In short, Peter had myriad reasons to remain affiliated with this church. Certainly, too, the AME church renewed and insulated him psychologically and spiritually: in essence, the church provided a refuge from the racism without, and solace when the racism touched within. It is no wonder, then, that he did not make a clean and immediate break from the church.

Despite the fact that it fed his soul, Clark needed something that fed his intellect as well. He hungered for a more rationalist theology and radical spiritual community that shared his vision of egalitarianism, universal humanism, and social justice. Unitarianism offered him that.

Clark's membership in a Christian church, his move toward Unitarianism, and adherence to a black humanist outlook were not necessarily irreconcilable, as their contradictions might suggest. According to Anthony B. Pinn, black humanism's "appeal to social justice is similar to that used historically within African American Christian churches minus one ingredient: justice is demanded and premised upon a humanocentric appeal to accountability and progress, not on the dictates of scripture lived through the Christ figure." In sum, Clark believed in the power of humans to transform their society and elevate African Americans' condition.[49] He towed the line between both congregations for more than a decade before finally joining the First Congregational Church in 1868.

Although the Cincinnati's First Congregational Church at Race and Fourth Streets may not have been as integrated as Clark may have liked, it offered him the opportunity to engage and interact with the city's most ardent social reformers. Between 1856 and 1862, when he began attending service, the church was led by freethinker-abolitionist-socialist Moncure Conway. Born into a slaveholding family in Virginia, Conway began to chart a new destiny for himself when he enrolled at Harvard's Divinity School. There, he learned about freethinking and Emerson's Transcendentalism, which set the groundwork for his eventual conversion to Unitarianism. He also came to believe that religion contradicted the premise behind slavery and became a committed abolitionist. At some point, Conway rejected his birthright by choosing not to become a Protestant Christian slaveholder, but a Unitarian abolitionist instead. He began his ministry in a Washington, D.C., Unitarian congregation, but was asked to leave because he denounced slavery and proslavery forces at Bleeding Kansas from the pulpit. Conway moved to Cincinnati in December 1856, where he took a position, at just twenty-four years of age, as minister of the First Congregational Church. Well-versed in German free thought, Paine's writings, and Transcendentalism, Conway caused a stir in the church when these radical ideas filtered into his teachings. While attending the 1857 Western Unitarian Conference, Conway asserted that the *Dred Scott v. Sanford* decision was one of several "deliberate assaults on religious and civil freedom in America." He called on Christians to fully and freely discuss this "crime against man, and . . . God." Conway's Transcendentalist beliefs, coupled with his radical social vision, ruffled many feathers in the otherwise conservative and traditional First Congregational Church and even led to a split in the body between the traditionalists and Transcendentalists.[50]

Clark began attending services at the First Congregational Church around the time of Conway's arrival, perhaps having been drawn there by the abolitionist social vision of its progressive-thinking young minister. Certainly, Conway, with his zeal and intelligence, made an indelible impression on the young Clark.

Conway's flock may have known about his association with well-known German American radicals and intellectuals, including the socialist labor leader and radical August Willich and the freethinking philosopher Johann Stallo. August Willich, a German-born freethinker, made his mark as a prominent member of the local Turnverein, and editor of the German-language free-labor journal *Cincinnati Republikaner* between 1858 and 1861. He used his press to advocate on behalf of the workingmen in their fight for better wages and working conditions. Considered even more radical than Cincinnati's other radicals because of his communist sympathies, Willich earned his nickname, "Reddest of the Red," honestly. Moreover, he personally knew Karl Marx and Friedrich Engels and had debated with them about communist ideology. Willich went further than most other radicals of his day with his views about race. He rejected any expansion of slavery into the new territories and advocated full racial equality. Unlike even most abolitionists, Willich accepted African Americans' humanity, asserted their capacity to progress intellectually, and advocated that they enjoy the same privileges as whites. His views earned him much contempt; the conservative German press called him a "German nigger worshipper."[51]

Stallo was no less controversial a figure. Although Catholicism was the predominant religion among recent German American immigrants, Stallo felt more at home in the First Congregational Church surrounded by other freethinking intellectuals and activists. A vociferous champion of religious freedom, Stallo challenged not only the Catholic church of his youth, but also the local Protestant community by speaking out against Sabbath laws and the practice of reading Protestant hymns and prayers in public spaces like schools. Like Willich, he earned himself much criticism within the German immigrant community and beyond for his pronouncements against Christianity. Stallo became one of Conway's chief advisors and dearest friends. Both Stallo and Willich knew Clark and likely engaged him in freethinking debates. Willich felt such an affinity for him that he came to Clark's defense several times in the local papers.[52]

The First Congregational Church also put Clark in contact with several well-heeled native whites. There, he met and started lifelong friendships with Alphonso Taft and future governor George Hoadly. Born in Vermont in 1810, Taft attended Yale College and Yale Law School. After graduating, he researched where he might have the greatest opportunity to launch his legal career. At the time, Cincinnati was an up-and-coming city with great possibilities for well-educated young New Englanders with ambition, so he moved there in 1839. A principled man who abhorred slavery on moral grounds, Taft first channeled his sentiments toward politics during Bleeding Kansas. The father of future president William H. Taft, the senior Taft would serve as the Judge of the Superior Court of Cincinnati in 1865, and later, the secretary of war and U.S. attorney general. George Hoadly had been born in New Haven, Connecticut, in 1826. He attended Western Reserve College and Harvard Law School. Hoadly arrived in Cincinnati in 1846 and assumed a position at Salmon P. Chase's law firm, where he became partner within two years. An active abolitionist, Hoadly spent the better part of his early career helping Chase prepare cases in defense of fugitive slaves. Like Chase, his career moved from abolitionism into politics. One of the most highly regarded attorneys in the city before the Civil War, Hoadly was appointed superior court judge in 1851, elected city solicitor in 1855, and elected judge of the superior court in 1859 and again in 1864. The height of his political career, though, would come in 1883, when he was elected governor.

Both Taft and Hoadly left their parties over the issue of slavery: Taft split with the Whig Party, while the Kansas-Nebraska Act drove Hoadly to leave his Democratic Party. Hoadly was present at the founding of the Republican Party. He and Taft attended its first convention in Philadelphia, and the two collaborated to organize the state Republican Party in 1855.[53]

Alphonso Taft (Courtesy of the Cincinnati Museum Center.)

Clark developed a business relationship with Taft, who acted as his attorney for real estate matters, but he and Hoadly developed a friendship that became the most significant in his life. Three years Hoadly's junior, Clark held a profound respect and loyalty to his friend that would guide every major political decision he made throughout his life. As a testament to the depth of his respect for Hoadly, Clark would follow him into some conservative political parties and alliances, including the Liberal Republican and Democratic Parties—even to the detriment of his reputation with his own community. For his part, Hoadly held an equally deep respect for Clark. He not only would consult Clark during his two gubernatorial campaigns, but would seek his advice on several key decisions as governor. Theirs is a good example of a nineteenth-century interracial friendship based on genuine mutual respect and admiration.

Still, Clark's occasional attendance at the First Congregational Church in the later 1850s must be underscored. Under Conway's leadership, the church became a fertile breeding ground for some of the most radical free-thinking minds in antebellum Cincinnati. Even more exceptional is the fact that the church fostered a living example of interracial, interethnic humanism that defied logic in a city that witnessed a near perpetual state of ethnic and racial conflict. Outside of his high school and the AME church, the Unitarian church played a pivotal role in developing Clark's intellectualism and humanism.

In 1855, Clark placed himself at the center of a national debate over African American education when he opposed Frederick Douglass's idea for an industrial college designed to uplift African American youth economically. Douglass believed the youth could "forsake menial employments" with industrial education. He first raised the idea at the 1853 National Colored Convention in Rochester, but it was not the first time African Americans had considered such a school. Several conventions of colored men beginning in 1835 had considered building an industrial school, but the idea had never gone beyond the planning stages. In 1853, a planning committee, named the National Council, was formed to organize this industrial college. The National Council conceptualized and planned the school: it would train men and women in the trades. According to an editorial in *Frederick Douglass' Paper,* the college "did not aim to make scholars, but workmen; not ministers or lawyers, but mechanics; it will be a school where colored youth . . . shall have a fair chance for making themselves master craftsmen." According to a leading member of the National Council, they did not intend to establish any "fat, lazy professorships, nor [would we] encourage the attendance of dressy droning students." The school would have a working farm so that "every man and woman, whether teacher or student, earn what they eat."[54]

The National Council hoped to raise $150,000 by selling ten-dollar shares and through donations from wealthy benefactors. Perhaps too naïve and idealistic, the National Council failed to consider that the free African American community in the North as a whole did not have the capital to raise that staggering amount; moreover, they had assumed that white abolitionists like Harriet Beecher Stowe would support the school. They were wrong. The council had to readjust its goals downward to $30,000. By the time it did, the idea for the school was already in jeopardy of failing because the council could not raise the necessary funds to even break ground.[55]

Clark exchanged editorials about the feasibility of the college with Dr. James McCune Smith, a Glasgow-trained New York physician, intellectual, writer, and member of the National Council. Their exchange was published in the *Cincinnati Herald of Freedom* and *Frederick Douglass' Paper.* Clark believed the idea of such a school to be wholly "impractical" and doomed from the start for several reasons. Obviously unaware of the initial $150,000 projected goal, he felt the National Council had grossly underestimated the cost of the project. He thought the $30,000 estimate "puerile," believing that the project would realistically cost no less than $500,000. He chastised the body for "forgetting the materials with which they must work, and the resources upon which they must rely," referring to the relative impoverishment of African Americans.[56]

Questioning the wisdom of the proposed site—100 miles from Erie, Pennsylvania—Clark believed it altogether too remote for the masses of African Americans to get there easily. Moreover, he argued that as long as the school was located so far from a major city, it could not offer anything but a few trades; students would, instead, have few options besides "broom and basket making, tailoring, and a few simple arts." Clark also wondered how many people the school realistically would serve since only a small percentage of African Americans were even free in 1855. He also doubted whether the school would benefit any but the "most enterprising" or the black elite. Moreover, he thought it ridiculous that African American leaders planned a school on the scale of white industrial colleges when their community simply did not have the resources for such an undertaking. He chastised them for coming up with ill-advised ideas that were doomed to fail.[57]

Infeasibility aside, Clark adamantly opposed industrial education on principle. With more than a hint of sarcasm, he insisted that African American youth needed to have better options than "barber shops, knife cleaning, and bone polishing." At the heart of that comment, though, is his disdain for any uplift program that focused on trades; Clark believed that African Americans needed higher options—especially since he doubted that anything but a limited number of "*respectable* trades" would be taught.[58] His own experiences may have dictated such a hard-line position: as a young man, he had been trained in printing and barbering; yet, his classical education at Cincinnati High had made the most difference in his life. Like W. E. B. Du Bois fifty years later, Clark insisted on a classical higher education for African Americans and rejected ideas that relegated them to menial, domestic, or industrial labor.

Although he never wavered from his support for "head learning," Clark did appreciate that the problem was really an economic one that centered on the fact that most whites refused to hire African Americans in the trades. Some white tradesmen had even unionized to block African Americans from the path in Cincinnati and other northern cities. As a remedy to that economic problem, Clark projected a socialist solution. According to James McCune Smith, Clark envisioned a cooperative form of economic development whereby African Americans with the same trades would form business cooperatives. Those cooperatives would then successfully compete with white businesses for large jobs. Clark projected that a cooperative could employ large numbers of African American youth. The owner of his own medical practice, Smith ridiculed the idea, rhetorically asking whether newspaper editors like Clark should also "unite their fortunes" and do the same.[59] Smith's sentiments are not surprising, especially since most African American entrepreneurs then subscribed, as they still do now, to individualistic and capitalistic ideas of free enterprise. Clark's vision of cooperatives was fundamentally socialist. Still, Clark opposed industrial *education,* not industrial jobs.

National Council members did not believe African Americans were ready for classical education. In a private letter trying to convince Harriet Beecher Stowe to offer financial support, Douglass explained that high schools and colleges that provided a classical education were "beyond our immediate occasions, and are not adapted to our present most pressing wants. High schools and colleges are excellent institutions, and will, in due season, be greatly subservient to our progress . . . [but] we, as a people, have not yet attained [that point]." He added, "Accustomed, as we have been, to the rougher and harder modes of living, and of gaining a livelihood, we cannot, and we ought not to hope that, in a single leap from our low condition, we can reach that of Ministers, Lawyers, Doctors, Editors, Merchants, &c." For Douglass, such goals might be achieved in the distant future, but not until African Americans have "patiently and laboriously . . . and successfully, mastered and passed through the intermediate gradations of agriculture and the mechanic arts."[60] Clark adamantly opposed Douglass's ideas that such jobs be an "intermediate" position; he did not think African Americans needed an intermediate position between slavery and real freedom.

Although Clark was one of the most vocal opponents of the industrial college, his was not the only voice of dissent. Garrisonians expressed outright hostility to the idea because they fundamentally opposed separate schools. One American Anti-Slavery Society official railed that this school promised to keep African Americans "ignominiously apart from the refining influence of association with the more highly educated and accomplished." Historians have speculated that Garrisonians may have discouraged Stowe from donating her much anticipated financial support to the school.[61] Worn down by the opposition and discouraged by the lack of finances to start the project, the National Council voted against the industrial college in July 1855.

Despite the fact that plans for the school already had been suspended, James McCune Smith, writing under the pseudonym "Communipaw" in *Frederick Douglass' Paper,* challenged Clark's objections on their merits in a series of editorials.[62] Confident that $30,000 would be sufficient to get the place started, he assured Clark and other readers that the college would "earn its own continued existence" through its working farm. While Clark believed racial uplift would be earned through classical education, Smith argued that men and women so trained in the trades would "go forth as men of enterprise, pith, resources and . . . there is no barrier of caste which they will not break down, no apathy on the part of their brethren which they will not kindle into emulous flame."[63] This is the same argument Washington would make later.

Clark's rejoinder to Smith on August 10 must have struck a nerve because the physician responded in a lengthy diatribe printed on September 21, 1855. Reflecting a touch of despondence, he lamented that African Americans lacked unity and instead harbored a "mutual repulsion"—self-hatred—toward members of their own race. Smith further detailed how many African Americans refused to patronize their own kind, preferring instead to support white businesses. Bemoaning how little the masses appreciate the work their leaders did to uplift them, he complained that they instead either "forget them, or if they remember them it is for the purpose of blame or ridicule." Smith added: "The galling pressure of the whites would be sad enough: but to have to endure the malignant spite of our own people, ever ready to lick the dust before our common oppressors, and to turn with venom upon their black vindicators ... is something which I cannot learn over again." Clark never responded.[64]

By 1855, Cincinnati's African Americans had begun to express discontent with their white teachers and the token Colored School Board. Weary of outside control, the community lobbied for the right to control their own schools. In addition, the Convention of the Colored Freemen of Ohio urged citizens to petition the legislature for the right to elect African American superintendents.[65] The Colored School Board, reconsidering whether it could manage both school systems, recommended that the city council cede control of the Colored Schools back to the African American community.[66] In the midst of such pressure, the Ohio legislature passed a law in 1856 that did just that.[67] Having control of these schools was essential. The black community believed that its governance over the administration, finances, curricula, and classroom instruction would ensure that African American children would receive the best education possible. In 1857, African Americans elected their own School Board members with John I. Gaines as superintendent. These board members were, in fact, the only elected African American officials in the city until the passage of the Fifteenth Amendment in 1870. One of the first things Gaines did as superintendent was to send for his nephew, then living and working in Rochester, to resume his position as a teacher in the schools after a four-year hiatus.[68]

A disabling illness plagued Gaines throughout his final years and ultimately cut his life short in 1859, at the age of thirty-eight.[69] John Mercer Langston delivered a glowing eulogy for him at the 1860 State Anti-Slavery Society meeting, extolling Gaines's integrity, enterprise, and promptness in business affairs, and held up his professionalism as a model for all African Americans. Langston remembered Gaines for his "deep, active, self-sacrificing interest in the welfare of [his] community." His work for Colored schools, he added, "should be recorded in granite, that posterity may know of his benevolent endeavors." Langston ended the eulogy by hailing Gaines's oratorical skills as "natural, perspicuous, animated and powerful"; and praising him for "originality, profoundness of thought, and accuracy of expression."[70]

Sadly, Gaines's untimely death ushered in the next stage of Clark's educational career, including his promotion to principal of the Western District Colored School. For the following seven years, Clark lobbied to obtain a high school for African Americans. When the first one opened in 1866, it was named Gaines High School in honor of his uncle and Clark was appointed as its principal. As the principal of both Gaines High and the Western District Colored School, Clark had a hand in the education of almost every African American child in Cincinnati before 1887. A few of these students went on to establish academic careers, including Charles Henry Turner, who was one of the first black scientists. In 1868, Gaines High opened a normal school to train black teachers and teach new skills to existing teachers.[71] Hence, before 1887, Clark trained nearly every African American teacher in southwest Ohio. This is significant because this growing teacher corps constituted the beginning of a black middle class in the city.[72]

Under Clark's leadership, the school eclipsed all other black institutions in Cincinnati as an agent for racial uplift and as a measure of black progress. Born out of the first extension of citizenship rights to African Americans by the State of Ohio, Cincinnati's Colored Public Schools represented decades of struggle. Running these schools and electing the trustees proved to be a preparation for African American participation in the body politic. Moreover, Colored Public Schools trained future generations of black leaders and civil rights activists, provided the means for the social and economic elevation of both individuals and the collective, and infused other black institutions with an educated membership. In sum, Peter Clark was the dean of black upward mobility in Cincinnati before 1887.

> How were Black teachers trained?
are Peter Clarks schools still standing?

Chapter Four

"The Silver Tongued Orator of the West"

> The institution of slavery . . . never had, has not now, and never can have, any foundation in justice, but is only the result of force and fraud, differing in no respect of principle from the early bondage of Western Europe, or from the serfdom of Russia, which are condemned by the voice of history as crimes against human nature.
>
> Resolutions of the Cincinnati John Brown Rally, December 1859

[handwritten annotation: → when did John Brown die?]

On May 28, 1856, Frederick Douglass did the honors of introducing Clark as a speaker at the Radical Abolition Party's nominating convention in Syracuse, New York; it was only the second national meeting of the new party. Clark's relatively short speech on the first day of the convention largely focused on America's failure to honor the concept of "universal brotherhood." According to him, the obligation to one's fellow human had been mandated by God and the Founding Fathers. Emphasizing the relationship between universal brotherhood and antislavery efforts, he concluded, "To this great doctrine underlies the anti-slavery movement, and whatever triumphs have been achieved, have been achieved because the friends of this movement have been faithful to this doctrine; and whatever remains to be achieved will be achieved by fidelity to this principle." Clark accused Americans of betraying the principle of universal brotherhood by failing to extend freedom or equal rights to African Americans. Moreover, he also blamed them for failing to honor the ideals laid out in the Constitution—a failure, he argued, that had further entrenched slavery: "Instead of forbidding Slavery to exist anywhere, we consented to let the African slave trade continue until 1808 and Slavery to live under the Constitution *till* [*sic*] *the people by the Constitution should see fit to abolish it.*" For the last third of his speech, Clark highlighted how unfree African Americans were in the so-called free states. Explaining why they were effectively powerless to liberate enslaved people, he ended by saying: "Had not we of the North been as much slaves as the blacks of the South, we should, ere this, have taken up the gauntlet the South has thrown down, and driven the slave power from the land."[1] In short, Clark's speech before the two-hundred-person assembly reiterated many of the Radical Abolition Party's positions. Disappointingly, he offered neither fiery condemnation of the Slave Power nor outraged indignation about what slavery had done to enslaved African Americans. Regardless, the important point is that he now publicly identified himself as a Radical Abolitionist.

Peter Humphries Clark walked into that Syracuse Radical Abolition Party convention at a critical juncture in American history. His address there—at the behest of Frederick Douglass—placed him in the vanguard of the most militant political abolitionists in the nation, including Douglass, Dr. James McCune Smith, J. W. Loguen, Gerrit Smith, John Brown, and Lewis Tappan. The Radical Abolition Party had been formed in 1855 in response to the Kansas-Nebraska Act. Passed in May 1854, the act not only repealed the Missouri Compromise, but decided that the question of slavery in Kansas and Nebraska territories should be settled through popular sovereignty. It radicalized antislavery activists and led to the birth of several new political parties, including the Republican and Radical Abolition Parties.

Not merely an abolitionist organization, the Radical Abolition Party was, first and foremost, a political party. As such, Radical Abolitionists believed politics was the best and most effective means to end slavery. They vowed to elect only those who would take the necessary steps to end slavery immediately. Radical Abolitionists can be distinguished from other abolitionists and political parties. First, their party's singular goal was ending slavery everywhere immediately. Not content with merely opposing the extension of slavery into new territories, Radical Abolitionists vowed to interfere with slavery in established slave states, as well. In this vein, they differed from the Free Soilers and Republicans who simply opposed the extension of slavery in new territories but did not believe the federal government had the authority to interfere with slavery where it already existed. Radical Abolitionists also refused to compromise with the Slave Power on any level. The final position that distinguished this party from others is that it advocated the extension of citizenship rights to African Americans.[2]

Radical Abolitionists believed the Declaration of Independence and Constitution were based on antislavery principles. They reasoned that the Founding Fathers—who used phrases like "all men are created equal" and "inalienable right to life, liberty, and the pursuit of happiness"—never intended for slavery to continue indefinitely in the republic. Such language provided incontrovertible proof that the Constitution and Declaration of Independence were antislavery documents. They also insisted that the documents proved that the federal government had neither a "moral [n]or political right" to tolerate slavery one minute longer. Rather than taking a neutral position on slavery, Radical Abolitionists believed the government had an *obligation* to "secure the blessings of liberty" for citizens and their posterity as the founding documents emphasized.[3]

Interestingly too, Radical Abolitionists like John Brown used the Bible to justify their crusade against slavery. One historian contends that Radical Abolitionists relied on "sacred self-sovereignty," meaning they envisioned that the Kingdom of God resided within humans. This concept of a God that dwells within is consistent with the writings of Transcendentalist thinkers such as Ralph Waldo Emerson and Walt Whitman, among others. Radical Abolitionists also rejected the idea that people are born into sin, believing, instead, that sin originates in institutions—in this case, slavery. Since social ills originated in society and its institutions, humans had the capacity to end that evil. Radical Abolitionists believed they were called to eradicate that evil in society. Imagining themselves as crusaders against sin made it easier for them to justify extreme measures, including violence.[4]

Because they saw abolitionism as a crusade, Radical Abolitionists expressed a willingness to use violence to overthrow the Slave Power and slavery, should political means fail—a position that clearly sets them apart from most abolitionists. For example, delegates at the first convention of the Radical Abolition Party in Syracuse in June 1855 had come to a consensus that armed resistance was the only recourse left in the battle for the soul of the Kansas and Nebraska Territories. They took a collection to fund antislavery forces in Kansas in 1854, and later would provide funds to John Brown for his raid on Harpers Ferry in October 1859.[5] The totality of their philosophy, zeal, politics, and militancy led William Lloyd Garrison to conclude that Radical Abolitionists were "madmen." But to what extent did Clark subscribe to armed revolt? Although he *preferred* political tactics to lobby for abolition and civil rights, he was not opposed to resorting to armed revolution when all other avenues failed.[6]

Clark did not affiliate with the Radical Abolition Party very long: he attended only one other Radical Abolition convention—the New York State Convention in September 1856—and left the party shortly thereafter.[7] As fate would have it, the 1856 New York Republican Party held its state convention in Syracuse during the same days as the Radical Abolition Party's nominating convention.[8] Since the two meetings were held within a few blocks of one another, Clark almost certainly attended that Republican meeting. Perhaps he had begun to doubt that the Radical Abolition Party could win at the polls or overthrow slavery, or perhaps he concluded that the Republican Party had a better chance of succeeding at the polls. Regardless of what moved him, sometime that fall Clark rejoined the Republican Party.[9]

Clark's brief affiliation with the Radical Abolitionists signals a defining moment in his development—when he began to endorse politics as an abolitionist and civil rights strategy. Although he and other political abolitionists also endorsed other strategies such as moral suasion, they believed politics to be the most effective weapon against slavery—bar none. As such, they focused on using the political system to effect change. Interestingly, Clark would use the lessons he learned as a political abolitionist to inform his other social reform activities throughout his life.

While African American abolitionists had a dual-pronged agenda of ending slavery and elevating the status of free African Americas, most placed greater emphasis on the former. By contrast, Clark's abolitionism focused less on ending slavery and more on securing full freedom, equality, and citizenship for free African Americans.[10] Although he did participate in typical abolitionist activities like antislavery lectures, conventions, and even the Underground Railroad, Clark's most significant contributions to that movement are those that allowed him to focus on the struggle for African American citizenship, specifically attending black conventions, memorializing for civil rights, Emancipation Day lectures, editing antislavery journals, and penning a history of a black Civil War brigade. He always found a way to insert the struggle for black citizenship into all of his abolitionist activities. Even his speech before the Radical Abolition Party's nominating convention partly focused on illuminating the condition of free African Americans.

Clark was introduced to the abolitionist movement through the black state conventions. These conventions were, in fact, a critical component of free African Americans' abolitionism. And Ohio was, perhaps, the best place for an African American to attend these conventions: it hosted one of the most tenacious, vocal, and engaged black convention movements in African American history. Convention delegates drafted petitions and addresses to the public, and lobbied legislatures. They debated the efficacy of various abolitionist tactics, including moral suasion, politics, and armed revolt. These meetings provided an opportunity for free African Americans to collectively agitate for emancipation for the enslaved and fuller rights for themselves. These conventions taught Clark how to use the political system to effect change.

He preferred this type of abolitionist work over all others, as evidenced by his robust participation in the black convention movement from 1849 through 1864. In no other abolitionist project did he sustain the same level of involvement and energy across such a long period of time. Furthermore, long after the walls of slavery came crumbling down, Clark continued to pattern his civil rights agitation on the models of organizing and lobbying he learned at the Ohio black conventions.

Despite Clark's active participation at Ohio black conventions, he did not officially get involved with the larger abolitionist movement until the mid-1850s. Although he played no official role at the 1851, 1852, 1853, or 1854 antislavery[11] conventions held in his city, he surely attended them.[12] There he would have heard addresses by some of the greatest abolitionist minds in the country and would have been influenced by what he witnessed at these conventions. He did not get actively involved in the mainstream abolitionist movement until the Western Anti-Slavery Convention held its 1855 meeting in Cincinnati. Not only did Clark serve as one of the convention's vice presidents, but he also stepped in for the convention chairperson, who had an unexpected absence. In that capacity, he delivered the keynote address, although unfortunately, local papers never recorded its substance.[13]

In addition to participating in formal, overt abolitionism, there are clues that Clark also belonged to the Underground Railroad network in Cincinnati, although concrete evidence of his involvement in a clandestine system in a city with severe reprisals for such activity is hard to find. Only a few remaining anecdotal clues support the conclusion that Clark did, indeed, assist in this type of abolitionist activity. He brazenly reported to the 1852 Convention of Colored Freemen of Ohio that 138 fugitive slaves had passed through Cincinnati the previous year, suggesting that he had personal experience and intimate knowledge of the system.[14]

Another indication of Clark's possible involvement in the Underground Railroad is his friendship with Levi Coffin, known to African Americans at the time as the "President of the Underground Railroad." Although not the most critical Underground Railroad operator in Cincinnati,

Coffin certainly was the most active of the city's white operators. His brick, three-story house, located on the corner of Sixth and Elm Streets, was an important way station for fugitives from 1847 through the Civil War.[15] Coffin and Clark met sometime in the early 1850s, either through that work or their service to the Colored Orphan Asylum, an organization Clark's father had helped found in 1844. Coffin had volunteered to run the orphanage free of charge because the institution had no money, while Clark served on its Board of Trustees throughout the 1850s.[16] Moreover, he would later serve as a pallbearer at Coffin's funeral in 1877—a testament to the depth of their personal friendship.[17]

More substantial evidence of Clark's Underground Railroad activity can be found in his involvement in a fugitive slave case in southwest Ohio involving George "Wash" McQuerry and three other bondsmen who escaped from Washington, Kentucky, in 1849. After moving around for a while, McQuerry eventually settled down just north of Dayton, in Troy, Ohio, where he worked as a boat hand. McQuerry's "owner," Henry Miller, diligently searched for him for four years, until finally discovering his whereabouts in 1853. According to the press, Miller traveled to Troy, seized his fugitive, and took him to Dayton without a writ of habeas corpus. In Dayton, Miller handed McQuerry over to a U.S. marshal, who then took him to Cincinnati. After learning of McQuerry's fate, Cincinnati's African American community mobilized to protest his return to Kentucky. Clark played a direct role in the events that unfolded next.[18]

In the wee hours of the morning, he and John Jolliffe, a local abolitionist attorney, drafted an application for a writ of habeas corpus. Writs of habeas corpus required anyone with possession of prisoner—or in this case, a fugitive slave—to appear before a judge to prove they had a legal right to keep them imprisoned. They guaranteed that even alleged fugitive slaves could not be deprived of their liberty without due process. In essence, writs of habeas corpus frustrated the efforts of "owners" to reclaim their bondspeople and safeguarded against the abductions of free African Americans. Hence, writs of habeas corpus proved to be not only powerful tools against the system of slavery but also safeguards of African American freedom and an assertion of their citizenship.

Clark then went to the Clifton home of Judge John McLean at 2:00 a.m. on August 16, 1853, and submitted the application on McQuerry's behalf. Clark's request, which appeared in local papers, stated that the U.S. marshal was guilty of "unlawfully depriving the said McQuary [sic] of his liberty, under the color and pretence that he has the authority to do so." The application asked that McLean grant a writ of habeas corpus so that McQuerry would be brought before the court, where his captors would be compelled to show just cause for his "unlawful imprisonment." Judge McLean granted the writ and granted the fugitive a hearing in district court. Abolitionists James Birney and John Jolliffe acted as his counsel. Their defense centered on two arguments. First, although McQuerry readily admitted that he had absconded from Miller four years prior, he was now entitled to his freedom because he was *reputed* to be free and had lived as a free man in a free state for four years. The second and strongest part of his defense centered on the presumed unconstitutionality of the Fugitive Slave Law. Although Jolliffe had a brilliant argument, Judge McLean decided that McQuerry should be remanded to his owner; within fifteen minutes of that decision, the fugitive was en route to Kentucky.[19]

Regardless of the poor outcome, Clark contributed to McQuerry's struggle for freedom when he applied for the writ. Had he not done so—and so quickly—McQuerry would have been taken to Kentucky without a proper hearing and never would have been given the opportunity to make his case for his freedom. By invoking the strongest safeguard of American liberty, the writ of habeas corpus, Clark ensured that McQuerry would be afforded certain rights which, heretofore, largely had been reserved for white prisoners. In an age when African Americans could not even testify in court or serve on juries, he operated with the assumption that African Americans *were* citizens with all the associated rights. Clark's petition for the writ affirmed African Americans' right to apply for writs of habeas corpus as citizens *and* to invoke them to protect their liberty. Still, despite his actions on behalf of McQuerry, Clark is not numbered among the most prominent or active Underground Railroad operators in the Queen City's history. His abolitionist activities, however, did not end there.

In June 1855, Clark launched the *Herald of Freedom,* an abolitionist weekly.[20] With no extant copies, it is difficult to gauge the politics of the paper, but according to another contemporary African American journal, the *Herald* adapted a "moderate anti-emigration" stance. Moreover, an editorial in the *Provincial Freeman* also noted that Clark had "peculiar notions about some things." Although deemed "moderate" and "peculiar" by the black press, Clark's *Herald* ruffled enough feathers that the conservative *Cincinnati Daily Commercial* printed an editorial in its June 19, 1855, issue accusing him of being too passionate about abolitionism and making it too prominent a feature in his journal. The *Commercial* editorial further criticized the journal for focusing too much on racial inequality and social and political rights for African Americans.[21] Still the consensus held that the *Herald* was a "well-conducted and useful journal" with "an extensive circulation throughout Ohio and adjoining States." *Frederick Douglass' Paper* liberally quoted *Herald of Freedom*—a testament to its success. Despite its fine reputation, the *Herald* survived just five months: like other antebellum African American newspapers, it suffered from limited and delinquent subscriptions, receiving just sixteen dollars per week.[22] Clark's efforts to use his own funds to support the paper proved inadequate to keep it afloat. Despite the failure of his journal, his experience as an abolitionist editor laid the groundwork for future opportunities.[23]

Clark's editorial experience—albeit limited—attracted the attention of Frederick Douglass, who, at the time, needed an editorial assistant for his journal, *Frederick Douglass' Paper,* an abolitionist weekly and the leading African American journal of the time. In early 1856, Douglass asked Clark to move to Rochester, New York, to assume a position as his assistant editor, while he promoted his autobiography, *My Bondage and My Freedom.* The invitation came as quite an honor for Clark, who had not yet established a name for himself outside of Ohio. Although Douglass might have selected nearly a half dozen other gifted editors from across the nation, he offered the job to Clark and William J. Watkins, Frances Ellen Watkins Harper's cousin. Clark did not hesitate to accept the opportunity—moving his young family to the Douglass's Rochester home in early 1856.[24] There he wrote for and edited *Frederick Douglass' Paper* for roughly a year under Douglass's guidance. Clark claimed that he ran the paper himself when Douglass's lecture or writing schedule called him away.[25]

Douglass invested his energies mentoring, grooming, and otherwise preparing his young protégé for leadership in the abolitionist struggle.[26] He introduced the Cincinnatian to the principles of Radical Abolitionism, took him to that 1856 nominating convention, secured him a place on the program, and formally introduced him to the body. It is no small thing to have been introduced to the delegation by Frederick Douglass—one of the most influential members of the new party, who also just had been nominated as the Radical Abolition Party's vice-presidential candidate. An introduction by someone of Douglass's stature increased Clark's political capital within the party and the larger abolitionist struggle. Most of what Clark learned about political abolitionism he learned from Douglass.[27] The elder statesman developed a deep affection and respect for his young assistant editor; the two would retain their bond for decades—a bond that would transcend and outlast their political differences.

Clark also tried, with limited success, to follow in his mentor's footsteps by becoming an abolitionist lecturer from 1856 to 1857. His speaking engagements extended as far east as the Hudson River and as far west as Ohio. Although there are few surviving records of the substance of these lectures, in April 1857 he delivered one before an African American church in Chatham, Canada, in which he spoke about the necessity of trades for the youth and the efficacy of moral suasion as an abolitionist strategy.[28] Lacking a sponsor, Clark covered his own lecturing expenses by selling an abolitionist dramatic piece he penned entitled *Sore Conscience*.[29] By all accounts, Clark proved himself an able and effective antislavery lecturer: the *Provincial Freeman* described him as a "ready and eloquent speaker" who held a captive audience.[30] The *Christian Recorder* nicknamed him "the silver tongued orator of the west."[31] Despite his eloquence, Clark could never realistically hope to be a *leading* antislavery lecturer, though. For one, he had never been enslaved so his lectures did not carry the dramatic or emotive force of the stories of fugitive slaves and former bondsmen like William Wells Brown, Henry Bibb, or Frederick Douglass. Henry Bibb, for example, not only held a captive audience when he spoke, but brought them to tears as he recounted horrific tales of brutality against his wife.[32] Antislavery audiences were especially moved by sentiment and firsthand experiences; hence, they expected and demanded to hear from African Americans who had personally experienced the horrors of slavery, not from free ones, like Clark, regardless of their eloquence. In fact, many antislavery audiences even preferred that the lecturers speak in slave dialect. For members of the American Anti-Slavery Society, Frederick Douglass appeared too "learned." They pressured him to use a little "plantation manner of speech" in his lectures.[33] In the final analysis, although a brilliant orator, Clark never rose to quite the same prominence and never obtained the same level of sponsorship in the antislavery circuit as Douglass and his other formerly enslaved contemporaries. He seemed better suited to deliver Emancipation Day speeches.

The August First and other Emancipation Day celebrations were part of a long tradition of African American public festivals, a tradition that included Pinkster and Election Day celebrations.[34] The festivals included parades, military displays, brass bands, the reading of the Declaration of Independence, music, dancing, and speakers, culminating with a picnic. Attended by every segment of the African American community irrespective of education, class, and political background, they provided one of the rare occasions for free African Americans to come together publicly.[35]

Where did Clark go to college?

Emancipation Day celebrations of all stripes prove that African Americans were conscious of the plight of enslaved people of African descent throughout the Diaspora. African Americans remained hopeful that the fall of a slave regime anywhere would be a victory for the enslaved everywhere. Moreover, the collapse of slavery in other parts of the Diaspora went far in convincing African Americans that it would end soon in the United States as well.

Not only were they festive occasions to bring the community together, but, unlike Pinkster and Election Day celebrations, Emancipation Day celebrations were deliberately and overtly political. In fact, festivals were important stages for abolitionist mobilization and forums to outline other uplift strategies, from respectability and self-help to black nationalist themes of economic unity.[36] Festivals also represent a public performance of racial politics. Emancipation Day festivals represent a vastly different type of abolitionist project than the antislavery lecture circuit.

Cincinnati and Dayton held some of the largest Emancipation Day celebrations in the country. Cincinnati's 1855 August First celebration—which up to that point was the largest in the city's history—typifies what took place at these celebrations. That celebration started with a parade that began at Sixth and Broadway in the heart of one of the largest African American neighborhoods in the city. Groups featured in the parade include Anderson's, an African American band; the Sons of Enterprise, a mutual aid organization; the Young Men's Temperance League; and Freedom's Choir, an interracial choir of sixty girls who wore white robes and sang "Freedom Songs." The procession made its way to the river, where reportedly seven hundred people embarked on a steamboat and continued their festivities. After keynote addresses at these events, someone might read the legislation that had emancipated bondspeople in the British West Indies.[37] Hence, these celebrations were powerful expressions of black cultural pride, which also emphasized a pan-Africanist perspective of black liberation.

The keynote address was the centerpiece of these public political gatherings; and the speaker proved to be the most essential propagator of racial politics and the primary vehicle of infusing the gatherings with political content and consciousness. Because the speakers were race men, they became a conduit to transfer racial pride and offer a vision to uplift the black masses. Speakers articulated collective values of racial uplift, imparted crucial lessons about the Founding Fathers and American history, and rallied the crowd toward renewed faith that freedom and equality were within reach. Emancipation Day speakers also fostered collective identity politics and encouraged respectability and responsibility.[38] Communities took great pains to find the most engaging and effective speakers—people like Peter Clark. He delivered his first Emancipation Day address at the 1853 August First celebration in Glendale, a village outside of Cincinnati.

Clark's physical build surely belied his commanding oratorical skills. Described by his contemporaries as a small, medium-built man with "thin, sharp features, bright eyes and rather dyspeptic appearance," he had the ability to captivate his audience with his magnetic charisma, verbal eloquence, and unparalleled intelligence. According to the *Cincinnati Daily Commercial,* "his intelligence is large, and embraces most subjects interesting to men of thought." The paper commended him for his verbal fluency.[39] Free black communities throughout Ohio and as far away as Maryland invited Clark to deliver addresses at Emancipation Day festivals—a torch undoubtedly passed to him by his uncle, John. By all accounts, Clark impressed and electrified his audiences. An observer at the 1872 festival in Zanesville, Ohio, applauded his speech for its "depths of research, selection of language, forcibleness of argument, and general arrangement." Clark rarely shied from unpopular topics in his Emancipation Day lectures. For example, at one address before a Dayton audience a year later, he used his platform to discuss the advantages of political independence. He insisted that African Americans free themselves from any obligation to the Republican Party since it had failed to live up to its promises and principles.[40] His Emancipation Day oratorical career spanned nearly four decades—from 1853 until at least 1880, around the time that the festivals declined in popularity, frequency, and political usefulness.[41] Without a doubt, Clark's Emancipation Day lectures made vital contributions to the African American abolitionist movement and black festive culture in Ohio by raising awareness about the African Diaspora, shaping the collective consciousness, and charting a political agenda for Ohio's African American community. When considered across a longer period, Clark's oratory career—particularly his Emancipation Day speeches—were important instruments for civil rights activism in the antebellum and postbellum eras.[42]

While living in Rochester, Clark had joined the New York black convention movement. Undoubtedly owing to Douglass's influence, he immediately filled a spot as one of Rochester's delegates to the 1856 state convention.[43] That same year, despite traveling and lecturing, he somehow managed to also attend the 1856 Ohio Convention of Colored Men, and even served on several of its committees. Most notably, he served on the Committee on Address, along with other prominent African Americans, including attorney John Mercer Langston, Charles H. Langston, and his cousin John J. Gaines. Despite the distinction of the other members of that committee, Clark served as the chairperson. In that capacity, he played an instrumental role in drafting an address to the Ohio legislature petitioning for the repeal of the remaining vestiges of the Black Law.[44]

Clark's Committee on Address requested the legislature to strike the word "white" from the Ohio constitution, thereby eliminating all racial inequality under the law. It specifically pointed to Article V, Section I. of the Constitution, which limited suffrage to white men. After promising not to insult the legislators' intelligence by attempting to prove African Americans' humanity, the address goes on to do just that. Attempting to refute the claims in the emerging field of scientific racism, the address asks a series of rhetorical questions: "Hath not the negro eyes? . . . If you prick us, do we not bleed? If you tickle us, do we not laugh?" After asserting the biological basis of black humanity, the address also demanded citizenship and suffrage—using the Declaration of Independence, the Ohio Bill of Rights, and the principles of the American Revolution as the basis for such claims. But instead of the typical memorial that adopted a posture of supplication, this address ended with an ominous warning. In no uncertain terms, it declared, "If we are deprived of education, of equal political privileges, [and] still subjected to the same depressing influences under which we now suffer, the natural consequences will follow; and the State, for her planting of injustice, will reap her harvest of sorrow and crime." The address further warned that if the African American population continued to endure such oppression it eventually would become "discontented" and "dissatisfied" and inclined to resort to "any revolution or invasion as a relief." Hence, instead of merely appealing to the legislature's morality and conscience, Clark's committee warned they would use violence as a means of seizing civil rights.[45]

Although this threat seems to be a strategy contrived to secure rights, the overall militant tone of the address suggests that Clark and other Ohio leaders had become, by the mid-1850s, less compromising and markedly more confrontational in their pursuit of civil rights. Although Clark had never been conciliatory and never had compromised with racism and discrimination, he had grown very impatient with the slow rate of progress. He proclaimed to the 1858 convention that he had decided not to petition for another right again, asserting that "if he could seize it [rights], he would do so."[46] His sentiment had not changed much a year later when he participated in a rally expressing solidarity with John Brown.

On December 3, 1859—just one day after John Brown's execution for his raid on Harpers Ferry while attempting to incite a slave insurrection—the Cincinnati German Freeman Society and the Arbiter Association held a rally at the German Institute in Over-the-Rhine to memorialize him.[47] African Americans entered the German Institute located at Vine and Mercer Streets carrying a banner decorated with crepe paper and pictures of Thomas Paine, George Washington, and the American flag, with a simple inscription that read: "In Memory of John Brown." The building overflowed with a multiethnic, multiracial, international crowd of men and women—two-thirds of whom were German, and one-third of whom were African American. The crowd's diversity is underscored by the editorializing of one witness who disdainfully remarked that the hall and galleries were filled with a "motley crowd of both sexes, diversified by every hue common to the human species." Complementing the physical diversity of the assembly is the fact that people lectured in three different languages. Clark, Moncure Conway, and B. Fromm delivered addresses in English; August Willich, editor of the *Republikaner,* delivered one in German; and Y. Montaldo gave one in French.[48]

Even more exceptional than the layers of diversity among the assembly of Brown sympathizers is the fact that the rally may have been one of only a few times in antebellum history that African Americans and radical German immigrants in Cincinnati crossed into each other's public spheres for activism.[49] Despite their different ethnic backgrounds and histories, Brown's martyrdom brought them together for a common objective. Most German radicals who attended that rally opposed slavery in principle because they thought it wrong to hold another human in bondage. Moreover, the slaveholding class reminded them of the despotism of the aristocratic class in the old country. Brown embodied the spirit of the Revolution of 1848 and those with the courage to stand against the landed elite and strike out for freedom for the common man. African Americans celebrated his life because he violently defended free soil in Kansas and tried to overthrow slavery in Virginia. By allowing himself to be martyred for the cause, Brown had made the ultimate sacrifice on behalf of African Americans. Given the spirit of the rally, it is no surprise, then, that the *Cincinnati Volksfreund* reported on the rally under the headline "Freedom, Equality, Brotherhood."[50]

Clark's freethinking Unitarian friends took the speakers' platform first. August Willich, speaking in German, encouraged his listeners to "whet

their sabers and nerve their arms for the day of retribution, when Slavery and Democracy [Democratic Party] would be crushed into a common
grave." Moncure Conway, minister of the First Congregational Church,
followed Willich. He had recently delivered a long sermon in support of
Brown, which had been printed in its entirety on the front page of the *Cincinnati Daily Commercial.* His rally address focused on Brown's sacrifice
and martyrdom. In Conway's mind, Brown would never die: "We too have
seen our Arnold die before us . . . and where there was one God-fearing
and man-loving heart in this land, there are now a thousand. John Brown
is not dead: last Friday he was born in a million hearts." Conway believed
Brown's actions signaled the start of a revolution—a revolution unparalleled in American history. He considered the American Revolution "a
mere squabble about taxes, unworthy [of] the name of revolution [when]
compared with the grand and noble one inaugurated by the heroic Brown."
Conway believed much was at stake in this real revolution against slavery:
according to him, "we must die or succeed."[51] Speaking after Conway,
Clark was one of five people and the only African American to address
the crowd. When he took the stage, he expressed how honored he was to
speak before a congregation of the "only freedom-loving people of this
city," and claimed that the rally was only the second time in his life he felt
truly free. Largely powerless himself as an African American, Clark told
the audience that he depended on white friends "do justice to his race" and
"vindicate the principle of freedom," by conferring citizenship rights onto
African Americans.[52]

And like Conway before him, Clark invoked American nationalism.
The American Revolution and the Declaration of Independence, he insisted, were intended to secure freedom for *all* people, regardless of race. For
him, the objective of the unfinished revolution was African Americans'
freedom. In front of the crowded hall, he echoed Conway's analysis about
the current turn of events: "We are in the midst of a revolution." Failure
was not an option; the revolution "must be fought to the death." As undeniable proof that their enemies waged a war to secure slavery, Clark pointed
to the recent *Dred Scott* decision by the Supreme Court, which denied African Americans' citizenship. Clark urged the assembly to counter such attacks with "all the weapons of freemen," implying the use of real weapons
and violence. He then threatened that those with hands bloodied by slavery
would be sent to "hospitable graves."[53] Although not a violent man under
other circumstances, Clark indicated here that he was prepared to use lib-
eratory violence "*if necessary.*"[54] With such threats against white elites, at

that moment—in the few years leading up to the Civil War—Clark possibly was one of the most radical free blacks in America.[55] Fortunately, he would never have to "seize" his rights himself or put slaveholders in "hospitable graves."[56] The Civil War would accomplish that for him.

In January 1862, less than a year into the Civil War, Clark attended the local Unitarian church's Sunday Night Discussion sponsored by Moncure Conway: the topic was emancipation. Clark frequently attended community dialogues and debates and even had sponsored some himself. But this discussion was different: the crowd's tone was hardly sympathetic to enslaved African Americans and even rose to the level of contempt at the prospect of their emancipation. The homogeneous crowd listened intently to the most vociferous proslavery speakers and even agreed with their sentiments. After having listening for some time to persuasive justifications supporting slavery from some of Cincinnati's most prominent citizens, Clark had had enough. Rather than allow the proslavery sentiment to carry the day, he put on his old hat as an abolitionist lecturer and delivered an impromptu lecture to a hostile all-white audience. By all accounts, his was the superior one that evening. According to one antislavery observer, his speech dwarfed all the others that preceded his. The "silver tongued orator of the West" gave his audience food for thought and even swayed some to reconsider their proslavery positions. While the specific content of Clark's commentary cannot be recovered, he unquestionably made quite an impression. The same observer noted that his eloquence and intelligence defied every prejudiced notion about African Americans. Moreover, the observer was deeply moved by Clark's "elegance of expression; such absolute mastery of his subject; such complete acquaintance with all the facts and figures; such perfection of style and pronunciation; such serenity and self-possession, which could not be betrayed into any violent remark; such wit, felicity and vigor carried the audience away by storm." The audience "sat breathlessly listening to his every eloquent word." When Clark tried to end his remarks, his captive audience encouraged him to continue. When he finally ended, he received rounds of "irrepressible applause." The chief unidentified proslavery voice in the discussion reportedly "turned pale, then purple, then red," clearly embarrassed about having been upstaged by a member of the "inferior race."[57]

   This moment is instructive because it illustrates that even as emancipation became a central issue in the war and appeared to some that it might become an inevitable consequence of it, many white Cincinnatians still shuddered at the thought. Perhaps owing to the city's southern sympathies, forums like this one in First Congregational Church did not reflect a city becoming increasingly sympathetic to emancipation, but rather the opposite. Many had to be convinced that emancipation was the right thing to do for society and for African Americans. Clark understood that when he rose to address the audience that evening.

By far, though, his most significant abolitionist effort during the Civil War was his thirty-page pamphlet *The Black Brigade of Cincinnati,* which chronicles African American men's impressment into service in defense of the city.[58] The history of the unit began ignobly on September 2, 1862, when African Americans were seized from their homes and streets in Cincinnati and forced to build fortifications in defense of an anticipated Confederate invasion of the city. Clark is one of the few who escaped this service.[59] More than likely, his class background and prominence shielded him from the otherwise indiscriminate seizure and impressment of most African American men throughout the city. Still, the irony of this type of forced service is that African Americans had previously volunteered their services but had been rebuffed by local whites.

The impressed black men were forced to labor at Fort Mitchell in Kentucky, where they were treated as prisoners of war, or worse. They labored incessantly and without sleep for thirty-six hours straight. They were provided only half rations of food. One witness observed that the white soldiers stationed at Fort Mitchell treated them as "abandoned property—to be seized and appropriated by the first finder." After considerable public outrage in the press about their "recruitment," the men were eventually allowed to return to their homes. Before they were released, William Dickson offered them a chance to volunteer for the Black Brigade he was forming. The men may have insisted on "the same treatment as white men" because Dickson promised them that. It is interesting that while black recruitment efforts worked, white recruitment proved to be disastrous and marred with racism.

Not only did the four hundred men return voluntarily the next morning, but three hundred additional men came with them—eager to serve in the Black Brigade. This time they were treated with decency. They were organized into companies, captains were selected, and they were named the "Black Brigade of Cincinnati." Although the Black Brigade was not recognized by Ohio or the federal governments as a real unit, its organizers tried to create the semblance of a regular military unit for these men. African American men were brought into duty with military formality, including a parade, patriotic speeches, symbols, and rhetoric. Never before had black Cincinnatians been greeted with such ceremonial or symbolic citizenship.

Seven hundred members of Cincinnati's African American male population served in the brigade. Despite the fact that their "Brigade" was no real brigade or officially part of any military or even state militia, the men cheerfully carried out their duties until the threat of a Confederate invasion subsided three weeks later. They did not engage in traditional combat, yet the men of the Black Brigade took great pride in knowing that they had contributed to the city's defense. They took what began as a harrowing and humiliating ordeal and redefined it. The State of Ohio neither authorized nor recognized the Black Brigade, but when they "mustered out" of service on September 20, 1862, they received a U.S. flag inscribed with the name of the regiment. Their commanders encouraged the men to: "Rally around it! Assert your manhood, be loyal to duty." Never before had African Americans been extended such an overt recognition of citizenship in Cincinnati. The Brigade's white commanders extolled their virtue, courage, and patriotism. Conscious of shaping and preserving its own history, members of the Black Brigade asked Clark to record their history for future generations. The men also chose to remember themselves as "the first organization of colored people of the North actually employed for military purposes."[60] That designation is itself instructive: African American men of Cincinnati wanted to have an honorable place in history, not a pitiable one.

The Black Brigade of Cincinnati is Clark's only definitive written work. It engenders a sense of collective pride about black Cincinnati's Civil War contributions that has survived to this day. The piece also had a grander objective: not simply a history of the events surrounding the raising of the Black Brigade, the pamphlet also underscores African American volunteerism, and patriotism. It defies the master narrative that erases them from this history and challenges assumptions about their cowardice, ignorance, and lack of patriotism. Most importantly, Clark's *Black Brigade* makes a compelling, if implicit, argument for African American citizenship and equality. In that vein, it is a crucial part of his civil rights activism.

Despite all of the distractions and trauma of war, Clark continued working to dismantle slavery and obtain citizenship rights for African Americans. He never used the seeming inevitability of slavery's destruction as an excuse to stop agitating; he never paused, rested, took a hiatus, or in any way stopped to wait for slavery to fall on its own. Not only did

Clark continue to give abolitionist lectures during the Civil War, but he also continued to attend black conventions. In early October 1864, he traveled to Syracuse, New York, to attend the National Convention of Colored Men, where he, Frederick Douglass, and William Wells Brown served on the Credentials Committee. It had been nine years since the body had met, but the Civil War created the urgent need to come together once again as a united, national voice. That meeting gave birth to the "Declaration of Wrongs and Rights," a statement of their rights "as men, patriots, as citizens, and as children to the common Father." The convention also established the National Equal Rights League, which aimed to secure, through moral suasion and legal action, "full enjoyment of liberties, protection of our persons throughout the land, complete enfranchisement" and equality before the law. The body installed John Mercer Langston as its first president. The National Equal Rights League is one of the first civil rights organizations in U.S. history.[61] The following year, at the January 1865 meeting of the State Convention of Colored Men, delegates established the Ohio State Auxiliary Equal Rights League, with roughly the same goals as the national body. Cincinnati was chosen as the permanent headquarters of the Ohio chapter, with Clark as its president.[62]

The Ohio chapter of the Equal Rights League adapted a long list of resolutions in its 1865 meeting. A significant number of them focused directly on the Civil War. The body expressed its opinion that "Divine Agency" had caused the United States to suffer through war as a "just retribution for its insults to justice and its inhumanity to colored people." All of the other war resolutions centered on the condition of African American Union troops. For example, in response to the Union policy of not promoting African American troops or allowing them to serve as officers, one resolution demanded that the path of promotion be opened to them. Another resolution expressed gratitude for how Major General Benjamin Butler treated African American soldiers under his command. Finally, the body also resolved that the government "promptly" retaliate for wrongs done to African American prisoners of war.[63] All of these resolutions centered on issues of equality in treatment, opportunity, and justice.

Interestingly, the Ohio Equal Rights League also made gestures to freed people in its resolutions. The body offered them the "right hand of fellowship" and promised to secure complete freedom under the law, including the right to vote. Finally, the body advised them to become respectable citizens through education, temperance, frugality, and morality and to legalize their marriages.[64] Under the auspices of the league, Clark also organized a suffrage club. At the very least, it is clear that Clark's chapter already was thinking about how to best integrate freed people into society.[65]

The Ohio chapter of the Equal Rights League accomplished far more than its national body. The National Equal Rights League organization failed to live up to its expectations, because as Clark said, Langston as the president-elect, "never called it together." Reflecting back about why the organization never reached its potential despite having three of the most intelligent and influential African American men in its leadership in Clark, Douglass, and Langston, Clark concluded that "the rivalry between Mr. Douglass and Mr. Langston prevented the wide usefulness of which the organization was capable." With that failed body, the golden era of antebellum black conventions would limp to a close. For the next several decades, these meetings would become fewer and farther between as they began to be eclipsed by political conventions.

Inasmuch as Clark made significant contributions to the abolitionist struggle, it nurtured his intellectual and political development. His political self, so to speak, was born of this movement. Black conventions heightened his racial consciousness and taught him how to advocate for social change. Moreover, the conventions, along with the antislavery lecture circuit and Emancipation Day speeches, honed his public-speaking and oratorical skills. Editing abolitionist journals also played a critical role in expanding Clark's intellect and consciousness. The abolitionist movement also introduced him to the nation's most prominent abolitionists of both races. The relationships and networks he fostered at various types of abolitionist conventions provided him with critical social and political capital he would need in the future. More than anything else, abolitionist activism prepared and catapulted Clark into position as a leader.

The chief objective of all Clark's abolitionist projects essentially boils down to securing full equality and citizenship for free African Americans. Perhaps owing to the fact that he had never experienced slavery himself, elevating the status of free African Americans remained his primary abolitionist concern. Even in the midst of the Civil War, while thousands of other free African American northern men volunteered their services and sacrificed their lives to the cause of freedom, Clark focused his efforts on using their service as an argument for citizenship.

Before the war, Clark largely pursued those objectives through moral suasion and rationalism. He believed in the possibility of racial elevation through education, middle-class respectability, and partisan politics as a strategy for change. He also held up the threat of emigration and revolutionary violence to secure African Americans' freedom and citizenship. General Emancipation proved to be a watershed in his long battle to secure equality and citizenship. After that, Clark abandoned moral suasion and threats of emigration and revolutionary violence and began to pursue partisan politics almost exclusively as a strategy to secure citizenship, political equality, and, ultimately, political power.

Chapter Five

Voice of Equality

I will never bind my hand so as not to vote for the proper man. I ask
you to stand fast in the liberty by which the Republican Party has made
you free, and don't throw it away by any foolish pledges.

Peter Clark, July 1873

On the evening of April 11, 1870, Cincinnati's African American community convened at Zion Baptist Church to discuss the upcoming local
election the following Monday. The Fifteenth Amendment, which granted
suffrage to African American men, had been ratified on February 3 of that
year. Eager to exercise these new rights for the first time in history, these
new voters and their families met before elections to outline the issues,
debate the positions, endorse candidates, and advise one another on how
to mark their ballots. According to one eyewitness, Zion was nearly filled
to capacity with all classes of African Americans from "the nearly white
persons, who have long been voters" to those who had only been recently
emancipated from bondage in the South. Although the newly acquired right
to vote was limited to African American men, this did not stop "scores" of
African American women from attending the meeting.[1] In many political
meetings following Emancipation, women voiced their positions, helped
define party loyalties, and weighed in about the way their male relatives
would vote. Cincinnati's African American men did not see voting as their
sole prerogative; each of their votes would benefit the collective whole.[2]

Several people spoke that evening, including J. H. Perkins, William
Parham, and Peter H. Clark. When he took the podium, Clark remarked
that he had been present when the Republican Party was organized and
had joined the party because of its antislavery position. He boasted that
he had voted Republican in every election since 1856. As a free African
American of mixed ancestry, Clark *had* been voting long before many of
his peers, which placed him among the small percentage of those who

voted before the Fifteenth Amendment. He exercised that right in Cincinnati, where mulattoes and African Americans with lighter complexions had been allowed to vote for decades.

Although he had long been Republican, Clark's speech at the suffrage meeting suggests he was neither a partisan nor blindly loyal. He made it clear that he believed in the "reserved or unreserved right of every Republican citizen" to vote as he pleased. Yet, he did not think newly enfranchised African Americans in Cincinnati were quite ready for that. Calling for black nationalist politics, Clark advised that they should vote for the Republican Party as a racial voting bloc until they fully understood Cincinnati's ward politics: he added, the "safe, straightforward rule for every colored man . . . [would be to] go and vote the clean Republican ticket."[3]

African Americans had had an interesting history with the Republican Party before 1872. When the party was organized in 1854, it generally did not appeal to free African Americans—largely because it took a comparatively lukewarm position on abolition. The Republican Party, primarily concerned with preventing the extension of slavery into the western territories, took no stand on the abolition of slavery where it already existed. The young party, desperate for voters, tried to woo black voters, but most of them remained reluctant to join a party that failed to condemn slavery *wherever* it existed. Quick to point out such limitations, Frederick Douglass editorialized that the party just did not "go far enough in the right direction," and urged it to take a firmer stand and not to make any concessions to the Slave Power.[4] With the decline of the Liberty and Radical Abolitionist Parties by the mid-1850s, the political options for African Americans *and* abolitionists shrank. The Republican Party—even with its comparatively weaker antislavery position—became the next best option. According to one scholar, the Republican Party was "more of a negative choice than a positive one, stimulated not so much by Republican party appeal and action, as by Democratic accusations and weakness in the antislavery parties."[5]

African Americans' initial ambivalence about the party gave way to increasing support over time. By 1858, African American voters enthusiastically threw their support behind the party and its candidates, forming Republican clubs, campaigning for candidates, writing favorable editorials, and endorsing the party at conventions. The nomination of Abraham Lincoln further cemented that antislavery marriage: by 1860, African Americans voted nearly solidly with the Republican ticket.[6]

African American partisanship solidified in 1865 when the shackles of slavery finally broke. They fully credited the Republican Party because a

Republican president had issued the Emancipation Proclamation in 1863, and a Republican Congress had passed the Thirteenth Amendment, which officially ended slavery everywhere in 1865. Furthermore, they also attributed to Republican efforts the passage of the Fourteenth (1868) and Fifteenth (1870) Amendments, which granted citizenship and suffrage for African American men, respectively. Hence, African American voters credited the Republican Party with their emancipation, enfranchisement, and citizenship. Consequently, they felt deeply indebted to the party and repaid that debt by overwhelmingly voting Republican. But blacks became Republicans out of more than just loyalty. At local and state levels throughout the nation, the party supported issues that African Americans cared about, including free public schools.[7] More often than not, the party also appointed African Americans to minor political posts. For more than a decade, Peter Clark firmly stood in the Republicans ranks, but by 1871, he had started to question the efficacy of the party as a vehicle for racial equality and began experimenting politically.

Just one year after the Zion Church meeting, Clark's politics again made the headlines, this time, as part of the Liberal Republican movement, a movement spawned from the Republican Party. Liberal Republicans hoped to redirect the focus of the party away from issues of race and toward civil service reform, free trade, and general amnesty.[8] In April 1871, three hundred Liberal Republicans assembled in Cincinnati for an organizing convention and set their agenda. First, they supported a tariff on imported goods to raise revenue for the financially strapped government. They also advocated civil service reform and a return to a national paper currency backed by gold or silver. Finally, Liberal Republicans advocated amnesty for all former Confederates, because they believed it would diminish animosity among southerners, blur sectional divisions, thereby fostering national unity.[9] Because they hoped to restore national unity, Liberal Republicans distinguished themselves from Radical Republicans, who wanted to deny citizenship and suffrage to those who had served in the former Confederate military or government.[10] Liberals strongly supported the restoration of power to white southerners: while they did support Reconstruction, they opposed any federal enforcement of it. People joined the Liberal Republican movement for other reasons, too. Some had a personal axe to grind with President Grant over ideological issues or the fact that they had not received patronage positions in his administration. Others protested the corruption in his administration and lobbied for civil service reform.

Moreover, the Liberal Republican movement also had an antiblack current. Some spewed inflammatory and racist rhetoric that held African Americans responsible for many of the nation's ills and ongoing divisions. Specifically, Liberal Republicans directed much of their antiblack rhetoric directly at African American voters and workers. They pointed to African Americans' newly expanded political power in the South as voters as the source of problems with Reconstruction, including the corruption and incompetence in southern governance. For example, they blamed African Americans for electing dishonest and unqualified candidates to office. According to Liberal Republicans, their poor choices proved that they were not prepared or educated enough to handle their new political rights and power. Essentially, Liberals believed that black voters threatened the republic. They also distrusted and resented African American workers and used several instances of them striking for better wages as evidence that they opposed free labor ideals and hoped to subvert the labor system altogether.[11] Casting African American voters and workers as the bogeyman proved to be an ingenious device that brought southern Democrats into the folds of this movement. Ironically, some of the Liberal Republicans included former abolitionists who had once advocated radical racial policies but now strummed the chords of racism. Horace Greeley, perhaps the most prominent Liberal Republican, routinely railed against "ignorant" African Americans who misused the vote.[12]

Not surprisingly, the Liberal Republican platform, especially as it related to African Americans' political power, leniency for former Confederates, and opposition to federal enforcement of Reconstruction, resonated with moderate southern Democrats, or "New Departure Democrats." Moreover, both sides shared contempt for what they believed was corruption and cronyism in President Grant's administration. Out of the striking similarity of positions across party lines, "New Departure Democrats" and Liberal Republicans formed a peculiar bipartisan coalition.[13] They were odd bedmates, which led many Republicans to believe the movement had been spawned by the Democratic Party. Pointing to the similarity in their platforms, some critics even believed that Liberal Republicans were actually Democrats in disguise, a belief that garnered even more credence after both the Liberal Republicans and the Democratic Party nominated the same man as their presidential candidate in 1872: Horace Greeley, the reform-minded editor of the *New York Tribune*. It seemed that the ideologies and destinies of Liberal Republicans and Democrats had converged.

Oddly enough, Peter Clark briefly joined this movement and even addressed the 1871 Liberal Republican Convention in Cincinnati.[14] It seems unfathomable that an African American could support a movement that blamed his people for the problems of Reconstruction. Clark may have been drawn into the movement at the urging of his dear Unitarian friend George Hoadly, one of the ideological fathers and national leaders of the Liberal Republican movement. In his defense though, Clark joined the movement while still in its infancy—before its rhetoric turned overtly antiblack. His address to the Liberal Republican Convention in 1871 offers insight into why he may have affiliated with this movement. He stated that the disorder in the South was a direct result of the "indecent haste with which the rebellious States were restored to their political relations with the Union." Clark argued that the former Confederate states should have been kept as territories for twenty-five or more years until they adjusted to the new order of things. Still, he reasoned, amnesty was the best course of action because it would ensure political stability and reform in the South. Reaching back to his political abolitionist philosophies, Clark insisted that political reform would precipitate social reform in the region. Regarding lawlessness in the South, he recounted how African Americans and Union sympathizers had suffered countless abuses at the hands of "the underclasses of secessionists" who governed the region after the war. For him, the terror and lawlessness reigning in the South then could be attributed to lower-class secessionists holding positions of power. Overturning the prevailing Liberal Republican and New Departure belief that Reconstruction had failed because of lower-class African Americans, Clark blamed lower-class Confederates, instead. Recommending that power be transferred from them back to the "guardians of social order"—in this case, the former planters and other elites—he concluded that "the order of nature is reversed" in the South, whereby it was "ruled by those who are fit only to be governed." According to him, the best way to protect African Americans and Unionists was to grant general amnesty to the "better class" of southerners, so that they could regain political power and become "friends of the Union [and] guardians of the law in their communities."[15]

On the surface, Clark's position seems very conservative, if not contrary, to the best interests of his race. After all, entrusting African Americans' security, safety, and civil rights to former slaveholders might seem imprudent to most. But Clark wanted to forgive and forget the past crimes of the Confederates: he advocated moving away from sectionalism and toward national reconciliation. This is a practical example of how American nationalism influenced him. He reasoned that if he, as an African American, could forgive, others should, as well. Not only did he consider general amnesty to be the right course, but he also believed it the best route to restore peace and order in the South and, ultimately, to protect African Americans and secure their citizenship.[16] Clark's decision to support an upstart political movement with apparent southern sympathies and to do so at such a tenuous moment in African Americans' history underscores his pragmatic approach to race relations.

Besides Clark, few other African Americans joined the Liberal Republican movement. In fact, many distrusted the new movement and believed it to be a Democratic ploy designed to destroy the Republican Party. The 1872 National Convention of Colored Men, which met in New Orleans, not only passed a resolution repudiating the Liberal Republicans, but the body also concluded that they essentially were Democrats.[17] Frederick Douglass, distrustful of any movement that threatened the Republican Party, once wrote, "I had better put a pistol to my head and blow my brains out, than lend myself in any wise to the destruction or defeat of the Republican party." The statesman believed the New Departure movement, in particular, schemed to "overthrow the Republican Party and found a new one." Douglass stated that while he knew new parties naturally arose when the old ones had fulfilled their missions, he judged the Liberal movement to be not only "untimely, mischievous and dangerous," but "the maddest illustration of our national haste."[18] So committed was Douglass to defeating the movement that he toured the country lecturing against it. According to one of his biographers, Frederick Douglass is the single reason African Americans did not bolt from the Republican Party at that time.[19] Others took a similar position, including John Mercer Langston, who stated that Liberal Republicans were "no good" for African Americans or the country.[20] Perhaps because of pressure from his mentors and role models, coupled with the increasing antiblack rhetoric from within the movement, Clark ended his involvement with the Liberal Republicans and returned to the folds of the regular Republican Party by August 1871, although he was notably more conflicted about partisanship.

During a keynote address at an 1871 August First celebration commemorating the British Emancipation Day, Clark told the New Richmond audience that he opposed the idea of a collective racial voting bloc for a particular party: "No man can abhor more than I do that clandish [sic] spirit which drives all, or nearly all, the men of a race to vote for the same political party. In approaching the ballot-box, then . . . a man should exercise the right of private judgment."[21] His frankness reveals that he was somewhat torn between the belief that African Americans had an obligation to the Republican Party and his wish that African Americans would have the freedom to vote as individuals—just like other Americans. However, Clark understood that independent political action was not yet feasible for African Americans in 1871 in a two-party state. Nonetheless, that dream never quite died in the man; until it could be realized, he committed himself to playing partisan politics—at least locally.

In March 1872, Clark devised a strategy to collectivize the African American vote in exchange for political patronage in the Cincinnati spring elections. He called a meeting of the African American community, where he proposed to create two three-person committees that would find and endorse local candidates willing to give African Americans a fair share of the street-cleaning and street-paving jobs. Clark stated that this plan offered the best opportunity to leverage some jobs. He also argued that the committees would hold politicians accountable and responsive to the African American community. Still, he cautioned African Americans against voting blindly for Republicans: "We must not take up blindly with everything that calls itself Republicanism"; he warned them against those in the party who might "climb into power on our votes" and then "treat us as any Democrat would." By encouraging them to scrutinize Republican candidates closely before they voted, Clark hoped to create informed, independent-minded voters, and not blind partisans.[22]

Uneasy about entrusting the interests of the entire African American population to six committee men who could be tempted to sell their votes, leading local African American leaders vehemently rejected Clark's plan, including his biggest local political rival, Colonel Robert Harlan, who served on the Republican State Central Committee. Although they were perfectly justified in their opposition, some objected for purely personal reasons. Because of Clark's past association with Liberal Republicans, some simply lacked confidence in him. Colonel Harlan charged that Clark had no rights or standing among true Republicans because he had been a "bolter" the previous fall and continued to follow his friend Judge George Hoadly and others who devised ways to defeat the Republican Party. Harlan added that if the body accepted Clark as a representative, it should only be on a probationary basis.[23] Clark's committee idea ultimately failed, proving that at this juncture, the majority of Cincinnati's African American community remained ambivalent about trusting those who did not have unshaken allegiance to the Republican Party. Despite this minor defeat, Clark quickly switched gears to focus on the 1872 national election.

The 1872 election marks the first time that African Americans were eligible to vote in a presidential contest. Throughout the nation, people speculated about how they would vote. Southern whites did not believe African Americans were intelligent enough voters to make good decisions at the polls. As such, they assumed that African Americans would vote Republican out of loyalty. By contrast, some northern whites presumed that southern black voters feared their former slave masters so much that they would vote the Democratic ticket with them. African American leaders weighed in on the debate, ending all speculation. In a letter to the press printed on May 16, 1872, Clark dismissed rumors that southern African Americans might vote Democratic, reassuring readers that they were loyal Republicans. He explained that they remained in the party not only out of indebtedness for emancipation and enfranchisement, but because it was an "ark of safety" against the reign of terror in the South. Clark, also confident that Charles Sumner's departure from the party posed no dilemma for African Americans, doubted any would follow him to the Liberal Republicans and vote for Greeley. In the same letter, he attacked the Liberal Republican movement, characterizing it as having been formed to break up the Republican Party.[24] Hence, one year after he had himself been a Liberal Republican, he now condemned them.

Clark vigorously campaigned on behalf of the Republican Party in the summer and fall of 1872, reportedly giving more than sixty speeches throughout Ohio, Kentucky, and Indiana. He also lent his energies to neutralizing Charles Sumner. Sumner, a former abolitionist and longtime advocate of equal rights and suffrage, had written an open letter to African Americans in the summer of 1872 urging them to support Liberal Republican candidate Horace Greeley for president.[25] Because Sumner had long been considered a trusted friend, his word carried a great deal of weight in the African American community. Clark quickly organized a meeting of the Cincinnati Grant Club to educate these voters about why they should not heed Sumner's wishes.

In its August 16, 1872, meeting, the club adopted several resolutions that, while acknowledging African Americans' indebtedness to Sumner, respectfully declined to accept his advice about Greeley. The resolutions affirmed the group's support for President Grant. In his presidential address before the club, Clark acknowledged Sumner's work on behalf of the race. Notwithstanding that, he condemned Sumner as a "disappointed and embittered politician" for wanting to "put the new wine of liberty into the old bottles of pro-slavery Democracy." Taking exception to Sumner's arrogant assumption that African Americans "would fall into line at the wave of his hand and vote as he might dictate," Clark proclaimed that no one could "claim our votes as his personal property." Refuting the idea that Horace Greeley had been an abolitionist and champion of African American rights, Clark recounted almost the entire history of the abolitionist movement and the Liberty, Free Soil, and Republican Parties to demonstrate that Greeley had not been a factor in *any* of it. In fact, he argued that Greeley often had stood under the mantle of conservatism and too frequently had appealed to southern ideals, including states' rights and the veneration of Robert E. Lee.[26] It took a great deal of intestinal fortitude and political courage for an African American to publicly criticize esteemed statesmen like Charles Sumner and Horace Greeley. For Clark, the African American vote would not be taken for granted by presumed "friends of the race." He was not ready to barter those votes to men with questionable antislavery pasts and uncertain antiracist futures.

By mid-1873, however, some of the GOP's recent failures regarding civil rights forced African Americans to reconsider their unfaltering loyalty. A growing number of leaders in Ohio believed the Republican Party had failed to live up to its own promises—namely, its Philadelphia Platform, which advocated full racial equality. And they had much evidence to support their charge. For example, in 1873 the U.S. Supreme Court, in the Civil Rights Cases decision (the so-called *Slaughterhouse Cases*) contended that the Fourteenth Amendment protected only federal citizenship; the Court found that the amendment did not grant the government the authority to intervene in the civil affairs of states. The decision was a major setback to African Americans, who had hoped that their citizenship rights would be guaranteed and protected at the federal level. Clark himself believed that federal power trumped state power. In 1872, he declared: "I, for one desire that the power of the entire Nation shall be enlisted in my behalf. I feel that to be a citizen of the United States is a grander thing than to be a citizen of Ohio."[27] African Americans instinctively knew that the individual states would do little to protect their rights. In fact, they had no confidence that the states could be trusted to protect them. Hence, the decision alienated Clark and others from the Republican administration.

African Americans also were dismayed that the Republican-dominated Congress had failed to pass Charles Sumner's civil rights bill at least five times. First introduced in May 1870, Sumner's bill prohibited discrimination and provided for equal access to public facilities, including cemeteries, theaters, schools, public inns, churches, and public transportation.

It also permitted African Americans to serve on juries. Sumner was persistent: each time the bill failed, he reintroduced it.[28] The bill's repeated failures were huge blows—even worse considering that Congress had a Republican majority throughout most of the five-year struggle.

Furthermore, the Republican Party also had failed to appoint or elect African Americans to public offices in northern states like Ohio. This failure was particularly acute since more than one hundred African Americans held high state positions in the South, while another eight hundred served in the southern legislatures.[29] While Reconstruction had made a huge difference in extending political positions to southern African Americans, those in the North remained alienated and powerless.

Clark had grown increasingly impatient with, and disillusioned by, the Republican Party—particularly its failure to extend political opportunities to African Americans. He recalled how he had gone to the White House in late 1872 seeking a patronage plum in exchange for his campaign efforts. But he had made it clear that he sought more than a symbolic appointment; he wanted a position that would give him the power to employ other African Americans, such as a ministry position. During Clark's visit to Washington, President Grant did promise to reward him for his efforts; unfortunately, no position materialized for quite some time.[30] In the spring of 1873, while waiting for the administration to make good on its promise, Clark was nominated as a Republican delegate to the Ohio Constitutional Convention. He received 13,913 votes. Although he received the smallest number of votes of any of the sixteen candidates, the fact that there were only two thousand African American voters in Cincinnati at the time means that he won more than eleven thousand votes from whites, which was a monumental feat for an African American in 1873. The *Cincinnati Daily Enquirer* concluded that the nearly fourteen thousand votes Clark received across all party affiliations was proof that "color is not . . . any obstacle to political advancement in Cincinnati." The *Cincinnati Commercial* commended him for earning votes from whites and Democrats and advised that he should be satisfied with his showing in the election.[31] Although Clark claimed to be "satisfied in having demonstrated to the Republican party that a colored nominee does not weaken the ticket," his defeat led him to conclude that no African American could be elected to an office in Hamilton County. His pessimism about African Americans' political prospects in the county and state was only compounded by the snub at the federal level: President Grant's administration still had not offered him the position it had promised. His sense of disillusionment festered.

Only after news circulated that Clark had organized a movement to criticize the party for its failures concerning African Americans was he finally offered a position in the Pension Bureau in August 1873. Admitting that he had lost his ambition for political office by then, he declined the offer. Besides that, the Pension Bureau post did not afford him the power he sorely wanted—the ability to hire other African Americans. Clark realized the implications of denying African Americans political opportunities loomed larger than his personal ambition. He, like Frederick Douglass, believed his political destiny was inextricably linked to the progress of African Americans collectively.[32] His failure to secure a post proved to him that African Americans' political prospects were grim. Certainly these personal political disappointments in 1873 are what prompted him to organize the Chillicothe Convention.

Clark and a group of other disgruntled black Ohioans organized a convention that would allow them to publicly express their grievances against the Republican Party.[33] On August 22, 1873, one hundred African American men convened in Chillicothe, Ohio, to discuss their dissatisfaction with their political status as well Republican Party failures. Many of those in attendance were lesser-known local activists like Alfred J. Anderson of Hamilton; Samuel W. Lewis and Lewis D. Easton, both of Cincinnati; and John Booker of Columbus, who acted as the convention's president.[34] Noticeably absent were the state's leading black Republicans, including the Rev. James Poindexter of Columbus, and William H. Parham and Rev. Benjamin Arnett of Cincinnati.

The Chillicothe Convention issued a damning critique of the Republican Party for, among other things, failing to fully embrace the full and equal extension of civil rights to African Americans. The convention based its claims on the platform the Republican Party had adopted at its 1872 convention in Philadelphia: the Philadelphia Platform. That platform stated that the party supported "complete liberty and exact equality in the enjoyment of all civil, political, and public rights." Furthermore, it outlined that liberty and equality should be acquired and protected through state and federal legislation. The Philadelphia Platform not only made equality and civil rights for African Americans central to the Republican agenda, but also asserted that legislation was the means by which that vision would be obtained. African Americans embraced this platform and considered it their contract with the party. For some, the party had broken that contract when it failed to uphold the Philadelphia Platform on so many fronts—including the Republican Congress's failure to pass Sumner's civil rights bill. Nonetheless, Chillicothe delegates used the Philadelphia Platform as the basis on which they would stake their claims within the Republican Party. The body declared: "The Republican Party . . . is pledged by the Philadelphia Platform and numberless other declarations of political principles, to do more than merely free him [African American males] and permit his approach to the ballot box."[35]

Moreover, the Chillicothe Convention also had specific grievances against the state Republican Party for denying African Americans political opportunities. The convention charged: "If a stranger visiting Ohio should . . . make a tour of the Court-houses, the State House, the asylums and other buildings controlled by the Republican Party, he would be justified in believing that there are no colored men in the State belonging to that party, so rigidly are we excluded from anything, which might look like an equality of right in office holding."[36] Consequently, one of the convention's resolutions released Ohio's African American voters from all perceived obligations to the party and urged them, instead, to "refrain from unconditionally pledging themselves" to Republican candidates and to "use their best discrimination" when voting.[37] The convention essentially granted African Americans the license to vote as they wished; delegates no longer wanted to obligate themselves to a party that did not have the same level of commitment to their rights.

The Chillicothe resolutions were the brainchild of Clark, the chief organizer and spokesman for the convention.[38] His involvement at this convention also represents a watershed in his own political thinking. Before the Chillicothe Convention, he had been a Republican who supported collective racial politics. Although he had expressed some reservations, he had advocated that African Americans should vote as a bloc for the Republican Party. But unlike others who advocated absolute allegiance to the Republican Party, Clark had never been a strict partisan. In fact, when the 1858 Convention of Colored Men of Ohio publicly denounced the Democratic Party as "abettors of Slavery" and "the great foe" to African Americans, Clark was the only person to oppose the pronouncement. He reserved his criticism for the Republican Party. He rhetorically asked that body, "When had the Republicans ever done anything for the black man?" He reminded the delegation that the Republicans had promised to repeal the Fugitive Slave Law but had failed to follow through on that promise. Clark ended his remarks with a scathing indictment, insisting that he "did not consider his rights any safer with Republicans than with Democrats." He, in fact, believed slavery would be *more* secure with the Republican

Party; to him, its goal to become a national party meant that it would not do anything radical for fear of alienating its base.[39] Clark's critique of the Republican Party contradicted what most Americans believed about it, underscoring his independent political thinking even then. Regardless, his 1858 comments are instructive because they underscore the fact that Clark's main political objective was to use politics as a strategy to secure rights for African Americans. Willing to criticize either party for failures, he affiliated with whatever party seemed most willing to extend rights to African Americans. And—despite his criticisms—for the moment, that was the Republican Party.

The sentiments Clark expressed at the Chillicothe Convention illuminate why he moved toward political independence by 1873. In his convention address, he adamantly denied the notion that the Chillicothe delegates had ignored all the Republicans had done for African Americans. Charging that none of those Republican deeds had been motivated purely by a desire to advance African Americans, he argued that "they were merely the steps needed to carry out the central purpose of the party—the preservation of the union." Clark also assailed the myth of Abraham Lincoln as the Great Emancipator by asserting that Lincoln had freed enslaved people only as a military necessity. Finally, he asked his audience to consider why African Americans still suffered gross abuses and mistreatment when Republicans led every department of the federal government. Such abuses, he asserted, could easily have been mitigated—if not eradicated—through civil rights legislation.[40]

Clark's chief grievance, though, was the wholesale exclusion of African Americans from political office. He firmly believed that political positions would be an "assurance that the last stronghold of slavery has fallen. It is the guarantee of . . . unmolested liberty." For him, this exclusion from political positions was tantamount to a denial of African Americans' full equality and citizenship. Nonetheless, he made it clear that he blamed party leaders—and not the party itself—for the discrimination. Clark asked several damning rhetorical questions of party leaders in his Chillicothe address. Responding to advice that African Americans wait until the next congressional session before agitating for their rights, he asked: "How long will these gentlemen have us wait? Until their prejudice subsides, or their greed of office is satisfied?" He continued, "[by] what authority have they set up their prejudices and selfish desires as a bar to my rights?" Clark declared that inequality "originates everywhere from the same source, and the feeling of prejudice which produces it must be combated by every colored man who is not entirely lost to self-respect." Challenging the presumption of African American inequality—reinforced by their exclusion from political office—was the cornerstone of Clark's battle for full equality at that time. After encouraging African Americans to use their ballots to persuade politicians to honor the Philadelphia Platform, he ended his address by advising African Americans not to let "any weak talk about being true to the party induce" them to vote for those who would not honor the principles of the Republican Party.[41] The convention ultimately decided to vote for the state Republican tickets, but independently for local candidates.[42]

Not only is this the first time that African Americans advocated a break from the party en masse, but it is the first time they advocated independent political action—a term that historians readily have acknowledged had various meanings when applied to African Americans of that era. One type of independence includes those who, though deeply critical of the Republican Party, remained tied to it. These people hoped their criticism would make the party more responsive to their grievances. Independent politics might include threatening to vote for other candidates or leave the party unless African Americans won certain rights or political positions, for example. Although they used the threats as leverage, people in this group still largely voted with the Republican Party on Election Day. Other independents actively supported viable third parties. The final type of independent politics was employed by those who avoided loyalty to any party, but who, instead, supported individual candidates who promised to fight for African Americans' interests, regardless of their affiliation.[43] People like Clark moved quite readily between these types of independent politics throughout his career. He used political independence as means to ensure that African Americans remained viable political actors and that their issues remained relevant until they received full equality.

The Chillicothe Convention had its critics from the beginning. Colonel Harlan, the newly appointed special agent of the Cincinnati branch of the U.S. Post Office and U.S. Treasury and half-brother of John Marshall Harlan, the future associate justice of the Supreme Court, arrived in Chillicothe the night before the convention with the sole purpose of undermining Clark's agenda. Harlan disrupted the reading of the convention's resolutions to proclaim his vehement opposition to them, and offered counter-resolutions of his own that asserted black Ohioans were actually "fully satisfied" with the "splendid administration" of President Grant. Colonel Harlan noisily declared from the convention floor that African Americans ought to be as "true" to the Republican Party as the party had been to them. He accused delegates of lacking appreciation for what the party had done for them. No one in attendance, though, took him or his antagonism seriously. Every time he tried addressing the convention, delegates interrupted him with jeers and tabled his proposals. Clark interrupted Harlan, accusing him of being out of order. He sarcastically declared that Harlan was there "earning his day's wages," alluding to the fact that the colonel may have had a vested financial interest in disrupting the convention, since he earned more than three thousand dollars annually in his Republican patronage position at the post office. One observer later underscored that point by joking that Harlan was the "self-appointed supervisor of General Grant's personal reputation among colored people of Ohio."[44] Before being permanently silenced at the Chillicothe Convention, Harlan accused delegates of being "soreheaded office-seekers" who had organized the convention because they were upset that they had been denied political office.[45] Despite the fact that none of the delegation took him seriously, no one present could have anticipated that Harlan did, in fact, represent a serious contingent of opposition to the Chillicothe movement.

Cincinnati's Democratic press endorsed the Chillicothe Convention—especially because it offered the possibility that African Americans might abandon the Republican Party.[46] A week before the convention, the *Cincinnati Daily Enquirer* editorialized that African Americans' right to vote might be "valueless" unless they could make the choice to decide for themselves instead of being "driven in herds to the ballot-box."[47] Using the same rhetoric as the Chillicothe Convention, the *Enquirer* echoed the criticisms of the GOP for failing to grant political positions to African Americans. The paper not only criticized the mayor for appointing only a select few African Americans to his administration, but also accused the party of "pay[ing] attention to the demands of the colored men only when their political necessities [were] sharp upon them."[48] To be clear, the *Cincinnati Daily Enquirer* did not make such charges out of concern for racial equality, but because it hoped disgruntled African American voters would defect from the party and vote the Democratic ticket.

It would be a while before the vision of political independence articulated by the Chillicothe Convention could be realized. Republican opposition quickly mobilized to thwart independent action. Upon his return to Cincinnati, Colonel Robert Harlan promptly organized a meeting at Allen Temple AME (formerly Allen Chapel) to formally declare that the African American community "repudiated [the Chillicothe Convention's] action."[49]

The audience sympathized with Harlan's position. Speaking before the assembly, Harlan reported on what he had witnessed at Chillicothe, claiming that the convention resembled the Liberal Republican Convention. He warned the audience, "If we follow them they will lead us into the Democratic camp where the Liberal Republicans went a year ago." He then told the audience that most of the Chillicothe Convention delegates had organized out of bitterness about being denied federal positions. He urged African Americans to remain loyal to the party that had opened doors of freedom and equality. Other local African American leaders in attendance, such as William H. Parham, reiterated Harlan's sentiments.[50] Ultimately, the assembly voted to denounce the Chillicothe resolutions and proclaimed complete satisfaction with the Republican Party.

As a testament to Colonel Harlan's influence among those in attendance, the Allen Temple assembly successfully passed the same resolutions that he had unsuccessfully raised at the Chillicothe Convention days earlier. One resolution insisted that black Ohioans approved of the "splendid administration of General Grant" and that their confidence in him was "still unimpaired." Another vowed they would patiently wait until the next session of Congress for the passage of a civil rights bill. The body admitted that while it, too, supported extending political positions to African Americans, it did not support any effort that hinged on disloyalty to the Republican Party. The Allen Temple assembly vowed to stand by the party as long as it remained true to its principles.[51]

These resolutions reveal that the assembly was, at once, blind to the party's failures regarding African Americans and singularly indebted to the Republican Party for Emancipation, the Thirteenth, Fourteenth, and Fifteenth Amendments, and the civil rights bill. Given the significance of this debt in the hearts and minds of African Americans, it would be a long time before they would be comfortable enough to publicly criticize the Republican Party, much less abandon it wholesale. Loyalty to the Republican Party eclipsed all other loyalties. For example, this group demonstrated its willingness to temporarily delay pursuing full equality in favor of partisan loyalty.

The vast majority of those at the Allen Temple meeting expressed indignation, if not outright contempt, for the Chillicothe resolutions and refused to listen to anyone who had participated in the convention. Clark courageously and defiantly emerged from the crowded assembly in an attempt to defend the Chillicothe resolutions. Each time he tried to speak, the crowd murmured, hissed, booed, and howled. People chanted "put him out" and "put him down"; others yelled, "renegade" and "traitor!" According to the press, people in the audience hurled violent threats at the principal. In spite of the crowd, Clark refuted the erroneous charges and asked the audience not to equate demanding that the Republican Party honor its own platform with endorsing the Democratic Party. He firmly believed that if African Americans released themselves from their sense of obligation to the Republican Party, each of them would be free—as individuals—to vote for candidates of their own choosing. He declared: "I will never bind my hand so as not to vote for the proper man. I ask you . . . [not to] throw it [the vote] away by foolish pledges."[52] Essentially, Clark encouraged African Americans to be informed citizens who voted for people based on their *substance*—not their party affiliation. Most of those at the church that night could not imagine anything except blind party loyalty. To suggest anything beside absolute loyalty to the Republican Party at that point in African American history was tantamount to being considered a race traitor. In fact, the opposition to Clark grew so fierce inside Allen Temple that night that he was not only unable to adequately convey the objectives of the Chillicothe Convention or the rationale behind its resolutions, but he was silenced after only a few minutes on the floor by an assembly not yet ready for his political vision.

To fully appreciate why Clark's political vision seemed so progressive when compared to that of his contemporaries, one must remember that he had a different—even exceptional—background. Unlike the majority of African Americans, Clark had never lived as a bondsman. As such, he did not feel personally indebted to the Republican Party for Emancipation as did former bondspeople. Furthermore, as a fair-complexioned African American, he had been voting most of his adult life in Cincinnati, where people who visibly had white ancestors were sometimes permitted to do so. And although Emancipation and suffrage were the primary reasons that most African Americans felt obligated to the Republican Party—and rightfully so—Clark had enjoyed those privileges long before most African Americans, so he did not attribute them to the party per se. Furthermore, because he had belonged to the Republican Party since its inception, his commitment to it had been born out of principle, not obligation or gratitude. And because his relationship to the party was based on principle rather than emotion or obligation, his criticism of it, too, was rooted in principle. Given his own exceptional history, it is not surprising that Clark was among the first African Americans to advocate thinking outside the proverbial (ballot) box.

The Chillicothe Convention was more than just a convention: it was nothing less than a political movement with Clark as its leader. According to the *New National Era and Citizen,* an African American journal published by Douglass and his sons in Washington, D.C., the Chillicothe Convention sparked a political movement with "enthusiastic endorsement throughout the state." Clark toured the state lecturing about its ideology, thereby increasing both his reputation and support for the movement. The *New National Era and Citizen* published several letters of support from prominent citizens.[53] Nor was the movement limited to Ohio: it caused a ripple effect throughout the nation. National African American leaders quickly weighed in and tried to counteract the momentum of the movement. Douglass visited Chillicothe with his son on September 16, 1873. In a public address, he denounced the Chillicothe resolutions as "premature" and warned that they could possibly hinder future gains.[54] John Mercer Langston, Ohio's first African American attorney and former president of the National Equal Rights League, delivered an address a week later at Chillicothe's city hall, challenging each of the resolutions without ever mentioning the Chillicothe Convention—or Clark—by name. Langston reminded his audience of the many things the Republican Party had done for African Americans, including "saving American liberty itself." He painstakingly refuted charges that the party had failed to extend political positions to African Americans, by offering detailed evidence of how many served at federal and state levels. Although Langston agreed with the Chillicothe delegates that the civil rights bill should have been passed earlier, he offered several explanations as to why it had not yet been passed, including divisions in Congress over whether civil rights should be addressed at the state or federal level.

Clark directly responded to Douglass's criticisms in what may have been his most powerful speech ever—delivered at Dayton's Emancipation Day celebration on September 22, 1873. Refuting Douglass's charge that the Chillicothe agitation was "premature," he pointed out how it was the great abolitionist himself who had taught him to demand immediate change: "The lesson I learned [from Douglass] was that it is never premature to demand justice." Clark also pointed out some inconsistencies in Douglass's criticisms. He reminded his audience that the Chillicothe resolutions had first been raised at the 1872 Convention of Colored Men in New Orleans. *That* body had resolved to use the impending elections as leverage to demand that Republicans pass a civil rights bill. Clark admitted that he had opposed such a move then because he did not wish to do harm to the party's chances of winning the presidential elections that year;

he had recommended that African Americans remain loyal to the par. until after the elections. According to him, a moving speech by Douglass persuaded the entire convention to move forward with their strategy. Clark found it somewhat contradictory that Douglass now judged the Chillicothe movement to be premature when it had not been so a year earlier.[55]

Clark firmly stood by his demands that African Americans be extended full political equality. In his 1873 Emancipation Day address, he declared, "We do not demand . . . any offices on the ground of color; but we do demand that color should not be a bar to office; that the political rights of the colored man shall not be exhausted when he has cast his ballot." That sentiment underscored the limits of African American citizenship and political power.

Believing that racial discrimination had proven to be an insurmountable obstacle to securing political power, Clark insisted that applicants for official positions have a "right to have his claims considered and the appointments made without regard to color." He also demanded that political positions be extended to African Americans under the "same conditions that it is accorded to other American citizens." Hence, he simply demanded that African Americans be treated equally and be afforded access to the same opportunities as whites. Although African Americans were discontented with their current inferior and disadvantaged political status, Clark made it clear that they did not seek any political *advantages* or privileges based on race. Nor did he support the idea that whiteness conferred certain advantages either. He declared, "The [political] offices do not belong to the whites of this land, but to the people of this land."[56] This comment echoes twentieth-century arguments for equal opportunity.

Clark's critics advised that he acknowledge that racism imposed real barriers to political equality, and that they should, therefore, temper or postpone their demands for immediate, full equality, but he stridently rejected this advice. He acknowledged the reality of racism, but refused to accommodate it. In what ought to be remembered as one of the most stirring speeches on American racism in the nineteenth century, Clark attested:

I do not forget the prejudice of the American people; I could not if I would. I am sore from sole to crown with its blows. It stood by the bedside of my mother and intensified her pains as she bore me. . . . It has hindered every step I have taken in life. It poisons the food I eat, the water I drink and the air I breath[e]. It dims the sunshine of my days, and deepens the darkness of my nights. It

every relation of life, in business, in politics, in
or as a husband. It haunts me walking or rid-
sleeping. It came to my altar with my bride, and
my children are attaining their majority . . . it stands by
and casts its infernal curse upon them. Hercules could have
as easily forgotten the poisoned shirt which scorched his flesh, as
I can forget the prejudices of the American people.[57]

Here, Clark depicts racism as an omnipotent, omnipresent force that
haunts African Americans from the cradle to the grave, across several generations, and in every facet of life. He portrays racism as almost super-
natural in its power to thoroughly oppress, repress, and depress African
Americans' opportunities. By painting such a chilling picture of how racism and discrimination had stifled his hopes and stunted his opportunities,
Clark conveys to his African American audience why it is important that
they not wait to demand equality. Clark's primary criticism of the Republican Party rested in its failures on that issue.

But Clark had a far more expansive vision of equality than just political
patronage. He fiercely advocated social equality, which he broadly defined
as "the right to qualify myself for first-class manhood in the same institutions and under the same circumstances that the white man pursues." In his
1873 Emancipation Day address at Dayton, Clark elaborated on his vision
of social equality: African Americans would have access to every institution that would foster their elevation, refinement, and cultural cultivation,
including schools, art galleries, music conservatories, theaters, and concert
halls. He insisted that there be no "reserved seats in the great amphitheater
of American life," in reference to the system of white privilege and African
Americans' exclusion and inferiority. Despite his vision of full social, legal, and political equality, Clark made it clear that he did not endorse "social mingling." He reasoned that once African Americans and whites were
"cultivated all alike," they would be "free to mingle or stray apart as they
please[d]."[58] Not a beneficiary of the language of the modern civil rights
movement, Clark clearly intended "social mingling" to mean integration;
for him, however, it should be an optional, and somewhat casual, *social*
interaction. He felt integration might be enjoyed *after* African Americans'
cultural and educational elevation; it was *not* a civil right in and of itself.
Unlike most civil rights leaders in both the nineteenth and twentieth centuries, Clark never defined integration as a fundamental objective of the
struggles for civil rights, social and political equality, or equal access.

Clark lobbied for state legislation that would guarantee the education of all African American children and removing racial distinctions in the laws—not integration. His broad civil rights agenda included: (1) eliminating laws that codified racial inequality; (2) prohibiting discrimination on public transportation; (3) guaranteeing equal education regardless of race; and (4) guaranteeing equal access to public places, including theaters and hotels.[59] Clark wanted no less than full and equal citizenship for African Americans. No one would doubt that his progressive objectives were designed to improve the condition of African Americans. Yet, they also demonstrate that in the Reconstruction era, advocacy for full and equal civil rights was not always inextricably linked to a demand for integration.

The only thing that came close to realizing Clark's civil rights agenda is the oft-tabled Sumner civil rights bill—passed as the 1875 Civil Rights Act. The act provided full and equal access to public accommodations, hotels, public transportation, theaters, and other places of entertainment. House Democrats had not only delayed passage of the bill, but deleted sections that prohibited discrimination in churches, cemeteries, and schools at the last minute.[60] Although the act signaled the walls of inequality and discrimination were crumbling, it proved to be much weaker than African Americans had hoped. Their disillusionment rapidly increased as Reconstruction breathed its last breath.

By the time Reconstruction had crawled to its death, many northern African Americans already had accepted its inevitable end, since it had been collapsing from within on a state-by-state basis since its inception. By 1876, Democrats had regained their pre-Reconstruction political dominance in every southern state except Florida, Louisiana, and South Carolina. When African American leaders met in Nashville, Tennessee, in April 1876 for the Colored National Convention, delegates debated the significance of the Democratic return to home rule in the South. The resolutions adopted at that convention included one that proposed extending an "olive branch" to southern Democrats asking for their protection against "mobs, assassinations, outrages, and violence." Apparently a number of delegates suggested that African Americans vote with that party as well—an idea that prompted swift condemnation.[61]

In a letter published in the *Commercial* on April 24, 1876, Clark vigorously defended those African Americans who proposed aligning themselves with the southern Democrats. He noted that northern African Americans were in no position to scorn southerners for how they dealt with the lawlessness and terrorism under which they lived. Moreover, he added, northerners could not truly imagine what it meant to live as an African American in the South. In the North, he wrote, "law is supreme" and courts were reasonably just: "Here, no powerful organizations exist, armed and strong enough to so intimidate State governments." By contrast, "The colored men of the South are in the hands of their enemies and must do the best they can under the circumstances." Referring to the countless political murders of African Americans, he added: "I would excuse them if they did not vote at all next autumn. . . . [T]heir attempt to vote would rouse that fell spirit of murder which broods over the South like a cloud."[62] Clark believed that southern African Americans should ultimately act in their best interests, even if that meant forming conciliatory alliances with Democrats to ensure their safety and survival, or not voting at all. Clark understood how sheer fear might force southern African Americans to accommodate their political castration. In some ways, his views were echoed later by Booker T. Washington. There are nuanced differences, however: Clark never recommended that African Americans forgo their political rights; he merely expressed his empathy for those living under conditions that made them choose between voting and living.

Clark's April 1876 letter to the press also happens to be the only extant evidence that provides insight into how he felt about the collapse of Reconstruction and the federal government's responsibility to protect African Americans, specifically. He lacked faith in the federal government to enforce civil rights or protect them. This sentiment actually may have been a residual effect of his time in the Liberal Republican movement. He pointed to several examples since the Civil War when African Americans had tried to seek assistance, justice, and redress from the federal government to no avail. He did not believe that either party, the Supreme Court, or its justices could provide relief. The swift collapse of Reconstruction taught him that state power reigned supreme: he concluded that African Americans must rely on the states to provide the assistance, justice, and redress they sought. Consequently, he concluded that the doctrine of states' rights "must eventually be adopted by the American people or the much-loved Union will prove a rope of sand." As the nation marched past Reconstruction, Clark's ideology increasingly became angular to the Republican Party and to other African American leaders.

In the 1870s, Clark repeatedly criticized the Republican Party because of his disillusionment, distrust, and impatience with its commitment to full equality and political power for African Americans. At a time when few

African Americans dared to criticize the party, this man demanded that it actualize its promises and honor its own principles. He believed that neither partisan loyalty nor debt offered enough reason to continue voting Republican. A practical man who did not see either party as African Americans' salvation, Clark thought African Americans should promise their votes to the party that offered them a measure of political power and civil rights.

Clark frequently embraced strategies designed to force the Republican Party to be more responsive and accountable to African Americans, as voters and citizens. His various political paths in the 1870s prove that he was unafraid to take hard, unpopular positions to advance his people. Above all, they prove that Clark was a visionary who used independent, pragmatic politics to leverage his quest for social equality and civil rights.

Chapter Six

Radical Voice

There is creeping into the consciousness of many of the wealthier class a conviction that such great accumulations of riches as mark our times are perilous to society, and that he who seeks to find a mode for the [re]distribution of wealth, which will prevent the great contrasts of poverty and opulence . . . is a friend, and not an enemy to society.

Peter H. Clark, 1881

One evening in late November 1875, Peter Clark rose to deliver an address before the Sovereigns of Industry. Although cooperation was the main topic of his address, the better part of it focused on denouncing the middlemen—merchants, grocers, and bankers—who "derived not only livelihood, but wealth, by coming between the producer and the consumer." For Clark, the middlemen were the chief culprits within the capitalist system. To illustrate how middlemen exploited people, Clark raised the example of groceries, which abounded in poor areas of the city and where grocers charged a premium on the inferior goods they sold. Defining cooperatives as "associations of earnest, sincere men, determined to mutually assist each other by doing the middle work for themselves," he recommended that poor people put their money together, buy goods wholesale, and then distribute the goods fairly among themselves.[1] For him, it was the surest way to eliminate, or at least, minimize the influence of the middlemen. Within a year of his 1875 Sovereigns of Industry address, Clark would join a socialist political organization for the first time, making him the first African American in history to do so.[2]

Between 1876 and 1879, Clark emerged as one of the most influential of the American socialists—a feat even more impressive given the fact that the American movement was dominated by German immigrants in the 1870s and included few other African Americans. Most of those who have written about Clark's socialist career focus only on that period, when he formally affiliated with socialist organizations. But that three-year stretch merely comprises his *documented* socialist career; a more nuanced examination of his life reveals that he openly associated with socialists and subscribed to the ideology much earlier. Although the exact moment that Clark subscribed to the philosophy cannot be determined with certainty, he once claimed that he had been a socialist "long before there was a Republican Party"; in other words, he embraced socialism before the birth of the Republican Party in 1854.[3] When one considers Clark's education in Gilmore's school, his apprenticeship with a socialist editor, his aunt's participation in a socialist commune, his efforts to form unions, and his association with German radicals, workingmen, and freethinkers, it seems nearly certain that Clark *had* embraced socialism before 1854. Each decade thereafter added a new layer to his socialist consciousness. In short, the year 1876 does not mark the beginning, but actually signals the start of the last chapter of his socialist career.

The labor struggle during the Civil War brought Clark's socialism into sharper focus. The end of the war and its subsequent period of rapid industrialization, created a new market and labor relationships. Too often these new relationships benefitted the capitalist class. Industrial laborers realized not only that they were powerless as individuals, but that the best way to lobby for better wages and shorter workdays, for example, was through collective action. Consequently, trade unionism increased exponentially, culminating in the birth of the National Labor Union (NLU) in 1866. NLU leadership, recognizing that African Americans had long been neglected by the labor movement, favored an open and inclusive policy. Consequently, the NLU's platform and constitution deliberately encouraged membership from all races and classes of labor in an effort to draw them into the movement. Andrew Cameron, editor of the premier labor journal of its day, the *Workingman's Advocate,* told the NLU inaugural convention that the interests of labor were the same, regardless of a worker's race or nationality. He added that if the body did not integrate African Americans into the labor movement, they would prove to be the bane of its existence. He rhetorically asked, "Can we afford to reject their proffered co-operation and make them enemies?"[4] But the recruitment of black workers faced resistance from rank-and-file NLU members who harbored deep-seated racial prejudices and tended to simply see them as competition. Owing to the divergent opinions, the NLU convention body did not pass a resolution to organize African American workers. Rather than forcing its affiliates to accept African Americans into trade unions, the NLU quietly encouraged them to form their own, separate trade unions.[5] Although African Americans had long been excluded from membership in local trade unions and considered employment discrimination to be one of their most pressing issues, they did not clamor to join the National Labor Union because they realized the organization was unwilling to draw any hard lines on race, inclusion, and unionism.

African Americans established their own national labor organization in 1869: the Colored National Labor Union (CNLU).[6] The organization held its first national convention in Washington in December that year; more than two hundred people from twenty-two states attended. The convention focused on improving the status of African American workers by organizing them in the South, lobbying for increased wages, working to end the importation of Chinese laborers, and forming "cooperative workshops, land, building, and loan associations."[7] One of the body's resolutions stated that such cooperative ventures would serve as a remedy against their exclusion from other organizations, as well as provide employment, sponsor self-sufficiency, and safeguard against the "aggression of capital."[8]

The Colored National Labor Union worked hard to improve the condition of African American workers. It pressed for political rights, lobbied for civil rights legislation, and provided trade education. The organization also encouraged African Americans to form cooperatives to purchase land. Its most crucial role, however, was raising awareness about labor unions and encouraging African Americans to form them. In February 1870, the Federal Bureau of Labor issued a report that emphasized that the failure to organize was responsible for African Americans' low wages. The *New National Era*—the mouthpiece of the CNLU—editorialized about the urgency to form unions. The CNLU began aggressively organizing and even sent Isaac Meyers to the South to organize southern African American workers.[9] Individuals responded to the call: Clark, for one, established a trade union of his own: the Colored Teachers Co-operative Association, one of the first teachers' unions in American history.[10]

The CNLU sent delegates to the NLU conventions in an effort to unite white and black laborers. Clark, John Mercer Langston, Isaac Myers (Colored Caulkers Trade Union Society), Josiah Weare (United Hod-Carriers and Laborers' Association), and P. B. S. Pinchback all attended the NLU 1870 convention in Cincinnati, with Clark representing his Teachers Co-operative Association.[11] At this 1870 convention, the NLU voted to make its transition from a union to a political party, the National Labor Reform

Party. African American delegates opposed a third political party, asserting that the Republican Party best served their interests. Only the Republicans, they argued, would secure legislation to protect the working class. Expressing no faith in the Democratic Party, the black delegates declared it an enemy to the working class. A third party, they felt, would do nothing to advance workers' interests.[12] They offered vociferous opposition on the convention floor. In addition, some controversy erupted over whether the NLU would allow John Mercer Langston the privileges of the floor. Several delegates moved against it, arguing that he was too much of a Republican partisan. Those members preferred that the NLU remain nonpartisan by disallowing any politicians or extreme partisans from having the floor. Furthermore, NLU leaders feared Langston would do his best to make the NLU "a tail to the Republican party kite." The convention proceedings also suggest, though, that racism may have played a role in Langston's exclusion. In a dramatic moment, one sympathetic white NLU delegate bellowed from the floor that "the real objection to . . . [Langston] was that the blood of Africa flowed in his veins!"[13] Although the contempt for Langston did ultimately lead to his exclusion, the controversy illustrates that African Americans—perhaps too narrowly—believed that the salvation of labor would come through the Republican Party.

Although Clark remained quiet at that particular labor convention, this moment marks when he began to link economic reform to political action. Others followed suit, for in the 1870s—as W. E. B. Du Bois notes in his seminal work on Reconstruction—African Americans began to see not only how their vote could be used to improve their economic situations, but how their rights, working conditions, and wages were also tied to the vote.[14] Clark also may have learned from Langston's mistakes that absolute Republican partisanship would derail any interracial labor movement. Nonetheless, labor unionism did increase his socialist consciousness and served as a precursor to his socialist political activism in the following decade.

The 1873 economic crash, or the Panic of 1873, provided another stimulant to Clark's emerging socialist consciousness. After years of unparalleled economic expansion in the railroad industry, railroad owners speculated and overestimated the industry's future growth. The problem was that much of the speculation had been financed through credit and bonds; by the early 1870s, however, many of the railroads could no longer pay the dividends, sparking a financial crisis of epic proportions in the railroad, banking, and credit industries. In 1873, the Northern Pacific Railroad failed. Shortly thereafter, Jay Cooke and Company, one of the nation's leading banks and one of the railroad's chief investors, collapsed after failing to sell millions of dollars' worth of railroad bonds. The collapse of Jay Cooke precipitated the failure of smaller financial institutions throughout the nation. Not only did railroad construction screech to a halt, but many of the industries that depended on railroad commerce were also affected by the downturn. Within one year, the Panic of 1873 had progressed to a full depression. Many of the budding manufacturing businesses failed. In 1876, nine thousand businesses failed; another nine thousand failed the following year. In 1878—the most difficult year of all—ten thousand businesses failed.[15] The economy suffered a severe contraction for more than five years, leading to one of the worst depressions in the nation's history. Workers were the real casualties. By 1877, 27 percent of the U.S. population was unemployed. Those fortunate enough to have jobs endured drastic wage drops in a short period of time. For example, cigar packers' average wages fell from $3.33 per day to $1.67 per day between 1872 and 1879.[16] The effects of the economic crisis were drastically felt in Cincinnati, where workers held "Bread or Blood" meetings to express their grievances with the owners of capital.[17] The enlargement of the working class occasioned by the emancipation of 4 million freed people also exacerbated the job shortage and wage depression.

Cincinnati's German neighborhood in Over-the-Rhine had a familiarity with radical solutions to suffering and starvation. The Forty-Eighters had a living memory of the exploitation and revolutionary spirit that informed Marx and Engels's *Communist Manifesto*. Radical socialist and communist solutions were discussed openly—whether among Forty-Eighters in beer gardens or taverns or in editorials in German-language newspapers. German workers were particularly receptive to these ideas; some publicly denounced the capitalist system, and others openly advocated Marxism. With his deep ties and friendships with German Forty-Eighters and labor radicals dating back to the antebellum era, Clark was easily pulled into the emerging socialist movement in Over-the-Rhine.

Beyond personal connections, Clark also had practical reasons to join this movement. Although he was educated and employed, he had long identified with the German working class in Cincinnati. He could relate to them because he once had been subjected to the demoralizing nature of capitalism. In a public address several years into the depression, Clark recounted how two decades earlier, he had been unemployed for months on end (referring to the time after he had been fired by the schools for Tom Painism) and unable to provide for his wife and child. He said his problems mounted so high that he considered "throwing himself in the river, and thus end[ing] all his misery." At that point, he began sympathizing and identifying with unemployed people.[18] Hence, his class identity and consciousness had been formed by what he experienced as a member of Cincinnati's working class, and through his own participation in what he called, "wage slavery." Although his *socialist consciousness* and awareness had been raised in the late 1840s through his personal associations with several socialists, including his aunt and her husband, and sharpened in the 1850s when he associated with German-born radicals, Clark did not fully embrace socialist political action until the depression, when he realized it could be a solution to the crisis facing the working class. He may even have hoped that a socialist revolution would also end class and racial inequalities.

By 1875, Clark was associating with William Haller, a former militant abolitionist, Underground Railroad operator, Cincinnati's chief socialist labor organizer, and editor of the *Emancipator,* the leading English-language socialist paper in the Midwest. The two had maintained a close relationship at least since the National Labor Union convention five years earlier. Haller had invited Clark to deliver that address before the local branch of the Sovereigns of Industry in November 1875.[19] The Sovereigns of Industry, still a bourgeoning socialist organization, had been founded in January 1874 by William H. Earle in Springfield, Massachusetts, to unite industrial workers in order to minimize the abuses of the capitalist class. The organization deliberately modeled itself after the National Grange of the Order of Patrons of Husbandry—or the Grange, for short.[20] Like the Grange, it organized cooperative stores where workers could exchange goods at very low prices.[21] The Sovereigns of Industry reportedly boasted more than forty thousand members at one point—75 percent of whom resided in New England. It promised to unite all laborers; its Declaration of Purposes extended membership without regard to "race, sex, color, nationality, or occupation." This inclusive membership made it among the most progressive of such organizations in the nineteenth century.[22]

The fact that Clark delivered the address before this body suggests that he sympathized with at least some of its tenets. In fact, many aspects of his address before the Sovereigns of Industry are consistent with the organization's ideology, including his scathing critique of middlemen. For Clark, middlemen were the *real* source of workers' suffering, and not the system itself. Moreover, he explicitly indicated that he did not entirely advocate a socialist revolution: he doubted the efficacy of socialist organizations that aimed to "take capitalists by the throat." Instead, Clark expressed confidence that the abuses of capitalism could be controlled "if men will go about it the right way." Capitalism was a "devil," he asserted, but "you can put a bit in its mouth and control it."[23] Hence, although Clark advocated the reorganization of labor, his critique of capitalism was comparatively mild; his solutions hinged on regulation and reform, not revolution.

Although he did not yet consider socialist revolution to be the solution to poverty and inequality, Clark was equally doubtful that charity or a welfare state could eliminate them either. He opposed all government-sponsored assistance: charity, he asserted, "crushed the manhood" and "degraded and debased" men. The only logical solution he could come up with was cooperation.[24] The term "cooperation" has meant many things within reform circles; certainly it was equally burdened by multiple meanings in the nineteenth century.[25] When Clark used the term during his Sovereigns of Industry address, he meant a cooperative store where consumers would unite to buy goods wholesale at a savings. For many socialists, cooperative stores represented a first stage in introducing and demonstrating socialist concepts to the working class.[26] Clark did not see socialism as an end itself; rather, socialist cooperatives would be the means to eliminate middlemen—the ultimate oppressors. Nonetheless, his advocacy of cooperation signals that he had begun to embrace socialism, although at this point, his views still were rather conservative.

Clark would later realize that socialist cooperatives alone would not work, leading him to seek more effective solutions to the growing economic crisis, including a Marxist political organization. In late 1876, he joined the Workingmen's Party of the United States, known simply as the Workingmen's Party.[27] The party had only been organized in July 1876, when the Social Democratic Workingmen's Party of North America (est. 1874) combined with other smaller socialist groups across the country.[28] The Workingmen's Party endeavored to abolish: (1) all unjust social and political conditions, (2) class rule and class privileges, and (3) laborers' dependence on capitalism by eliminating the wage system and replacing it with cooperative labor.[29] Although compromised of Lassalleans and Marxists, the party largely adopted a Marxist approach, albeit with some concessions. It emphasized that the first and most crucial step toward socialism was the development of strong national and international trade unions. Political action would come only *after* the unions were well organized. Therefore, the Workingmen's Party eschewed electoral politics, except lobbying for laws that would benefit the working class. Special provisions, though, could be made to enter local elections.[30]

The Cincinnati branch of the Workingmen's Party envisioned that "equality of all men" would be realized through a socialist local government that would—among other things—set a uniform wage for all local government employees and ensure that people were not charged exorbitant amounts for essentials like housing and coal.[31] It is easy to see why someone like Clark would have been attracted to this party: its mission would have been particularly attractive to someone who had labored his entire life for equality and justice. Although the Workingmen's Party never explicitly articulated racial equality as an objective, its rhetoric of equality certainly appealed to Clark, himself a champion of equality.

Although he belonged to a Marxist party, all existing evidence indicates that Clark was, by 1876, a Lassallean Socialist Democrat, meaning he believed that democratic political power would liberate workers from the inherent and inevitable negativity of capitalist market forces. Unlike Marxists, Lassalleans saw the ballot box as the *only* way forward. They envisioned that workers, using democratic political power, would demand a socialist economic system. Capital and industrial production would then peacefully shift from private hands to the government without a revolution. The government—not private owners—would reap the profits from its industries and would distribute those profits for the mutual benefit of members of society.[32] It is not surprising that Clark believed in the power of politics as a means of liberation. After all, he had learned this lesson so many years earlier as a member of the Radical Abolitionist Party.

Although members of the Workingmen's Party were forbidden to belong to any political organization of the propertied class, Clark towed the line between it and the Republican Party for as long as he could.[33] Although he came close to disavowing the Republican Party when he predicted, in March 1877, that the Workingmen's Party would ultimately "triumph over the dominancy of the . . . [Republican] party," the truth is that Clark had trouble making a clean and certain break with the Republicans.[34] Indeed, he *never* officially left or publicly repudiated the Republican Party,[35] but remained active in it through late 1876, and even campaigned for Rutherford B. Hayes in the summer and fall of 1876. He identified politically with the party even longer—trying to secure Republican patronage through mid-1877.[36] Certainly, though, the party's failure to extend him a political post *did* lead him to reduce his Republican activities, while more fully embracing the Workingmen's Party.

In the 1870s, politicians routinely rewarded their best supporters with jobs and political positions: in other words, the spoils system reigned. The spoils system was, in fact, so common in American political life in the 1870s that most people blindly bought into it without questioning its ethics. While New York's Boss William Marcy Tweed is the epitome of political graft and corruption in this era, New York was not alone; this political corruption also extended to Ohio politics. Clark understood these unwritten rules of the political game and wholeheartedly complied.[37]

Not only did Clark subscribe to the spoils system, but he had a keen sense of entitlement to it. After having campaigned at a dizzying pace for the Republican Party through the election season of 1876, he had received nothing for his efforts. The Hayes administration failed to appoint him to any position, as he had hoped. Rather than sit back and wait for an offer of a position, he decided to use his political capital to obtain a position of his own choosing. And in the fall of 1876, he set his eyes on the presidency of Howard University.

Soon after the election, Clark wrote an editorial in the *Advocate,* insisting that the vacant presidency post at Howard University be filled by an African American. After decades of almost exclusively white leadership, Clark asserted that an African American must lead the historically black university in Washington, D.C. Other race men voiced the same concerns.[38] Although he stopped short of announcing his own interest in the position, every *Advocate* reader knew that Clark wanted the job. His friends and fans rallied to support his candidacy as soon as the letter appeared in print. AME Bishop Henry M. Turner wrote a glowing editorial praising Clark for being "learned, polished, dignified, indomitable, prudent, sagacious, fearless and well-experienced" and suited for the Howard presidency.[39] Even Attorney General Alphonso Taft endorsed Clark, judging him to be "an excellent teacher, a good speaker, and a gentleman of large intelligence . . . [and] thorough education."[40] Apparently, even such glowing praise from an esteemed white Republican politician was not enough to restrain the spirit of opposition against him. Some of Clark's detractors feared that white benefactors would be distrustful of African American leadership and would withhold financial support and threaten the school's financial stability. Others took a more personal stand against Clark's candidacy, charging that his Unitarian faith disqualified him to represent the masses of African Americans—a recurring theme throughout his career.[41]

More than anything, timing doomed Clark's candidacy. Howard University was in a precarious point in its history, and African Americans were quite sensitive and protective of the institution. A nasty public dispute between the school's president, John Mercer Langston, and its Board of Trustees led to Langston's resignation in 1875. Saddled with the debt caused by reduced student enrollment and income, the university was forced to close its doors for two academic years between 1876 and 1877.[42] People had good reason to fear the school might never reopen or might be forced to close again if it did. Hence, concerns about the school's financial solvency lay at the center of question of leadership; Clark's candidacy was fiercely debated precisely because of the precarious position of the school. Some felt that an African American president would lead to a serious reduction in funding from white benefactors.

The press aired all these concerns, and that coverage all but guaranteed that Clark would not get the job as Howard's president. Seeing the writing on the wall, he only half-heartedly tried to defend his faith and his suitability for the position. In an October 1876 letter to Alphonso Taft, Clark wrote, "I do not think my prospects brilliant," although he admitted that he believed he could lift Howard "into a condition of usefulness and make it, as it deserves to be, the great educational institution of the country for colored people." A few months later, he had abandoned all hopes of securing the coveted position: "It would be a miracle if I am proferred the position," he solemnly wrote.[43] Although he did make the short list, Howard's trustees overwhelmingly voted to hire William W. Patton, a white Congregationalist minister, instead.[44] Although Clark abandoned hopes of getting the Howard University position, he held fast to his belief that the Republican Party owed him. He took advantage of a divisive political moment the following spring to stake his claim.

The 1876 presidential election results had been close enough in some states to cause controversy about which candidate had won the election. In South Carolina and Louisiana, the votes were so close that neither side wanted to concede defeat, so dual governments were established by both parties. The U.S. House of Representatives had the arduous responsibility of determining which candidate had won the disputed electoral votes and, ultimately, the presidency. The resolution of this controversy, known as the Compromise of 1877, centered on southern Democrats conceding the presidency to Rutherford B. Hayes; in exchange, Republicans agreed to effectively end Reconstruction. Not only were the last of the federal troops promptly withdrawn from the South, but federal intervention and influence in local politics and society ceased. Southern whites regained control of their local and state governments and committed themselves to stripping

African Americans of their hard-earned civil rights. Many African Americans felt the Hayes administration had simply abandoned them.

Outraged and disappointed by the end of Reconstruction, Cincinnati's African American community held a public meeting in late July 1877 to express indignation about Hayes's southern policy, vociferously resolving: "The so-called Southern policy of President Hayes is a desertion of the cause for which the war was waged, is an abandonment of the principles and doctrines of the Republican party, and leaves the colored citizens of the South unprotected and exposed to the assaults and oppressions of the Southern people; . . . President Hayes has neglected the rights of colored voters of the South, and left them at the mercy of relentless foes."[45] Another resolution condemned the local Republican Party for failing to extend patronage to African Americans. Clark only reluctantly agreed to address the audience. When he finally took the floor, he *defended* President Hayes's decision to effectively end Reconstruction by withdrawing troops from the South; Clark insisted that the president had no alternative because Congress had refused to make appropriations for federal troops.[46]

Clark's address to the body revealed his myopic interpretation of African Americans' Reconstruction experience. Expressing little sympathy for the plight of southern African Americans, he insisted that "much of the blame for the saddening condition of public affairs in the South is chargeable to the colored people themselves and the carpet-baggers, who have kept in office men who have shamefully robbed those communities." Selectively ignoring the disfranchisement and other forms of political repression suffered by African Americans throughout the Reconstruction South, Clark chose to highlight, instead, the political corruption of Republican governments. Even then, he blamed African Americans themselves for electing people who corrupted those governments.[47] For him, they were not victims, but conscientious political agents who by willfully electing corrupt politicians had precipitated the end of Reconstruction themselves.

This interpretation contradicted that of most African Americans, who concluded that the Republican Party had failed them. Nonetheless, Clark persuaded the Cincinnati audience to accept his interpretation of why Reconstruction ended; according to the *Cincinnati Commercial,* Clark's "sensible little speech" had quieted the discontent among Cincinnati's African American community. The paper stated that Clark had convinced the audience that southern African Americans were not in as bad a position as they had imagined. The body subsequently voted to rescind its initial resolutions, underscoring how persuasive he had been.[48]

Although in a minority among African Americans, Clark was not alone in his support for Hayes's southern policy; other African American leaders in Ohio staunchly defended the withdrawal of troops. But unlike Clark, who overlooked African Americans' oppression in the South and blamed them for the region's political climate, men like Cincinnati's George Washington Williams and Columbus's James Poindexter considered Reconstruction a failed policy because the federal government had been unable or *unwilling* to enforce laws or protect African Americans' rights. They recommended that the Hayes administration abandon the policy and seek different and more innovative solutions to elevate the condition of African Americans and to protect their rights.[49] Interestingly enough, many African Americans in Ohio who supported Hayes's policy sought political positions, and one must wonder if that lay at the root of their support for the end of Reconstruction.[50] If so, they essentially traded the political rights of southern African Americans for their own political power. In fact, political aspirations explain why Clark had taken such a conservative stand applauding the end of Reconstruction.

Although he had long criticized the Republican Party for failing to extend patronage to African Americans and even had led an independent movement in 1873, Clark vigorously defended the party against those same charges four years later. Insisting then that the local party *had* extended patronage to African Americans, he provided several examples of African Americans who had been appointed to political positions throughout the state in recent years—including his old nemesis Colonel Harlan, and his son. In response to those who believed the party could have done more to help them, Clark asserted that African Americans themselves were guilty of not fully taking advantage of the patronage system. Specifically, he pointed to those who exchanged political service to the party on Election Day for cash, beer, or other benefits. Failing to appreciate how the material needs of the masses surely outweighed any political aspirations, Clark focused on the lost political opportunities. The problem with accepting cash rewards for political service, he reasoned, is that it frees the politician from being bound to reward those people with patronage.[51] Hence, he chastised African Americans for not using the patronage system in ways that would render the greatest benefits to them politically. Clearly his sudden switch had been motivated by political ambition. But to what end?

At precisely the same moment as Reconstruction drew to a close, Clark was rising within the ranks of the Cincinnati socialist movement. In an address delivered on December 10, 1876, before the Cincinnati branch of the Workingmen's Party and entitled "Wages, Slavery, and Remedy," Clark decried the extreme concentration of wealth in the hands of a few, stating that it threatened the welfare of society. A champion of the working class, Clark decried the excesses that created unscrupulous millionaires at one end of the spectrum and homeless people at the other. He called for a *gradual* socialist remedy through government reform and legislation that would recognize the rights and duties of labor. To that end, Clark recommended "thorough, intelligent, honest and faithful" labor organizations that would provide research to educate their membership about the benefits of certain occupations. All of the stated measures, he believed, would eliminate market speculation and panic, as well as business failures. In sum, he hoped that through socialist reform, capitalists would relinquish some of their "assumed selfish rights" and give labor its rightful share of the power and profits. Clark made it clear that he did not, however, endorse any socialist program that would hold everyone to the same level (communism) and that he believed there should be some room within the socialist system for meritocracy.[52]

In another address to the Cincinnati Workingmen's Party at Robinson's Opera House the following March, he observed that the middle class was being "crushed out," while the number of millionaires and "tramps" steadily increased. He lamented that the workers who "toiled and moiled to make the city what it is, have passed away in poverty and obscurity."[53] For the first time, Clark called for the end of all private ownership of capital, including industrial machines and railroads; instead, he advocated that the government should own and control these resources. In his socialist vision, all future profits generated from the government-owned industries would be distributed to the community. Rejecting the laissez-faire argument that government should be minimized, Clark believed that government's role should, in fact, be expanded under socialism. He argued that the government should take responsibility not only for controlling and regulating the economy, but also for minimizing the number of destitute workers and providing relief for the unemployed. "Capital," he asserted, "must not rule, but be ruled and regulated. Capital must be taught that man, and not money is supreme, and that legislation must be had for man." He emphatically stated that "nothing short of a radical reorganization of society" based on socialist principles would eliminate the economic disorder and inequality in society. The *Emancipator,* edited by Haller, boasted that Clark's speech was "decidedly the best of the evening."[54]

At the same time that he was shining as a star of the Workingmen's Party, Clark still held out hope for a Republican patronage position. After John Mercer Langston received the widely coveted appointment as minister to Haiti in July 1877, Clark and other African American men with political aspirations in Hamilton County, including the political upstart George Washington Williams, Alfred Anderson, and Colonel Robert Harlan, sent a telegram to the White House insisting that the ministry position be given to a black Ohioan because their fifteen thousand votes had helped deliver the presidency to Hayes.[55] Naturally, these men felt the administration owed them *something*, and what better than the most lucrative and high-powered political post available to African Americans? All the men who signed the telegram had a personal interest in the position. Although Clark never explicitly expressed his interest, his actions suggest he secretly coveted the post. These men used residency as a way to justify an underhanded attempt to wrest the position from Langston, who *had* lived in Ohio for many years and had cut his teeth in the state's politics, before moving to Virginia. Regardless, these machinations underscore the fact that so few political positions were available to African Americans then that some were willing to go to any lengths to secure them—even betraying a childhood friend.

These men made more than a little noise about Langston's appointment. The political disaffection among black Cincinnatians proved sufficient enough that William H. West, state Supreme Court justice and former Ohio attorney general, advised President Hayes that unless he appointed someone from that community to either a mission or consulate position, "We [Republicans] shall have a fearful struggle." Ultimately, though, black Ohioans failed to wrest the appointment from Langston.[56] Clark would be forced to focus his political ambitions elsewhere: for now that meant the Workingmen's Party.

Later that summer, during the Great Railroad Strike of 1877, Clark moved from ordinary to phenomenon within socialist ranks. The strike earned the distinction of being not only the first national labor strike, but also the most combative contest between capitalists and the middle and working classes in American history up to that point. The strike also catapulted him onto the center stage of Cincinnati's socialist circles. The seeds of labor unrest were sown when the Baltimore & Ohio Railroad announced a 10 percent wage cut—the second 10 percent wage cut in eight months. In addition, the company had laid workers off, reduced the length of the work week, and increased the number of trains headed to Pittsburgh without hiring more workers. The railroad employees resented the fact that while they suffered, the company continued to pay generous dividends to stockholders. On July 16, laborers walked off their jobs in Martinsburg, West Virginia. The striking workers blocked the trains leaving the station and refused to move until their wages were restored. Word of the strike spread quickly, as the strike moved to Pittsburgh and other stops along the railroad route. From the east coast to Chicago, strikers disrupted rail service, destroyed equipment, and rioted. Sympathetic workers in other industries joined the strike in solidarity. More than ten thousand workers across the nation joined the strike. They were joined by the unemployed and destitute. Because so many other industries relied on railroads, the strike brought commerce to a screeching halt, further crippling an already depressed economy. President Hayes, acting in the interests of the railroad owners, ordered hundreds of federal troops to protect strikebreakers and suppress the uprisings. In Baltimore, the militia killed ten protestors. In Pittsburgh, on July 21, the state militia opened fire, killing twenty workers, their wives, and children who had been blocking the rail.[57]

Laborers throughout the nation immediately staged demonstrations, issued resolutions affirming solidarity with the railroad strikers, and voiced outrage at the state-sponsored slaughters. Cincinnati's Workingmen's Party issued a resolution vowing to "stand by them . . . to the end of the struggle." On July 22, 1877, the organization held a massive rally in the Court Street market space between Walnut and Main Streets. The *Cincinnati Commercial* estimated that four thousand people attended the rally, making it one of the largest Great Railroad Strike rallies in the nation. The paper reported that the Workingmen's Party marched into the market space carrying its red flag. The rally was divided into three sections, two for English-speakers and one for German-speakers. The German section of the rally drew the largest portion of the crowd—a fact that underscores how German immigrants dominated the socialist movement in Cincinnati. At one of the sections designated for English speakers, an excited audience quieted down only after Clark ascended the podium to deliver his historic address.[58]

Clark wasted no time expressing his sympathy for the strikers and lamenting the plight of the laboring poor:

> I sympathize in this struggle with the strikers and I feel sure that in this I have the co-operation of nine-tenths of my fellow citizens. The poor man's lot is at best a hard one. His hand to hand struggle with the wolf of poverty leaves him no leisure for any of

the amenities of life; his utmost rewards are a scanty supply of food, scanty clothing, scanty shelter, and if perchance he escapes a pauper's grave he is fortunate. Such a man deserves the aid and sympathy of all good people especially when he is pitted against a powerful organization such as the Baltimore and Ohio Railroad, or Pennsylvania Central.[59]

After painting this picture of the day-to-day hardships workers faced, Clark railed against the Baltimore & Ohio Railroad for reaping stock dividends of at least 10 percent, while reducing workers' wages to what he called "starvation rates." He concluded that the railroad owners' greed had put the workers in such an untenable position that their only recourse was to strike. He also resented the fact that the government had quickly suppressed the labor movement in order to protect the interests of the capitalists. He bemoaned that the president of a private company could, "by the click of a telegraphic instrument," summon state and federal troops to "shoot down American citizens guilty of no act of violence."[60]

Moreover, Clark commended the strikers for not cowering in the face of government repression: "The sight of soldiery fired the hot blood of the wronged men, and they met force with force. Whether they are put down or not, we are thankful that the American citizens, as represented by these men was not slave enough to surrender without resistance his right to appeal for redress of grievances. When that day comes that a mere display of force is sufficient to awe a throng of Americans into submission, the people will have sunk too low to be entrusted with self-government."[61] Hopeful that the Great Railroad Strike would lay bare the problems with capitalism, and ultimately validate socialism, Clark stated: "These men will be avenged—nobly avenged. Capital has been challenged to the contest; and in the arena of debate, to which in a few days the question will be remanded, the American people will sit as judges, and just as surely as we stand here, their decision will be against monopolists and in favor of the workingmen."[62] Confident that the tide of public opinion would flow toward socialism, Clark predicted that in twenty years railroads would be owned by the government and that "cooperation instead of competition will be the law of society."[63]

Clark, a self-described "law-and-order man" who asserted that he hated "violent words and violent deeds," counseled the audience of disquieted laborers against violent retribution for the slain strikers. He reminded the audience, instead, that the civil liberties of free speech, free press, the right to assemble, and the vote were more effective weapons.[64] His plea for peace went far to subdue the possibility of violence in the city.

Throughout his speech, Clark underscored why poverty is unfavorable and, ultimately, detrimental to the republic. He believed poverty and ignorance were linked. Perhaps looking at society through an educator's eyes, he noted that he had been "alarmed . . . [by] the spread of ignorance and poverty in the past generation." He feared entire cities and states were "at the mercy of an ignorant rabble who have no political principle except to vote for men who pay the most on election days, and who promise to make the biggest dividend of public stealings."[65] Clark asserted that each person should own enough wealth so that they could have time for schooling.

In addition to eradicating ignorance, socialism, he asserted, provided the only solution to end the dispute between laborers and their employers. Charting the highs and lows of a capitalist economy, Clark noted that periods of prosperity in the economy actually were times of "unrestrained speculation." In such periods, capitalists grow wealthier, while the promise of prosperity encouraged others to invest. According to Clark, the period of prosperity continues until overproduction leads to a saturation of the market which, in turn, is followed by a period of intense competition. As a consequence, prices are reduced below costs, shops close, and workers underbid each other for wages. Strikes were the culmination of this struggle to maintain jobs and wages. Far from being a remedy to the labor problems, trade unions, Grangers, Sovereigns of Industry, cooperative stores and factories—solutions he had once championed—were all "futile," in his opinion. Clark had come to believe that these cooperatives too closely replicated the practices of capitalism: "They are simply combinations of laborers who seek to assume towards their more unfortunate fellows who are not members the attitude that the capitalist assumes toward them." Furthermore, Clark added, they "incorporate into their constitutions all the evil principles which afflict society"—namely, competition and overproduction. In sum, he believed workers' cooperatives too often succumbed to the same attitudes toward workers and business practices as the capitalists and, therefore, could not be their salvation. He concluded that "all these plans merely poultice the ulcer in the body politic, which needs constitutional treatment."[66]

Clark argued that the only way to stop the inherent contest between laborers and capitalists was for the government to control capital and machinery and to distribute it for the benefit of the whole. He posited that "future accumulations of capital should be held sacredly for the benefit of the whole community"; while past accumulations of capital could remain in private hands until they became a "burden." Then, he reasoned, the owners would "gladly surrender" it. He envisioned that every railroad would be government-owned; private ownership would be completely eliminated; and capital would "vested in the people."[67] Clark's speech made such an impact that it appeared in its entirety in the local papers.

Although the first national strike ultimately was crushed and the workers silenced, Clark's stirring speech opened some political doors for him.[68] First, it increased his standing within the Cincinnati socialist movement and primed him for a political career in the Workingmen's Party. His was the first widely publicized socialist speech by an African American and the most significant Great Strike speech by any Cincinnatian—regardless of race. Clark's contemporaries understood its significance. Moreover, just as significant is the fact that he is the only African American on record in the nation to speak publicly about the Great Railroad Strike of 1877. The Workingmen's Party prepared to utilize that to its advantage.

As a native-born American, Clark was in a minority among Cincinnati's socialists, who largely consisted of German immigrants; even fewer African Americans identified with the movement. Given Clark's local reputation and influence, his membership in the party undoubtedly won some African American converts to the movement. In the August 7, 1877, issue of the *Enquirer,* someone—most likely Clark—writing under the name "Justice" asserted that some African American voters had "thrown off the spirit of submission" to the Republican Party and would in the future act as "free and independent voters." "Justice" went on to state that because Republicans had failed to offer patronage to their community, some would vote Democratic, "a large number will follow Peter Clark and vote with the Workingmen," and others would not vote at all. Justice's letter is significant because it suggests that for some African Americans, the Workingmen's Party proved to be a viable option, although it is difficult to determine how many followed Clark into the party or how well socialist ideology generally resonated in that community.

Not everyone was as enthused about Clark's speech. Cincinnati's elite criticized the strike and the larger socialist movement. Local newspaper editors decried the speech and attacked Clark for defending the striking workers. With the exception of the *Emancipator,* the official paper of the Workingmen's Party, the coverage of the strike in local papers reflects a bias against the striking laborers, depicting them as a class of desperate, irrational, lawless arsonists and looters who destroyed the property of others without provocation. Newspaper editors also pursued a smear campaign against socialists. According to Clark, local papers denounced socialists as "destructives" and "fools" who threatened the order and stability of society. In a lengthy response to these charges that appeared in the *Cincinnati Commercial,* Clark vociferously defended himself, socialists in general, the strikers, and the Workingmen's Party, specifically, against the false, but common perception that they were violent, destructive, or even anarchists. Strikers, he wrote, were neither "destructives nor men of blood."[69] His letter emphasized how many of the same people who criticized the strikers for violence had provoked them through violent words and deeds. Clark blamed the press for incendiary, irresponsible editorials that provoked some readers to aggression. He wanted readers to know in no uncertain terms that some of the violent acts carried out by discontented workers were "the product of newspapers, not of communistic teachings."[70] Still, winning converts in this climate surely proved to be an uphill battle.

Undoubtedly enthused about having one of the most visible local leaders in their folds—one who also happened to be an extremely gifted orator *and* African American—socialists immediately tried to reward their star with a political position.[71] In the late summer of 1877, the Hamilton County branch of the Workingmen's Party nominated Clark to serve as state school commissioner, making him the first African American in history to run for political office as a socialist. Within months of joining the organization, the party positioned him to fill a higher political position than he ever had been offered as a Republican. William Haller insisted that Clark "most thoroughly represents the contest between laborers and capitalists, [as a member] of the proscribed race." In fact, according to Haller, Clark's nomination was "the finest vindication of the claim, that the 'Workingmen's Party' is a purely cosmopolitan organization."[72]

In a speech delivered at a campaign rally in Columbus on August 24, 1877, Clark insisted that there is "no remedy" for the troubled economy and suffering among the laboring classes except through socialist reform. Government, he asserted, "must stand as firmly for the rights of humanity as it has heretofore stood for the rights of property." In other words, the state had to be an agent of humanity and justice. For their part, workers had an obligation to resist—not through strikes and riots, which led to anarchy, but through the ballot box. Clearly, he had changed his position on strikes: just one month earlier, he had supported the Great Railroad Strike. Now, he considered strikes futile as well. Clark increasingly believed that the only path to revolution would come through the ballot, proclaiming, "If he [workers] did not resist at the ballot box we shall have a Nation of industrial slaves or paupers, governed by an aristocracy of capital."[73] His campaign speech proved that he did not advocate Marxist revolution. Instead, he advocated reform through politics: only politics would lead to economic transformation.

The October 1877 elections marked a golden year in socialist politics in Cincinnati. The Workingmen's Party won 24 percent of the votes for Congress. As for Clark, he ultimately lost his bid for state school commissioner, although he did win an impressive 8,129 votes in Cincinnati, plus an additional 318 votes from the areas surrounding the city. His biggest support came from Wards 7, 10, 11, 12, 13, and 14, which included Over-the-Rhine and wards with heavy African American and German-immigrant populations. Despite his defeat, the number of votes he won proved troubling for the GOP. Every vote for Clark was one vote fewer for the Republican Party. Republicans realized that because Clark was such a well-known and respected leader throughout the state, he had enough power to convince some African Americans to vote with him or *for* him. (The *Emancipator* had already reported that African Americans were starting to support socialist functions.)[74] And that was the last thing the GOP wanted or needed in a tight election.

Republican Party leaders also realized that between the Chillicothe movement and the Workingmen's Party, Clark had drawn African Americans away from the party; if he lured more away, it could be enough to make a difference in an election. GOP leaders, eager to do something to shore up black votes for good, nominated the first African American for the legislature in the fall 1877—Cincinnatian George Washington Williams. Not only did Williams's nomination serve as an act of good faith toward African Americans, but it also nullified the primary premise behind Clark's complaints about the party's failure to offer African Americans political posts. Still, the nomination must have been a huge slap in Clark's face, because Williams—who was not yet even thirty years old—had not cut his teeth in Ohio's politics. In fact, he had only moved to Cincinnati a little more than a year earlier to serve as pastor of the Union Baptist Church. Despite decades of laboring for the GOP around Ohio and beyond, it would be Williams—not Clark—who would reap those benefits and earn a place in history as the first African American to serve in the Ohio legislature when he was elected in 1879.[75]

For now, Clark could only hope that the Socialists could deliver something similar to him. When the Workingmen's Party reorganized and changed its name in December 1877 to the Sozialistische Arbeiterpartei—

which literally translates in English to be the Socialistic Labor Party (SLP)—Clark was named to its National Executive Committee.[76]

The following fall, in 1878, the party took a leap and nominated him for Congress to represent Cincinnati's First Congressional District. The ticket did poorly. Clark received just 281 out of 25,386 votes cast in the district. Solomon Ruthenberg, the other SLP congressional candidate, running in the Second Congressional District, received just 181 of more than 25,000 votes. Hence, collectively, the Clark-Ruthenberg ticket received just 462 out of more than 50,000 votes cast in the city.[77]

Fall 1878 Congressional Elections: Cincinnati First District

Candidate	Votes Won	% of Votes
M. Sayler (D)	12,032	47.4
B. Butterworth (R)	12,793	50.4
Spohn (N)	137	0.5
W. G. Halpin (N)	143	0.6
P. Clark (S)	281	1.1
Totals	25,386	

Considering that the SLP candidates had received 10 percent of the votes cast in the spring 1877 elections, and 24 percent in fall 1877, this 1878 election defeat was stunning. It is less of a reflection on the candidates personally, though, than on local political conditions and the infusion of Greenbackers into Cincinnati politics. Nationally, the Greenback movement was led by farmers and debtors who had suffered the most from the Panic of 1873 and its ensuing depression. These groups demanded that the government not only continue to circulate greenbacks, or fiat paper money, but also print more. They also called for an unlimited coinage of silver. Greenbackers, as such people called themselves, reasoned that increasing the amount of greenbacks in circulation would lead to inflation, which would make it easier for them to repay their debts. Their calls spawned a political movement and the birth of the National Greenback Party in 1876. The Democratic Party quickly aligned itself with the fledging party. According to a socialist journal, Republican "business men united to crush the 'inflationists' [Greenbackers] and prevent the financial anarchy which they believe would ensue should the 'fiat' money plan be inaugurated." Members of the SLP correctly suspected that the Greenbackers sought to absorb workingmen into their ranks by holding itself out as friendly to laborers. The SLP pointed to how the National Greenback Party had inserted the term "labor" into its name in 1878 (Greenback Labor Party) and began recruiting workers just in time for the congressional elections as a way to divide the working class. According to the socialist journal the *Socialist,* Cincinnati German trade unionists and workingmen were forced to make tough choices that election: they could support the SLP on principle— although each vote for a third party risked a Democratic-Greenback victory—or vote for the Republicans to prevent that. Although most German immigrants in Cincinnati trusted neither of the two major parties, they preferred the Republicans. Cincinnati's Germans chose to vote en masse for the Republican ticket in the 1878 elections. The effect on the SLP proved "disastrous" and explains why Clark and Ruthenberg received so few votes.[78] The precipitous political decline of the local SLP continued. Despite the fact that they had run for nearly every open office in the city, SLP candidates won just 2,586 collective votes out of more than 429,000 votes cast—or 0.6 percent—in the spring 1879 local elections.[79]

By then, the local SLP showed signs of deep internal divisions over platform, ideology, and strategy. One faction was led by William Haller, a prominent party member who tried to move the party toward almost immediate radical political action. He had no faith in trade unions. In an editorial in the *Socialist* on July 12, 1879, Haller insisted that such organizations were "political rings" that "have exhibited all the traits . . . [of] *robbers.*" Haller was quite vocal and public about his opposition to the official party position on politics. Another faction believed trade unions to be "the most appropriate form of crystallization for the economic interests of wage labor." This faction, which included Philip Van Patten, the secretary of the National Executive Committee, argued that the time was not yet ripe for political action. The official party position was that "the political action of the party [should be] confined generally to obtaining legislative acts in the interest of the working class proper." Van Patten reminded his body of the official platform of the SLP, which indicated that the party would "not enter into a political campaign before being strong enough to exercise a perceptible influence." If that were not already enough division, the SLP membership also divided on the Greenback issue. Those workingmen who supported the Greenback position worked to unite the SLP and Greenback Labor Parties in 1878. William Haller resisted that move, a position for which he received sharp criticisms by Greenbackers. This group of self-identified "Anti-Communistic workingmen" became openly "hostile to the [SLP] organization and platform of the Workingmen's Party" and worked against its success.[80]

These internal divisions, coupled with yet another political blow in spring 1879 elections, seemed to be a bad omen for the Cincinnati SLP.

The string of political defeats led to widespread disillusionment within the ranks about the potential for revolution through democratic politics. Many local socialists now realized that the movement might not survive without cooperating with trade unions. Van Patten's faction gained more power as a result; the local party reiterated that strong trade unions must precede political action. Van Patten tried to force Haller to accept this strategy, to no avail. Haller was brought before the body, interrogated about his views, censured, and reprimanded for refusing to subscribe to the party's platform. After being subjected to a series of humiliating public trials, Haller was finally expelled in early August 1879.[81]

Although he resigned from the party on July 21, 1879, during Haller's trials, Clark had stopped attending meetings long before. As early as the previous January, the National Executive Committee had passed a resolution demanding that Clark explain his "repeated absence[s] from our meetings without offering excuse."[82] The resolution reveals that he was no longer invested by then, although he did not officially quit the party for several more months.

In his farewell address to the body in July 1879, Clark declared in no uncertain terms: "I am a Socialist." He buttressed that statement by expressing his enduring faith in socialism's political viability. Clark told his audience that although he held onto socialist principles, he would "cease to operate *politically* as a Socialist [his emphasis]." To justify his decision, Clark pointed to Republican efforts to expunge him from the SLP election ticket in the fall 1878. Republican leaders had given him an ultimatum: get off the socialist ticket or resign as the principal of Colored Schools. It was an untenable choice. Clark recounted how the African American community mobilized and came to his defense: They "laid aside political prejudices and religious prejudices, and came out as one man and protested against my removal." Naturally, he felt indebted to the community for standing by him and coming to his rescue: "I really belong to that people; I really belonged to them from my childhood; I have served them in every capacity that they wanted me." Clark told his socialist audience that he intended to affiliate with the Republican Party "because my people so generously, nobly and unanimously came to my rescue."[83]

Although Clark framed his justifications for resigning in the rhetoric of racial indebtedness and loyalty, he obviously had other, more compelling political and ideological reasons for quitting the SLP. He did not leave the party, as some contend, because it grew unresponsive to African Americans.[84] He did not become a socialist to solve racial problems; and race is not the reason he left the SLP. Clark himself hardly ever mentioned race in any of his socialist speeches. Although he did believe African Americans comprised a distinct class of laborers, he did not consider their plight as exceptional or hyper-oppressed. For example, at a mass meeting before socialists in March 1877, he had declared that those who produced the nation's wealth were "slaves, white and black." Although the term "slave" was part of the nineteenth-century socialist lexicon, it is interesting that Clark missed the opportunity to educate his comrades about the critical differences between racial slavery and wage slavery. In the same speech, he mentioned southern labor issues as part of a larger discussion on wage slavery around the world. "Go into the South," he railed, "and see the capitalists banded together over the poor whites." Those same capitalists, he argued, "carefully calculate how much, and no more, it will require to feed and clothe the black laborer and keep him alive from one year to another. That much they will give him for his hard labor . . . and not a cent more will they give him. Not a foot of land will they sell to the oppressed race who are trying to crowd out the degradation into which capital has plunged them."[85] Here, Clark does make a distinction between African American and white laborers, particularly in relation to wages and the opportunity to buy land. This marks one of the only times he made such racial distinctions as a socialist. Yet, even then, he did not emphasize how race compounds the class issues or how African Americans have a more peculiar relationship to capital than other southerner laborers. Moreover, his statement that the "degradation" suffered by African American southern workers had been caused by capital suggests that Clark had no analysis of how racism dictated the class position of African Americans. More than likely, his silence about an issue that had been his life's work suggests he may have not wanted to alienate white workingmen with too forceful a stand on race.

    Clark quit the SLP for several reasons. First, the party did not prioritize political action. He long had believed that politics was a panacea for all manner of inequalities. He made it abundantly clear that he thought the organization had taken the wrong course by holding fast to the idea that political action must be delayed until *after* a strong organization had been built: "I do not see that a set of men have any right to assume a political organization until they are prepared to announce and fix a political policy, and I do not know that Socialists as yet have any distinctive political policy." Moreover, he also considered the SLP overly rigid in its doctrine, and was particularly unsettled by how the organization held members to a "certain routine of ideas." Nor could Clark stomach how the section had brought Haller, his friend and mentor, up on charges and then expelled him from the organization. Alluding to Haller's expulsion, Clark stated, "Here is this man expelled, and that man expelled from the organization for some independence of thought, [and] some independence of action."[86] Hence, it had become increasingly clear to him that the organization no longer held promise as a vehicle for change. Finally, the timing of his exit coincided with party's rapidly declining numbers at the polls. Given how important political power had been to him throughout the decade, it is highly plausible that Clark lost interest when the party ceased to offer the possibility of political power. Nonetheless, by the time he resigned, the Cincinnati branch of the SLP was no longer relevant. In fact, it imploded within a few years of his departure.

Clark had been introduced to socialism as a philosophy and worldview by his mentors and relatives during his formative years. Although he had been a socialist in thought for decades, he had no need to put the philosophy into practice until the 1873 depression. Even then, he embraced it for practical reasons—namely class grievances. Clark soon catapulted himself into the local leadership of that movement and left a powerful legacy with his speeches.

When he realized that the SLP had lost faith in radical democratic politics as the primary means for reform, he quickly ended his affiliation. After all, his belief that radical political action could effect change dated back to his time with the Radical Abolitionists.

As the father of black socialism—and one who had been informed by black radicalism—Clark held ideas about black socialism that were surprisingly *white*. He never developed a racial critique of socialism: he never criticized either the Workingmen's or Socialistic Labor Parties for being conspicuously silent on the issue of race or for failing to make any substantive efforts to recruit or organize African American workers.[87] Nor did he denounce these parties for ignoring the unique and troubling position of African American southern farmers trapped in a form of debt peonage as sharecroppers. Did he simply fail to see the connections?

Clark was unable to formulate a racial critique of socialism because he had failed to acknowledge or embrace African Americans' distinctive history or its troubled historical relationship to capital in this country. Moreover, he never offered his own interpretative theory on the development of American history that challenged the received notions about the intersections of race and class.[88] Without a consciousness and application of *that* theory of history, Clark subconsciously endorsed the white workers' view of history *and* capital. His brand of socialism fell squarely within the parameters of nineteenth-century American socialism and therefore offered no possibility of being revolutionary for African Americans.

Clark never believed socialism to be a remedy for racial inequality. He had not been drawn to socialism because of its potential to "redeem the race as it liberated class" or because of its potential to liberate African Americans, as some have argued.[89] He did not expect socialism to solve African Americans' problems specifically, although he did expect it to solve the problems of the working class. Moreover, Clark never criticized socialists for unresponsiveness to African Americans' plight. In fact, he hardly mentioned race or racism during the time he formally affiliated with socialist political organizations and actually grew more conservative on the issue of race during that time.

For him, socialism offered a solution to *economic* inequalities—not racial ones. Hence, he never tried to insert an African American agenda into the socialist movement, despite how some historians have framed it. Nor did he ever press the Workingmen's Party or the SLP to be responsive to African Americans or to become vehicles to obtain racial equality. He asked for no special privileges or considerations for them as a distinct group of workers with a distinct relationship to capital. Never did he utter any criticism for the parties' failures regarding race. The truth is, Clark never tried to change the color of socialism; but socialism had, in fact, changed him. If nothing else, it brought him tantalizingly close to the possibility of elected office. Running for office and garnering votes seemed to whet his appetite for political office. And it is *that* possibility that forever changed Clark and created a watershed in his politics thereafter. From this point forward, he would wage a relentless campaign for personal political power.

Chapter Seven

Voice of Dissent

We will learn that all the friends of the colored man are not in the Republican Party, nor all his enemies in the Democratic Party.

Peter H. Clark, 1885

No sooner than announcing his resignation from the Socialistic Labor Party (SLP) in July 1879, Clark immediately revived his membership in the Republican Party. He earned a place within the party's local leadership in short order—proof that he had lost very little political ground among Republicans during his time as a socialist.[1] In a speech before the Ninth Ward Republican Club one night in late September 1879, Clark rose to the podium. In what was only his second Republican speech since his break from the socialists two months earlier, he spoke at length about Democrats' use of political murder and intimidation in the South; by contrast, in the North "their only chance," he asserted, "is fraud." Clark urged the general audience to vote a straight Republican ticket. He had special advice for African American voters, though. He cautioned them to resist Democratic efforts to court their votes and to tell them: "Yes, I will vote the Democratic ticket the day that you assure me that in every State every black man can go to the ballot-box and vote his sentiments just as he pleases, and not till then." Clark added one last caveat: "For every vote you give the Democratic party sanctions the [political] murders of your fellow-men in the South."[2] In Clark's view, African Americans should never forget the crimes committed against them by southern Democrats when they went to the polls. In short, Republican loyalty had been forged through blood.

Few public intellectuals vocalized their contempt for the Democratic Party as loudly as Clark. Earlier that same month in a meeting of the city's Republican Executive Committee, he had lectured about the Democratic Party's misdeeds and undemocratic schemes, including all manner of voting fraud, voter intimidation, and murder.[3] There is little indication in 1879 that Clark would *ever* become a Democrat one day, much less within a few years of uttering such sentiments. But he did.

Peter H. Clark's decision to become a Democrat in 1882 could be categorized as a stroke of hypocritical amnesia. He not only seemed to forget or ignore his own words from that 1879 address, but the heinous atrocities the party had committed against his people as well. Despite the fact that African Americans largely remained loyal to the Republican Party in 1880, a growing number were becoming Democrats. Many of those men continued to be respected in their communities despite their political affiliation; not so with Clark. He became an object of disdain, scorn, hatred, and contempt and reduced to the label of race traitor. A closer analysis of his political career reveals that it was not his political affiliation, but his *politics* as a Democrat that opened the dam of antagonism toward him. His actions as a member of the Democratic Party between 1882 and 1884 drove a wedge between him and African Americans—and ultimately, between him and his conscience. This chapter charts his loss of conscience and commitment toward his people even as he embraced the Democratic Party and the dream of personal political power.

Although he did not become a Democrat until 1882, there were some previous clues that Clark would head down that road long before then. The earliest significant clue that he did not feel entirely committed to the Republican Party dates back to the 1873 Chillicothe Convention, where he had condemned absolute loyalty to the Republican Party and encouraged independent political action, instead. He authored the convention's resolutions that urged voters to "use their best discrimination" when voting for candidates.[4] The Chillicothe Convention marked a defining moment in Clark's thinking. Independent political action became his trademark strategy for securing political positions and civil rights for African Americans. He reasoned that if they voted independently, both parties would be forced to compete for their votes and would be more responsive to their issues. In fact, his advocacy of political independence made it possible to imagine himself as something other than a Republican.

Another clue that Clark would eventually bolt from the Republican Party is found in a letter to the *Cincinnati Commercial* editor printed on April 24, 1876. In it, he admonishes those who criticized African Americans who vote with the Democratic Party. Encouraging the African American community to be more open-minded, his letter went on to state that a number of African Americans had an interest in joining the Democratic

Party but were "repelled." He concluded that "it is to be regretted that the Democratic party disdains to leave open an honorable way by which colored men may enter its ranks." The tone and scope of this letter suggests that political designs fueled Clark's defense of black Democrats. At the very least, his letter intended to make Democrats more palatable. By trying to convince African Americans to embrace the Democrats among them, he tried to make it easier for people to join that party without fear of reprisals or rejection from their community. Clark also may have hoped to make white Democrats receptive to the idea: He informed them that those interested in affiliating with their party could not do so either because they were "repelled" or because their conscience would not allow them to affiliate with a party that sponsored racial terrorism. He believed that voting as a bloc for one party amounted to political suicide for African Americans; some had to become Democrats: "[African Americans'] political rights will never be secure from attack until a portion of our people are found voting with that party."[5] Clark's comments suggest that as early as 1876, he had seriously begun pondering becoming Democrat as a political expedient. Still, there is a big difference between talking about a political strategy and actually executing it. Clark remained in the Republican Party.

The 1880 Garfield presidential campaign proved to be yet another watershed in Clark's political career. He tirelessly worked for the campaign through the 1880 election season. Republican politicians mentioned his name for at least two patronage positions in Garfield's administration should he win: minister to Haiti and assistant United States treasurer in Cincinnati. After waiting patiently several months after Garfield's victory for a patronage position to materialize, Clark, in April 1881, formally notified that administration about his interest in the Haiti ministry position—a position that had been occupied by John Mercer Langston since 1877. Eagerly anticipating that his childhood friend would either resign or be removed from the post, Clark mobilized all of his social and political capital to apply for the job. His letter of application included the signatures of Cincinnati's leading Republican citizens endorsing his candidacy. For good measure, he followed up his letter to the president with another to the outgoing U.S. secretary of the treasury John Sherman, requesting his assistance in securing the Haitian post. Sherman's initial response to Clark indicated that he would be unable to assist him; Clark followed with another letter reiterating the fact that he had the endorsement of prominent businessmen in Cincinnati for the position, obviously confident that his endorsements would all but guarantee his appointment. Sherman's two

Were Black Dems in the 1800s Called traitors?

letters of response not only reflect a level of disinterest in Clark's candidacy, but annoyance with him. Apparently not even the signatures of Cincinnati's leading men would make the administration force Langston to resign or appoint Clark to the vacant ministry post if he had. Sherman's final letter to the principal stated in no uncertain terms that he had already selected another Cincinnatian to serve as the minister to Haiti.[6] Langston did not resign for years to come, though, so the issue of who would replace him became moot. Certainly, though, a disgruntled Clark may have been even more insulted by how dismissive his party had been regarding his application. The Garfield administration sent an undeniable message that it did not think him worthy of a political post, in spite of his endorsements from prominent Cincinnati Republicans.

The whole situation convinced Clark that the Republican Party did not play fairly—especially regarding patronage. He firmly believed that those who worked hard in service of their party ought to be aptly rewarded.[7] Spoils were the most appropriate reward for such service. After all, he had worked tirelessly for his party for years—stumping for the presidential candidates and organizing local political clubs, yet all that work had yielded nothing. Bitter memories of how he had been shortchanged for both the position at Howard University and the Haitian ministry post by the Hayes administration surely still tormented him. As fate would have it, James Garfield succumbed to an assassin's bullet in 1881, just months into his presidency. No one can be certain whether he ever intended to give Clark a position, but it is unlikely since he secretly harbored deep-seated racist views, dating back to 1865.[8] Although President Garfield's death, coupled with the fact that Langston continued on as the minister to Haiti, provided the party with a legitimate justification for why it had snubbed Clark, the snubs had become all too common. The fact that another political position proved elusive seemed to him to be a glaring indictment of the Republican Party that confirmed its unwillingness to commit to full political equality for African Americans. Republicans had no problem using him and other African Americans to help win elections, but repeatedly snubbed them after securing a victory on their backs. But this would be the last time he would ever try to obtain a patronage plum from the Republican Party. He had had enough.

Clark could no longer overlook the countless snubs he had suffered by the GOP dating back to the mid-1870s. He wanted political power—collectively and personally—more than anything, and it had eluded him as a Republican.[9] All of his old friends and enemies alike had been rewarded

Why didn't he get Howard position?

by the party including John Mercer Langston, Frederick Douglass, Colonel Robert Harlan, and recently, Cincinnati's George Washington Williams, a political upstart. And still he had nothing. Clark had no choice but to resign from the Republican Party for good and align himself with the Democratic Party. In October 1882, he attended a meeting hosted by Cincinnati's Colored Democratic Club. It was his first public event as a Democrat.[10]

Personal political ambitions aside, Clark also had other reasons for becoming a Democrat. In an 1885 interview with the *Washington Bee*, he explained that he became a Democrat because he did not think it wise for the majority of African Americans to vote in a single party. It had been a recurrent mantra in his political career. He also concluded that the Republican Party "ceased to be useful" to African Americans because it no longer advocated on their behalf. Clark also realigned himself because he resented how Republicans expected African Americans to be loyal to that party. And with that expectation, they also seemed to take black voters for granted. Writing a few years later, he went into detail about why black Democrats such as him were offended by Republicans' insistence that African Americans should remain loyal to the party: "We repudiate the gratitude argument by which Republicans bind us to their party. A man may be and sometimes ought to be grateful to individuals who have aided him, but never to parties. Parties are the instruments which a wise man uses to accomplish political ends and lays aside when they cease to be useful." This comment about political expediency explains why he switched parties so often in his life. Clark felt it futile "to waste our votes upon candidates who can do us no good if elected."[11]

Clark now believed that citizenship rights could only be enforced and protected by state governments.[12] Because he believed states had the ultimate authority, Clark began privileging local politics. He always had acted for African Americans' *national* interests before, but when he began understanding that citizenship rested in the states, Clark's political focus became increasingly local.

Clark numbered among a growing minority of leading African Americans who had broken ranks with the Republican Party by early 1880. George T. Downing, a successful restaurant entrepreneur; Timothy Thomas Fortune and W. Calvin Chase, editors of the *Washington Bee;* James Milton Turner, former minister to Liberia; and Clark are among the earliest prominent African Americans who became Democrats. The first significant black political realignment came in the days following the *what is this?*

Black Independents in 1880s

Compromise of 1876, when a growing minority of African American voters, sorely disappointed and disaffected about the party's southern policy
and its abandonment of Reconstruction, either became independents or
Democrats. Clark did not criticize the Republican Party's southern policy
because it abandoned freedmen, though. He had a problem with its commitment to use "defiance and threats of force" to convince whites to respect African Americans' civil rights; for him, that approach was simply
too antagonistic. He reasoned that such an approach would pit Americans
against one another along strict racial-partisan lines.[13]

Like Clark, many black Democrats did not take a straight path to the
Democratic Party. Some first tried to reform the Republican Party; others
became independents before becoming Democrats. Chase, for example,
wavered back and forth between the Republican and Democratic parties
throughout his career. A profile of black Democrats in the 1880s illustrates
that most had been reactionaries who joined the party not out of commitment to Democratic ideology or policies, but because of Republican
failures; hence, their political realignment can be seen as a gesture of defiance. For example, in 1883, Chase declared that African Americans had
been blindly loyal to a [Republican] party that had "deserted, disowned,
and frowned upon [them] . . . in 1876." Fortune, too, had not been so much
drawn to the Democratic Party as repelled by Republican Reconstruction failures.[14] Hence, these early African American Democrats were not
strict partisans, but men who hoped to leverage their votes with the party
that placed African American issues on the agenda. Fortune, for example,
urged African Americans to act on the motto of "Race First, then party."[15]

In the 1870s, northern Democrats adopted various strategies to attract
disaffected black Republicans. Some Democratic candidates simply pointed out Republican hypocrisies related to African Americans, while others
projected themselves as racial moderates, or even made antiracist gestures
to appeal to African Americans. Ohio's Democrats attempted all of these
tactics and gestures to mine the considerable black electorate for votes. In
1880, for example, House Democrats voted in favor of a report that condemned discrimination against any member of the House after an incident
in which newly elected representative George Washington Williams was
denied lunch at a Columbus restaurant because of his race.[16]

Cincinnati's Democrats, enthused with Clark's decision to bolt from
the Republican Party, rewarded him with small political plums. First, they
made his son, Herbert, a deputy sheriff in Hamilton County.[17] The party also
provided funds for the Clarks to begin publication of the *Afro-American*

in 1883, with Herbert as its editor. The *Afro-American* acted as the mouth-piece for black Democrats in the state. At the time, African American Democratic journals were few and far between (in fact, only a handful existed in the nation, making the *Afro-American* one of the premier organs of its kind). Mindful of the primary objective—increasing the number of black Democrats—the Democratic Central Committee provided free copies of the journal to every African American voter in Cleveland, Cincinnati, and Toledo, cities with high African American populations.[18] By publishing a paper that competed with the Republican-leaning *Cleveland Gazette,* the other major African American political journal in Ohio, Herbert and his father earned themselves some determined political enemies at the other end of the state—namely, Harry C. Smith, the editor of the *Gazette,* who seized every opportunity to criticize Clark for nearly every political move he made after joining the Democratic Party in 1882.[19] Smith's editorials sometimes bordered on malicious character assassination. While some of the anti-Clark commentary in the *Gazette* must be taken with a grain of salt since the two wrote for rival papers and belonged to rival parties, the tenor and ferocity of the political exchange between the two editors nevertheless illuminates the extent to which African Americans felt they had a stake in Ohio politics.

When Clark joined the Democratic Party, most African Americans still felt a great deal of contempt for it. The *Cleveland Gazette* summarized the myriad reasons African Americans opposed the party: "We hate it because it was the proslavery party, and bought and sold human beings. . . . We hate it because since the war it has opposed every step of the colored American [to get] out of the pit of degradation." Reverend Dr. Derrick, bishop of the AME church, labeled the party "Satanic."[20] Moreover, most believed black Democrats to be among the most objectionable people. Derrick called them "Judases" and ranted that he could not understand how "Colored Democrats [could] cling [to] a party that have done nothing for them. . . . [I]t had always been their purpose and endeavor to perpetuate our servitude!"[21] Frederick Douglass, speaking in Washington in April 16, 1888, stated, "I am unable to see how any honest and intelligent colored man can be a Democrat or play fast and loose between the parties."[22] An editorial in the *Cleveland Gazette* lamented: "We cannot understand by what process an honest colored man can be changed into a Democrat. We are perfectly aware that there are some 'Black Democrats,' but to our mind they are as horrible as the gnomes and giants and monsters of divers sorts that we read about . . . when we were boys."[23]

Indeed, despite the fact that most African Americans were then growing increasingly critical of the Republican Party, few were willing to abandon it altogether. Even in the aftermath of the collapse of Reconstruction
and the repeal of the Civil Rights Act of 1875, African Americans remained
loyal to the party of Lincoln—even if apprehensively. It was then that esteemed statesman and Republican loyalist Frederick Douglass labeled
himself "an uneasy Republican" and criticized the party for not standing
for justice. Only a small minority of African Americans determined that
abandoning the party was a sensible alternative—especially to join the
ranks of a party with a history of sanctioning African American oppression
and the denial of civil rights. Hence, Peter H. Clark the Democrat contradicted every principle most conscientious African Americans held dear.
The idea people could not stomach is how he could be a champion of his
people while belonging to a party with such a record of oppressing them.
The *Cleveland Gazette* questioned how Clark could associate with a party
that bore responsibility for degrading and killing African Americans.[24]

Yet after black Republicans learned of Clark's affiliation with the
Democratic Party, many found themselves torn between their respect for
him as an educator and leader and contempt for his politics. For the most
part, black Republicans still held Peter H. Clark, the man, in high esteem,
even if they could not respect his political choices. Although the *Cleveland
Gazette* voiced the loudest criticism of Clark's politics, the press initially
maintained that he was a man of unassailable character.[25] But anti-Clark
sentiment grew as he started committing what the community believed to
be indefensible political sins in early 1884. And since racial and political ties conflated in post-Reconstruction America, some of Clark's actions
in the name of the Democratic Party were deemed traitorous to African
Americans.

Clark first tarnished his reputation as a race man when he took an unpopular position on the issue of school integration. In the first session of
the Democratic-controlled Ohio legislature in 1884, John Littler, a white
Republican and "staunch friend of the colored man," introduced a bill to
repeal the Black Law mandating separate public schools. Supporters of the
bill believed that separate schools denied African Americans the opportunity to benefit from the best educational facilities and resources. They
pointed to the inferior facilities in Cincinnati's African American schools
as proof that separate schools bred inferiority. Hence, long before the idea
had been codified in the *Brown v. Board of Education* decision, proponents
of integration believed that separate schools and substandard resources

advanced the notion that African Americans were inferior and "unfit for association" with whites.[26] Hence, most African Americans in the state believed integrated schools would diminish racial prejudice and secure racial equality and equal opportunity.[27]

African Americans hoped the Littler Bill would go further to end racial distinctions than the state Civil Rights Law, passed on February 5, 1884. The state Civil Rights Law provided protection for African Americans' civil rights in most public places, but excluded restaurants and barber shops. It did not address the issue of intermarriage or, more important, schools. Many African Americans almost immediately raised their voice in condemnation, calling for an amendment. Chief among the critics was the Equal Rights League, which condemned the law as "proscriptive in character." Members of that organization believed it did not go far enough because of the exclusions. Not only did it fail to provide a sufficient penalty for those who violated the law, the league charged, but the maximum penalty allowed under the state law was only one hundred dollars— significantly lower than the five-hundred-dollar penalty under the federal law. Moreover, there was no minimum fine for violation, which meant that the law would not adequately punish or deter potential offenders. In short, the law had no teeth, a fact not lost on the African American leadership. The Equal Rights League considered the law to be a Democratic ploy passed merely "for the purpose of hoodwinking our people." The league argued that the law stood merely as a "shallow pretense of friendship" intended to engender African American loyalty to the party.[28]

With the obvious limitations of the Ohio Civil Rights Law, African Americans focused their hopes for equal rights and legal protections on the success of the Littler Bill, which faced stiff opposition. African American teachers and principals emerged as the most vocal and determined opponents of the bill. Clark wrote a letter to the state legislature voicing his opposition to the bill and organized the teachers' lobby, supported by some of the most prominent and accomplished African American educators, including William Parham and Samuel Lewis of Cincinnati, S. T. Mitchell of Springfield, and James Guy of Zanesville.[29]

By the time Littler introduced his bill, nearly every community in the state except Cincinnati already had dismantled its separate school systems. African Americans enjoyed the privileges of integrated schools throughout the state, but in Cincinnati, support for maintaining separate school systems remained strong. Since the antebellum era, African Americans had managed their own separate schools—the Colored Schools—elected their school board themselves, and exercised full authority in the school's operation. Deeply proud of these schools, many parents and leaders decided that the advantages of integration did not outweigh the advantages of maintaining control of their own schools, from curriculum to finances. They also reasoned that a strong black school board, black principals, and black teachers all ensured that African American children would receive a respectable education in Cincinnati—despite the unequal resources.[30] It surely must have been hard for Clark as a principal and leader of the fight for access to support any measure that would close these schools—especially because they had proved so highly beneficial to African Americans.

His opposition to the Littler Bill does not mean he supported either segregation or state-sanctioned inequality between the Colored Schools and white public schools. As an administrator in Cincinnati's Colored Schools, he, more than anyone else, must have realized that the schools remained wholly inferior to the white public schools. Even his good friend Governor George Hoadly had acknowledged that. Oddly, Clark refrained from publicly commenting on the inequality of the school systems.

Once the layers are peeled back, it becomes clear that Clark really only fought to preserve an institution that, in his opinion, possessed more intrinsic value to black uplift than integration. He took a conservative position on integration and had often publicly reassured whites that he had no interest in "social mingling." Ten years earlier, he had said, "No colored man nor any colored man's friend demands that social mingling shall be enforced, either by law or otherwise; but they do demand the opportunity to make themselves the equal of any man in the land."[31] This statement makes it abundantly clear that Clark did not place integration central to any civil rights agenda; social equality was far more important to him. The irony, of course, is that inasmuch as he advocated full equality in every aspect of life, he had endured unequal resources in the Colored Schools since day one.

Clark's endorsement of separate schools while tolerating resource inequalities within them could be perceived as an accommodation to racism and inequality. Considering his earlier black nationalist stance in the early 1850s, his position on schools could be seen, in part, as another manifestation of black nationalism. Clark never felt particularly hopeful about how African American children might fare in integrated schools, at least as long as discrimination persisted in society. His stand on separate schools represents the same ideological conflict that would emerge many times later in the African American community between integrationists and separatists over which schools could or would effectively serve African American children. Separatists argued that the persistent discrimination and hostility in society would result in a hostile educational environment for African American students, in which they would be taught by white teachers who might discriminate against them. Clark predicted that only a few of them in such an environment would "persevere" to graduation.[32] He believed that until African Americans secured full equality and civil rights throughout all levels of society, separate schools represented the best means to educate African American children effectively. The paradox is that the same black nationalism that had once seemed radical now presented itself as conservative and somewhat accommodationist.

Still, Clark is not the only one who doubted whether integrated schools would best serve African American children. In fact, his position on integrated education is one side of a contentious and public debate among African American leaders nationwide regarding separate education in the 1880s and 1890s. John W. Cromwell, Alexander Crummell, and Dr. James McCune Smith all supported separate schools. Francis L. Cardozo, South Carolina's former secretary of state and treasurer, flatly rejected the idea that separate schools led to internalized inferiority. Cardozo, Clark, and Calvin Chase, editor of the *Bee,* supported separate schools as a temporary strategy until African Americans obtained full citizenship.[33] Clark would never move from this position; he taught in separate schools his entire career.

Clark and the teachers lobby also had vested professional and economic reasons for opposing the bill. Historian August Meier once stated that "individual leaders with vested interests in them [separate institutions] are inimical to real integration."[34] That is certainly true of Clark and the teachers lobby, who feared their jobs would be casualties of an integrated school system. They correctly predicted that they would not be allowed to teach white children in integrated schools. Explaining why he opposed integration in an April 1884 letter to the *Christian Recorder,* Clark wrote, "I do not advocate schools in which colored pupils are tolerated and colored teachers shut out." In sum, the principal's vision of integration included an integrated student body *and* teaching corps. He stated that he could only support integration if it were implemented thoroughly: "I stand for separate colored schools, until they can be really mixed."[35] While the teachers' lobby primarily fretted about losing their own jobs, Clark's concerns extended beyond the typical; he had an additional burden of worrying about how the loss of the black teachers would affect the struggle for racial uplift. Specifically, integration promised to wipe out all black teachers, eliminating that professional path. In fact, teaching was one of only a handful of professional paths open to African Americans and created the foundation of a growing black middle class in the nineteenth century. Clark reasoned that if educated African Americans lost the opportunity to teach, the only sure path of upward mobility would be blocked, leaving them with few occupational choices beside menial labor and servile positions. He expressed his fears that "the [only] occupations open to them [graduates] will be those of coachmen and laundry maids to their white schoolmates."[36] And since he had spent the better part of his life training teachers and fighting for increased professional opportunities for African Americans, he could not, with good conscience, endorse any plan that would contract those opportunities.[37]

Realizing that the majority of black Ohioans now leaned toward integration, the teachers' lobby compromised. They decided to, instead, push for an amendment to the Littler Bill—one that would guarantee positions for African American teachers in the integrated schools.[38] After the legislature struck down its proposal, the lobby then pushed for an amendment that might give each community the option to preserve African American schools if they so chose.[39] Again, the intention was not to maintain segregation or inferiority—as Clark's critics cried—but jobs. Fortunately for them, the teachers' lobby found a powerful ally in Clark. The state's Democratic legislature respected him and looked to him for guidance on how to proceed. At Clark's urging, the assembly amended the Littler Bill to provide for separate schools if a majority of African Americans in a district presented a petition asking for such. While the original bill ended segregation in Ohio's schools, the amendment allowed certain Colored Schools to remain open if a community chose that option. The amended Littler Bill went before the House for a vote on April 9, 1884. Although the legislature voted 50 to 32 in favor of repealing the separate school law, the amended Littler Bill fell three votes shy of obtaining a constitutional majority.[40] The defeat was quite a stunning blow to the civil rights struggle in nineteenth-century Ohio.

Disillusioned integrationists looked for someone to blame for the failed bill; they found a worthy scapegoat in Clark—the champion of the teachers' lobby. Many deeply resented that he had opposed the bill so vociferously, and they were unsympathetic with his reasons for doing so. In their minds, he had endorsed segregation. Many African Americans even concluded that he had personally and directly orchestrated the bill's defeat because they knew he wielded considerable political power within the state's Democratic Party. Furthermore, they knew that party leaders made few decisions concerning African American voters without his advice. In their minds, he had convinced the Democratic legislature to vote against the Littler Bill. Regardless of the veracity of such a charge, Clark's actions *had* left much room for contempt. Even those who may have given him the benefit of the doubt now wondered why he continued to support a party responsible for defeating a bill that would have eliminated racial distinctions under the law. Moreover, many African Americans were deeply troubled by the fact that he maintained his political affiliation with the Democratic Party even though it had closed the door to racial integration and, consequently, equality under the law. As late as April 1884, he claimed that Cincinnati's African American community "stand[s] by the [separate school] law as it is." However, the reality is that by then, that community had begun complaining about the teachers' lobby and organizing to get the separate school law repealed.[41]

Even if initially reluctant to crucify Clark on the Democratic cross, the *Cleveland Gazette* and his other political enemies grew increasingly at ease with casting him as an enemy to his own community—especially after the failure of the Littler Bill in early 1884. He only further alienated himself from the masses of African Americans when he tried to defend his actions in the April 26, 1884, issue of the *Cleveland Gazette.* In one of his rare responses to the attacks, he wrote that he opposed neither the repeal of the black law, nor integration, on principle; he insisted that he supported integration if based on "terms of equality."[42] For him, anything less than full equality and full employment of African American teachers in the integrated schools would be unacceptable. He then drew an uneasy analogy between separate churches and schools, stating that the AME church had been founded "upon the color line," just like the Colored Schools. He encouraged those who attended separate churches to understand that the issues were the same. And in many ways they were.

But Clark's attempt to invoke an analogy fell on its face; in fact, he *offended* African Americans when he invoked the black church as a way to justify his opposition to integrated schools. A *Christian Recorder* editorial responded by condemning him for belonging to a church (Unitarian) without any African American ministers. The *Recorder* advised: "To be consistent he must leave that church and join one that practices equality, not only in the pews, but in the pulpit."[43] A *Cleveland Gazette* editorial went a step further by questioning whether Clark's Unitarianism made him too out of touch with African Americans: "How can a man be in sympathy with his people when he scoffs at their religion, and turns his back upon their churches? P. H. Clark is an infidel! Has always been an infidel! He is now an infidel Democrat!!"[44] Although intended to indict his religious faith, these comments, nonetheless, illustrate that by mid-1884, Clark's leadership was being questioned on all fronts. The Republican press held up every aspect of Clark's life—even his faith—as evidence that he was no longer a suitable leader of his people.

In the wake of his opposition to the Littler Bill, the *Cleveland Gazette* leveled some of its most vitriolic anti-Clark attacks yet. The journal portrayed him as an obstacle to African Americans' racial progress, charging that he had, in fact, "retarded its efforts to secure full citizenship for African Americans." The paper exaggerated and mischaracterized Clark's opposition to the Littler Bill, claiming that he had "stood for years to bear all the influence he and his friends can command" to prevent African Americans from access to all the best schools—even those enjoyed by whites. Moreover, the *Gazette* likened Clark to a Judas—someone who sold his racial loyalty for political power. That editorial characterized him as "a man who would give thousands of his own race [*sic*] educations inferior to the whites' that he and an insignificant few might gain a few paltry dollars, is indeed a traitor to his race." In another issue, the paper labeled him and other opponents of the bill a "gang of God-forsaken blatherskites and low, contemptible sordid hucksters who bartered the highest welfare, prosperity and advancement of their race for a mess of pottage."[45] By mid-1884, as news of Clark's perceived opposition to integrated schools spread across the nation, other journals joined the chorus of anti-Clark venom. A Louisville paper charged that he had "sold his manhood" to keep his job. The *Detroit Plaindealer* railed that he was "a thing foul and rotten, whose political stench is unbearable: whose record is so damnable that decent men turn from it with disgust and loathing."[46]

While much of the anti-Clark sentiment emerged in direct response to his position on the school issue, some of it also had been prompted by his decision to remain loyal to the Democratic Party even during the high-stakes 1884 presidential campaign, with Democratic candidate Grover Cleveland running against James G. Blaine, the Republican nominee. The 1884 presidential race offered the first such contest in decades in which a Democratic candidate was more popular than the Republican one. Throughout the campaign, it was clear that Cleveland had a realistic chance of winning the presidency. Despite some campaign scandals, including a paternity charge, Cleveland remained a wildly popular candidate. But not everyone was excited about his impending historic victory. For African Americans, a Cleveland victory spelled doom; using the Democratic Party's history to guide them, they feared that a Democratic administration would overturn every gain they made since 1865. As the election drew closer, the fear increased to the point of near-hysteria. Precisely because they believed their destiny hung in the balance, African Americans grew increasingly antagonistic to the Democrats among them—even more so with the vocal, active ones like Clark. Having someone of his stature and reputation help secure a Republican defeat was unbearable for some African Americans. In an open letter to Clark appearing in the *Commercial Gazette,* J. H. Meriwether, a prominent black resident of Washington, D.C., implored him to stand behind Blaine for president. Meriwether clearly posted the letter out of fear that Clark's influence might cause enough African Americans to follow him into the Democratic Party to yield a Republican defeat in the presidential race. He not only cast doubts about whether Cleveland would protect African Americans' rights as promised, but predicted that his victory would lead to their further oppression in the South. In his letter, Meriwether reminded Clark what Democrats had done to deprive African Americans of political positions, which had long been a special concern to the teacher. Unfortunately, though, Meriwether's pleas fell on Clark's deaf ears.

What is certain is that before 1882, Clark's political moves had been calculated to benefit the whole, and not him, personally. His affiliation with the Democratic Party after 1882 made people less confident about his motivations or commitment to African Americans. Moreover, people believed that Clark's separatist position on schools contradicted the best interest of the masses. Furthermore, many were deeply troubled by the fact that he maintained his political affiliation with the Democratic Party at a time when it was directly responsible for the contraction of African American rights in the state and beyond. Many simply concluded that Clark had placed political ambition before their progress. Perhaps he had. In any case, by 1884, Ohio's African American community no longer believed that Clark had its best interest at heart. In fact, that community no longer felt it could trust someone it believed had sold them out for personal economic interests.

Chapter Eight

Voice of Betrayal

> Does Peter Clark think that by becoming a Democrat he has changed
> his skin, and that by serving the Democratic party in its oppression of
> his people he has become a white Democrat?
>
> *Cincinnati Commercial Gazette,* 1885

On the eve of the 1884 presidential election, a "mob" led by Mike Mullen, a Cincinnati police lieutenant, raided the home of John Venable, a black boarding home operator who also happened to be president of the Colored Blaine and Logan Club—a political club dedicated to securing the election victory of Republicans James G. Blaine and John A. Logan ticket for president and vice president, over their Democratic opponent, Grover Cleveland.[1] Operating without warrants, Lieutenant Mullen and his squad seized twenty-four African American men from Venable's home on Gilmore's Landing, near the Ohio River, that evening. These men then were marched to the Hamilton Street station house and confined to the cellar from midnight on the eve before elections, until well after the polls closed on Election Day. The police never charged them with any crimes and made no record of their arrests or confinement.

Apparently, the lock-up of Venable's boarders constituted only a small part of a larger scheme to deny African Americans the right to vote that election. As the truth unfolded, it soon became clear that Mullen and other police officers, acting under the presumed authority of the mayor, seized every African American man they could find from streets, carriages, theaters, and even their homes. While in custody, they were denied food, water, and communication with the outside, and none were informed of their charges or given writs of habeas corpus.[2] Not only were several of their civil liberties violated in the detention, but they were denied the most important civil right of all: the franchise.

When the whole story came out in the press, papers reported that Mullen had illegally arrested and detained a total of 152 African American men that night—a detention that effectively prevented these men from exercising their Fifteenth Amendment right to vote the following day. Papers reported that the police had offered to release those who promised to vote for the Democratic ticket.[3] And while terrorism, false imprisonment, and other schemes to deny African Americans the franchise were common in the South, people were shocked to learn that it had happened in a northern city.[4] Even more shocking was the fact that one of Cincinnati's leading African American citizens, Peter H. Clark, was implicated in the raids. His name was spoken in the same breath as tales of voter intimidation, disfranchisement, and bribery—a fact that hastened his loss of status and respect as a race man.

What could have possessed Clark to participate in such a sordid political scandal that included disfranchising and discrediting African Americans—the very people for whom he had tirelessly worked his entire life? What could have possessed a man with an impeccable professional reputation to risk everything by attempting to bribe someone? The answers to these questions begin with Clark's decision to become a Democrat in 1882 and his calculated decisions as a member of that party afterward. In the mid-1880s, Peter Clark's thirst for personal political power, coupled with his desire that Democrats retain local political dominance, eclipsed all other goals. He understood that the changing demographics and political culture dictated that he venture into political waters that few African Americans ever had: machine politics.[5] But to enter that world—as it was constructed in Cincinnati—he had to leave behind his own identity politics even as he embraced a party dominated by working-class ethnics. Unfortunately, his decision to play machine politics led to Clark's very public and embarrassing fall from the pedestal of race leadership.

The mass disfranchisement of African Americans in Cincinnati exposed the dirty schemes and widespread corruption in Gilded Age politics in the city. The Queen City reigned over little more than political fraud and corruption. Local officials accepted bribes, politicians purchased votes, and parties purchased elections. In 1881, a councilman went to the press with charges that the city council had been offered bribes to vote for the Union Depot ordinance. Papers reported that a local gubernatorial candidate admitted spending fifty thousand dollars purchasing votes in the 1883 primary.[6] The most common and widespread form of political corruption in the city, though, happened every Election Day. The *Cleveland Gazette* charged that "Democratic ruffians" long had dictated how people would *why do you sell a vote?*

vote in certain wards in Cincinnati. On the day of any given election, voters could be bulldozed—or intimidated by the police or mobs of political
thugs—who demanded that they either not show up at the polls or vote a
certain way when they did. Repeaters moved through the city on Election
Day voting more than once. Nor was it uncommon for Kentuckians to
cross the river and illegally vote in Cincinnati elections. According to one
politician, all manner of voting fraud and schemes were practiced, including repeating, ballot-box stuffing, and ballot burning. As the newest voters
who had no political power, African Americans were the most vulnerable
segment of the electorate and, consequently, the most victimized group
in election scams and frauds. Since most African Americans identified
themselves with the Republican Party, Democrats schemed to victimize
them. One paper alleged that African Americans were sometimes shot and
wounded, brutally beaten, and driven from the polls.[7] This was politics as
usual in Cincinnati.

Nothing did more to muddy the political waters in Cincinnati, though,
than the influence of money. Charles P. Taft noted that money first became a critical factor in local elections and conventions in the early 1880s
around the time that Clark became a Democrat.[8] Money bought and sold
candidates, votes, political alliances, and elections. Because of the conflu-
ence of poverty and politics, it was easy to convince poor, desperate people
to sell their votes for a dollar or two; others, for a warm bed and a meal.
The *Cleveland Gazette* indicated that in Cincinnati, African American
votes were "purchasable and for sale to the highest bidder." For example,
the black tavern operator Henry Pickett, who fed and housed dozens of
unemployed levee workers in his tavern on "Rat Row," secured votes for
the Democratic Party in exchange for cash. The paper editorialized about
the disgrace to be found in the fact that African American voters would
sell their "political birthright for a mess of Democratic pottage" to smiling
demagogues who charmed them with smiles, cheap whiskey, and cigars
in addition to the money.[9] Nor were African Americans the only ones se-
duced by money. Politicians and city leaders routinely succumbed to the
temptation of kickbacks and bribery. And no one seemed to benefit more
in this climate than "bummers" who bought and sold votes to the highest-
paying party.[10] In the end, neither the vote nor party loyalty proved sacro-
sanct—only money.

As bad as Cincinnati may seem, it was not exceptional. The buying
and selling of votes dominated Gilded Age political life. People willing to
sell their votes for cash or withhold votes if the cash failed to materialize

lurked at every polling place on Election Day. And such corruption was hardly clandestine activity; it was done in the open. Moreover, contemporary party correspondence made veiled references to the practice, while local newspapers around the nation speculated about the exact dollar amounts spent to buy elections. In Cincinnati, thirty or forty votes went for $150.[11]

By the mid-1880s, a new type of politician that fostered a local political system based on ward politics and "unorganized bipartisan corruption" governed the Queen City. Ward "bosses" catered to the needs of a growing influx of Irish and German working-class immigrants.[12] One of the earliest Cincinnati bosses was John R. McLean, publisher of the Democratic paper the *Cincinnati Daily Enquirer.* As the leader of the Democratic machine, McLean and his chief political operative, Lewis Bernard, controlled the local government power centers, including the mayor, the county sheriff, and much of the police force.[13] Moreover, as the publisher of the leading paper in the city, McLean wielded a great deal of influence in Cincinnati society: he had the power to build and ruin reputations with one run of his paper.

Not only did many of the local government officials belong to the Democratic Party, but many of them sponsored corruption. Former governor Joseph B. Foraker claimed in his autobiography that corruption plagued the Democratic Cincinnati police force then. According to him, not only did convicted criminals, professional gamblers, and those who routinely associated with the "criminal classes" serve on the police force, but a few officers even committed crimes while on duty and in uniform. Foraker also contended that the police routinely committed election fraud.[14] The *Ohio State Journal,* a Republican paper printed in Columbus, accused the Hamilton County sheriff, a Democrat, of ignoring the voter intimidation and election frauds committed by his officers.[15] Hence, not only did the Democratic Party wield unchecked power in Cincinnati, but there was little hope that the party could be defeated until 1883 when Republicans mounted a serious challenge to its supremacy. After that, a glimmer of hope emerged that the Cincinnati Democratic machine could be broken.

Moreover, Republicans also benefitted from a national climate that grew increasingly intolerant of such political practices. A faction of Republicans—"Mugwumps"—aggressively lobbied for civil service reform. By the late 1870s, local Republican complaints about Democratic corruption in Cincinnati led to federal intervention. In 1878, U.S. marshals were stationed at the polls to ensure a fair election. Moreover, congressional committees came to Cincinnati in 1878 and again in 1884 to investigate election fraud.[16]

The 1884 election seemed critically important to Cincinnati politicians in both parties. Republicans thought they could use it to break the Democratic machine. Democrats feared as much; in addition, they hoped to help the national party send a Democrat to the White House for the first time since 1856. Observers in both parties regarded the African American vote as the key swing bloc in the election. This is especially true in Ohio, where both parties recognized that the more than 22,000 African American voters could very well be the decisive factor in the contest.[17] Joseph Foraker and other Ohio politicians openly acknowledged that African Americans were the single reason Republicans won state elections in the late 1870s and early 1880s. Democratic politicians hoped that if they could wrest the African American vote from the Republicans, a Democratic victory would be secured.[18] With so much more at stake, Democrats worked to suppress the black vote.

To guarantee the integrity of the 1884 election, the U.S. marshal Lot Wright sent 3,000 regular and "special" policemen, deputy sheriffs, and marshals into the streets of Cincinnati to prevent or deter election schemes and voter intimidation by the Democratic machine.[19] Not surprisingly, McLean's *Enquirer* criticized this show of force, fearing it would break the party's control of local politics. The paper claimed that those deputized by the U.S. marshal consisted of "murderers, burglars . . . common thieves," and others "of the extremely ignorant and vicious class." Some of those deputized included African Americans. *Enquirer* editorials complained that these "roughs" had been instructed by the U.S. marshal and the Republican committee to freely use their weapons on behalf of the Republican candidates. In reality, those complaints were founded. Democrats denied countless African American men the right to vote by challenging their legal residential qualifications. Many of these men were, in fact, transients or river workers who had no stable homes and simply boarded for weeks at different places in Cincinnati; although they could claim no other city as home, Democrats claimed they were not residents of Cincinnati. Other black voters could not adequately prove their legal residences either, because they had only recently arrived in Cincinnati. All of these potential voters were conveniently rejected as legal voters and turned away from the polls. Rather than allow these men to be prevented from voting, armed Republican deputies would pull guns on the Democratic poll workers and demand that the men be given the right to cast their votes.[20] This practice of protecting black votes with guns helped to ensure some Republican victories in Cincinnati.

After the election, losing Democratic candidates not only leveled accusations that Republicans had won certain elections through fraud and intimidation committed at the hands of the deputized marshals, but they also called for an investigation themselves, particularly of the U.S. marshal, Lot Wright. After extensive testimony before the House of Representatives, William H. Taft, the inspector of elections, concluded that the character of the deputy marshals had led to *some* voting irregularities, but those irregularities had benefitted both parties.[21] It was hard to tease out who did what because fraud, money, intimidation, and corruption were ubiquitous and rampant. At the very least, the presence of three thousand deputized election agents undoubtedly exacerbated the election mayhem, fraud, confusion, and intimidation in the streets of Cincinnati.

Nonetheless, the heightened oversight and "policing" of the election did little to deter Mullen and his gang, who still managed to seize, detain, and disfranchise 152 African American men.[22] And this he did with little regard for the law. After the mass arrests, leading Republicans George B. Cox, chairman of the Republican Campaign Committee; Colonel S. A. Whitfield, U.S. postmaster; and J. C. Harper, U.S. commissioner, went to the police station to inquire about the charges and post bonds for the men. Lieutenant Mullen reputedly refused to answer their questions and even insulted them.[23] Judging from his brazen actions, Mullen probably never expected to answer for his crimes since Democrats controlled the local government at the time of the mass arrests. The media attention, however, made it difficult to let him go unpunished. And the indignant African American community was clearly moved to mobilize. On October 21, 1884, the *Cincinnati Commercial Gazette* reported that upward of five hundred African Americans met at Union Baptist Church and passed resolutions condemning the mass arrests.[24]

Lieutenant Mullen, along with Lieutenant John Burke and two other officers, were subsequently arrested, indicted, and tried for violating election laws for their roles in the illegal confinement and disfranchisement of those African American voters.[25] Mullen, the ring leader of the operation, justified his actions by claiming that the twenty-four men seized at Venable's home legally resided in Kentucky and, therefore were not legally able to cast ballots in Ohio. He and other Democrats accused Venable of being a "bleeder" who supplied Kentucky residents as voters in Cincinnati elections for the party that paid him the most.[26]

There is a small possibility that Venable *had* been transporting Kentuckians across the state lines to vote in Ohio. After all, there was a long precedent for such practices in border politics dating back to antebellum contests over the issue of popular sovereignty. Witness testimony from both sides makes it clear that Venable was being truthful about the men being boarders. His enemies may have leveled this accusation to diminish his credibility and delegitimize him as a political actor. Besides that, focusing the attention on Venable proved to be a crafty way to detract from the larger disfranchisement of nearly 130 *other* African American male voters; these men were forgotten in the debates carried out in the press.

What *is* certain is that Lieutenant Mullen acted on a false, and even racist, assumption when he made those arrests in 1884: he presumed that the majority of African American men in the city could not legally vote in Ohio. Mullen never asked the men to prove their legal residence; moreover, he did not discriminate as to who he arrested and detained that night; the only qualification was that they be African American men—and thus, qualified voters. It is clear that Mullen intended to diminish the African American vote, which leaned Republican. The *Cincinnati Commercial Gazette* confirmed this when it asserted that the seizure of Venable's men was part of a larger Democratic voting scheme to reduce the number of Republican votes.[27]

Nonetheless, the body of evidence against Mullen forced him to admit guilt at his own trial. He subsequently received a one-year sentence and a severe reprimand from U.S. Circuit Court judge John Baxter. Judge Baxter admonished Mullen for seizing men he personally knew to be legal residents, "without inquiry, complaint or proof . . . [in order to] prevent them from exercising their constitutional right to vote." Baxter concluded, "You not only outraged the imprisoned parties, but you stuck a traitorous blow to the fundamental and vital principle that underlies our republican institutions."[28] Partly owing to voter fraud and intimidation in Cincinnati and elsewhere, Democrat Grover Cleveland easily won the 1884 presidential election, placing the presidency back into the hands of that party for the first time in almost thirty years.[29]

In the wake of Cleveland's victory, various African American leaders published their analyses of the nature and significance of the election in the *AME Church Review.* In an article entitled "The Democratic Return to Power—Its Effect?" Frederick Douglass concluded that the Republican Party had lost the election because of internal weaknesses and divisions. He also attributed some part of the Democratic victory to the fact that

Find this!

the party had "by bullet and bludgeon, by midnight assault and assassination" shored up its power in the South through voter intimidation. Yet, he remained hopeful that the party would ascend again.[30] Prominent African American Democrats also joined the discussion. Timothy Thomas Fortune, while acknowledging the past wrongs of the Democratic Party, asserted that the present party was not the same as it had been in its past. "It is wiser; more politic," he offered. Fortune argued that the Republican Party had changed as well: it no longer stood for "the grand principles of right and justice as enunciated by Lincoln and others." He believed the Republican Party was comprised of selfish, greedy, status-seeking leaders; moreover, corporate interests now trumped those of the masses.[31]

Clark's reflections in the *AME Church Review* focus less on condemning the Republican Party and more on defending the Democratic Party. He admonishes African Americans for mistakenly thinking that all of their friends were in the Republican Party and all of their enemies were in the Democratic Party. Such thinking, he writes, made African Americans the "ready tool of the demagogue," not to mention "narrow in his political ideas, bitter, intolerant" and "vindictive and murderous." Clark's condescending comments illuminate his growing impatience and frustration with the African American community for its continued loyalty to the Republican Party. He insisted that Democrats were not the "devilish creatures" that many African Americans believed they were. He also warned that such thinking reflected a major "defect in the character of [African Americans]" because it prevented them from trusting their "fellow-men—white or black" who belonged to that party. Clark also had a larger message about the danger of assuming that most whites were racists who plotted to deprive them of their freedom and rights. He implored African Americans to see the humanity in Democrats, in particular, and in whites, in general.[32]

In addition to attempting to humanize Democrats, Clark also tried to allay their overwhelming fears by making several projections about how African Americans would fare under Cleveland's administration. First, he proclaimed that they would lose none of their rights under the Democratic administration—at state or federal levels. He also emphatically asserted that on the Democrats' watch, African Americans would not only enjoy an expansion of their civil rights, but would have those rights protected by state legislation. Moreover, he added, there would be a positive shift in the public sentiment toward African Americans.[33] Hence, Clark intended to convince African Americans that the Democratic Party would protect their current rights, elevate their status, and expand their civil rights.

Clark's *AME Church Review* article is significant because it reflects a significant evolution in his ideology. Although he had spent the larger part of his political career pushing for federal protection of civil rights; by 1883, after the overturn of the Civil Rights Act, he no longer had faith in the capacity of the federal government to protect African Americans' civil rights. Civil rights legislation not only had to be won at the state level, he reasoned, but it could only be effectively *protected* at that level. African Americans, he felt, had done themselves a disservice by holding onto partisan animosities. Clark urged them to ingratiate themselves with Democrats in their homes states in order to secure state civil rights legislation rather than relying on "the vain hope that we will have the aid of the Washington government." Clark cautioned his readers that even if they were fortunate enough to secure federal civil rights legislation, there was no guarantee that it would not be undone by the next administration or war. Arguing that only changing the mind-set of society would ensure that legislation would have some meaning and permanence, Clark asserted that "constitutions, amendments, and laws which are not sustained by public sentiment are as worthless as blank paper."[34] This comment also demonstrates why he began to act politically at the local level.

Clark's vision of African Americans transcending partisan politics and working with local whites to secure state legislation is pragmatic, and may have worked—in a later era. Perhaps he was a bit naïve to think that African Americans would vote—in the name of political pragmatism—with a party that only had recently resisted their emancipation, opposed critical amendments, overturned civil rights legislation at the federal level, and sponsored their disfranchisement, while encouraging lynching and terrorism against them at the state level. For most African Americans, contempt for the Democratic Party was not purely a question of partisan loyalty or narrow-mindedness, but of principle. They felt the party's history of antagonism toward African Americans was a predictor of its future actions. Not even Clark's haughty charges that most African Americans were narrow-minded, "bitter," and "intolerant" induced them to embrace that party.

Despite Clark's best efforts, most African Americans could not reconcile his portrayal of the Democratic Party and their own perceptions of it, nor could they easily stomach his role in securing the party's victory at the national level. The *Detroit Plaindealer* labeled Clark a "man without principle" because of his political affiliation.[35] Given the stakes in that 1884 election, African Americans undoubtedly blamed people like him not only for the Democratic victory at the national level, but also for the disfranchisement of African American voters at the local level in Cincinnati. It did not escape anyone that Clark, the city's most vocal proponent of civil rights, had failed to denounce either the Cincinnati police or Lieutenant Mullen for the unlawful imprisonment and disfranchisement of African American voters. Instead, he found every reason to defend Mullen's actions in his journal, the *Afro-American*. He singularly and narrowly focused on convincing his readership that the twenty-four African Americans seized from Venable's home were not legal residents and therefore not entitled to vote. The fact that nearly 130 other African Americans also had been detained and disfranchised that night seems to have escaped him. A *Cincinnati Commercial Gazette* columnist accused Clark of endorsing the presumption that African Americans were noncitizens or illegal voters who were not entitled to the same rights as whites.[36] His defense of actions that denied African Americans their rights suggests that he put the Democratic Party above the very issues for which he had labored throughout his career. Consequently, his credibility as a race man increasingly diminished toward the end of 1884.

Clark's waning influence as a race man after 1884 proved unfortunate for him because in early 1885 Governor Hoadly, his old friend and fellow Democrat, launched an assault on racially discriminatory legislation, including the legislation that sanctioned separate schools for African Americans and prohibited intermarriage. Before taking any action to that end, he first tried to win over the support of Clark and other prominent African Americans who advocated separate schools. On January 2, 1885, Hoadly sent a letter to James Guy of Zanesville, one of the most vocal advocates of separate schools in the state, urging him to reconsider his position. Hoadly wrote, "I am very sorry to find a colored man taking the view that you do, for I am persuaded that it is hostile to your duty, and to the interests of your people." The governor concluded his letter by telling Guy that "the foundations of distinctions in Ohio should be correct conduct, good behavior, merit, and not color."[37]

In an address to the people of Ohio a week later, Governor Hoadly declared that discriminatory laws were "relics of prejudice" that had their origins in slavery and that "had no relation to moral worth [or] fitness for civic usefulness." He pointed to Cincinnati's Colored Schools as evidence that separate schools impeded racial progress. He acknowledged that despite the fact that some of the schools had excellent teachers, taken as a whole, they were inferior to the integrated schools and provided African Americans with inferior opportunities.[38]

George Hoadly (Courtesy of the Ohio Historical Society.)

Acting on the governor's suggestion, Senator George Ely of Cleveland presented another bill repealing all remaining discriminatory laws, including the separate school law. This time, African Americans mobilized and organized to support the school integration bill. Black Cincinnati, which had historically supported separate Colored Schools, held a mass meeting at Zion Baptist Church that February to discuss the advantages of school integration. Oddly enough, Clark did not attend, but his position remained as it had been the previous year: once again, he opposed any bill that would threaten teachers' jobs. And once again, his teachers' lobby opposed the bill because it made no provision for them to retain their jobs in the integrated schools. They supported provisional integration; they lobbied for an amendment that would have provided the option to retain Colored Schools if a local community so desired. But that mass meeting at Zion made it clear that the tide had turned sufficiently enough that teachers, Clark, and others who opposed the bill were now in a minority in the Queen City and the state. People criticized them for placing self-interest above racial interest. The community now no longer preferred separate schools, and Peter Clark and all those associated with opposition to this bill—regardless of their reasons—grew increasingly unpopular in the city. At the same time, those who supported the bill—including Colonel Robert Harlan and Jesse Fossett—now had the dominant voices in the community.[39]

Despite the activism and support from African American communities across every part of the state, the Ely bill failed.[40] Many black Ohioans outside of Cincinnati also could not fathom what had possessed a man of Clark's stature to seemingly depart from his core values and work against his own community in so many ways. The *Cleveland Gazette* had an answer to this burning question: political power. The journal accused him of "regarding his own [political] interests paramount to the interests of his race" and alleged that Clark and other leading Ohio black Democrats had joined the party only because they had been denied offices or jobs in the Republican administration.[41] The editor repeatedly reminded his readers that Democrats had rewarded Clark for his partisan work "against his own race" with political appointments.[42]

The truth is that the Democratic Party did value Clark—as a black Democrat—and positioned him to receive political rewards for his loyalty to the party. To a certain extent, Democrats took advantage of his reputation and influence among African Americans, which they harnessed for the party's benefit. Records illustrate that as early as 1883 the party had actively pursued a strategy of securing the African American vote. Peter Clark helped deliver that vote in Ohio.[43] Not only had he been instrumental in Hoadly's victory, but his continued alliance with the party, along with his politics, had cost him his standing among African Americans. If any African American stood to reap the tangible benefits for diligent service to the Ohio democracy, it should have been Clark. And the party did reward him at key moments. For example, after the 1883 election, Hoadly appointed Clark as trustee of Ohio State University. The following year, the Democratic Party sent him to the Democratic national convention as the African American delegate-at-large.[44]

Governor Hoadly sought to reward Clark in other ways as well. In March 1885, Hoadly wrote a self-congratulatory letter to a White House staff member, praising himself for the work he had done as governor for African Americans. Moreover, he credited himself with having recommended that the General Assembly pass a state civil rights bill. The governor also gave himself credit for recommending the repeal of the Black Laws and for forming African American military companies (although some would argue that the segregated military companies belied his commitment to full integration and equal rights for African Americans). The governor also emphasized how he had appointed African Americans to high-profile positions throughout his administration, including the board of trustees at the leading state universities, Ohio State University and Miami University, and the board of the State Blind Asylum. Hoadly summarized his accomplishments by stating that he had "in all ways and methods open to me . . . made manifest the determination of the Democracy of Ohio to obliterate the color line." He concluded by asserting that his activities on behalf of African Americans in Ohio made him "a sort of champion of the colored race."[45] He may have been a bit out of touch with reality when he made these assertions in 1885, because by then, three significant events at the state and local levels in 1884 and 1885 overshadowed his accomplishments and compromised his reputation among the state's African American population: a weak state civil rights law, the repeated defeat of the Littler Bill in the legislature in 1884 and 1885, and the 1884 mass arrests in Cincinnati.

Clark still hoped to land the patronage plum of the Haitian ministry post in President Cleveland's administration. Under the spoils system, the victorious party routinely released political appointees from the previous administration from their civil service positions, filling the vacated positions with loyal members of its own party. Hence, Langston finally would be forced to relinquish the coveted ministry position for which Clark had waited eight long years. And Clark fully expected the outcome would be different this time since he belonged to a different party. In fact, he had been so confident that he would get the position that he had traveled to Washington to make his wishes known to the new administration. But the Republican Party had one last trick of its own. Only days before he left office and within hours of Langston's retirement, President Chester Arthur nominated George Washington Williams, author of *History of the Negro Race in America* and Ohio's first black legislator, to fill the position. In a whirlwind, the Senate confirmed Williams's nomination the same evening, and he was sworn in within two days, on March 4. The appointment came as an utter surprise to everyone, including Clark, who was completely blindsided by the news.[46]

It was especially galling to Clark that the position went to Williams, a man he considered his political nemesis. The two had had a long competitive history in Cincinnati's politics. Their rivalry began when Williams became the direct beneficiary of Clark's affiliation with the SLP. Republicans, fearing Clark might draw African Americans into the SLP, nominated and elected Williams to serve in the Ohio legislature in 1879. After Williams bowed to pressure by wealthy Avondale whites to introduce a bill that would have prohibited African Americans from interring bodies in their own Colored American Cemetery, Clark led the strenuous objections raised against Williams in Cincinnati's African American community, saying of his rival: "Williams seemed to be the man to do anything that anybody put in his hands. . . . Now here is a man who should have staid [sic] by the interests of the colored people while there remained a drop of blood in his veins."[47] With African Americans from his own district aligned against him—and Clark the most vocal among them—Williams had a short political career, serving just one term in the legislature. There was no love lost between the two men.

Outraged by the fact that he had lost the position and to his local political rival, Clark voiced his concerns to President Cleveland in a private meeting. At the president's suggestion, he wrote to Thomas Bayard, the newly appointed secretary of state, indicating that he believed Williams would be a poor representative for the country. Framing his letter in concerns that Williams might dishonor both the office and African Americans, Clark did not provide Bayard with specific allegations, but did provide him with a short list of names of prominent Ohioans who could verify his claims. A few days later, he wrote Bayard a second letter elaborating on Williams's character. In it, Clark accused him of being "a notoriously untruthful man" who possessed "utter unreliability in word and deed." He added that any honest person who knew Williams longer than three months could attest to that. Clark then took his assassination of Williams's character to another level by writing that he "neglects his family shamefully," accusing Williams of living "luxuriously at hotels" throughout the Northeast while his wife and child lived "at the expense of her poverty stricken mother or of friends." The letter included an even longer list of names of others who concurred with this assessment of Williams. Clark's mentor and friend Frederick Douglass was at the top of the list.[48] In his drive to wrest the coveted position from Williams, Clark proved he would resort to anything, including character assassination. Surely at his urging, even the former mayor of Cincinnati, William Means, sent a telegram to the White House characterizing Williams as a "deadbeat . . . unfit to represent [the] present administration."[49] People far more prominent than

Clark and the former mayor of Cincinnati with the misfortune of knowing Williams personally also wrote letters to the secretary of state vehemently protesting his commission and citing his poor character, including
the U.S. diplomats to Switzerland and Germany. These letters told tales
about pathological lying, the failure to repay loans, and wanton neglect
of his family. The stature of these complainants must have given Bayard
cause for concern because he refused to give Williams orders to leave for
Port-au-Prince. In fact, the position remained functionally vacant. Bayard
never told Williams the exact nature of the charges leveled against him or
who raised them. He never knew that Clark had been one of the instiga-
tors.[50] Regardless, Williams was the second African American man Clark
tried to undermine.

While he was busy disparaging Williams in Washington, D.C., Governor Hoadly sent a letter to President Cleveland urging him to make "a few
conspicuous appointments among colored people." He offered the names
of Clark and George T. Downing, another prominent black Democrat of
Newport, Rhode Island, as possible recipients of those political positions.[51]
In a series of letters to the president, the Ohio governor praised Clark for
being "a most accomplished man, learned and eloquent, honest and sober,"
calling Clark "a ripe scholar, and an orator of rare power." Hoadly admittedly invested so much effort into securing a political appointment for
Clark because he believed it would serve the interests of the Democratic
Party. He advised President Cleveland that a Clark appointment would not
only assure African Americans that their rights "will not be violated by a
Democratic administration," but that it would help "break the color line,"
both of which would ultimately increase African American support for
Cleveland.[52] While Hoadly never specifically mentioned the Haitian min-
istry position, it is obviously the position to which he refers in his letters.

Finally, on May 7, 1885, President Grover Cleveland ended all the
controversy surrounding the post by appointing John Edward West Thompson, an African American physician from New York, to serve as the next
minister to Haiti. Dr. Thompson's appointment officially ended Williams's
tenure, although the latter never did even one day's work as minister. Clark
had been snubbed yet again. Even after all of his underhanded, backroom
maneuvers against George Washington Williams, he failed to secure the
very same position he had sought two times before as a Republican. The
record is silent about why the president decided against giving the job to
Clark, but perhaps his own tarnished reputation among African Americans in his home state played a role. Dr. Thompson, by contrast, received

universal approval from all quarters. Few could find anything to protest about him, while at least one person had advised the president to avoid people like Clark.[53] Or perhaps Clark's calculated and aggressive efforts to disparage Williams had turned the administration against him as well.

Feeling sympathy for him, Clark's Democratic friends in Cincinnati and elsewhere lobbied to secure another patronage position for him. In a desperate letter to the president dated September 9, 1885, Governor Hoadly urged him to make no appointments in Cincinnati except to appoint Clark to "as high an office as you can find for him."[54] The timing of this letter, coupled with its expressing a greater sense of urgency than was shown in the previous letters, suggests that Hoadly felt a great deal of indebtedness to Clark for his continued loyalty and support, which only intensified as the election drew near. The only way he could see to repay him was through the patronage system. Neither Hoadly nor Clark had come to terms with the fact that the spoils system did not work the same way for African Americans as it did for whites. Even with all of his endorsements from people in high places in Cincinnati and beyond, a federal position eluded Clark. His questionable racial politics in the fall elections surely had not helped his case.

In the summer of 1885, newspapers reported that Governor Hoadly had signed a petition requesting a presidential pardon for Lieutenant Mullen. Prominent state Democrats who sought to overturn Mullen's conviction soon after the 1884 election drafted and circulated the petition. In fact, a conspiracy to exonerate him extended to the highest ranks of state and national office. Perhaps succumbing to political pressure, President Grover Cleveland pardoned Mullen in August 1885, setting off a political firestorm in Cincinnati and beyond. The *Cleveland Gazette* railed that the pardon represented "an outrage upon civilization." Hoadly excused Mullen's actions claiming that Venable had sponsored illegal voters. The governor reputedly acknowledged that he was "proud" to stand by Mullen, a "worthy officer." Even more stinging is the fact that the governor convened a police board to consider Mullen's full reinstatement to the Cincinnati police force, and expressed full confidence that he would, in the future, exercise more "discrimination" in distinguishing legal and illegal voters. With Hoadly's endorsement, the board promptly granted Mullen's reinstatement to the force. The *Cincinnati Commercial Gazette* warned African Americans that Hoadly could not be trusted: "any man who would defend the suppression of the ballot anywhere as Hoadly does . . . would suppress or corrupt it everywhere they could." The *Cleveland Gazette* encouraged African Americans to hold the governor personally responsible for Mullen's pardon at the next election by voting against him.[55]

The Mullen pardon came right before the 1885 gubernatorial election, which ended up being a rematch between Democratic governor George Hoadly and Joseph Foraker. Hoadly had won the 1883 election largely because state Republicans had divided over the issue of temperance; seventy thousand of them refused to vote in that election, thus giving Democrats the numerical advantage.[56] To a lesser extent, though, his victory is also attributable to the fact that significant numbers of African Americans voted for Hoadly thanks to Peter Clark, who had vigorously campaigned for his Unitarian church friend. Although Hoadly defeated Foraker by only a slim margin in 1883—just 12,529 votes—by all accounts, African Americans had tipped the balance in his favor. Hoadly acknowledged that "in nearly every Northern state the colored people hold the balance of power." In a private letter to the White House, he noted that the African American vote had been "distinctly divided" for the first time during his bid for the governor's office in 1883. He estimated that he received from "3,000 to 7,000 of the 25,000" African American votes in the state, and readily acknowledged that those votes had led to his victory over Foraker.[57] Because African Americans clearly held the balance of power, both parties recognized they were the swing voting bloc for the 1885 election.

Democrats worked hard to prove Hoadly was a better candidate for African Americans because he had a stronger record on racial issues. They pointed to the fact that he had been an ardent abolitionist, Radical Republican, and in every way, a proven "friend" of African Americans dating back to the antebellum era. In addition, he also had been mentored by Salmon Portland Chase, a known abolitionist attorney and champion of black freedom in the antebellum period. That alone seemed to be enough to prove him a "friend." In fact, Hoadly had "impeccable egalitarian credentials." Democrats also leveled a flurry of charges of racism aimed at discrediting the Republican candidate, Joseph Foraker, among African American voters. The rumor mill they set in motion accused Foraker of having transferred from Ohio Wesleyan University as a young student because the school had admitted an African American. Some found that unacceptable. African Americans also took exception to the fact that Foraker had acted as the defense attorney in two anti–civil rights suits.[58] In the 1883 campaign season, Democrats had reputedly distributed cards in the black community accusing Foraker of refusing to vote for George Washington

Williams, a candidate for representative, simply because he was an African American.[59] African Americans faced the dilemma of voting either for a candidate who was a proven ally but who belonged to a party with a long history of antagonism to them, or for a candidate who reputedly held antagonism toward them but who nonetheless belonged to a party that had historically advocated on their behalf. Republicans tried to ensure African American loyalty by keeping the memory of the Mullen election scheme and his subsequent pardon fresh in their minds. Mullen's pardon *had* reopened some old wounds; most African Americans certainly would heed the *Gazette's* advice and hold Governor Hoadly responsible for that.

In an October 10, 1885, gubernatorial debate with Foraker, Governor Hoadly, trying to secure the loyalty of African American voters, reminded the audience that a Democratic legislature had given them equal rights, the right to testify in courts, and had abolished Black Laws. When a heckler in the crowd retorted that Hoadly could not get the African American vote that way, he promised that he would treat African Americans fairly whether they voted for him or not. He reminded African Americans that Democrats were their "friends" and expressed full confidence that the party would not betray them. In his rebuttal, Foraker asked a rhetorical question: If Hoadly be "the friend of the colored race, how can he reconcile consistently with that position what he has done for Mullen, who perpetrated upon colored people the grossest outrage ever known north of the Ohio River?"[60] The question elicited wild applause from the audience. Certainly the Mullen issue exposed the governor's hypocrisies.

Clearly, even one year later, Mullen remained anathema to African Americans. He embodied not only the 1884 mass efforts to deny them their vote, but also the terror of the Democratic machine in Cincinnati—one enforced by mobs and police officers. By reminding African Americans that their "friend" had pardoned their enemy, Foraker hoped to persuade them to cast their votes for him instead. The very nature of the campaign suggests that the 1885 Ohio gubernatorial election outcome rested squarely in the hands of African American voters. Mullen's pardon and subsequent reinstatement, coupled with Hoadly's other political missteps regarding African Americans, proved too much for the incumbent to overcome at the polls. Joseph Foraker won the 1885 gubernatorial race, his victory a testament to the significance of the black vote in Ohio.

Even before Election Day, however, John Venable found himself at the center of yet another controversy after a shooting on his property in September. According to him, mobs had come to his home for several days beforehand, trying to intimidate him. He claimed that he had tried to go through the legal avenues by seeking protection from the magistrate and local police. All his requests for protection were in vain because the Democratic machine did nothing to uphold his constitutional rights. Venable claimed that on the fifth mob visit, someone hit him with a brick and nearly cut him with a knife. In the scuffle, he fired his gun, wounding Dominic Podesta, a mob participant who had trespassed onto his property. It was Venable, however—not Podesta—who was arrested. After being arrested and charged with attempted murder, Venable insisted that the shooting had been in self-defense.[61]

One must question both why mobs repeatedly targeted Venable's home and the timing of the attacks. Certainly it was no coincidence that conflict between Republicans and Democrats erupted at his home in the days preceding two different elections: in 1884 and 1885. Democrats claimed that Venable's home was "a convenient place for the assemblage of illegal voters who had come into the state from Kentucky." By his own admission, Venable typically boarded between sixty to one hundred African American men, although he claimed the men legally resided in Ohio. Many of the men worked on steamboats and boarded at Venable's home between trips on the river. Regardless, his home became a natural target for those hoping to intimidate scores of African American voters—legal or otherwise.

A short editorial that had run in the *Cincinnati Daily Enquirer* on September 25, 1885, just days before the attack, may have incited nervous Democrats to target Venable's home for the second time in two years. The piece warned its readers that he might attempt to register more than one hundred men to vote again; if he did, it read, "there may be a pressing demand for Mullen's services once more."[62] Essentially, the paper demanded more Democratic police repression of the black vote. But instead of the police, this time a politically inspired mob attacked Venable's home shortly after the editorial appeared. According to the *Cincinnati Commercial Gazette,* mobs comprised of "Democratic bummers" intended to "intimidate colored voters with impunity." Venable himself told a reporter that he believed the mob had persecuted him for two reasons: to make him pay for prosecuting Mike Mullen and to make sure that he did not vote for the Republican ticket.[63] Certainly the dozens of other potential voters who resided with him were a bonus target.

But what makes this case even more controversial is that Venable accused Peter H. Clark of taking advantage of his predicament to force him to recant his 1884 charges against Mullen. After all, Venable's testimony had led to Mullen's conviction for election fraud a year earlier. He claimed that prominent Democrats Samuel Lewis and Clark had approached him one evening shortly after officials released him on bond for the Podesta shooting. Clark allegedly offered him five hundred dollars if he would help exonerate Mullen by going to the magistrate and signing a prepared affidavit stating that the twenty-four men taken from his home in 1884 were "repeaters and had no right to vote." Venable reported that when he expressed reservations about perjuring himself, Clark returned a couple of hours later, stating that he had spoken to the magistrate, who had promised not to press perjury charges if Venable signed the affidavit. Clark also allegedly promised him that if he complied, McLean, the machine boss, would put him on the police force; if he failed to do so, he would be indicted and sent to the penitentiary. Venable claimed that he neither accepted the bribe or offers of patronage nor voted for Democrats in the election.

Although he escaped conviction on an attempted-murder charge, the jury did convict Venable of shooting with the intent to injure. In retrospect, he stated that his refusal to comply with the terms of the payoff had led partisan police officers to "swear [his] liberty away" by perjuring themselves in his trial. After being convicted and sentenced to a two-year prison term, Venable lamented: "My God, what justice can a man get in Hamilton County under the present Gang rule?"[64] Venable may have been right: the Democratic machine controlled the city government, police force, and prosecutor's office. Once Venable was entangled in the machine-controlled justice system, there would be no mercy for him.

Interestingly, Venable did not raise the issue of Clark's attempted bribery until *after* he had been convicted and sentenced to two years in prison for Podesta's shooting. Then, at the end of November 1885, Venable, speaking from his jail cell, shed light on the alleged corruption that delivered his conviction. The two-month delay in raising these accusations may lead some to wrongly conclude that he fabricated these claims—the deceptions of a desperate and vengeful convict. But thoughtful analysis of the political climate in Cincinnati reveals that Venable had every reason to delay leveling such accusations until after his trial. The political culture surely made it unwise for a relatively powerless black Republican to level allegations of corruption against high-ranking members of the Democratic machine before his trial—especially since the machine wielded so much power in the city, including in the justice system. Such claims before the trial might have sealed his fate and guaranteed his conviction. A black Republican, Venable may have hedged a bet that silence about the bribery would benefit him at his trial and return a decision of not guilty. When that did not happen, he no longer had anything to lose by revealing the Democratic attempts to induce him to sign an affidavit exonerating Mullen.

Republicans and Democrats rushed to spin the story to their best political advantage. Venable's Republican friends rallied around him and used the press to wage a campaign against the Democrats. They linked his legal troubles to a wider pattern of Democratic election fraud. According to one *Cincinnati Commercial Gazette* editorial: "It is within the personal knowledge of each citizen of this city . . . that the Democratic Gang's fraud machine was worked up to at least six thousand votes." The editorial went on to add that Democratic candidates were fraudulently elected to state and county office in the 1885 election.[65]

Republicans also tried to rally popular sympathy for Venable. An editorial in the *Cincinnati Commercial Gazette* concluded that the Democratic mob believed it could terrorize Venable "because he was a poor colored man who held his own in one of the hardest wards in America." According to the writer, he was "a better citizen than any of the Gang who have grown rich out of the spoils of Cincinnati." Another editorial went as far as to label him "a hero and a martyr" for "daring to defend himself heroically against the bummer bullies of his ward," and for declining the "Boodle Boss's money." The paper applauded Venable for refusing "to barter his integrity" to escape prosecution.[66]

Democrats waged a counterattack on his character. Not a member of the African American middle class, Venable certainly could not be considered respectable. In fact, the *Advance Courier* described him as a "rough and uncultured man." Even the *Cleveland Gazette* called him naïve and "illiterate." A December 1, 1885, editorial in the *Cincinnati Daily Enquirer* entitled "Hoghead John" took exception to the *Cincinnati Commercial Gazette*'s portrayal of Venable as a martyr. The paper attacked his character, claiming that he "kept the very lowest dive in the city; a resort for thieves of the lowest character, murderers, and low prostitutes." The same editorial portrayed Venable as an unscrupulous "bleeder" who not only had no loyalties to Republicans, but who sold votes to the party that paid him the most. The *Cincinnati Daily Enquirer* reported that an anonymous member of the Republican Campaign Committee stated that local Republicans had such contempt for Venable that many would delight to have his sentence *increased*.[67] The Democratic press latched onto his class background as a way to discredit him and diminish the gravity of the charges against Mullen and their party a year earlier.

Clark had an opportunity to defend his own character against Venable's allegations. Despite the fact that he long had been regarded as a man of "unimpeachable integrity," the charges had a ring of truth.[68] At the time, money and politics went hand in hand in Cincinnati, especially among Democrats. Bribery not only is a reasonable allegation in that context, but in fact, a common occurrence. More than anything else, though, Clark's response to Venable's allegations left little question about his guilt. The December 1 issue of the *Cincinnati Commercial Gazette* printed Clark's version of the events. In it, he claimed that at Venable's request, certain "parties" had contacted him for an affidavit attesting that the men taken from his home in 1884 were illegal voters. According to Clark, when the two met, Venable admitted the men were illegals, but he allegedly refused to admit this fact publicly because he "did not want any notoriety in the newspapers." Clark cherry-picked which of Venable's accusations he would address, refuting parts, but not all, of the accusations. Specifically, he insisted that Venable had willfully approached him, not the other way around. He also maintained that he had not persuaded Venable to make any statement regarding the legal status of his boarders in 1884. The principal also denied having mentioned Hoadly or McLean at all in his conversation with Venable.[69]

Curiously, though, Clark never explicitly denied that he had offered Venable a bribe. That more than anything suggests that he had, indeed, done so. The press concluded that his failure to directly address Venable's bribery allegations conceded his guilt. According to the *Cleveland Gazette,* Clark's statement left enough holes to "show a blind man that he is guilty." Another strong indication that he may have been guilty of the allegations is that after giving his version of the events to the paper, he admitted that he *had* offered to use his influence with Governor Hoadly to get the governor to pardon Venable for the shooting. It is somewhat peculiar that Clark would offer to help a man he had accused of having contemptible character in his own newspaper, the *Afro-American,* just months before.[70] Clark's offer to help Venable appears more like a bribe itself. Adding even more credence to the bribery allegation against Clark is the fact that although Venable also implicated John R. McLean, the *Cincinnati Daily Enquirer* editor and machine boss never addressed the claims one way or the other. His silence is telling: that, coupled with the fact his paper barely covered the story, and when it did, it focused more on attacking Venable's character than on openly refuting the bribery allegations, not only suggests that Venable had told the truth, but that McLean had been complicit along with Clark.

Venable's story also seems plausible because the Democrats had a powerful motive for inducing him to sign the affidavit before the election. If they could vindicate Mullen and the party in the minds of the public, they might have been able to lure some African Americans away from the Republican Party and secure the votes needed to guarantee a Democratic victory in the 1885 gubernatorial race. Hence, when all the evidence is tallied, it is clear that Clark, acting as an agent of the Democratic machine in Cincinnati, had indeed tried to persuade Venable to recant his testimony against Mullen. What is less certain is whether the bribe consisted of actual cash, Venable's exculpation from the shooting charges, or both. Regardless, the fact that Clark had any role in trying to exonerate those implicated in the 1884 mass arrests seemed unconscionable to most African Americans.

So, with that mountain of evidence suggesting his guilt, Clark's political career crumbled. After his version of the events appeared in the press, people were not easily convinced that his was the truthful one. On December 6, 1885, the *Cincinnati Commercial Gazette* printed a scathing condemnation of Clark in an editorial entitled "A Colored Judas." The editorial expressed outrage that he had been instrumental in trying to secure an affidavit attesting to the illegality of the African Americans at Venable's home in 1884. The editorial asked, "Did Peter Clark ever hear of a descent on the domiciles of white persons, and the abduction of them to hide them away from the law for a night and an election day, upon the presumption that they were not entitled to vote?"[71]

In the ensuing months, Clark endured severe censure from his own community and beyond. The white press accused him not just of being a traitor to his own community, but of wishing to *change* his skin color. The *Cincinnati Commercial Gazette* blasted in December 1885: "Does Peter Clark think that by becoming a Democrat he has changed his skin, and that by serving the . . . party in its oppression of his people he has become a white Democrat?" Such charges of Uncle Tomism leveled by a white journal further discredited Clark as a race leader. The editorial concluded that his "self-seeking abasement" had dishonored his people.[72] These accusations of bribery on the heels of his opposition on the school issue made him the scourge of Ohio politics. In the ensuing years, it became obvious that Clark no longer had either credibility in his community or political capital within his party. He soon ceased to be relevant in Cincinnati and Ohio politics.

Although it is clear that high-ranking Ohio Democrats intended to reward him for his loyalty to the party, it is harder to decide whether Clark's

disconcerting politics had been motivated solely by the prospect of positions and power within the Democratic administration. In a climate in
which political patronage abounded, he naturally expected a degree of political compensation for his troubles. Despite his rather drastic attempts to
secure the Haitian Ministry post, he never got that, or any other federal appointment. And unlike other beneficiaries of patronage, Clark never grew
fat from political booty. A survey of his career illuminates that despite the
fact that he proved himself to be one of the most important players in Ohio
politics between 1865 and 1885, he reaped practically nothing in the way
of political patronage—from either party.

A cursory view of Clark's political life in the 1880s suggests that the
bribery scandal at the end of 1885 overshadowed his countless contributions to African American political life in Ohio in the late nineteenth century. But that only partly explains why history has forgotten him. Even
more than the bribery scandal, his political career had been killed by his
efforts to defeat two bills that would have eliminated racial distinctions under the law. Moreover, his determination to help exonerate someone who
had helped disfranchise African American voters also worked against him.
His apparent role in the Venable scandal only accelerated his fall from
grace and drove the nail into his political coffin.

Clark's decision to become a Democrat, in and of itself, is not the
reason he fell from grace and lost power and status as a race man; what led
to his undoing is that his politics as a Democrat radically diverged from
the masses of African Americans. His position on integrated education,
among other things, went against the deepest aspirations of his community: full equality. Clark's politics contradicted the core values and goals
the African American community envisioned for itself—and that cost him
its trust and respect. By mid-1884, most African Americans in Ohio believed that Clark had done everything in his power to hold them back.
Although that could not have been further from the truth, it remained the
prevailing perception of him. Many believed that he had become a selfish
status-seeker willing to betray his community for personal political gain.
As such, African Americans deemed him unacceptable as a race leader.
The party had taken advantage of his good reputation to help pull other
African Americans into the party. But Clark's now sullied reputation in
that same community meant he no longer had usefulness to his party as
a representative man; it would be a while before he realized this himself.

Contemporaries of Clark and Frederick Douglass often depicted the
two as equally great intellectuals and politicians. Without a doubt, both

made important contributions to their community. But one must question why Douglass's memory and legacy have stood the test of time, while Clark has only recently been re-remembered. Perhaps the *Cleveland Gazette* stated it best in 1887: "Mr. Douglass is a patriot and philanthropist; Mr. Clark is neither. Mr. Douglass will never die. Mr. Clark is already dead, so far as his race is concerned."[73] Perhaps that sentiment goes the farthest in explaining why his influence waned, his memory faded, and his legacy died.

Chapter Nine

A Still Voice

Mr. Clark suffered more for his politics from his colored brethren than from whites.

William J. Simmons, 1887

On March 10, 1886, Reverend Benjamin W. Arnett, of Greene County, and Jere A. Brown, of Cuyahoga County, delivered speeches before Ohio's House of Representatives praying for the passage of his bill to repeal the state's odious Black Laws. These laws, which mandated separate schools and prohibited intermarriage, had stalked African Americans' freedom in the state and denied them equality under the law for decades. Since 1884, a few Ohio legislators had persistently tried to introduce bills to repeal the legislation. In his speech before the House, Representative Arnett decried the pernicious role that race played in society: "One would think that at this time of our civilization, that character, and not color, would form the line of distinction in society, but such is not the case. It matters not what may be the standing or intelligence of a colored man or woman, they have to submit to the wicked laws and the more wicked prejudice of the people."[1] He went on to recount the numerous ways that segregation limited African Americans' freedom, in general, while highlighting some of his personal encounters with segregation:

> I have traveled in this free country for twenty hours without anything to eat; not because I had no money to pay for it, but because I was colored. Other passengers of a lighter hue had breakfast, dinner, and supper. In traveling we are thrown in "jim crow" cars, denied the privilege of buying a berth in the sleeping coach. This monster caste stands at the doors of the theatres and skating rinks, locks the doors of the pews in our fashionable churches, closes the mouths of some of the ministers in their pulpits which prevents

the man of color from breaking the bread of life to his fellowmen. This foe of my race stands at the school house door and separates the children, by reason of "color" and denies to those who have a visible admixture of African blood in them the blessings of a graded school and equal privileges.[2]

Arnett urged the body to repeal the legislation that sanctioned racial inequality. The *Cleveland Gazette* concluded that his speech was "the finest delivered in the House" during that session. The House responded with a 62 to 28 vote on the bill that repealed the discriminatory laws.[3] The bill finally passed the Senate nearly a year later on February 16, 1887, with a vote of 24 to 7.[4] The "Arnett Law" signaled a new era in race relations for Ohio.

No one would have predicted that an AME minister and first-time politician would be the person to deliver the death blow to Ohio's Black Laws. Benjamin Arnett had had a meteoric rise in his political career. Born in Fayette County, Pennsylvania, in 1838, he began his professional career as a schoolteacher, and his activist career as a member of the Pennsylvania State Equal Rights League. He received his preacher's license in 1865 and moved to Cincinnati two years later to assume his first ministry position at the AME church in suburban Walnut Hills. In the ensuing decades, Arnett led AME congregations throughout Ohio, including Toledo, Columbus, Urbana, and even the historic Allen Temple in Cincinnati. He ventured into politics in 1885, with a successful run for the Ohio legislature, representing Greene County. In the spring of 1886, Representative Arnett walked into the pages of Ohio's history when he introduced the final bill destined to repeal the laws mandating separate schools and prohibiting intermarriage.[5] Although the school desegregation bill had been previously brought before the House without success, by 1886, the tide had changed; the Ohio legislature had a Republican majority, which created a favorable climate for the erosion of these laws.

Throughout the state, African Americans and their white allies marked the erasure of the Black Laws with jubilee celebrations. Even the state's governor participated in the jubilee celebration in Columbus, The *Cleveland Gazette* reported that more than two thousand attended the Springfield celebration on February 28, 1887, concluding that it was one of the "grandest demonstrations" in recent memory. The most prominent citizens attended that jubilee. The audience heard from Ohio's most distinguished speakers, including Benjamin Arnett; Senators Ely and Pringle;

[handwritten annotation: I would [illegible] this]

Rev. James Poindexter of Columbus; Professor William S. Scarborough of Wilberforce; C. M. Nichols, editor of the *Republic;* and Harry C. Smith, editor of the *Gazette.*[6] Peter H. Clark noticeably absented himself from the event. His voice fell mute, quieted by the deafening cries of victory heard throughout the state. With his opposition to the school desegregation bills still fresh in the minds of most, Clark received no invitations to speak at any of these celebrations.

This historic moment in Ohio's history had passed him by; for the first time in decades, black Ohioans had accomplished a significant equal rights victory without his direct involvement. Clark had been a formidable and persistent opponent of school desegregation legislation in the past. But the Venable bribery scandal at the end of 1885 negated him as a credible voice of opposition and rendered him politically impotent in state politics; his silence allowed the legislation to be passed that following spring without his interference. Undoubtedly aware of the significance of the moment, Clark tried to revise the history of the repeal of the Black Laws. In a letter to the editor of the *New York Freeman* published a month after the passage of the Arnett Law, Clark inserted himself more centrally into the history of the repeal—despite his vigorous opposition to integrated schools at various junctures. He contends that "kickers"—Democrats and others who "threw off [Republican] party shackles"—had actually dismantled Ohio's Black Laws.[7] Clark vehemently insisted that Republicans should not get credit for the historic victory—noting that in the twenty years that Republicans ruled the House, the party had never moved to repeal the Black Laws. Emphasizing his own interpretation of what had initiated the repeal, he credited kickers with helping to elect a Democratic governor who, along with a Democratic legislature, took the initial steps to dismantle the Black Laws. Through the omission of certain truths, he gave the Democratic Party more credit than it deserved. First, Clark's letter to the *New York Freeman* omitted the fact that the Democratic Senate had failed to pass the bill that would have repealed the separate school law sooner. He also failed to acknowledge that a *Republican* legislature took the final steps to repeal the Black Laws. Insisting that the repeal of the Black Laws had been part of a master plan, he wrote: "The 'kickers' of Ohio are satisfied with the results of their plan and are prepared to recommend it to their brethren in other States. Indeed, some of them are asking if there is not a chance for the use of their tactics on the broad field of National politics."[8] This is the first and only time that Clark ever suggested that he had a larger plan to have both parties vying for African Americans' votes in order to

Blacks on indep. POL should be studied

secure civil rights. Such a strategy is not uncommon; African Americans previously had engaged in independent political movements to end slavery or to secure the right to vote. Certainly Clark's independent politics in the mid-1870s fall into such a category. But his actions after 1882, while a member of the Democratic Party, are questionable; more often than not, he actively worked *against* the policies and practices that would have elevated African Americans' status, like school integration. But the fact that he chose to remember the history this way is illuminating. Conscientiously inserting himself into a history that did not actually include him allowed him to engineer his own legacy—a legacy that had been largely overshadowed by his recent activities. Perhaps, too, it suggests that he understood that history already had begun to forget him.

why did Clark oppose it?

Clark would never teach in Cincinnati's integrated schools. He and other African American teachers were the first casualties of integration. As he once had predicted and feared, white parents opposed the idea of African Americans instructing their children, so the school district could no longer keep them.[9] But Clark's dismissal cannot be framed in racial terms: his termination was purely political.

At its first meeting on May 24, 1886, the new Republican school board moved to dismiss him from his position as principal of Gaines High and the Western District Colored Schools, a position he had held for nearly thirty years. The board offered no justification for the decision, although the minutes revealed that citizens had sent a petition demanding that he be fired. Nonetheless, it is obvious that partisan politics dictated his termination. According to the *Cincinnati Commercial Gazette,* the Board of Education, like so many other government organizations, had been run "purely on party politics" and had been controlled by the Democratic machine for several years. Clark had been able to retain his job as principal even after the Venable scandal because Democrats dominated the board. It had been nearly impossible to break the party's stranglehold on local government. Only a concerted and determined campaign by U.S. marshals to end political corruption in the city broke the domination of the Democratic Party. Newspapers reported after the 1886 elections that citizens had voted safely and their votes had counted for the first time in a while.[10] With the changing of the guard, Clark's job became vulnerable.

The newly constituted Republican school board nominated one of its own African Americans, William H. Parham, to replace Clark as principal. In the official vote cast two weeks later, Parham defeated Clark, 19 to 13.[11]

Soth of the Parham family @ minutes?

what drew him to Unitarians?

For years, Clark had enjoyed relative job stability despite the fact that his job *had* been seriously threatened at least twice: once in the 1850s because of his Unitarian faith, and the second time in the later 1870s because of his socialist politics. Both times, the African American community had rallied to support him. That community supported the educator despite his various angular affiliations. Even during Clark's most radical point as a socialist, his community never questioned his suitability to head the Colored Schools. Black Cincinnatians compartmentalized their confidence in him as an educator from their general disdain for his politics.

However, following his actions in 1884 and 1885, certain parts of the local African American community could no longer stomach those politics and demanded his termination from the school system. The *Cincinnati Commercial Gazette* reminded its readers of the transgressions that warranted his removal, including his affiliation with John R. McLean, the Democratic editor of the *Cincinnati Daily Enquirer,* his "outrageous open defense of Mike Mullen, and attempted 'quieting' of his chief victim" (in reference to the alleged bribery). But no calls for his dismissal were louder than those coming from the *Cleveland Gazette,* which reenergized its fierce, decade-long anti-Clark campaign. The June 26 editorial in that journal contended that Clark had "antagonized the most vital interests of the colored people of this State, in his foolish effort to serve [the] Democracy." The editorial also blasted him for other myriad offenses against his own community, including "his affiliation with the notorious Democrat McLean; his outrageous open defense of that miscreant, Mike Mullen ex-Lieutenant of Police," and using his influence in the legislature to block the dismantling of the Black Laws. The paper urged African Americans to demand and secure Clark's dismissal for these egregious actions. All of these deeds, compounded by the Venable bribery scandal, seriously diminished his reputation in his own community, and forced some to rethink whether he was suited to be principal. At the very least, some African Americans may have shared the sentiments of the *Cleveland Gazette,* which declared that "school teachers are not to be partisans." The paper claimed that 75 percent of the African American population in Hamilton County and the majority of African American population in the state supported Clark's termination. While those estimates likely are unfounded and exaggerated, they are somewhat plausible given the widespread disdain for the principal's politics.[12]

In a letter published in the *New York Freeman* on June 19, 1886, Clark insisted that his political affiliation was the only reason he had been dis-

why would he support Black Laws?

missed. Offering as proof the fact that he had been dismissed without any charges against him, Clark contended that his enemies falsely asserted that the African American community had initiated the demands for his dismissal. He also insisted that the scheme to terminate him had been initiated by powerful white men in the Republican Party—specifically William Smith, a local party leader, who influenced other members of the school board to vote against him. According to Clark, the experience taught him that "the conduct of the white men who have perpetrated this outrage upon free thought and free speech, shows that in the North as in the South, the colored man is only free to think and act with the majority of the white fellow-citizens." In sum, Clark not only viewed his termination in political terms, but in racial ones.[13] The truth is, however, that his political affiliation accounted for only part of the reason he was terminated.

Clark appears a bit out of touch with how the masses felt about him and his past deeds. Few people objected to his dismissal. None of the local Cincinnati newspapers or any of Clark's political friends raised objections to his termination. In fact, all kept noticeably silent about the dismissal of a man who had been such a dedicated public figure. The local Democratic Party had been rendered impotent by the scrutiny of the elections and its subsequent loss of power. T. Thomas Fortune, editor of the Democratic journal the *New York Freeman,* was one of only a few of Clark's friends who rose in his defense. Fortune published an editorial that not only lauded his friend's career as an educator, but also depicted Clark's termination as retaliation for his political affiliation. Similarly, the editor of the *Chicago Observer* expressed concern for what he described as an injustice committed against Clark.[14]

But Clark's cries of injustice relating to his termination are partly based on a misguided, privileged assumption that the job belonged to him indefinitely. Civil service jobs, at the time, could hardly be long-term; in most cities civil service positions lasted only as long as the party who granted them remained in power. The *Cleveland Gazette* reassured its readers that this was especially true for Clark given that he was an "offensive partisan."[15] Hence, he unreasonably assumed his job would outlast his party's local domination *and* his reputation and standing in the city. The *Cleveland Gazette* repeatedly blasted Clark for bringing politics into the schools and then invoking a double standard when used against him: "Mr. Clark carried [politics] into the school and the School Board is only taking it out."[16] But the *Gazette* was wrong on that point: although Clark became a formidable political force, he never did anything to turn the Cincinnati

Colored Schools into his own political forum. He always kept his job completely separate from his politics.

Were he not such a partisan, Clark might have lasted another couple of years in Cincinnati's Colored Schools despite the Arnett Law: the city did not integrate its schools overnight. In fact, according to the 1887 annual report of the Cincinnati Board of Education, integration posed "a serious difficulty" and might have become quite a contentious issue were it not for a citizens' petition. The school board reported that African Americans petitioned to reopen the colored schools as "branch" schools in order to circumvent the Arnett Law, so determined were they to retain separate schools. The school board heeded this "petition," and separate schools in Cincinnati survived a while longer. According to one report, 90 percent of the student population continued to attend these schools.[17]

Despite the continuation of the Cincinnati Colored Schools, Clark never got his job back as principal. In the late spring of 1887, he accepted a job offer as the principal of the Alabama Colored Normal School at Huntsville, Alabama (later, Alabama A&M University), replacing William Hooper Councill (1849–1909).[18] A former bondsman who had received his first education in a freedmen's school, Councill previously had worked as principal of a local school, editor of the *Huntsville Herald,* and receiver of public money for the Grant administration. He had run the State Colored Normal School at Huntsville since 1875, investing much of his own resources, energy, and ideology into the institution.[19] Although he and Clark shared much in terms of their teaching and editing careers, they had strikingly different worldviews. Councill, for one, was a master at making bargains with the local and state white power elites to get what he wanted. He reputedly had "sold his black soul for white Conservative favor" when he agreed to become a mouthpiece for the Democratic Party in exchange for his position at the Normal School. Both their contemporaries and historians have compared Councill and Booker T. Washington, but many regard Councill not only as the better speaker, but far shrewder than Washington at bargaining with the white power structure. A master at disarming southern whites, Councill could make them feel as if they were African Americans' best friends and allies while also criticizing "radical" northerners. He performed the dutiful and loyal Negro persona so well that white, powerful Alabamians considered him a better representative colored man than even Booker T. Washington.[20] Clark seemed to be an unsuitable substitute for someone like Councill.

Like most African American leaders at the time, Councill moved in the gray areas between the two extremes of accommodation and militant resis-

Council was more accommodating than Booker T. Wash

tance. One of his acts of resistance came at a considerable price. On April 7, 1887, he and some teachers from campus attempted to board a first-class train car on the Western and Atlantic Railroad. Although the group had tickets for the first-class section, the crew removed them because African Americans were not allowed in the first-class cars.[21]

Councill's resistance is part of a larger civil rights struggle in Huntsville, Alabama, in the 1880s, of which attempting to integrate railroad cars is a huge part. The *Huntsville Gazette* is filled with complaints from African Americans about being forced into second-class, or Jim Crow, cars even after having paid for first-class tickets. They resented the fact that besides denying them "comforts, privileges and advantages" equal to those enjoyed by white passengers, second-class cars were filled with drinkers, smokers, and otherwise unrespectable people. The irony here is that these civil rights activists did not object to Jim Crow cars per se (thinking them fitting for unrespectable people), but to being placed on them after having paid for better service. Hence, the root of their objection is that "second-class" should not be defined by race, but by respectability. Black Huntsville residents also resisted their second-class status by filing formal complaints to the Interstate Commerce Commission (ICC), which oversaw interstate travel. Established in 1887, the ICC was the first regulatory agency for railroads. Although people were not clear whether its authority covered the treatment of passengers on trains, African Americans hoped it would. Another strategy this community used was filing lawsuits against railroad companies in an effort to obtain equal treatment. The *Huntsville Gazette* reported that a Mrs. E. F. Logwood sued in federal court for damages against the Memphis and Charleston Railroad for relegating her to a smoking car despite the fact that she was "enfeebled by sickness and a surgical operation." Although Mrs. Logwood's suit decried her mistreatment on the train despite her illness, the lawsuit—like others—essentially boiled down to African Americans' desire to be treated with decency, dignity, and equal service while traveling on trains.[22]

It was in such a climate that William Hooper Councill and his teachers staged their resistance to the Jim Crow system. After his experience on the train that April 7, Councill filed a grievance with the ICC, requesting twenty-five thousand dollars in damages for discrimination. The commission ultimately determined that although segregation itself was not illegal, Councill and other African Americans who purchased first-class tickets *were* entitled to first-class accommodations. Although he technically won his ICC suit, the victory was bittersweet because white Huntsvillites considered civil rights activism of any kind radical—if not subversive—to the racial order there. Councill's agitation for equality so offended the local white leaders that he was pressured to resign, which he did in spring 1887. Councill's letter of resignation, which was subsequently published in African American newspapers, explained that his act of civil disobedience had generated such hostility that the legislature threatened to close the school unless he resigned. Unsettled by the news that Clark had accepted his former job, Councill remarked that he could not understand how "Clark got the consent of his manhood to accept the place."[23]

But perhaps Councill did not fully appreciate Clark's desperate situation: he certainly could not afford to be selective about any job or to refuse one on principle. After all, he had not worked for more than a year by then. Clark surely missed the generous $2,200 annual salary he had earned as principal in Cincinnati. Besides that, positions for African American principals were few and far between. Councill himself was nearly destitute just one month after his own resignation. In a letter to Booker T. Washington in September 1887, Councill admitted that he had no resources besides the small tokens of assistance he had received from several individuals and organizations; nor did he have any "plans . . . [or] prospects" of any other employment.[24] Certainly Clark suffered similar tribulations during his own year of unemployment.

Clark accepted the position, resigned as trustee of Ohio State University, and moved to Alabama.[25] His tenure as principal of Alabama's Colored Normal School did not last long, though, owing to Councill's determined efforts to get his position back. And Councill well understood that he had to appease the white powerful elite to do so. In his resignation letter from the Alabama school that spring, he claimed, "I have always been, am now, and shall ever be, opposed to it [social equality] in all its phases." This statement contradicts everything Councill had done to integrate the railcars, but he undoubtedly assumed this unsettling conciliatory position as a last-ditch effort to stem the retaliation against his career and the school. In a desperate September 3, 1887, private letter to Booker T. Washington, Councill complained that he had few options and begged Washington to "kindly suggest something," although it is not clear if he sought a job opportunity at Washington's Tuskegee Normal School or advice about how to get his old position back. Regardless, Councill's appeal to the accommodationist leader of Tuskegee suggests that he wanted advice about how best to placate the white power elites in Huntsville. He would use the tactic of accommodating powerful whites more often as the years progressed.[26] Just before the school's Board of Trustees met in June 1888 to decide whether to retain Clark, Councill reversed his earlier civil rights position and openly denounced African American memorials to the Alabama legislature demanding decent railroad accommodations. He also gave a speech in which he condemned liberal education for African Americans, stating that they were "educated beyond their legitimate sphere."[27]

Councill also focused on making things difficult for Clark. The Cincinnatian had enemies no later than his arrival in Huntsville. Although there is a possibility that his reputation as a Democrat and opponent of integrated schools in Ohio may have preceded him, it is more likely that Councill and his local supporters waged a jealousy-inspired smear campaign against Clark. The *Birmingham Era,* an African American newspaper, attacked Clark early in his first month on the job for allegedly planning to implement a policy of expelling students who challenged the color line. After comparing the activism of the two men, the paper concluded that Councill was better suited to serve as principal of the school. After describing Councill as a racial "conservative" who had always been "foolishly blind to the greater of the outrages perpetrated upon the race" throughout his thirteen years at the normal school, the *Era* noted that he had openly denounced social equality. Councill's questionable record aside, though, the *Era* determined Clark to be "ten times worse as a social equality advocate" for allegedly planning to implement a policy of expelling students who challenged the color line.[28] If the newspaper reports can be trusted, Clark may have implemented such a policy not to accommodate inequality, as the paper suggested, but to protect the school and its students from retaliation, reprisals, or closing. And in that state, reprisals often proved particularly deadly. In August 1887, a mob tracked Jesse Duke, the accomplished editor of the African American journal *Montgomery Herald* after he wrote an article condemning lynching. Duke barely escaped the state with his life. Certainly any northerner—even Clark—would have been afraid in such a climate. Nonetheless, the *Era* relentlessly attacked the principal for alleged accommodation to social inequality; the paper sarcastically labeled Clark as "Ohio's great social equality man" and challenged him to fight against Alabama's black laws as he claimed to have done in Ohio. The *Era* ultimately accused him of "compromising principle for the sake of a few dollars" and advised that he no longer deserved a place among "respectable people."[29]

Councill's scheming worked. However, not everyone was pleased by his strategies: one southern journal remarked that Clark had been "ousted by the humiliating and unmanly conduct" of Councill.[30] Still, Clark's reputation bowed under the virulence of the *Era*'s charges, eliminating his prospects of serving as principal long-term. He lost his bid for reappointment in June 1888, despite the fact that he had remained politically neutral, avoided local politics and major controversies during his tenure, and had spent most of his energies running the school and organizing teachers. For example, he not only joined the Madison County Teachers' Institute but also helped organize the Teachers' Association for North Alabama. And despite Clark's own classical education and past strenuous opposition to a proposed industrial college in the antebellum era, he made plans to hire instructors in woodworking, dressmaking, cooking, printing, and gardening. The highlight of his year was when Booker T. Washington invited him to lecture at Tuskegee.[31]

Clark apparently did nothing that might warrant a termination in a rural southern community. Nonetheless, at its June 1888 meeting, the Board of Trustees fired him and reinstalled Councill, apparently acting under the pressure of a petition signed by Alabama's leading teachers, of both races.[32] Clearly Clark's termination had been initiated by the powerful white elite in the state—a group that included the school's Board of Trustees—who may have reasoned that a chastened Councill who had learned his lesson about challenging Jim Crow in Alabama, was a less risky option than Clark. Councill's behavior in the year following his resignation convinced the white power elites that he finally had accepted and internalized an inferior social and legal status for himself and African Americans. Clark must have realized that he was no match for Alabama, where the triple oppressions of Jim Crow, lynching, and disfranchisement dogged African Americans, so he returned home.

By 1888, African Americans increasingly began switching their affiliation to the Democratic Party. This minor, but significant wave of political realignment was precipitated by Democratic moderates like President Grover Cleveland who, in the interest of winning their votes, conscientiously decided to build a more positive relationship with northern African Americans. Cleveland demonstrated a greater willingness than previous Democratic candidates to appoint them to political positions. Consequently, he earned a good reputation among black voters.[33] This moderate approach successfully wrested some of the same disgruntled elements that had participated in the Chillicothe movement away from the GOP by the mid-1880s.

The most concrete evidence of success in the post-Reconstruction era for ambitious and educated African Americans proved to be political power. For the politically ambitious, the journey toward political power on the Republican Party path seemed obstructed and impassable: fewer and fewer of African Americans received even petty patronage positions at the local level. As repugnant as the Democratic Party still appeared to be to the masses, a corps of talented and successful African Americans thirsty for political power began to hitch their wagon to the Democratic star.

Interest abounded. Local clubs and state chapters of the Democratic Party sprang up everywhere in black communities. Yet, the chapters devoted themselves to little more than compiling lists of people to be recommended for patronage positions. Without coordinated efforts, African Americans wielded very little power within the party. Hence, when Peter Clark's son, Herbert A. Clark; Charles H. J. Taylor of Kansas; James Milton Turner of St. Louis, a former Republican minister to Liberia between 1871 and 1878; and others summoned all black Democrats to convene in St. Louis, it signaled a new phase in the history of the party. When they convened in June 1888, the more than one hundred African Americans established the National Negro Democratic League (NNDL). The NNDL was designed to serve as an umbrella organization for local and state Democratic clubs, coordinate black Democratic efforts at the national level, and provide a larger forum for their activism.[34]

After that initial organizing meeting, James Milton Turner issued a wider call for black Democrats to convene for a conference in Indianapolis in July. Turner had had a long career as a Republican, but like so many others, he had become disillusioned by his unsuccessful bids to get a Cherokee bill passed. He saw ripe political opportunities for himself in the Democratic Party. Thirsty to reap such opportunities, Turner took the lead in the planning stages of the NNDL and issued the call for the convention. Desperate to gain legitimacy, he added the names of eighteen prominent black Democrats—presumably as endorsers. Turner used thirteen of the eighteen names without the knowledge or consent of their owners. When those named in the call discovered his deception, they accused him of being driven by selfish interests. In his own defense, he claimed to have acted under the instructions of the chairman of the Democratic National Committee. Still, Turner's action cast a dark cloud over the convention. In addition, rumors abounded that labeled him a "boodler" who aimed to betray African American interests for political power and that the convention simply served as a tool to that end.[35] Thus, controversy and suspicion swirled around the convention even before the first address. Veteran Democrats debated whether to give in to Turner's scheming by attending the convention, but ultimately, many decided that any opportunity to convene outweighed the selfish designs of one man. Others set out for the convention with the express intention of disrupting the proceedings, usurping Turner's presumed power, and frustrating any ulterior motives.[36]

Turner convened the convention on July 25, 1888, in the Indianapolis Hendricks Clubs Rooms. In his introductory remarks, he explained that he had issued the call because the time had come for African Americans to "assert themselves" and "think independently." Reporting on the proceedings, the black Democratic journal the *Indianapolis Freeman* declared that Turner was "one of the finest orators of the country and one of the most brilliant men of the race."[37]

Despite such praise for the new upstart in local papers, contempt for Turner proved so pervasive throughout the meeting that a local newspaper reported that delegates "denounced [him] in all kinds of epithets." Charles H. J. Taylor, whose political success afforded him a level of respect and standing among black Democrats, emerged as Turner's most outspoken critic and nemesis.[38] To this esteemed veteran, Turner's audacity to initiate the call for the meeting, organize a national body, and then assume leadership of the NNDL and the conference affronted his own presumed right to lead. Despite the fact that all the men were relatively new converts to the party, divisions between veteran Democrats—people like Taylor, Clark, and Fortune who had been Democrats before Cleveland's first term—and newer ones threatened to divide the meeting and overshadow its historic importance. The veteran Democrats resented the recent converts, especially their aggressive and calculated pursuit of power and patronage. These tensions came to a head over the election of a conference chairman, a conflict that symbolized a larger generational struggle. Customarily, the person who issued the call for a conference would serve as its permanent chairman, but that did not happen at the 1888 Negro Democratic National Conference. Although Turner received the initial nomination for the position, Taylor rallied people to vote against him. He strongly objected to Turner serving as the conference's chairman and declared, "I do not propose . . . to allow gentlemen who have just entered our ranks to take charge and lead." Nor did Taylor trust that Turner had pure motives: he accused Turner of organizing the conference solely for his personal interests—specifically, to get money from leading Democrats in exchange for his efforts. Turner responded by calling Taylor "a national buffoon and a national ass." "Taylor," he said, "is an empty barrel rolling down a rocky hill." He added, "I have no words to waste on him."[39]

T. Thomas Fortune, impatient with Turner's superciliousness, nominated Peter H. Clark for the permanent chairperson position. People quickly rallied behind this nomination. Clark's unexpected nomination and swell of support suggests that despite the fact that the Democratic establishment no longer needed or valued him, black veteran Democrats still did. After listening to speeches by supporters of both candidates, the body voted. Although Clark defeated Turner by a slim and contested margin, both sides claimed victory and cried foul. According to several newspapers, "opprobrious epithets were bandied," "blows were exchanged," and "revolvers were drawn." Despite how heated this battle over conference leadership became, it was not the defining moment of the conference; yet, the media chose to focus on it. The local press perhaps overstated the divisions and predicted the entire conference "would come to naught." The black Republican press concluded the conference was a "big farce" that would "only serve to destroy the influence [of] the independent colored vote." Delegates spent the second day of the meeting trying to refute the press's unfavorable assessment of their conference. Turner took the floor to reassure the public that no internal divisions existed among black Democrats. In a gracious speech, he acknowledged Clark's victory and emphasized that he harbored no ill feelings.[40]

Clark addressed the Negro Democratic National Conference twice. His speeches both outlined reasons African Americans should become Democrats. In terms of substance, they contained many of the same ideas he had articulated at previous engagements. For example, he highlighted the difference between how Republicans and Democrats interpreted the Constitution on the issue of civil rights. The Republican Party, according to him, had been misguided for its persistent insistence that the federal government confer and protect civil rights. Instead, he and other Democrats believed in the superiority of state power and its ultimate power to grant and protect civil rights, so he instructed African Americans to agitate for civil rights at the state level, advising, "The negro should assume that the laws of the State are on his side, and let him appeal not once, but continually until an authoritative decision is given for or against him."[41]

Clark also pointed to the parties' respective position on tariffs as another key difference between them. In 1888, President Grover Cleveland had catapulted the tariff issue to the top of the Democratic agenda with his strong opposition to duties. In fact, that year the tariff became *the* defining issue for the Democratic Party. Democrats believed the tariff would prove detrimental to the common man since it would prevent cheaper imported goods from reaching the market. The party advocated free trade. Democrats believed that reduced tariffs would keep prices low for the consumer and reduce the surplus in the treasury. Clark subscribed to these purely economic arguments, but he also saw the issue through the lens of race. He stated, "On the question of maintaining the high tariff . . . which is pauperizing thousands and rendering the struggle for life difficult for all, the Democratic negro stands with the party which proposes a wise reduction of the tariff."[42] Hence, he implied that he believed the plight of African Americans could be alleviated through a reduction of the tariff. Neither the tariff issue nor states' rights were racial issues, fundamentally; the Democrats hardly had a reputation for promoting a problack agenda. What is interesting is that Clark tried to make these traditionally (read, white) Democratic issues relevant to African Americans. Despite his best intentions, his conference speeches would never have convinced black Republicans that the Democrats held the keys to a better future.

Clark's address to the convention did something else, though: it outlined a path of salvation for African Americans. Noting that not all the problems facing African Americans were political in nature, Clark reasoned that politics, then, could not be a "the universal panacea." Certainly this pronouncement represents a drastic departure from his days as a Radical Abolitionist and Socialist. While he never eschewed political activism as some of his contemporaries would later do, his observations that politics was not the "universal panacea," at the very least, encouraged African Americans to seek other solutions to their problems. He advocated racial uplift through increased morality, intelligence, and wealth. In other words, he believed that African Americans must shoulder the responsibility for ending racism; through "respectable" behavior and achievements, they would prove they deserved equal rights and treatment. Hence, this speech reveals that Clark abandoned his long-held views that politics could effect change and now embraced the idea that moral suasion and racial uplift provided the best remedy.

However, Clark believed that this prescription of moral suasion would only erode racism slowly: "It will require generations of intercourse with full, progressive, self-respecting negroes to remove from the white man's mind that taint of prejudice which floods his conscience . . . [and] justifies him in defying [sic] common rights and privileges to his colored fellow citizens." The local black press reported that Clark's "treatment of the race problem was very masterly and made a deep impression" on his audience.[43]

The conference included speeches by several other prominent Democrats, including T. Thomas Fortune and Charles H. J. Taylor. Fortune also read a letter from George T. Downing of Rhode Island, the details of which were not published. Before the conference ended, the body issued several resolutions. The first resolution applauded President Cleveland for reassuring African Americans that their rights would not contract during his administration and vowing to do everything in his power to uphold the Constitution. Two other resolutions focused specifically on economic issues: the body decried the "unnecessary" and "unjust" practice of heavy taxation—a burden that "threaten[ed] the prosperity of the people and menac[ed] . . . the business interests." Another resolution advocated a reduction of the tariff in exchange for heavy taxation on whiskey and tobacco. By far, the most inconsistent resolution endorsed Ireland's right to independence and self-determination. This resolution seems to have been a contrived attempt to express solidarity with Irish nationalism and with supporters of Irish independence—a curious position, given the history of violent contests between Irish immigrants and African Americans on American soil. Of the remaining resolutions, one condemned the tariff for protecting the same businesses that denied African Americans jobs, while the other—which was nearly incoherent—seems to encourage citizens to acquire skills, education, and wealth.[44]

Notwithstanding these resolutions, the conference illustrates that a critical mass of those who joined the Democratic Party did so not as a reaction against the Republican Party, but because they supported the Democratic Party's principles and agenda. Second, the conference energized the debate on the utility of African Americans voting as Democrats or independents. The press coverage also made people aware of the growing numbers and strength within the black Democratic and independent movements. While Democratic journals lauded the conference as a success, black Republican papers like the *Washington Bee* called it a "boodle conference"—an accusation suggesting that conventioneers sought political office or cash for their efforts. The *Cleveland Gazette* argued that it "demonstrated clearly to the people . . . that without an exception, the leaders of the movement are not men to be looked upon, much less trusted as leaders."[45] The Negro Democratic National Conference was one of the last times Clark would be active on the national political stage.

Clark relocated to St. Louis, Missouri, shortly thereafter in November 1888. The historical record provides no clues about why he chose St. Louis as his new home. He taught in St. Louis district schools for a few months until he was hired to teach at the all-black Charles Sumner High on Eleventh and Spruce Streets. Sumner High—named after Charles Sumner, the great champion of African American civil rights—had been established in 1875 as one of the first high schools for African American youth in the nation. By all accounts, Clark seemed content with his employment. Although his daughter Ernestine wrote to Frederick Douglass and begged his assistance in securing a job for her father in the Baltimore schools, Clark reassured Douglass that he was satisfied with his position in St. Louis. He wrote: "I am on excellent terms with the school authorities and the people do not oppose me. The prospect of steady employment and ultimate promotion is good."[46] In St. Louis, black teachers did not have to fear losing their jobs because the city seemed fairly committed to segregated education. Although Sumner High already had a principal in Oscar M. Waring— who also happened to be the city's first African American public-school principal, Clark's letter to Douglass illustrates his optimism that he would be promoted to principal one day. But he would never be a principal again; he would have to find satisfaction working as a regular teacher over the next twenty years.[47]

Clark resided at 1909 Goode Avenue and then at 4581 Garfield Avenue in St. Louis for the next thirty-seven years. He must have felt comfortable in the city because in many ways, it bore a streak of familiarity to him. No other city so closely mirrored the spirit and essence of Cincinnati as St. Louis. First, St. Louis, like Cincinnati, was situated on a river; moreover, steamboat trade had been the main source of the city's economic vitality in the antebellum era. Both St. Louis and Cincinnati were border cities geographically, economically, and politically. The Mound City, much like the Queen City, was torn between three competing, and sometimes warring, identities—northern, western, and southern. Both cities became "havens for European immigrants": German and Irish immigrants made up a significant portion of both cities' populations. At times, the combination of the diversity and competition for resources sometimes boiled over to rioting. Sadly, too, Missouri borrowed a page from early nineteenth-century Ohio's playbook with its laws requiring African American settlers to post bonds and others that initially denied them a public education.[48]

By the time Clark moved to St. Louis in 1888, the city contained a sizeable number of the African American elite, characterized there by family background, education, wealth, and respectability of its members. Of all the criteria, family background loomed largest. Though not a wealthy

Clark and students at Sumner High School, April 1893. (Courtesy of Clark N. Jones.)

man or well-bred by birth, Clark met the other criteria because of his ed-ucation, respectability, and national reputation. Clark enjoyed the ranks of St. Louis's nineteenth-century black elite with James Milton Turner, the Vashons, Arthur D. Langston, and other families that boasted some pedigree or another, including the Clamorgans, Mordecais, Hickmans, and Curtises. The black elite dominated the social, political, and economic life of black St. Louis and filled the ranks of race men and women.[49]

Although none of their children moved to St. Louis immediately, Peter Clark and his wife, Frances, never were lonely. After years of correspond-ing with his former student Charles Henry Turner, the first black animal researcher, Clark convinced him to relocate to St. Louis. Turner had spent the intervening years pursuing a doctorate at the University of Chicago and teaching at Clark College (now Clark Atlanta). He secured a teach-ing position at Sumner High School alongside his former teacher; he and his family settled down within a few doors of the Clarks. In addition to the Turners, Susan Paul Vashon, George B. Vashon's (1824–1878) widow, settled in St. Louis in 1882 along with their four children, including sons

John B. Vashon and George B. Vashon Jr. By the early twentieth century, the Vashon and Clark families lived next door to one another. Clark became like a father to the Vashon boys, mentoring them as they entered their adulthoods and pursued professional careers. The elder Vashon son, John, taught at Sumner High with Clark until John's death in 1924. John Mercer Langston's son, Arthur D. Langston, also lived in St. Louis. Despite the fact that they were a generation younger than he, Langston and the Vashons provided Clark and his wife with a sense of community and a piece of their former lives in Cincinnati. He certainly got some sense of satisfaction from being able to mentor his deceased colleague's children.

As a newcomer, Clark quite noticeably retreated from the national African American political scene and partisan politics for four years after settling in St. Louis. More than likely, his retreat from political activism had been precipitated by embarrassment stemming from the Venable affair, fatigue after the Huntsville situation, and some disillusionment with the Democratic Party. Cincinnati Democrats had abandoned him during the Venable affair, while the national party never extended him the patronage he so deserved. Furthermore, Clark had been battered and bruised in the black press from Cleveland to Birmingham for taking unpopular positions and advancing unpopular strategies. It is no wonder that he took a reprieve from politics and activism.

The tragic thing about Clark's retreat from public life is that it was ill-timed, intersecting the lowest point in African American history, the "nadir of race relations." Southerners stripped African Americans of the franchise through terrorism, intimidation, legislation, and threats of economic reprisal. They codified Jim Crow at the local and state levels, and the color line thoroughly entrenched itself into the mind-sets of white and black southerners alike. Hundreds of African Americans who dared to defy southern customs by voting, intermarrying, or through economic or educational success were lynched every year. African Americans witnessed the swift erosion of their rights and social status. Clark could not have picked a worse time to retire from political life. But that did not mean he had stopped thinking about the status of African Americans in the South.

In a personal letter to Frederick Douglass in 1889, Clark commended him for his lecture entitled "The Nation's Problem," delivered before the Bethel Literary and Historical Society on April 16, 1889. Clark agreed with Douglass's acknowledgment that all African Americans' problems were not political, telling his friend that African Americans needed "industrial, pecuniary independence as much as or more than they need political independence."[50] This private acknowledgment that economic independence took primacy over the political marks a major shift in Clark's ideology. Electoral politics, political activism, and political power long had been his definitive strategy for uplift. But his views were evolving.

During the nadir of race relations, between the end of Reconstruction and the turn of the century, strategies of racial pride, racial unity, self-help, separate institutions, and economic advancement became increasingly common. These black nationalist strategies found resonance and popularity at a time when civil rights and political opportunities and power contracted almost daily. Some hard-line integrationists like Douglass expressed grief and alarm about the trend toward black nationalism.[51]

In his Bethel Literary and Historical Society address, Douglass vehemently denounced most aspects of black nationalism. First, he asserted that "race pride" was a "positive evil" built on a "false foundation." For him, it was too similar to white supremacy: both arose from the same sentiments. Douglass encouraged African Americans to reject it and to be proud only of their own accomplishments as individuals. He also railed against separate neighborhoods, churches, schools, and other institutions—all of which had become increasingly popular among African American leaders as race relations reached their nadir in the late nineteenth century. As the paths of equality and inclusion into American society became littered and obstructed by white supremacy, black racial pride, forming separate institutions, and conscientiously supporting black businesses represented, in part, a practical response to wholesale exclusion from mainstream institutions, as well as social, economic, and political life. Although he supported some aspects of black nationalism at different times in his own career, Douglass now rejected all of them in favor of assimilation and integration.[52]

Having read the speech, Clark stated in his letter that he agreed with Douglass's views on racial pride, which he labeled "froth" and an "ocean of twaddle." He wrote, "Until the colored people of the country generally see this point as clearly as you now see it; Until they cease to be led by such froth as that which characterizes the speech [sic] of the several gentlemen who spoke on the same day and on the same subject, there will be no legitimate basis for race pride."[53] Clark's comments are curious given how black nationalism, in its various forms, had informed many of his strategies to uplift African Americans and demand civil rights. He had embraced everything from the most conservative forms of black nationalism to the most radical, including emigration, establishing a black nation, and race-based voting blocs at times. Clark aggressively pursued black political power for decades—collectively and individually—and clung to the institutional side of black nationalism his entire life. He could not bring himself to support school integration without full and equal citizenship. Moreover, he embraced black history as a source of racial pride *and* as a basis to claim equality, inclusion, and citizenship, and had written a historical text himself. Clark even had endorsed cultural black nationalism in a speech about the Allen Temple AME in 1874, when he boastfully acknowledged their distinctive black religious folk culture; he advocated black pride during his 1875 address before the Convention of Colored Editors and in countless Emancipation addresses. History is littered with examples of African Americans who did not subscribe to the "entire complex" of black nationalist ideas in this period, and Clark is one of them.[54] Hence, his private remarks to Douglass seem remarkably disingenuous. They must be understood as a function of his wanting to show his friend support.

After moving to St. Louis, Clark's vocal and visible agitation declined precipitously. Then, in 1892, during the worst year on record for lynchings, he reemerged from the shadows to denounce this heinous ritual, calling on African Americans and their friends to dedicate a day to "humiliation, fasting, and prayer" to request divine intervention to stop the lynching of African Americans. Clark apparently had lost faith that governments—state or federal—would protect African Americans. In fact, he had lost faith that *any* human force could or would help. He rhetorically asked, "To whom, then, can we turn, save to the Lord, God; to him who has the power to enlighten and soften men's hearts."[55] In an appeal published in papers across the country, Clark implored African Americans to leave their jobs for the day, meet in churches, and pray collectively about their plight on May 31, 1892, the day designated for the Day of Prayer. Many of the nationally known African American leaders publicly endorsed his call for a national Day of Prayer, including Frederick Douglass, Bishop Daniel A. Payne of the AME church, Benjamin T. Tanner, Augustus Tolton, J. C. Price, T. Thomas Fortune, William S. Scarborough, Francis Ellen Harper, George T. Downing, and John Mercer Langston.[56] The leaders who supported this call held different racial ideologies and represented different political and religious affiliations. None of those superficial divisions mattered in the face of the extensive loss of African American lives.

Clark outlined three specific prayer requests on the day. First, "if it is our fault that the hearts of our fellow countrymen are so cruelly turned against us, He will show us the evil, and give us the wisdom to remove it." The second prayer request was that God show whites that the security for American institutions was dependent on "the observance of law by all, however powerful, and by the extension of its protection to all, however weak." The final prayer request asked that whites would "remember our lately enslaved condition, that they will not forget our centuries of toil," and that they would be "patient with our short-comings and encourage us to rise to that level of intelligence and virtue which marks the character of a good citizen."[57] Interestingly, none of the prayer requests demanded divine justice or retribution. They neither condemned lynching as an evil, inhumane act, nor did they make any demands of the perpetrators to immediately stop the egregious injustices. Instead, the tone and substance of these prayers are conciliatory and reflect a degree of accommodationism. In fact, in two of the requests he suggests that African Americans themselves may have played a part in provoking lynchings through either some "evil" that had turned whites' hearts against them or "short-comings" of intelligence and virtue. Essentially, the prayer requests place more responsibility on African Americans than on the offenders. Conciliation is not characteristic of Clark; he always had made militant demands for justice and equality. But he may have adopted this tone because he understood how vulnerable southern African Americans were. He simply could not afford to make militant demands or issue too strong a condemnation of southern whites, lest he risk their lives in the process.

Although it is impossible to determine how many people participated, the National Day of Prayer received hearty support from African American communities—especially religious ones—all around the country. People met in churches and fervently prayed for deliverance from this peculiar persecution. Community leaders and ministers presided over the local meetings. Those in attendance listened to choirs and addresses by various local leaders. Communities in Cleveland and elsewhere passed resolutions that stated that after years without redress from state and local governments, the prayer warriors would now refer the matter to a higher authority.[58]

The fact that Clark conceived of the idea of a national day of humiliation, fasting, and prayer is out of character for him. Although a devoted Unitarian, Clark had never been devout, by any means. At no other point in his political career did he advocate a spiritual strategy to combat African Americans' problems. Rather, he had always insisted on pragmatic, tangible, secular strategies. Furthermore, his strategies typically were grounded in a general faith in humanity to solve its own problems and in society to cure its own ills. But on the question of lynching, he had opted for divine intervention instead. On the surface, it would seem that the problem of lynching had literally brought him to his knees. Perhaps it had. But closer analysis reveals that the national Day of Prayer was much more than a simple collective plea for divine intervention. Clark invoked old abolitionist ideologies in this antilynching effort. Always the pragmatist, he may have calculated that a massive religious act such as this not only would make people sympathetic to African Americans and the injustice they endured, but also would establish the stance of moral superiority necessary to launch an attack on the practice. And the Day of Prayer did garner some expressions of sympathy and acknowledgment of past wrongs committed against African Americans. An editorial in the *New York Evangelist* acknowledged, "The fact is too plain for controversy that we have not meted out to them that equality before the law." The writer declared, "It is a solemn thing when seven million souls, however poor and humble they may be, carry their appeal from man's injustice to the bar of the Almighty." The article concluded, "It is a serious matter for a nation when any body of people, however, few, betake themselves not to revolt, but to prayer."[59] Although Clark's Day of Prayer did not lead to any real reduction in the number of lynchings, its most tangible sign of success was how African Americans across the nation mobilized around the issue.

Lynching remained a concern to Clark long after that day of reflection. In May 1900, he publicly commended his old nemesis Harry C. Smith, the *Cleveland Gazette* editor-turned-legislator, for proposing antilynching legislation in Ohio in 1894. Smith's bill stated that a county that hosted a lynching or mob violence could be liable for from five hundred to one thousand dollars in damages for survivors and for five thousand dollars for the families of murdered mob victims. The bill represented one of the most comprehensive pieces of legislation against mob violence of its day, and actually served as a model for antilynching legislation in other states. The Smith bill ultimately became law in 1896, but it was held up in court for a few more years with legal challenges. After a favorable resolution in the Ohio Supreme Court, Clark celebrated its success in a court he considered to otherwise be a "graveyard of liberal legislation." Clark assured Smith that because the bill had made it through Ohio legislature, with its tough opponents, it certainly would succeed in other states. He insisted that "it is time for action" on the lynching issue.[60] Despite his urgent rhetoric, Clark had a decidedly more conservative and passive approach to antilynching activism than most of his contemporaries.

The Day of Prayer did elevate Clark's national profile to a small degree. At the very least, he gained some moral capital—enough to make people forget about his infamy in his final days in Cincinnati. He tried to convert that moral power to political power when former Democratic President Grover Cleveland ran for reelection in 1892. Upon being elected to a second term, the president made it clear that he intended to reward deserving African Americans who had helped with his campaign. Since Cleveland's administration had never adequately rewarded his efforts during his first and second presidential campaigns in 1884 and 1888, Clark may have had higher expectations this time; he applied for an unspecified position within that administration.

The National Negro Democratic League endorsed Clark by supplying the administration with a list of worthy candidates, with his name at the top. Charles H. J. Taylor, who had been Clark's most vocal supporter during the 1888 conference, now publicly challenged his commitment to the party. He editorialized in the *Cleveland Gazette:* "[Clark] is not entitled to any political recognition from Mr. Cleveland. If he is a democrat he did not show it in the last campaign." According to Taylor, Clark and others had "sat like bumps on a log through the hot campaign" and "should not be given anything." He concluded the diatribe by assailing Clark's potential for leadership: "We helped make Clark chairman of a Negro democratic convention in 1888 and in that position he was a first-class failure."[61] Whether or not Clark had been a "failure" as Taylor charged does not represent the sentiments of other black Democrats. And given Taylor's pattern of attacking political rivals—as he had done with James M. Turner—it seems more likely that he attacked Clark because he wanted a position himself. As long as Clark, the front-runner, remained in the candidate pool, Taylor did not stand a reasonable chance of securing a position over him. Nonetheless, the noise Taylor made ruined Clark's possibility of obtaining the position. Frederick Douglass himself personally put in a good word for Clark directly to the president, but even that was not enough. After several months waiting for the appointment, an extremely disappointed Clark thanked his mentor for his efforts. With his spirit battered from all the attacks he had endured over the years at the hands of men from his own community, Clark wrote Douglass: "The truth is . . . [m]ore than once that tide which leads to fortune has swelled under my feet and I have failed to float upon its crest. I beg you to consider this a misfortune, not a fault."[62] Sadly, the man who had given so much to political parties across several decades never was rewarded with a political appointment at the national level.

In 1890, the editor of the prestigious *New York Age,* T. Thomas Fortune, organized the Afro-American League as a national, nonpartisan protest organization that would coordinate and organize legal challenges to Jim Crow. Following the spirit of the Colored Convention movement, the Afro-American League held annual conventions that provided a national forum for African Americans to discuss pressing racial issues and a venue in which to chart a course of action. Fortune identified six areas of focus for the league, including disfranchisement, lynch and mob rule, school inequality, injustice in the legal system, unequal treatment on railroads, and lack of access to places of public accommodation.[63] While it had great potential as a civil rights organization, the Afro-American League suffered from numerous internal issues. Fortune cited a lack of funds, the lack of mass support, and the leadership's indifference as the reason for the organization's demise after three short years. In 1898, after a five-year hiatus, the league was revived and renamed the Afro-American Council, although it had the same mission. The council boasted the most respected African Americans among its members, including Monroe Trotter, W. E. B. Du Bois, Ida B. Wells, Ferdinand Barnett, N. F. Mossell, and Booker T. Washington, all of whom addressed the council's annual conventions. T. Thomas Fortune allowed his friend and benefactor Booker T. Washington—who had emerged as a "representative man" after his famously conciliatory Atlanta Exposition address in 1895, in which he denied any interest in social equality—to dictate the tone of the organization. The Afro-American Council increasingly reflected the philosophy of accommodationism and conciliation. Philosophical differences about the best approach to solving the African Americans' problems led to internal strife. Ida B. Wells, Monroe Trotter, and other radical voices of the Afro-American Council resented and resisted Washington's influence within the organization. They rallied against him and others who favored a more conservative approach. An exodus of the radicals ultimately gave birth to two other civil rights organizations, the Niagara Movement (1905) and the National Association for the Advancement of Colored People (1909).[64]

By the time of its 1904 convention in St. Louis, the Afro-American Council had become almost irrelevant. Very few of the nation's most respected African Americans even attended the 1904 convention. In fact, most of the eastern race leaders were noticeably absent, having abandoned the council by that time. A new cadre of leaders hailing from the southern and midwestern states assumed the helm. Many of them, like George L. Knox, the editor of Democratic journal *Indianapolis Freeman,* were decidedly conservative and supportive of Washington's philosophies. Although he was not even present, Booker T. Washington's financial and ideological domination was apparent to everyone present at that convention.[65]

The 1904 convention, as had so many Afro-American Council meetings before it, condemned the lynching of African American men, the rape of African American women, the disfranchisement of African American citizens, and all other crimes that denied African American civil rights. The council condemned mob rule, decried the absence of justice, and lamented the enactment of racist legislation throughout the South. It also issued an appeal—directed specifically at ministers, the press, and legislators—to enact laws against such crimes. The convention strategically capitalized on the fact that the Louisiana Purchase Exposition and the Olympic Games both were being held in St. Louis at the same time: the convention's message to the nation underscored how every group in the international community received attention except African Americans, who were treated as inferiors in the exhibits and as tourists.[66]

Seventy-five-year-old Clark was one of the speakers at the annual National Afro-American Council convention in St. Louis; few marquee names attended, underscoring the council's waning significance. Since the contemporary press neither recorded nor summarized his speech, the content of his address is unknown.[67] The fact that he addressed the convention suggests that he was more than a casual and indifferent delegate: he supported the mission, culture, and strategy of the Afro-American Council, which was, by then, an extension of Booker T. Washington's philosophies. Those who remained in the organization at that point most certainly subscribed to Washington's ideology or personally held him in high regard.[68] Hence, Clark's active role in the 1904 convention and the fact that he performed the honors of introducing Washington when he spoke in St. Louis in 1899 suggest that Clark's loyalty rested with Washington. Certainly the fact that he did not join the Niagara Movement or the NAACP gives credence to that theory.[69]

The St. Louis convention marks one of the council's last; by 1908, the National Afro-American Council organization faded once again. Unfortunately, neither that 1904 convention nor the National Afro-American Council, in general, ever fully realized its potential. It did, though, chart the path for the NAACP, which carried on the twin battles against racial injustice and advancing racial progress.[70] Unfortunately, Clark did not follow that more progressive, racial path into the twentieth century. Instead he continued to participate in state conventions like the one held in Missouri in 1907.

In July 1907, Clark participated in what seems to have been his last black convention: the Negro State Convention of Missouri. The body formed the Negro Constitutional League of the State of Missouri, which aimed to cultivate "good fellowship between the races and to prevent legislation and judicial infringement" upon African American rights. Specifically, the organization committed itself to encouraging interracial cooperation as the most effective strategy to protest racial discrimination. In its published statement and proceedings, the convention used battle-worn tactics of moral suasion and patriotism to try to convince whites that African Americans had a stake in the racial policies in America and, ultimately, to convince them to take a stand against discrimination and racist legislation. The convention declared that racism was a disease that corrupted the whole republic: "It is lowering the tone of national morals; it is brutalizing and corrupting the whole land"—including religion. The convention warned, "Such a policy will ultimately rob millions of loyal citizens of their patriotism and weaken the republic." Moreover, it continued, "sooner or later all the people will reap the bitter fruits of injustice." Despite these ominous warnings, black Missourians clearly believed that the battle could not be waged alone: the convention's resolutions also struck a conciliatory note, thanking specific whites for their philanthropy on behalf of African Americans' educations.[71] Neither the resolutions nor the strategy of this convention fundamentally differed from the black conventions of the nineteenth century. It echoed the same denunciation of racist legislation of the Ohio conventions in the antebellum era without offering any new strategies or approaches. This convention, like Clark, remained a relic of the antebellum black convention movement.

The young activist who had once electrified and empowered mixed ethnic audiences with speeches about radical heroes like John Brown and Tom Paine and who had threatened to "seize his rights" had taken a long journey to his National Day of Prayer. He had traded his alliances with August Willich, Levi Coffin, and Moncure Conway for one with Booker T. Washington. The same Clark who had started off his journey witnessing communitarian schemes and rejecting trade colleges on principle would one day embrace Washington's boot-strapism as the saving grace. The irascible barber who once had dashed a shaving cup to the ground, threatening to cut a white man's throat if he ever shaved one again, is the same man who would later refer to expressions of racial pride as "froth." How could such vastly different ideologies inhabit one body in one lifetime?

Clark entered into his conservatism the day he ceased to believe in political power for the benefit of the whole and began selfishly seeking it for himself. The deal was sealed when he ceased to believe in a political strategy for social change. That was the day Peter H. Clark the radical became Peter H. Clark the conservative.

Unlike scores of other charismatic, educated, vocal, and politically engaged African Americans in the nineteenth century, Clark never enjoyed political office—either elected or appointed. Becoming a Democrat had not gotten him any closer to securing a political position. If nothing else, his decision to participate in Democratic machine politics alienated him from his own community. In the late 1880s, he abandoned his aggressive political agitation in favor of moral suasion and economic independence. Alas, even that yielded no fruits for the aging activist.

While he never secured a political appointment as he had wished, Clark could take comfort in the fact that he had earned the respect and esteem of hundreds of students he had taught throughout the years. To celebrate his seventy-fourth birthday and honor him as an educator, the African American community of St. Louis presented him with a silver "loving cup" in 1903.[72] Peter Humphries Clark retired from the St. Louis Public Schools in 1908 after more than fifty years in the classroom. He outlived his wife, Frances, who died after a long illness in 1902; his son, Herbert; his daughter Consuelo; and his entire generation of African American leaders. His eldest and only surviving daughter, Ernestine, moved to St. Louis after her mother's death to care for her aging and forlorn father in his own home. Clark lived the remainder of his life under her care; he died on June 21, 1925, at the age of ninety-six. He was buried in St. Peter's cemetery in St. Louis. As his only surviving child, Ernestine inherited her father's entire estate.[73]

George B. Vashon Jr., the son of George B. Vashon, wrote a glowing obituary for the *St. Louis Argus* that revealed the depth of his reverence and admiration for his father's dear friend. The obituary situated Clark within the larger pantheon of great African American intellectuals. Comparing Clark to the greatest minds of his day, Vashon wrote: "[John Mercer] Langston was cultured with the culture of ripe scholarship; Douglass was titanic with native mental power. Peter Clark was both. . . . He was, above them all, a philosopher." Vashon's tribute acknowledged, too, that Frederick Douglass and Peter Clark had a deep mutual respect and love—feelings Douglass held for few people. Vashon wrote, "Peter Clark was the only mention that I know of that softened the face and tones and words of

Mr. Douglass to unmistakable affection." According to him, Clark's fearless stand for justice—with courage unmatched in common men—is what earned Douglass's respect and admiration. Vashon lauded Clark as an "intrepid warrior" who "never begged for justice; [but] he demanded it." His outrage at injustice "filled his being with ire and left no room for fear." Of his passing, Vashon regretted that Clark left a "space so vast no score of leaders of today can fill it."[74]

Chapter Ten

"A Painted Lie"

Autobiography and Historical Memory

In early 1885, Peter Humphries Clark relayed his life story to Timothy Thomas Fortune, editor of the African American journal the *New York Freeman.* Fortune devoted two-thirds of the front page of his January 3 issue to Clark's biography, signifying Fortune's respect for his friend and political ally.[1] Although this was not the first time anyone had published Clark's biography, he rarely ever discussed his personal life story publicly, especially his family history.[2] In that issue of the *Freeman,* Clark briefly recounted how his maternal grandfather, Samuel Humphries, a teamster by trade, had traveled to Erie, Pennsylvania, to help build the famous fleet of ships that Commodore Oliver Hazard Perry used to defeat the British during the War of 1812. He maintained that after the ships were complete, his grandfather served as a sailor on one of them, and had been present at one of the most famous battles in that war, the Battle of Lake Erie.[3]

In that same article, Clark expressed his annoyance at society's failure to acknowledge the role African Americans played in that war. It seemed to be—at least to him—a deliberate attempt to erase their contributions. For him, even William Henry Powell's 1873 famous painting *Battle of Lake Erie* contributed to African Americans' erasure from the history of the War of 1812. That painting depicts Oliver Perry standing in a rowboat with several oarsmen. In the midst of battle, with cannon fire all around them, all the men except one are depicted as brave: the African American is shown cowering. Clark complained that "although colored men were in the hottest of that fight and bore themselves bravely too, the only one whom the artist represents as showing trepidation is the black sailor." Outraged by the depiction and the message it sent about African American bravery, Clark blasted Powell's rendition as a "painted lie."[4] By critiquing Powell's interpretation of the battle, he directly challenged American [white] nationalist history, which places whites at the center of nation forming, and either relegates African Americans to the margins or erases them altogether. By painting trepidation into the face of the black sailor, Powell subtly asserts that African Americans had not *valiantly* served in the War of 1812 and therefore represent the antiheroes. Clark felt that the painting mocked African Americans' service, and that their apparent trepidation and cowardice defined them as unpatriotic—and therefore undeserving of citizenship. Powell's *Battle of Lake Erie* obviously hit a nerve; Clark's commentary is his attempt to disrupt and challenge the master narrative of American history, while simultaneously using his own family history as a basis to prove that African Americans had valiantly served in the war and, consequently, deserve the rights of citizens.[5]

Although scant records from that battle survive, historians have verified that African Americans comprised somewhere between 10 and 20 percent of those who served in that historic battle.[6] It seems perfectly plausible that Clark's grandfather may have numbered among them, but a closer look at the records of the Battle of Lake Erie suggests that there is only a slim chance that his maternal grandfather, Samuel Humphries, actually served under Commodore Perry on Lake Erie. The muster rolls at Lake Erie Naval Station cannot be found, but there are some other surviving records that provide a near-complete list of names of those who served, including Samuel Hambleton's Prize List, compiled so Congress could disburse compensation for those who served in that campaign. Humphries's name is not found on this list or on the list of those wounded or killed in battle.[7] Although the Hambleton's Prize List is incomplete and contains not only spelling errors but also errors of omission, it is the most definitive extant list of men who served under Commodore Perry during the War of 1812. Moreover, although there is a slight chance that Samuel Humphries's name may have been omitted or recorded incorrectly, it is doubtful that he served at all, as Clark claims. His story bears remarkable resemblance to the real story of William Anderson, his wife Frances's grandfather, who heroically served in the American Revolution.

Clark also led people to believe that his paternal grandfather was the American frontier explorer William Clark, who, along with Meriwether Lewis, led a pioneering transcontinental expedition through the American Northwest to the Pacific Coast from 1803 to 1806. Lewis and Clark's expedition is significant in American history because it expanded knowledge about the geography, natural resources, and native peoples of that territory, sparking interest in the westward expansion of the United States. Every history textbook includes this quintessentially American story. Clark first inserted himself into William Clark's family in 1900, when the Oregon historian Eva Emery Dye contacted him to inquire about his kinship to the explorer. At the time, Dye was researching the details of William Clark's life for her forthcoming book, *The Conquest: The True Story of Lewis and Clark.*[8] Apparently she had already contacted several members of the explorer's family in St. Louis. In the course of that research, someone must have suggested to her that the explorer had an African American grandson in Peter Clark. His written response to Dye's inquiries read:

> Dear Madam—The William Clark of the Lewis and Clark expedition sustained to my father the double relation of master and father. When he moved to Missouri he emancipated his mulatto children, sent them to Ohio and made some provision for their care and education. I was born in Ohio, not Missouri. We, I speak for myself and brothers and sister, have never cared to claim kinship with the white branch of the family. Nor do I now, court any notoriety in that connection.
>
> Yrs, Peter H. Clark.[9]

Clark, clearly mindful of the explorer's personal history, inserted his grandmother's story into it.

This tale of false kinship, like the tale about his grandfather at the Battle of Lake Erie, is so credible because it sticks closely to the actual details of William Clark's life. There are quite a number of overlaps and coincidences in the biographies of the explorer and Peter Clark's grandmother Elizabeth, leaving open the possibility that the explorer did have an enslaved concubine. Elizabeth—then Betty—had been born in 1784 in Hanover County, Virginia. Coincidentally, that county neighbored Caroline County, Virginia, where William Clark, the future explorer, had been born in 1770. Being in such close proximity, it is plausible that the two could have met at some point. Moreover, Betty's owner was a man named John Clarke; the explorer's father had the same name, but without the "e." Betty's owner, John Clarke, had a son named William S. Clarke. Hence both families had a patriarch named John and a son named William Clark/ Clarke. But both names were quite common then. Another coincidence: both Betty's owner and the explorer's family eventually relocated to Kentucky, albeit to different parts of that state: William Clark and his family to Louisville and Betty Clarke and her owner to Cynthiana. Only ninety-two miles separated Betty, the bondswoman, and William, the explorer, in Kentucky. That distance could be covered in a day's journey, leaving open the possibility that they had a relationship then. Moreover, William Clark's family owned bondspeople, so it is not too far outside the bounds of the imaginable to think that his family may have purchased her at some point. In addition, the possibility that William Clark, the explorer, may have fathered Betty's children is made more plausible by several periods of unaccounted time in his travel journal, periods that would have given him ample time to take the woman and her children to Cincinnati before he went west, as Peter Clark asserted in a 1919 private letter. For example, Meriwether Lewis arrived in the Louisville area to meet William Clark on October 14, 1804, but the men did not start their expedition for another two weeks. Historians have not yet determined why their trip was delayed for so long.[10] That two-week time frame would have given Clark more than enough time to take Betty and her children to Cincinnati. The final fact that seems to give credence to Peter Clark's claim is that he eventually relocated to St. Louis, the very same city where the explorer settled and lived until his death in 1838. The multiplicative effect of these coincidences and parallels seems rather convincing. It is no wonder historians have gotten this all wrong.

Despite the coincidences, the historical record simply does not support the possibility that Peter Clark *is* the explorer's grandson. The two Clark(e) families may have been one family at some earlier point in history, but this was not the case at the time the explorer and Peter's grandmother Betty were born. In order to include the explorer as a probable father of Betty Clarke's children, one would need to prove he had access to her. There is no evidence that their paths ever crossed, much less enough to produce five children. Two of the children in question, Elliott and Evelina, were born in 1806. William Clark and Meriwether Lewis left on their expedition in 1804 and did not return until September 23, 1806, making it impossible for Clark to have fathered either of Betty's children born in 1806. Moreover, Peter Clark, writing in 1919, claimed that his white grandfather took his African American family to Cincinnati himself. Yet, the explorer's national celebrity and visible government positions as a territorial governor of Missouri and, later, the superintendent of the U.S. Office of Indian Affairs would have made him too conspicuous to have resettled an African American family in Cincinnati in 1816 without major papers noticing. There is no evidence that William Clark ever came to the city that year.[11] A more telling piece of evidence that disproves this relationship is the will of John Clark, the father of the explorer. His 1799 will provides a very detailed account of the property left to his sons and sons-in-law, including the names of every single bondsman and bondswoman the elder Clark owned at the time of his death. Moreover, when the estate was appraised in 1811, the three Bettys listed among the inventory are distinguished as "black," "yellow," and "younger." By then, Peter's grandmother was nearly thirty years old—too old to be considered "young." While either of the other two women named Betty might have fit the bill, none of the names of her children are listed in the inventory, suggesting that none of these three women named Betty is Peter's grandmother.[12] Second, there is no evidence that William Clark, the explorer, ever purchased any more bondspeople after his initial inheritance.

The evidence not only disproves the claim but also suggests that Peter Clark fabricated this tale of fictive kinship. One sign of a conscious fabrication is how he spoke about his own lineage over the years. Several biographies of Clark were penned during his lifetime. In that era, African American history largely consisted of volumes that chronicled the lives of great men; Clark is almost always included in them. Some interesting patterns emerge in the biographies of him written by his contemporaries while he was still alive. The first biographical profile of Clark ever printed appeared in William Wells Brown's *Rising Son,* published in 1874. Not only is there no implicit or explicit reference to a kinship to William Clark in that piece, but it makes no reference to his lineage at all—not even the Humphries tale. Clark said absolutely nothing about his lineage publicly until he was fifty-six years old. And then, in a biography dictated to, and penned by Fortune in the January 3, 1885, issue of the *New York Freeman,* he mentions only his mother's lineage—the Humphries tale. That article is one of the most thorough biographies ever printed about Clark during his day. However, subsequent reprints of it, published in the *Cleveland Gazette,* omit all references to his ancestry, even the Humphries tale. Clark is also profiled in William J. Simmons's 1887 tome *Men of Mark.* Simmons had asked those featured to write their own biographies. Yet even in that profile, Clark fails to mention that he descended from William Clark, the explorer, or Samuel Humphries, the valiant and fictionalized veteran of the Battle of Lake Erie.[13] If Clark really were related to these very important, *historic* people, he would have mentioned that fact in these biographical profiles. The fact that he did not speaks volumes about the veracity of his assertion to Dye in 1900.

Not only did Clark never mention his famous explorer kinsman until 1900, at the age of seventy-one, but he never did so publicly. Offering historian Dye an explanation for why he had never before claimed kinship to the explorer he wrote, "I speak for myself and brothers and sister, [we] have never cared to claim kinship much with the white branch of the family, nor do I now court any notoriety in that connection."[14] Even though he claimed to want to keep his lineage secret, Clark surely must have known that making such an assertion to a historian would certainly make his allegations public. Interestingly, though, Dye chose not to include this claim in her biography of the explorer published two years later. Either she remained skeptical of his claim or did not want to tarnish the image of an American icon with an unverified tale of miscegenation and illegitimate children with a bondswoman.

In 1919, William Clark Breckenridge, an esteemed Missouri historian and trustee of the State Historical Society of Missouri, contacted Clark to inquire about his life. Peter Clark must have thought better of falsifying his lineage to Breckenridge, an expert in Missouri history and a far more accomplished historian than Dye. Breckenridge certainly would have immediately recognized anything falsely ascribed to the explorer's biography. In Clark's handwritten autobiographical answers to Breckenridge's questions about his ancestry, he made no explicit mention of his kinship to the explorer, although he did allude to it: Clark wrote that people called his grandfather "Major Billy Clark." Clark stopped short of claiming that "Major Billy" is the same person as William Clark, the explorer, but the military reference is highly suggestive since the explorer held several titles during his long military career, including captain, lieutenant, and brigadier general, although never a major. In the same document, Clark also mentions that Major Billy had gone "West."[15] This is yet another veiled reference to the explorer. Moreover, too many of the details of the family history he constructs bear resemblance to the explorer's biography to be coincidental. To his credit, though, Peter Clark did not tell Breckenridge or any other historian besides Dye that he was the explorer's grandson. When all is said and done, he seems to have told that story to only one person outside of his own family. Such a seemingly harmless untruth might have gone unnoticed had it ended there.

Historical memory is how people remember their past. Memory is not created or preserved the same way it is when a disciplined professional is involved, nor does memory satisfy the same needs. Much of what has been written in this book falls within the guidelines of the discipline of history, but Clark's entire story cannot be told that way. A part of his story is about how he tried to manufacture his own legacy and how, in the process, he created historical memory that became a proxy for the historical truth until now.

If historical memory is how people remember their past, then a large part of what people remember about their past and how they remember it is imagined. So is memory fictional? Not exactly. For those who embrace that imagined past, it becomes their truth. And they will even offer "evidence" to sustain that truth. For example, people tend to offer "genetic" clues to defend their truth about blood relationships: Peter Clark's family members offer as evidence the fact that his daughter, Ernestine, had red hair, just like William Clark the explorer. For them, the red hair is irrefutable proof that she is his great-granddaughter. Because historical memory is so deeply personal, it necessarily creates fierce loyalists and staunch defenders of that "truth," even in the face of evidence to the contrary. Clark's descendents, for example, remain resolute in their devotion to the idea that he was William Clark's grandson to this day.[16]

A few of Peter Clark's relatives and descendents have defended this truth in print and converted memory to history. This is not uncommon since memory often provides the material for professional historical inquiry. In other words, historians are often inspired by the remembered past. But memory must be validated. After stories are collected, historian David Blight instructs historians to then "get thee to an archive!"[17] Otherwise false memory becomes false history.

Dovie King Clark, Clark's former student at Gaines High and the wife of his nephew Edward, became the first person to convert that memory to history when she published a biographical sketch of him in an academic journal, the *Negro History Bulletin,* in 1942. In that sketch, she asserts that pioneer frontiersman William Clark is Peter's grandfather.[18] It is obvious that she got this story and the details from a family source—possibly even Peter Clark himself—and believed it to be true. She provides no historical research to validate this claim, and therein lies the problem. With one hum of the printing press, the fictive kinship at the center of Clark family memory passed as oral history. The integrity of Dovie King's biographical sketch was not questioned by the journal's editors, possibly because of her relationship to the family. That is not surprising since, by then, oral testimony was fast becoming a more accepted way to recover African American family history. But once the story appeared in print in a trusted academic journal, historians did not stop to challenge it or check the facts;

they simply accepted the story as truth. Hence, this legend been replicated in most biographies of Peter Clark ever since.[19] Even more unsettling is the fact that that false claim has nearly eclipsed all of Clark's accomplishments and colored how we remember him.

In 1995, another Clark relative, Ernestine Garrett Lucas (her grandmother was his cousin), wrote a book that examines African American history through the lens of her own family. In it she proclaims: "Many people who have heard bits and pieces of this story have said it was only a fairy tale, and not very true at all. I have personal knowledge and proof that it is very true."[20] Her book, *Wider Windows to the Past: African American History from a Family Perspective,* is an eclectic mix of family legend, oral testimony, and written evidence. The only problem is that she, like King, does not interrogate the mythic kinship to William Clark nearly enough—probably because it is so deeply personal to her.

The evidence strongly suggests that Clark actively tried to construct his own historical legacy. For example, not too long after Dye had contacted him, he submitted his history of the Black Brigade to the State Historical Society of Missouri. Then, in 1906, he applied for membership in the society—undeniable proof that he understood how important it was to preserve history, especially his own. Yet, the historical society ultimately denied Clark membership because of his race.[21]

Clark is not the only prominent nineteenth-century African American political figure who fabricated stories about his ancestry. James Milton Turner, former minister of Liberia, once claimed to have descended from African royalty on both sides of his family tree. He told a reporter that his father's ancestry could be traced to a Moorish prince, while his mother descended from the Vey people, who, according to him, developed a system of writing. Not content with that the grandiosity of that, he also claimed to be the great-nephew of Nat Turner.[22] Like Clark, James Milton Turner was an accomplished man who had fallen out of favor with his people decades earlier. Both men made up these stories after a very public fall from grace and an extended period of irrelevance in black political life.

Still, one must wonder why a man as accomplished as Peter Humphries Clark would *need* to lie about one grandfather being in the Battle of Lake Erie with Commodore Perry and the other being the great American explorer. It is necessary to analyze his motivations because historians must "interpret both history and memory in order to write good histories of memory."[23] Both tales of fictive kinship emerged during moments of extreme self-reflection about his legacy. For example, at the time he fabricated the Battle of Lake Erie story in 1885, he was embroiled in controversy about his politics as a Democrat. Perhaps he feared how historians would remember him. Fifteen years later when he told Eva Emery Dye that he descended from the explorer, the seventy-one-year-old was no longer relevant in African American political life. He had witnessed the meteoric rise of others like W. E. B. Du Bois and Booker T. Washington, who had eclipsed him as public intellectuals. He may have wondered whether history would remember him as fondly as it did Douglass or Langston, if at all.

Humans endlessly revise memory to fit our deepest needs and desires. People sometimes need "an ennobling past through which to establish our identities." The memory we construct provides a comforting and romantic safe haven in the past.[24] In this vein, Clark's myths may have been created to link him to nobler ancestors. His real—albeit, humble—ancestry may have been a source of shame for him. Pretending to be related to an explorer so central to U.S. history is far grander than saying that one's father was a product of rape or an otherwise illicit and unequal sexual relationship between a teenaged bondswoman and her owner. Moreover, these tales of "grandfather" William Clark leading an expedition into the frontier and of Samuel Humphries as a heroic veteran of the War of 1812 are quintessentially *American*. After all, themes of rugged frontiersmanship and heroic military service had defined the American story for a long time. These tales invoke a heroic version of the history of the American frontier, Manifest Destiny, and the nation's triumph over all enemies who might challenge its right to expand from coast to coast. To be a part of *that* history is to hold an indisputable claim to American citizenship. By writing himself into the family of a famous American explorer and writing his African American grandfather into the history of the War of 1812, Clark constructed a personal history that placed his family at the center of defining moments in American history. In this, he would be—finally and undeniably—an American.

Acknowledgments

The late Walter P. Herz, a lay historian living in Cincinnati, resurrected Peter H. Clark. A member of Clark's Unitarian church, Walter was completely fascinated by the life Clark led, so he decided to tell the world about him. After retiring from another career, Walter spent more than ten years familiarizing himself with the literature, methods, and the discipline of History, and searching for primary sources by and about Clark. Despite the fact that no collection of Clark's papers exists, he left no stone unturned in his research. I am grateful for the years of research time he saved me.

When Walter approached me about coauthoring this project, I initially declined. Although I had mentioned Clark in my first book, I was not sure I shared Walter's enthusiasm for him. Moreover, I was none too excited about coauthoring because I feared losing my voice and interpretation in the negotiations. Biography as a method also gave me reason to pause because I tend to privilege communities over individuals. Only after Walter gave me Clark's 1873 Emancipation Day address to read did I reconsider my decision. Clark's words penetrated me to my core and energized my passion for this era. I have never looked back. I realized that his life is a great way to tell a larger story about black radicalism and political and intellectual strivings in this period. Unfortunately, shortly after I agreed to do this project, Walter's failing health prevented him from moving forward. I only hope that I have done Walter and Clark justice in these pages.

The First Unitarian Church of Cincinnati (the same one Clark attended) largely funded this book. Its minster, Reverend Sharon K. Dittmar, and congregation have been incredibly supportive of me and the project through the entire process. The church has provided funds at various stages of this research. I understand why it appealed to Clark and Walter. I also thank the History Department at the University of Cincinnati for supplementing production costs.

234

I would like to thank the staff at the following archives and libraries for their generous assistance: the Library of Congress, Cincinnati Historical Society, Ohio Historical Society, Oberlin College Archives, Fisk University Special Collections, Schomburg Center for Research in Black Culture, and the Public Library of Cincinnati and Hamilton County. The late Beth Madison Howse, librarian at Fisk University Special Collections, was very generous with her assistance and patience. Dan Aren, librarian at the Public Library of Cincinnati and Hamilton County, not only helped me locate *Volksfreund* articles mentioning Clark, but translated them for me. It certainly pays to be in a city with fluent German speakers. Carrie Nelson provided me with copies of Clark's correspondence that she stumbled upon at an estate sale in St. Louis decades ago. The historian in me wishes she had purchased more of his papers at that estate sale, but I am grateful for what she did buy. I encourage her to deposit the materials at an archive, where future historians can access them.

Few academic presses want to publish books about black nationalist-socialists from Cincinnati, which is why I am eternally indebted to Dr. James Ramage and the other trustees and editorial staff at the University Press of Kentucky for agreeing to publish this book. In particular, I owe special thanks to Ashley S. Runyon, Acquisitions Editor and Development Coordinator, who believed in my vision and in me as a historian and made the appeal before the board. She has been very efficient, professional, and supportive throughout this process. My only hope is that this book lives up to all of our expectations.

I am very fortunate to be at a good institution with outstanding colleagues, which is infinitely better than being at an outstanding institution with good colleagues. I would like to thank all of my UC Colleagues in the Departments of History and Africana Studies. Special thanks to Mark Lause, Shailaja Paik, John Brackett, Elizabeth Frierson, Carolette Norwood, Michele Reutter, Thabiti Asukile, Joseph Takougang, Willard Sunderland, Tracy Teslow, Faraha Norton, and Holly McGee.

Several people have read this manuscript at different stages; most were too kind to let me know the worst. Mark Lause and I engaged in countless conversations about Cincinnati's nineteenth-century radicals, socialists, and Spiritualists. He demonstrated great patience in helping me navigate Fourierism, the land-reform movement, and the nuances of the SLP. I am fortunate to have someone with his expertise literally two doors away. When I asked Zane Miller to critique my manuscript, I fully expected the typical page or two of comments. Instead, he painstakingly went through the 325-page manuscript line by line, commenting on everything from word choice to organization and analysis. It is one of the most thorough reads my work has had in years. Even more remarkable is the fact that he did all of that for someone he has never met. A long list of others read and commented, including Tim Messer-Kruse, Wilson Jeremiah Moses, Jim Stewart, Bruce Mousser, Richard J. M. Blackett, Eric Jackson, and the anonymous readers of the University Press of Kentucky.

I would like to thank my friend and mentor Paul Finkelman, on whose shoulders I stand. He has helped me manage my career, read drafts of my work, given me publication and speaking opportunities, and written countless recommendations for me. Peter Wood remains a source of support as well.

I owe a great deal of emotional debt to a woman who has been like a mother to me for nearly two decades, Phyllis Wadley. A soror and friend, she has been my emotional rock, the person I turn to for matters large and ridiculous. Her prayers and words of encouragement have gotten me through countless storms. I profoundly admire her dignity, class, substance, and integrity. By extension, I also thank her entire family—especially, James Wadley Sr.—for embracing me and my daughter as their own and showing us what a family should be. My friendship with Stacia Parker has endured longer than most. We were drawn to one another because we are sister-spirits. What I most admire is her generosity of spirit and a commitment to our friendship. Another kindred sister-spirit and soror, Sheila Ferguson Booker, has been a daily source of encouragement and support. We have endured a great many heartaches and disappointments together, which has forged an even stronger bond between us. I am very fortunate to have met a handful of real friends in my life; she is one of them. I also thank her mom and all of the other Fergusons, one of the most loving families I have ever met.

I am happy to have a host of friends and students who inspire, encourage, and uplift: Ashley Brassfield Adams, Johnny Bailey, Bryant Barner, Colleen Bonnicklewis, Brittany Brantley, Dan Baum, Scot Brown, Justin Christopher, Nelson Collins, Stephanie Creech, Deon Cromwell, Karen Getter, John Owusu, Kyanna Perry, and Kurt Windisch. Although he began as my student fifteen years ago, Allen Thomas has become family. I am immensely proud of the man he has become and honored that he and his lovely wife, Felicia, have asked me to be the godmother of their child, Allen Jr. I am deeply indebted to Eric Jackson, a dear friend and colleague who played a huge role in connecting me with the University Press of

Kentucky. Beyond that, he has read drafts and patiently listened to me go on and on about the project. It has been a one-sided friendship for a while, with him doing all of the giving, but I hope to repay him soon.

Although I consider all the people I have already thanked my family, I also have some blood relatives I must acknowledge. First are my two brothers, Anthony Allen and Jamie Cox, of whom I am extremely proud. Both represent models of manhood that are admirable, respectable, and courageous. I applaud them for remaining committed to their college education. My niece Adrianna is an angel who, with one word, can melt my heart.

My mom, Ladonna Taylor, fulfills roles as mother, sister, friend, and motivational force. She has instilled me with such great reserves of strength, courage, perseverance, and ambition that I do not think I will exhaust them in this lifetime. My daughter and her future children and grandchildren will build on her legacy. Mom also made sure that I did not drift too far away from the people who matter most in my world, and she is one of them.

I must thank my amazingly precious daughter, Kaia Marie, who offers daily words of love and encouragement. She cheerfully serves as my live-in research assistant (often unpaid), file organizer, printer, library errand-girl, and proofreader. At times, it probably seemed to her that Peter H. Clark was a living, breathing man who occupied her mother's time and thoughts, had his papers and photos sprawled in eight of the nine rooms in our home, and traveled on vacations with us. She is not too resentful of the years he lived with us without doing any chores or paying any bills. Kaia ensured that the book never became hagiography by reminding me that "most people won't care about him like you do, Mom." Sometimes we all need reality checks from our teens. Still, I thank her for her patience, encouragement, flexibility, and unwavering faith and pride in me.

Notes

Introduction

Epigraph: *Cincinnati Commercial,* 23 September 1873.

1. *Dayton Evening Herald,* 22 September 1873.

2. Ibid.

3. According to Edward W. Said, the main "purpose of an intellectual's activity is to advance human freedom and knowledge" (Said, *Representations of the Intellectual* [New York: Vintage, 1994], 17, 22).

4. On the power of words to the black intelligentsia, see Cedric J. Robinson, *Black Marxism: The Making of the Black Radical Tradition* (Chapel Hill: University of North Carolina Press, 1983), 183.

5. Nell Painter defines a "leading colored man" as someone selected by whites to lead African Americans. Although these "leading colored men" represented "what whites thought Black people should think and be," Painter adds that they can hardly be considered African Americans' *real* leaders or spokespersons (Painter, *Exodusters: Black Migration to Kansas after Reconstruction* [New York: Norton, 1976], 26–29 passim). A "leading colored man" is the same as a "representative man." Joy James defines "race man" as someone "obligated to further emancipation projects" (James, *Transcending the Talented Tenth: Black Leaders and American Intellectuals* [New York: Routledge Press, 1997], 8). Clark's contemporary Dr. James McCune Smith, writing under the pseudonym "Communipaw" for *Frederick Douglass' Paper* and responding to Clark's editorial in *Herald of Freedom,* insisted that African Americans had no leaders. In his opinion, even the race leaders were not real leaders because they "never had the masses to support them, nor even to give an approving cheer or God's speed to their well meant efforts." Moreover, Smith was not hopeful that African Americans could *ever* have leaders, especially considering their "repulsion" for one another (*Frederick Douglass' Paper,* 21 September 1855).

6. For the bootlicking phrase, see Wendell Dabney, *Cincinnati's Colored Citizens: Historical, Sociological, and Biographical* (Cincinnati: Dabney, 1926), 114).

7. According to James, the quality of those projects was measured by "political courage and efficacy" (see James, *Transcending the Talented Tenth,* 8).

8. Ibid.

9. Historian Vincent Harding offers the most articulate explanation of the black radical tradition. He argues for a unified tradition that includes slave rebels and free black abolitionists (Harding, *There Is a River: The Black Struggle for Freedom in America* [San Diego: Harcourt Brace Jovanovich, 1981], 50–51). See also Robinson, *Black Marxism,* 73.

10. This comment is a reference to Ohio senator Thomas Corwin's controversial commentary in opposition to the Mexican War, a war that many abolitionists believed had been provoked by the U.S. government in order to seize territory for the expansion of slavery. Corwin said: "If I were a Mexican I would tell you, 'Have you not room in your own country to bury your dead men? If you come to mine, we will greet you with bloody hand[s], and welcome you to hospitable graves.'" On the role of violence in the black radical tradition, Robinson asserts that black revolutionary violence is committed by those who desired to "live on their own terms, die on their terms and obtain freedom on their terms" (Robinson, *Black Marxism,* 170).

11. Wilson Jeremiah Moses concludes that antebellum black nationalism actually was conservative. He argues that there was no clear-cut distinction between it and assimilation. Black chauvinists, he argues, hoped to "civilize" and Christianize the continent, while many integrationists defended all-black institutions at times. According to Moses, separate institutions and emigration, more often than not, were defense mechanisms and therefore disingenuous. Finally, according to him, black nationalism in that era also failed to challenge Western cultural values and racial stereotypes (see Moses, *The Golden Age of Black Nationalism, 1850–1925* [New York: Oxford University Press, 1978], 44–46). Although Clark's was a reactionary response to the 1850 Fugitive Slave Law and the intractability of racism, his attempts to realize it were radical. He was not motivated by an attempt to civilize, Westernize, or Christianize Africans when he formed an emigration society and made a genuine attempt to move to Africa. Moreover, he envisioned a sovereign black republic in Central America that had enough power to negotiate the release of enslaved African Americans. Finally, he was prepared to use revolutionary violence, if necessary.

12. Sterling Stuckey contends that David Walker had an anticapitalist critique, while Henry Highland Garnet developed "an economic interpretation of oppression," although neither was an admitted socialist (Stuckey, *Slave Culture: Nationalist Theory & the Foundations of Black America* [New York: Oxford University Press, 1987], 168–69).

13. Winston James, "Being Red and Black in Jim Crow America: On the Ideology and Travails of Afro-America's Socialist Pioneers, 1877–1930," in *Time Longer Than Rope: A Century of African American Activism, 1850–1950,* ed. Charles M. Payne and Adam Green (New York: New York University Press, 2003): 336–99.

14. See resolutions 17–19 of *Proceedings of the Convention of the Colored Freemen*

of Ohio, Held in Cincinnati January 14–18, 1852 (Cincinnati: Dumas and Lawyer, 1852), 7. For more on Kossuth, see Mischa Honeck, *German-Speaking Immigrants and American Abolitionists after 1848* (Athens: University of Georgia Press, 2011), 26–27.

15. *Cleveland Gazette,* 19 April 1884 and 19 June 1886.

16. Lawrence Grossman, "In His Veins Coursed No Bootlicking Blood: The Career of Peter Clark," *Ohio History* 86 (Spring 1977): 94.

17. Juan M. Floyd-Thomas defines black humanism as "a canon of philosophical, historical, and religious knowledge by, for, and about people of African descent with the ultimate goal of achieving social justice for all people." According to him, the "black humanist tradition invariably has one penultimate goal: the redemption and liberation of Black people and thereby all humanity" (Juan M. Floyd-Thomas, *The Origins of Black Humanism in America: Reverend Ethelred Brown and the Unitarian Church* [New York: Palgrave MacMillan, 2008], 172–73).

18. Darlene Clark Hine and Earnestine Jenkins, eds., *A Question of Manhood: A Reader in U.S. Black Men's History and Masculinity* (Bloomington: Indiana University Press, 1999), 31. Clark credited the AME church for celebrating African Americans' culture, demonstrating their capability to lead, and increasing their collective confidence. See his speech about the AME church in Rev. Benjamin Arnett, *Proceedings of the Semi-Centenary Celebration of the African Methodist Episcopal Church of Cincinnati* (Cincinnati: H. Watkin, 1874), 97–102.

19. David Gerber, "Peter Humphries Clark: The Dialogue of Hope and Despair," in *Black Leaders of the Nineteenth Century,* ed. Leon Litwack and August Meier (Urbana: University of Illinois Press, 1988), 174; Grossman, "In His Veins Coursed No Bootlicking Blood," 79.

20. Wilson Jeremiah Moses, *Creative Conflict in African American Thought: Frederick Douglass, Alexander Crummell, Booker T. Washington, W. E. B. Du Bois, and Marcus Garvey* (New York: Cambridge University Press, 2004), 15.

21. Ibid., 6; Louis Harlan, ed., *The Booker T. Washington Papers* (Urbana: University of Illinois Press, 1972), 2:118–19.

22. For more on O'Hara, see Eric Anderson, "James O'Hara of North Carolina: Black Leadership and Local Government," in *Southern Black Leaders of the Reconstruction Era,* ed. Howard N. Rabinowitz (Urbana: University of Illinois Press, 1982): 101–25 passim; and August Meier, "Afterword: New Perspectives on the Nature of Black Political Leadership during Reconstruction," in *Southern Black Leaders of the Reconstruction Era,* ed. Rabinowitz, 401.

23. Jeffrey P. Perry, ed., *A Hubert Harrison Reader* (Middletown, CT: Wesleyan University Press, 2001), 14; Jeffrey P. Perry, *Hubert Harrison: The Voice of Harlem Radicalism, 1883–1918* (New York: Columbia University Press, 2009), 269; David Levering Lewis, *W. E. B. Du Bois: The Fight for Equality and the American Century, 1919–1963* (New York: Owl Books, 2000), 28, 241; Moses, *Creative Conflict in African American Thought,* 6, 11. George Edwin Taylor ran for president on the

National Liberty Party ticket in 1904 against Theodore Roosevelt. See his biography in Bruce L. Mouser, *For Labor, Race, and Liberty: George Edwin Taylor, His Historic Run for the White House, and the Making of Independent Black Politics* (Madison: University of Wisconsin Press, 2011).

24. Other nineteenth-century African American socialists include George Mack, Frank J. Ferrell, and Charles G. Baylor. See Philip S. Foner, *American Socialism and Black Americans: From the Age of Jackson to World War II* (Westport, CT: Greenwood Press, 1977), 58, 64, 73.

25. Gerber, "Peter Humphries Clark: The Dialogue of Hope and Despair," 174. Moses is right when he asserts that uncovering these philosophical contradictions is not nearly as stimulating as trying to understand how people reconciled them (see Moses, *Creative Conflict in African American Thought*, 6). For other biographies, see Dovie King Clark, "Peter Humphries Clark," *Negro History Bulletin* 5 (May 1942); Wilhemena S. Robinson, "Peter H. Clark," in *Historical Negro Biographies* (New York: Association for the Study of Negro Life and History, 1969); Paul McStallsworth, "Peter Humphries Clark," in *Dictionary of American Negro Biography*, ed. Rayford W. Logan and Michael R. Winston (New York: Norton, 1982); Herbert Gutman, "Peter H. Clark: Pioneer Negro Socialist, 1877," *Journal of Negro Education* 34 (September 1965); Philip S. Foner, "Peter H. Clark: Pioneer Black Socialist," *Journal of Ethnic Studies* 5, no. 3 (Fall 1977); David Gerber, "Peter Humphries Clark: The Dialogue of Hope and Despair," in *Black Leaders of the Nineteenth Century*, ed. Leon Litwack and August Meier (Urbana: University of Illinois Press, 1988); and Lawrence Christensen, "Peter Humphries Clark," *Missouri Historical Review* 88, no. 2 (January 1994).

26. *Indianapolis Freeman*, 20 September 1890; also quoted in John Hope Franklin, *George Washington Williams: A Biography* (Chicago: University of Chicago Press, 1985), 234. The poll was sent to the *Freeman*'s 8,000 subscribers. The paper's full list of ten winners consisted of: Frederick Douglass, Blanche K. Bruce, Peter H. Clark, Toussaint L'Ouverture, Daniel Payne, Joseph C. Price, James Milton Turner, George Washington Williams, Timothy Thomas Fortune, and Edward E. Cooper. Although the *Freeman* reports that Clark made the list of ten, historian Gregory Bond's careful analysis of the results prove otherwise. See "Jim Crow at Play: Race, Manliness, and the Color Line in American Sports, 1876–1916" (Ph.D. diss., University of Wisconsin-Madison, 2008), 156.

27. Moses, *Creative Conflict in African American Thought*, 21, 31, 55.

28. Ibid., 56.

29. Peter H. Clark, "Emancipation Day Speech," delivered at Emancipation Day Celebration, Dayton, Ohio, 22 September 1873. Reprinted in *Cincinnati Commercial*, 23 September 1873.

30. Historian August Meier acknowledged this benefit to writing biographies of local politicians thirty years ago in "Afterword: New Perspectives on the Nature

of Black Political Leadership during Reconstruction," in *Southern Black Leaders of the Reconstruction Era*, 403.

31. Moses, *Creative Conflict in African American Thought*, 18.

1. Launching a Life

Epigraph: *Cincinnati Commercial*, 23 September 1873.

1. *Western Star* (Lebanon, Ohio), 29 August 1829, quoting the *Cincinnati Sentinel*.

2. *Western Times* (Portsmouth, Ohio), 22 August 1829.

3. Patrick A. Folk, "'The Queen City of Mobs': Riots and Community Reactions in Cincinnati, 1788–1848" (Ph.D. *diss.*, University of Toledo, 1978), 55.

4. According to the 1829 city directory, there were 2,258 blacks in the city. A year later, in the 1830 census, there were only 1,090 African Americans in the city, suggesting that at least 1,100 left (see United States Census for 1830: Ohio, Hamilton County; and Robinson and Fairbank, *The Cincinnati Directory for the Year 1829*. See also *Annual Advertiser* (Cincinnati: Whetstone and Buxton, 1829). We would be remiss to ignore the fact that between 1820 and 1829, there was a 15 percent per annum increase in the black population. If the black population had been allowed to increase at that rate without molestation, the 1829 population of 2,258 would have naturally grown to 2,597 by 1830. Instead, there were only 1,090 blacks in the 1830 census. The difference would suggest that 1,507 African Americans were forced to leave the city. This is the best way to ascertain the low and high numbers of population flux after the forced migration. These numbers may be grossly underestimated considering the number of fugitive slaves in Cincinnati who did not allow themselves to be enumerated in the city directory or census. In addition, those who compiled the city directories admitted to undercounting many blacks because of living situations that made it difficult to do an accurate count. It is also possible that many of the families who left the city in 1829 only left temporarily and returned to be counted in the census the next year.

5. Robinson and Fairbank, *Cincinnati Directory for the Year 1829*, 155. These numbers grossly underestimate the number of fugitive slaves residing in the city. Fugitive slaves would have been unwilling to allow themselves to be enumerated by either census takers or city directory compilers. Even free blacks who housed fugitive slaves would have underreported the number of people in their households, making it difficult to provide a more accurate number of blacks in Cincinnati in these years.

6. The city directories record 690 African Americans in 1826 and 2,258 in 1829 (B. Drake and E. D. Mansfield, *Cincinnati in 1826* [Cincinnati: Morgan, Lodge, and Fisher, 1827]; Robinson and Fairbank, *Cincinnati Directory for the Year 1829*, 155).

7. Robinson and Fairbank, *Cincinnati Directory for the Year 1829*, 155.

8. Nikki Taylor, *Frontiers of Freedom: Cincinnati's Black Community 1802–1868* (Athens: Ohio University Press, 2005), 50–58, 63–64.

9. Ibid., 32–34.

10. Ibid., 46.

11. Peter H. Clark, "Biographical Sketch of Peter H. Clark," n.d., William C. Breckenridge Papers, Western Historical Manuscript Collection, Columbia, Missouri.

12. Eugenia G. Glazebrook and Preston G. Glazebrook, *Virginia Migrations, Hanover County: 1723–1850* (Baltimore: Genealogical Publishing, 2000), 23–26; *Donald Scott & Co. v. Clarke Admir.,* in Federal Records, Unrestored, U.S. Circuit Court Box 65 (November 1805); *John Murdoch and Co. v. Admir.,* in Federal Records, Unrestored, U.S. Circuit Court Box 7 (November 1807); Fayette County Tax List for 1797; Harrison County Tax List for 1799; Henrico County Deeds 1750–1767: 111–12; Harrison County Clerk Wills, 1795–1832: 245; Harrison County Tax List, 1799, 1800, 1809; *The Third Census of the United States, 1810* (New York: Norman Ross, 1990).

13. Will of John Clarke, Harrison County, KY Will Book A, 245; William S. Clarke, Manumission of Elliott, 22 May 1815, Harrison County, KY Deed Book 4, 346. Peter Clark claimed that all five of Betty's children were fathered by John Clarke (see Peter H. Clark, "Biographical Sketch of Peter H. Clark," n.d., William C. Breckenridge Papers, Western Historical Manuscript Collection, Columbia, Missouri).

14. One reason he may not have freed them during his life was because Kentucky laws made it difficult to do so. Kentucky counties could require former owners to post bond to ensure that their freedpeople did not become indigent (see Robert M. Ireland, *The County Courts in Antebellum Kentucky* [Lexington: University Press of Kentucky, 1972], 30).

15. Will of John Clarke, Harrison County, KY Will Book A, 245. The will indicates that the deeds for Betty, Eliza, Michael, and Evelina were placed in the hands of Benjamin Mills. Peter Clark indicated that the deeds were taken to the Hamilton County Courthouse, which burned down at least twice in the nineteenth century ("Biographical Sketch of Peter H. Clark").

16. William S. Clarke, Manumission of Elliott, 22 May 1815, Harrison County, KY Deed Book 4, 346.

17. *New York Freeman,* 3 January 1885. Michael Clark does not appear in any Cincinnati records, including the census or city directory, until the 1830s.

18. For biographical details of Elizabeth, see *Cleveland Gazette,* 6 March 1866; *New York Freeman,* 3 January 1885; Restored Hamilton County, Ohio Marriages 1808–1949; and Clerk of the Court of Common Pleas of Hamilton County, Ohio, 16 December 1819.

19. Cincinnati Colored Public Schools, *Tenth Annual Report of the Board of Trustees for the Colored Schools of Cincinnati, for the Year Ending June 30, 1859* (Cincinnati: Wrightson, 1859), 9.

20. *Cincinnati Daily Gazette,* 23 October 1832.

21. Harrison County Circuit Court, Bundle 4653, *Free Betty v. Clarke,* filed 28 February 1829; Harrison County Order Book, March 1829, 11 March 1829.

22. Harrison County Circuit Court, Bundle 4653, *Free Betty v. Clarke,* filed 28 February 1829; Harrison County Order Book, March 1829, 11 March 1829.

23. *Robinson & Jones' Cincinnati Directory for 1846;* Benjamin W. Arnett, *Proceedings of the Semi-Centenary Celebration of the African Methodist Episcopal Church of Cincinnati, Held in Allen Temple February 8th, 9th, and 10th, 1874* (Cincinnati: H. Watkins, 1874), 64; Wendell P. Dabney, *Cincinnati's Colored Citizens: Historical, Sociological and Biographical* (Cincinnati: Dabney, 1926), 129; John Mercer Langston, *From the Virginia Plantation to the National Capitol or The First and Only Representative in Congress from the Old Dominion* (Hartford, CT: American, 1894), 60–61. More biographical details on Woodson can be found in William Cheek and Aimee Lee Cheek, *John Mercer Langston and the Fight for Black Freedom 1829–65* (Urbana: University of Illinois Press, 1989), 53, 58; and Taylor, *Frontiers of Freedom,* 132–33.

24. On Harbeson's role in the Allen Chapel AME church, see Arnett, *Proceedings of the Semi-Centenary,* 20, 22, 25, 30, 56. On the couple's role in the Colored Orphan Asylum, see ibid., 130.

25. For example, after a cabinet shop hired an African American cabinetmaker in 1835, white journeymen threw down their tools and vowed to "never work with a Nigger" (Ohio Anti-Slavery Society, *Report on the Condition of the People of Color in the State of Ohio* [Putnam: Beaumont and Wallace, 1835], 3; Taylor, *Frontiers of Freedom,* 100–101).

26. *New York Freeman,* 3 January 1885; William J. Simmons, *Men of Mark: Eminent, Progressive and Rising* (Cleveland: George M. Rewell, 1887), 374; Henry D. Shaffer, *The Cincinnati, Covington, Newport, and Fulton Directory for 1840* (Cincinnati: Donogh, 1840), 469; Charles Cist, *Cincinnati Directory for the Year 1842* (Cincinnati: E. Morgan, 1842), 441; *Robinson and Jones' Cincinnati Directory for 1846.*

27. *New York Freeman,* 3 January 1885.

28. Ernestine Garrett Lucas, "Wider Windows to the Past: African-American History from a Family Perspective" (Decorah, IA: Anundsen Printing, 1995), 96; "Wives of Distinguished Churchmen Laid to Rest," *Pittsburgh Courier,* 31 March 1934; United States Census Bureau, *The Seventh Census of the United States 1850* (Washington: Robert Armstrong, 1853); Jefferson County Marriages, Book II.

29. Henry D. Shaffer, *The Cincinnati, Covington, Newport, and Fulton Directory for 1840* (Cincinnati: Donogh, 1840), 469.

30. Arnett, *Proceedings of the Semi-Centenary Celebration,* 129; Taylor, *Frontiers of Freedom,* 128, 265n.

31. *Robinson & Jones' Cincinnati Directory for 1846* (Cincinnati: Robinson and Jones, 1846), 190; *Cincinnati Directory and Business Advertiser for 1850–51* (Cincinnati: C. S. Williams, 1851), 122; Hamilton County Recorder, Series 1, Book 12: 368; Hamilton County Deed Book, R-2, p. 17; United States Census Bureau,

The Fifth Census of the United States for 1830 Hamilton County (Washington: Duff Green, 1832).

32. "A Threatening Letter from Kentucky," quoted in David Grimsted, *American Mobbing 1828–1861: Toward Civil War* (New York: Oxford University Press, 1998), 59.

33. Reprinted in *Philanthropist*, 8 January 1836.

34. Ohio Anti-Slavery Society, *Narrative of the Late Riotous Proceeding against the Liberty of the Press in Cincinnati with Remarks and Historical Notices Relating to Emancipation* (Cincinnati: Ohio Anti-Slavery Society, 1836), 13.

35. *Philanthropist*, 15 July 1836.

36. Ohio Anti-Slavery Society, *Narrative of the Late Riotous Proceeding against the Liberty of the Press,* 39–40; Grimsted, *American Mobbing 1828–1861,* 61.

37. Taylor, *Frontiers of Freedom,* 120–25 passim.

38. *Cincinnati Daily Enquirer,* 2 September 1841.

39. *Cincinnati Daily Gazette,* 6 September 1841.

40. Ibid.

41. Langston, *From the Virginia Plantation to the National Capitol,* 65.

42. *Dayton Evening Herald,* 22 September 1873.

43. Langston, *From the Virginia Plantation to the National Capitol,* 11, 59, 61; Cheek and Cheek, *John Mercer Langston and the Fight for Black Freedom,* 14, 17–22 passim.

44. Langston, *From the Virginia Plantation to the National Capitol,* 73–4; Cheek and Cheek, *John Mercer Langston and the Fight for Black Freedom,* 68.

45. Peter H. Clark to Carrie Langston, 11 December 1897, John Mercer Langston Collection, Fisk University Archives, Nashville, Tennessee.

46. *Cincinnati Commercial,* 31 March 1867; Cincinnati Colored Public Schools, *Eighth Annual Report of the Board of Trustee for the Colored Public Schools of Cincinnati, for the School Year Ending June 30, 1857* (Cincinnati: Moore, Wilstach, Keys, 1857), 10.

47. "Biographical Sketch of Peter H. Clark"; *Weekly Herald and Philanthropist,* 26 June 1844; *Philanthropist,* 22 September 1841; Samuel Matthews, "John Isom Gaines: The Architect of Black Public Education," *Queen City Heritage* (Spring 1987): 44.

48. *Cincinnati Weekly Herald and Philanthropist,* 26 June 1844; John Wattles, *Annual Report of the Educational Condition of the Colored People of Cincinnati* (Cincinnati: n.p., 1847), 8.

49. *Cincinnati Weekly Herald and Philanthropist,* 9 August 1844, 26 March and 11 June 1845.

50. Martin Delany visited Cincinnati High School in 1848 and wrote about the school in the 9 June 1848 issue of the *North Star.* Deeply critical of the school,

he concluded it was "far from being a good school." He reported that most of the students had learned "comparatively nothing" and "know but little about those branches of education [sciences]." Moreover, he added that most of them "write as though there was no such letter as capital I." Delany concluded that teachers spent too much time preparing the students for exhibitions and not enough time on the lessons. What is interesting is that this editorial was penned during Clark's final year at the institution. But this review is overly critical. By all other accounts, Cincinnati High was every bit as effective as others claimed.

51. *Weekly Herald and Philanthropist,* 26 June and 9 August 1844.

52. Arnett, *Proceedings of the Semi-Centenary Celebration,* 63; *New York Times,* 15 March 1875; John B. Shotwell, *A History of the Schools of Cincinnati* (Cincinnati: School Life, 1902), 453, 455; Carter G. Woodson, *The Education of the Negro Prior to 1861* (New York: Putnam, 1915), 124–29; Wattles, *Annual Report of the Educational Condition of the Colored People of Cincinnati,* 8; Matthews, "John Isom Gaines: The Architect of Black Public Education," 44; Taylor, *Frontiers of Freedom,* 162–63.

53. *New York Freeman,* 3 January 1885; *Cleveland Gazette,* 6 March 1886; *Cleveland Gazette,* 3 September 1887; Simmons, *Men of Mark,* 374.

54. Robert Owen first proposed the formation of cooperative communities whereby all members would work together to secure their collective needs and would equally benefit from the fruits of that labor. But these communities were more than a mere concept for him; Owen landed in New Harmony, Indiana, in 1825 to launch such a community. Although New Harmony failed within a year or so, Owen's communitarian vision lived on through the hearts and minds of his followers, who were popularly referred to as Owenites. A second wave of utopian socialist communities was inspired by the writings and ideas of the French national Charles Fourier. New Yorker Albert Brisbane learned about Fourier's ideology while traveling in Europe in the early 1840s. He imported the ideology to America after his return, enthusiastically educating others about Fourier's concepts through lectures and editorials, even writing his own book, *The Social Destiny of Man.* Hence, he popularized the idea among Americans, which gave birth to the second wave of socialism in America after 1842 (see Edwin Charles Rozwenc, *Cooperatives Come to America: The History of the Protective Union Store Movement, 1845–1867* [Philadelphia: Porcupine Press, 1975], 1–7 passim). Although the Owenite and Fourier movements had critical differences, their commonalities made them a national movement.

55. On the differences between communism and joint-stock principles, see John Humphrey Noyes, *History of American Socialisms* (New York: Dover, 1966), 194–99. Noyes breaks down these terms to the simplest ideas. "Every family," he writes, "is a little example of Communism; and every working partnership is an example of Joint-Stockism. Communism creates homes; Joint-stockism manages business." For more on Fourierism, see Carl J. Guarneri, *The Utopian Alternative: Fourierism in Nineteenth-Century America* (Ithaca: Cornell University Press, 1994), 2–3.

56. *Circular,* 24 May 1869; Noyes, *History of American Socialisms,* 316, 366, 377.

57. On the mysticism of the Universal Brotherhood, see *National Era,* 27 April 1848; and *Herald of Truth, A Monthly Periodical, Devoted to the Interests of Religion,* 1 February 1847.

58. The organization has been alternately called the Cincinnati Brotherhood, True Brotherhood, and Universal Brotherhood in primary sources. For information on the organization, see *Miscellany,* 14 December 1846; *Univercœlum and Spiritual Philosopher,* 21 October 1848; and *Harbinger,* 2 October 1847 and 22 January 1848.

59. Guarneri, *Utopian Alternative,* 69.

60. Carl J. Guarneri, "Brook Farm and the Fourierist Phalanxes: Immediatism, Gradualism, and American Utopian Socialism," in *America's Communal Utopias,* ed. Donald E. Pitzer (Chapel Hill: University of North Carolina Press, 1997), 161.

61. *Cincinnati Daily Commercial,* 22 December 1847; *National Era,* 30 December 1847.

62. *Cincinnati Daily Commercial,* 22 December 1847; *National Era,* 30 December 1847.

63. Louis H. Everts, *History of Clermont County, Ohio, with Illustrations and Biographical Sketches of Its Prominent Men and Pioneers* (Philadelphia: Lippincott, 1880), 343.

64. *Cincinnati Daily Commercial,* 22 December 1847; *National Era,* 30 December 1847; Everts, *History of Clermont County, Ohio,* 343.

65. Everts, *History of Clermont County, Ohio,* 344.

66. *Univercœlum and Spiritual Philosopher,* 21 October 1848.

67. There are only a few clues about where he went after that, but according to John I. Gaines, he moved from place to place, seeking "a more perfect state of society"—an obvious reference to his quest to find or found a successful utopian socialist scheme. Cincinnati Colored Public Schools, *Eighth Annual Report of the Board of Trustee for the Colored Public Schools of Cincinnati, for the School Year Ending June 30, 1857* (Cincinnati: Moore, Wilstach, Keys, 1857), 11.

68. *Christian Recorder,* 17 July 1873. Regardless, even a high school education in that era meant that Clark still ranked among the African American elite.

69. *New York Freeman,* 3 January 1885; Simmons, *Men of Mark,* 374.

70. Taylor, *Frontiers of Freedom,* 133–34.

71. In 1845, tuition at Cincinnati High was between three and seven dollars, depending on the course of study. Board was one to two dollars per week (see *Cincinnati Weekly Herald and Philanthropist,* 26 March 1845).

72. Stereotyping is a type of printing that is radically faster than the old way of making words and sentences from individual, movable letters. Stereotyping creates a mold of the entire page of text, significantly decreasing the time involved in the regular printing process and enabling mass production of books or newspapers.

73. Mark Lause, *Young America: Land, Labor, and the Republican Community*

(Urbana: University of Illinois Press, 2005), 3, 30, 80, 116, 160. Land reformers advocated a prohibition on farm foreclosures. They also championed a radical redistribution of land by settling landless people on public lands and limiting the amount of land an individual could own.

74. Consumers could deposit goods and were able to "purchase" others through labor notes that equaled the time they had invested in their products. For details on how the prices of goods in this store were determined by labor-time, see Rozwenc, *Cooperatives Come to America,* 9. On Warren, see Guarneri, *The Utopian Alternative,* 359, 364; and Noyes, *History of American Socialisms,* 94–97. On the Varneys' relationship with Warren, see Lause, *Young America,* 81, 202 n. 23.

75. For more on NRA activities, see Lause, *Young America,* chap, 8. On Masquerier, see ibid., 73, 81; and John Pickering, *Working Man's Political Economy, Founded upon the Principle of Immutable Justice and the Inalienable Rights of Man* (Cincinnati: Thomas Varney, 1847). For Maria L. Varney's articles, see *Herald of Truth, A Monthly Periodical, Devoted to the Interests of Religion, Philosophy, Literature, Science, and Art* (Cincinnati: John White, Printer, 1847), 81–87, 231–37; and William H. Venable, *Beginnings of Literary Culture Ohio Valley: Historical and Biographical Sketches* (Cincinnati: Robert Clarke, 1891), 95. Horace Greeley allowed Albert Brisbane—the primary propagator of Fourierist ideology in America—space to write editorials in the *Tribune.* For that relationship, see Rozwenc, *Cooperatives Come to America,* 7. On the Varneys, see Simmons, *Men of Mark,* 374–75; Lause, *Young America,* 81, 202 n. 23; and *New York Freeman,* 3 January 1885.

76. *New York Freeman,* 3 January 1885; Simmons, *Men of Mark,* 374.

77. Ibid.

78. The couple left Cincinnati in February 1849, judging from Thomas's travel diary. He traveled alone and took a circuitous route down the Ohio and Mississippi Rivers to Panama and then on to California. Maria went back East to spend some time with her mother. During that time, she got involved in the women's rights movement. She joined Thomas three years later in San Francisco. For the next few decades, Thomas spent his time inventing and conducting experiments in explosives, while Maria continued to write and became a clubwoman (Thomas and Maria L. Varney Papers, California Historical Society).

79. *New York Freeman,* 3 January 1885; *Cleveland Gazette,* 3 September 1887; Simmons, *Men of Mark,* 374–75.

80. When Michael Clark passed away in 1849, his wife, Eliza, inherited fifteen thousand dollars' worth of property, making her one of the wealthiest African American women in Cincinnati (Taylor, *Frontiers of Freedom,* 133, 134; United States Census Bureau, *The Seventh Census of the United States 1850* [Washington: Robert Armstrong, 1853]; Last Will and Testament of Michael Clark, in Hamilton County Will Book, 5).

81. Simmons, *Men of Mark,* 375; *New York Freeman,* 3 January 1885.

82. *New York Freeman,* 3 January 1885; *Cleveland Gazette,* 6 March 1886 and

3 September 1887; Simmons, *Men of Mark,* 375. Unfortunately, historian Mischa Honeck has mischaracterized this exchange, ignoring the sexual implications. Honeck asserts that the argument between Clark and this customer stemmed from "Clark's policy of providing equal service," which is incorrect (Honeck, *German-Speaking Immigrants and American Abolitionists after 1848* [Athens: University of Georgia Press, 2011], 90).

83. Matthews, "John Isom Gaines: The Architect of Black Public Education," 44.

84. *New York Freeman,* 3 January 1885; *Cleveland Gazette,* 6 March 1886 and 3 September 1887.

85. More than likely, Clark penned the biography of Gaines included in William Wells Brown, *The Rising Son; or The Antecedents and Advancement of the Colored Race* (Boston: A. G. Brown, 1876), 450–52. *Liberator,* 27 April 1860; Matthews, "John Isom Gaines: The Architect of Black Public Education," 41–42.

2. Voice of Emigration

Epigraph: *Voice of the Fugitive,* 12 February 1852.

1. *Minutes and Address of the State Convention of the Colored Citizens of Ohio, Convened at Columbus on January 10, 11, 12th and 13th, 1849* (Oberlin: J. M. Fitch's Power Press, 1849), 8.

2. Benedict Anderson, *Imagined Communities: Reflections on the Origin and Spread of Nationalism* (London: Verso, 1983), 28; Geoff Eley and Ronald Grigor Suny, *Becoming National: A Reader* (Oxford: Oxford University Press, 1996), 8; Patrick Rael, *Black Identity & Black Protest in the Antebellum North* (Chapel Hill: University of North Carolina Press, 2002), 213, 235.

3. He asserts that many black nationalists also had internalized notions about the degradation and inferiority of African and African American culture. Such an assertion explains why they were preoccupied with privileging white American values and transmitting them to the black community in the name of "uplift." For a fuller discussion of the characteristics of black nationalism before the Civil War, see Wilson Jeremiah Moses, *The Golden Age of Black Nationalism, 1850–1925* (New York: Oxford University Press, 1978), 10–11, 45–47.

4. George A. Levesque, "Interpreting Early Black Ideology: A Reappraisal of Historical Consensus," in *African-American Activism before the Civil War: The Freedom Struggle in the Antebellum North,* ed. Patrick Rael (New York: Routledge, 2008), 123; Moses, *Golden Age of Black Nationalism,* 33, 45–46.

5. Constitution of the American Society of Free Persons of Colour . . . Also the Proceedings of the Convention with Their Address, in *Minutes of the Proceedings of the National Negro Conventions 1830–1864,* ed. Howard Holman Bell (New York: Arno Press, 1969), 9.

6. Minutes and Proceedings of the First Annual Convention of the People of Colour, in *Minutes of the Proceedings of the National Negro Conventions*

1830–1864, ed. Howard Holman Bell (New York: Arno Press, 1969), 5–6. African American leaders first met on 20–24 September 1830 in Philadelphia to discuss emigration and the general condition of the race. The American Society of Free Persons of Colour was born from that meeting, with Richard Allen as president and Austin Steward and Dr. Belfast Burton as vice presidents. The following year, leaders attended the First Annual Convention of the Free People of Colour, held 6–11 June 1831 also in Philadelphia. Its president was John Bowers, and the vice presidents were Abraham D. Shad and William Duncan. This time the convention focused on racial uplift and improving the condition of the race, instead of emigration. Education was one of its main focuses, along with temperance and moral reform.

7. James Oliver Horton and Lois E. Horton, *In Hope of Liberty: Culture, Community and Protest among Northern Free Blacks 1700–1860* (New York: Oxford University Press, 1997), 208. After 1835, the conventions were suspended due to low attendance.

8. August Meier, *Negro Thought in America 1880–1915: Racial Ideologies in the Age of Booker T. Washington* (Ann Arbor: University of Michigan Press, 1963), 4.

9. William Cheek and Aimee Lee Cheek, *John Mercer Langston and the Fight for Black Freedom 1829–65* (Urbana: University of Illinois Press, 1989), 133–34; Peter H. Clark to John W. Cromwell, 21 December 1901, in *The Negro in American History: Men and Women Eminent in the Evolution of the American of African Descent,* ed. John W. Cromwell (Washington, D.C.: American Negro Academy, 1914), 37.

10. David Gerber, *Black Ohio and the Color Line, 1860–1915* (Urbana: University of Illinois Press, 1976), 22; William F. Cheek, "John Mercer Langston: Black Protest Leader and Abolitionist," in *Blacks in the Abolitionist Movement,* ed. John H. Bracey Jr., August Meier, and Elliott Rudwick (Belmont, CA: Wadsworth, 1971), 26.

11. *Minutes and Address of the State Convention of the Colored Citizens of Ohio, Convened at Columbus, January 10–13, 1849,* 18.

12. Thomas D. Morris, *Free Men All: The Personal Liberty Laws of the North* (Baltimore: Johns Hopkins University Press, 1974), 130–47 passim.

13. Nikki Taylor, *Frontiers of Freedom: Cincinnati's Black Community 1802–68* (Athens: Ohio University Press, 2005), 154–55.

14. The African American emigrationist tradition in the United States dates as far back as the Revolutionary era, when the first emigrationist societies were formed. Early black emigrationists were motivated by the belief that racial oppression precluded the possibility of enjoying freedom or equality in the United States. Only by returning to Africa could African Americans be free from racism and have control over their own lives and destinies. Those who supported emigration to Africa also believed that African Americans would help "civilize" and Christianize Africa.

The African Union Society of Newport, Rhode Island, established in 1780, was the first to actively formalize plans to establish a settlement of African Americans in Africa. In 1787, seventy-five black Bostonians took steps to realize their desire for emigration when they petitioned the Massachusetts General Court for assistance in helping them relocate to Africa. The Providence, Rhode Island, African Union Society even sent agents to Sierra Leone to survey land for the colony. That same society also attempted to nationalize the emigration movement by communicating with groups in Newport, Rhode Island, and Philadelphia and inviting them to assist in the efforts. Unfortunately, these plans were hindered by the inability to locate and secure land in Africa and to win popular support among African Americans (see Floyd J. Miller, *The Search for a Black Nationality: Black Emigration and Colonization 1787–1863* [Urbana: University of Illinois Press, 1975], 3–20 passim).

15. Rael, *Black Identity & Black Protest in the Antebellum North,* 213; Richard Bardolph, *The Negro Vanguard* (New York: Rinehart, 1959), 42.

16. The State Convention of the Colored Citizens of Ohio, which had resolved in 1849 to "never submit to the system of Colonization to any part of the world, in or out of the United States … to those soliciting us … their appeals to us are in vain," changed its position the following year (*Minutes and Address of the State Convention of the Colored Citizens of Ohio, Convened at Columbus, January 10–13, 1849,* 17).

17. Taylor, *Frontiers of Freedom,* chap. 3 passim; "Movement among the Colored People of Cincinnati," *African Repository* 26 (July 1850): 219, in *Black Nationalism in America,* ed. John H. Bracey Jr., August Meier, and Elliott Rudwick (Indianapolis: Bobbs-Merrill, 1970), 85–86.

18. Peter H. Clark to the American Colonization Society, 17 September 1850, in "Letters to the American Colonization Society," *Journal of Negro History* 10 (April 1925): 285–86; Cheek and Cheek, *John Mercer Langston and the Fight for Black Freedom 1829–65,* 173.

19. The specifics of what was discussed are unknown (*Cincinnati Daily Enquirer,* 22 November 1850; *African Repository* 27 [January 1851]:21).

20. "Movement among the Colored People of Cincinnati," in *Black Nationalism in America,* ed. Bracey, 86; *African Repository* (March 1851): 72.

21. The Will of Charles McMicken of Cincinnati, Ohio, 1858, University of Cincinnati; *Memorial of the Ohio Committee of the American Colonization Society to the Senate and Ohio House of Representatives of the State of Ohio,* 8 January 1851, Ohio Historical Society, Columbus; *Cincinnati Daily Enquirer,* 22 November 1850.

22. The ACS had been established in 1816 to settle freed African Americans in Liberia, a colony it established in Africa. Its founding members included Henry Clay, Andrew Jackson, Daniel Webster, and scores of other influential and powerful men. Those who joined the ACS had a variety of motives: some were opposed to slavery yet empathized with slaveholders who feared that the presence of freed

slaves would make slavery more unstable. These antislavery ACS members hoped slaveholders would be motivated to emancipate their bondspeople and send them to Liberia. Other whites joined the organization because they believed African Americans would never receive equality or rights in a racist America. For them, settlement in Africa seemed to be the only option. Ministers and other Christians joined the ACS because they supported the idea of an American Christian outpost in Africa. In their vision, African Americans would lead the effort to Christianize a "savage" Africa. The ACS also had a significant share of slaveholders as members. These members hoped that removing free African Americans would make slavery more secure. They reasoned that presence of free blacks planted notions of freedom in the minds of enslaved people, making them more eager to secure it for themselves. Still others who joined the ACS were ardent racists who hoped colonization would ultimately rid America of its African American population (see *African Repository,* October 1832, passim; and Horton and Horton, *In Hope of Liberty,* 187).

23. In Philadelphia, more than three thousand African Americans met at Bethel AME Church in 1817 to draw up a resolution denouncing the American Colonization Society. As third- and fourth-generation Americans—some of whom had served in the American Revolution and the War of 1812—these Philadelphians believed they had earned their right to call the United States home. They felt as American as members of the ACS and resented efforts to banish them to far-off lands. This community also distrusted the motives of the ACS, believing that it was "a deportation society whose members believed in both black inferiority and in the necessity of ridding the country of its free black population in order to preserve the institution of slavery." Other African American communities also denounced the organization. As many as two-thirds of African Americans living in Baltimore in 1826 opposed the ACS (see Horton and Horton, *In Hope of Liberty,* 188; Miller, *The Search for a Black Nationality,* 54; and Christopher Phillips, *Freedom's Port: The African American Community of Baltimore, 1790–1860* [Urbana: University of Illinois Press, 1997], 214).

24. In March 1839, the African American community met at the New Chapel (formerly Deer Creek Methodist Episcopal) to protest white efforts to revive the Ohio chapter of the American Colonization Society (ACS). The community raised its voice in "unmitigated and unqualified opposition" to this organization. A resolution adopted at this meeting and published in the 5 March 1839 issue of the *Philanthropist* charged the ACS with being "unjust," "unchristian," "anti-republican" and "unworthy [of] the patronage of Christian and republican people." The notice charged that the ACS not only "fosters and sustains that prejudice, which they now declare to be invincible, by stigmatizing us as a worthless and inferior race," but "apologizes for the sin of slavery, and thereby so far as its influence operates, tends to the perpetuity of that accursed system." The notice also asserted that free African Americans would not "consent to become an instrument of slaveholders, and their

co-adjutor [*sic*], the American Colonization Society, to fasten more permanently upon the necks of our brethren, the galling yoke of bondage" (*Philanthropist*, 5 March 1839; see also Taylor, *Frontiers of Freedom*, 115–16).

25. Eric Burin, *Slavery and the Peculiar Solution: A History of the American Colonization Society* (Gainesville: University Press of Florida, 2005), 17.

26. Leon Litwack, *North of Slavery: The Free Negro in the Free States 1790–1860* (Chicago: University of Chicago Press, 1961), 29; Ira Berlin, *Slaves without Masters: The Free Negro in the Antebellum South* (New York: Vintage, 1974), 355; Burin, *Slavery and the Peculiar Solution*, 29.

27. Martin R. Delany, *The Condition, Elevation, Emigration, and Destiny of the Colored People of the United States Politically Considered* (New York: Arno Press, 1968), 169–70; Taylor, *Frontiers of Freedom*, 59.

28. On black nationalism, see Tunde Adeleke, *UnAfrican Americans: Nineteenth-Century Black Nationalists and the Civilizing Mission* (Lexington: University Press of Kentucky, 1998), 1, 8.

29. V. P. Franklin, *Black Self-Determination: A Cultural History of the Faith of the Fathers* (New York: Lawrence Hill, 1992), 87; Jane H. Pease and William H. Pease, *They Who Would Be Free: Blacks' Search for Freedom, 1830–1861* (Urbana: University of Illinois Press, 1990), 261.

30. Moses warns us that the "distinction between colonization and emigration was not as clear as the emigrationists would have liked it to appear" (Moses, *Golden Age of Black Nationalism*, 45).

31. Peter H. Clark, "Biographical Sketch of Peter H. Clark," n.d., Breckenridge Papers, Western Historical Manuscript Collection, Columbia, Missouri; *Cincinnati Daily Enquirer*, 22 November 1850; *African Repository* 27 (January 1851): 21; *Cincinnati Daily Commercial*, 11 February 1851; *African Repository* (March 1851): 152.

32. Moses, *Golden Age of Black Nationalism*, 35–36.

33. *Daily Times*, 16 January 1851.

34. *African Repository* (March 1851): 104–5.

35. Peter H. Clark, "Biographical Sketch of Peter H. Clark," n.d., Breckenridge Papers, Western Historical Manuscript Collection, Columbia, Missouri; *Daily Times*, 16 January 1851; *Annual Report of the American Colonization Society* 27 (March 1851), 71; *New York Freeman*, 3 January 1885; *Cincinnati Daily Commercial*, 11 February 1851; Will of Charles McMicken of Cincinnati, Ohio, 1858, University of Cincinnati; Rev. William J. Simmons, *Men of Mark: Eminent, Progressive and Rising* (New York: Arno Press and New York Times, 1968), 375–76.

36. *Minutes of the State Convention of the Colored Citizens of Ohio, Convened at Columbus, Jan. 15th–18th, 1851* (Columbus: E. Glover Printer, 1851), 3.

37. *Proceedings of the Convention of the Colored Freemen of Ohio, Held in Cincinnati January 14–18, 1852* (Cincinnati: Dumas and Lawyer, 1852); *Voice of the Fugitive*, 12 February 1852.

38. H. Ford Douglass had been born in Virginia. He had been active in the African American communities of Columbus and Cleveland. In 1850, he had sold subscriptions for Henry Bibb's *Voice of the Fugitive*. For a biography of Douglass, see Miller, *The Search for a Black Nationality*, 150. *Voice of the Fugitive*, 12 February 1852; *Proceedings of the Convention of the Colored Freemen of Ohio ... 1852*, 5.

39. Pease and Pease, *They Who Would Be Free*, 258–59; Rael, *Black Identity & Black Protest in the Antebellum North*, 262.

40. *Cincinnati Daily Gazette*, 19 January 1852; *Ripley Bee*, 31 January 1852; *Voice of the Fugitive*, 12 February 1852; Peter H. Clark to John W. Cromwell, 21 December 1901, in *Negro in American History*, ed. Cromwell, 37–38.

41. *Voice of the Fugitive*, 12 February 1852; *Proceedings of the Convention ... 1852*, 5, 9.

42. *Voice of the Fugitive*, 12 February 1852; *Proceedings of the Convention ... 1852*, 9.

43. *Voice of the Fugitive*, 2 February 1852; Miller, *Search for a Black Nationality*, 127–28; Delany, *Condition, Elevation, Emigration, and Destiny of the Colored People of the United States*, chap. 22 passim.

44. *New York Freeman*, 3 January 1885.

45. Quoted in Cheek and Cheek, *John Mercer Langston and the Fight for Black Freedom*, 231.

46. *Voice of the Fugitive*, 12 February 1852.

47. *Proceedings of the Convention ... 1852*, 5; *Voice of the Fugitive*, 12 February 1852; *Frederick Douglass' Paper*, 5 February 1852.

48. For convention resolutions, see *Proceedings of the Convention of the Colored Men of Ohio ... 1852*, 5–8.

49. Ibid., 7. For more on Kossuth and his American tour, see Mischa Honeck, *We Are the Revolutionists: German-Speaking Immigrants and American Abolitionists after 1848* (Athens: University of Georgia Press, 2011), 26–27. Kinkel was involved in the Communist League and published a revolutionary newspaper called the *Bonner Zeitung*. He joined the armed revolution in Palatinate in 1849, for which he was arrested and sentenced to life in prison. Kinkel eventually escaped and moved to London.

50. Lajos Kossuth arrived in New York on 4 December 1851 and toured New England, the South, and Midwest (see Honeck, *We Are the Revolutionists*, 26).

51. Miller, *Search for a Black Nationality*, 151–52, 159–61.

52. Howard Holman Bell, *A Survey of the Negro Convention Movement 1830–1861* (New York: Arno Press, 1969), 166; *Proceedings of the Colored National Convention, Held in Rochester, July 6th, 7th, and 8th, 1853* (Rochester: Frederick Douglass' Paper, 1853), in *Proceedings of the National Negro Conventions 1830–1864*, ed. Holman Bell (New York: Arno Press, 1969), 5, 11.

53. *Proceedings of the Colored National Convention, Held ... 1853*, 36; Moses, *Golden Age of Black Nationalism*, 39.

54. *Proceedings of the Colored National Convention, Held ... 1853,* 56. On Douglass's black nationalist views, see Moses, *Golden Age of Black Nationalism, 1850–1925,* 39.

55. In 1877, he chaired a local planning meeting to consider emigration to Arkansas. But that, perhaps, had been a romantic, but disingenuous, return to an earlier position and not representative of his actual views (see *Cincinnati Daily Enquirer,* 7 August 1877).

56. Clark was also a delegate at the 1857 State Convention of Colored Men of the State of Ohio, which opposed colonization and emigration in its resolutions (*Proceedings of the State Convention of Colored Men of the State of Ohio Held in the City of Columbus, January 21st, 22nd & 23nd,* 1857).

57. The withdrawal of Clark's support had little impact since nationally recognized emigrationists like Martin Delany and Henry Highland Garnet certainly never counted him among their ranks. Not only was he not invited to address the 1854 National Emigration Convention, but he did not attend it either.

58. *Proceedings of the National Emigration Convention of Colored People, Held at Cleveland, Ohio on ... the 24th, 25th, and 26th of August 1854* (Pittsburgh: A. A. Anderson, 1854), 37; *Frederick Douglass' Paper,* 20 October 1854.

3. Voice of Purpose

Epigraph: *Cincinnati Daily Times,* 11 August 1853.

1. State Convention of the Colored Citizens of Ohio, Minutes and Address of the State Convention of the Colored Citizens of Ohio, Held at Columbus September 18th, 19th, 20th, and 21st, 1844.

2. Ohio General Assembly, An Act to Provide for the Support and Better Regulation of Common Schools (1829), in Stephen Middleton, *The Black Laws in the Old Northwest: A Documentary History* (Westport, CT: Greenwood Press, 1993), 34.

3. See ibid., 34–35.

4. *Colored American,* 16 January 1841.

5. African Americans were again denied the right to vote at the 1850–1851 state convention.

6. Samuel Matthews, "The Black Educational Experience in Nineteenth-Century Cincinnati 1817–1874" (Ph.D. diss., University of Cincinnati, 1985), 83; Frank Quillin, *The Color Line in Ohio: A History of Race Prejudice in a Typical Northern State* (Ann Arbor: George Wahr, 1913), 38–39.

7. Ohio General Assembly, An Act to Authorize the Establishment of Separate Schools for the Education of Colored Children, and for Other Purposes (1849), in Middleton, *Black Laws in the Old Northwest,* 39; Matthews, "Black Educational Experience in Nineteenth-Century Cincinnati 1817–1874," 86.

8. Cincinnati Colored Public Schools, *Eighth Annual Report of the Board of Trustees for the Colored Public Schools of Cincinnati, for the School Year Ending*

June 30, 1857 (Cincinnati: Moore, Wilstach, Keys, 1857), 12; Cincinnati Colored Public Schools, *Eleventh Annual Report of the Board of Trustees for the Colored Public Schools of Cincinnati, for the School Year Ending June 30, 1860* (Newport: Free South Office, 1860), 24; *New York Freeman,* 3 January 1885.

9. Matthews, "Black Educational Experience in Nineteenth-Century Cincinnati 1817–1874," 83.

10. Cincinnati Colored Public Schools, *Eleventh Annual Report of the Board of Trustees for the Colored Public Schools of Cincinnati,* 24.

11. Ohio General Assembly, An Act to Provide for the Maintenance and Better Regulation of the Common Schools in the City of Cincinnati (1853); An Act to Provide for the Reorganization, Supervision and Maintenance of Common Schools (1853); An Act to Amend the Act to Provide for the Maintenance and Better Regulation of Common Schools, in the City of Cincinnati (1854), all in Middleton, *Black Laws in the Old Northwest,* 40–42.

12. The members of the Board of Trustees for 1854–1855 were Rufus King (president), George Rice, and Josephus Fowler. For 1855–1856, the board consisted of James Johnson (president), Peter Harbinson, Lovell Flewellen, Henry Boyd, Daniel Gibson, and Joseph Fowler (see Cincinnati Colored Public Schools, *Second Annual Report of the Board of Trustees for the Colored Public Schools of Cincinnati, for the School Year Ending June 30, 1856* [Cincinnati: Jacob Ernst, 1856], 30).

13. Cincinnati Colored Public Schools, *First Annual Report of the Board of Trustees for the Colored Public Schools of Cincinnati, for the School Year Ending June 30, 1855* (Cincinnati: Moore, Wilstach, Keys, 1855), 5–6.

14. Cincinnati Colored Public Schools, *Second Annual Report of the Board of Trustees for the Colored Public Schools of Cincinnati, For the School Year Ending June 30, 1856* (Cincinnati: Jacob Ernst, 1856), 13.

15. Mischa Honeck, *We Are the Revolutionists: German-Speaking Immigrants & American Abolitionists after 1848* (Athens: University of Georgia Press, 2011), 75, 78.

16. *Cincinnati Daily Gazette,* 24 March and 25 March 1854, quoted in Honeck, *We Are the Revolutionists,* 79.

17. *Cincinnati Daily Commercial,* 5 December 1859.

18. Bruce Levine, *The Spirit of 1848: German Immigrants, Labor Conflict, and the Coming of the Civil War* (Urbana: University of Illinois Press, 1992), 90–91, 119; Honeck, *We Are the Revolutionists,* 75, 78.

19. Levine, *Spirit of 1848,* 154–55.

20. Apparently, the local Turnverein may not have accepted Clark into membership had he tried. In 1859, the organization turned away three African American men who simply tried to enter a Turner fair because of their race. When the situation was reported by the press, it not only made the local Turnverein appear racist and hypocritical, but seriously challenged the alliance between German radicals and

African Americans. For more on this event, see Honeck, *We Are the Revolutionists,* 95–96.

21. *Western Christian Advocate,* 17 August 1853.

22. *Voice of the Fugitive,* 12 February 1852; *Proceedings of the Convention of the Colored Freemen of Ohio, Held in Cincinnati January 14–18th* (Cincinnati: Dumas and Lawyer, 1852), 8. It is not clear whether Clark envisioned the teachers' association to be a kind of protective union that would provide assistance to sick, unemployed, and elderly teachers or whether it was a trade union designed to advocate for better working conditions.

23. *Proceedings of the Convention of the Colored Men of Ohio … 1852, Proceedings of the Convention of the Colored Freemen of Ohio, Held in Cincinnati January 14–18, 1852* (Cincinnati: Dumas and Lawyer, 1852), 7.

24. *Cincinnati Daily Times,* 6 August 1853.

25. Philip S. Foner, ed., *The Life and Major Writings of Thomas Paine* (Secaucus, NJ: Citadel Press, 1974), 475.

26. Craig Nelson, *Thomas Paine: Enlightenment, Revolution, and the Birth of Modern Nations* (New York: Viking, 2006), 266–67; Foner, *Life and Major Writings of Thomas Paine,* 460.

27. John A. Buehrens, *Universalists and Unitarians in America: A People's History* (Boston: Skinner Books, 2011), ix–x.

28. Juan M. Floyd-Thomas, *The Origins of Black Humanism in America: Reverend Ethelred Brown and the Unitarian Church* (New York: Palgrave MacMillan, 2008), 172.

29. Thomas Paine, *Rights of Man: Being an Answer to Mr. Burke's Attack on the French Revolution* (London: J. S. Jordan, 1791), 46–47.

30. Stephen E. Maizlish, *The Triumph of Sectionalism: The Transformation of Ohio Politics 1844–1856* (Kent, OH: Kent State University Press, 1983), 180.

31. *Cincinnati Daily Commercial,* 11 August 1853.

32. *Cincinnati Daily Gazette,* 3 and 6 August 1853.

33. Ibid.

34. *Cleveland Plaindealer,* 8 August 1853, quoted in *Cincinnati Daily Times,* 11 August 1853.

35. *Cincinnati Daily Commercial,* 11 August 1853; *Western Christian Advocate,* 17 August 1853.

36. *Cincinnati Daily Times,* 8 August 1853.

37. *Western Christian Advocate,* 17 August 1853; *Cincinnati Daily Times,* 6 August 1853.

38. *Cincinnati Daily Commercial,* 11 August 1853.

39. *Cincinnati Daily Times,* 11 August 1853.

40. Waldo E. Martin Jr., *The Mind of Frederick Douglass* (Chapel Hill: University of North Carolina Press, 1984), 179.

41. *Frederick Douglass' Paper,* 26 August 1853.

42. William Anderson's service has been documented in both the Military Service

and Pension records at the National Archive (see *Military Service Records of the U.S. Regular Army: William Anderson* [MD] M860 Roll 1, National Archives; Pension Records of William Anderson, M804, Roll 59, National Archives; and Robert Ewell Green, *Black Courage 1775–1783: Documentation of Black Participation in the American Revolution* [Washington, D.C.: National Society of the Daughters of the American Revolution, 1984], 29, 42, 47, 48). Details of his service are also included in the *Cincinnati Commercial,* 31 March 1867 (with some factual errors). When Anderson applied for a pension in 1818, he initially was denied because he could hardly remember the details of his service, including the names of people under whom he served. Eventually, Capt. Jeremiah Collins was deposed as part of Anderson's pension claim and testified to Anderson's service, confirming his injuries.

   43. Peter H. Clark to Azariah Root, 9 January 1888, Oberlin College Archives; "Minority Student Records," Oberlin College Archives; Ellen N. Lawson and Marlene Merrill, "The Antebellum 'Talented Thousandth': Black College Students at Oberlin before the Civil War," *Journal of Negro Education* (Spring 1983): 151.

   44. *New York Freeman,* 3 January 1885; *Cleveland Gazette,* 3 September 1877; Simmons, *Men of Mark,* 377.

   45. Bishop Daniel Alexander Payne, *Recollections of Seventy Years* (Nashville: Publishing House of the AME Sunday School Union, 1888), 133.

   46. United States Census Bureau, *The Seventh Census of the United States 1850. Population Schedules for Hamilton County;* United States Census Bureau, *The Eighth Census of the United States 1860. Population Schedules for Greene County, Xenia Township.*

   47. Rev. Benjamin W. Arnett, *Proceedings of the Semi-Centenary Celebration of the African Methodist Episcopal Church of Cincinnati, Held in the Allen Temple February 8th, 9th, and 10th, 1874* (Cincinnati: H. Watkins, 1874), 55, Cincinnati Historical Society.

   48. Nikki Taylor, *Frontiers of Freedom: Cincinnati's Black Community 1802–1868* (Athens: Ohio University Press, 2005), 46.

   49. On African American humanism, see Anthony B. Pinn, "Anybody There?: Reflections on African American Humanism," www.huumanists.org/publications/journal/journal-articles/summer-fall-1997/anybody-there-reflections-on-african-american-humanism.

   50. Honeck, *We Are the Revolutionists,* 81–84 passim, 91, 93; Levine, *Spirit of 1848,* 91, 223; Roger Burns-Watson, "The Unitarian Clergy and Anti-Slavery in Antebellum Cincinnati" (Cincinnati: First Unitarian Church, n.d.), 7–8; Moncure Daniel Conway, *Autobiography Memories and Experiences of Moncure Daniel Conway* (Boston: Houghton, Mifflin, 1904), 1:251; Walter P. Herz, "Influence Transcending Mere Numbers: The Unitarians in Nineteenth-Century Cincinnati," *Queen City Heritage* 51 (Winter 1993): 10–11.

   51. On Willich's background, see Honeck, *We Are the Revolutionists,* 83–84,

95–97. Willich nicknamed "German nigger worshipper" can be found in *Cincinnati Volksfreund*, 25 December 1859, cited in Honeck, *We Are the Revolutionists*, 97.

52. Roger Burns, "The Unitarian Clergy and Anti-Slavery in Antebellum Cincinnati," published locally by the First Unitarian Church of Cincinnati, n.d. For more on Stallo, see Honeck, *We Are the Revolutionists*, 81–82. According to Honeck, Stallo was a freethinker and one of the nation's leading philosophers in that era. Stallo also championed religious freedom and frequently spoke out against Sabbath laws and the requisite reading of Protestant hymns and prayers in public schools and other public spaces. On Willich's defense of Clark in the Cincinnati press, see Honeck, *We Are the Revolutionists*, 96–97.

53. Conway, *Autobiography Memories and Experiences of Moncure Daniel Conway*, 254; Herz, "Influence Transcending Mere Numbers," 5–8 passim; Walter P. Herz, "Such a Glaring Inconsistency: The Unitarian Laity and Anti-Slavery in Antebellum Cincinnati," published locally by the First Congregational Church of Cincinnati, n.d., 8–9.

54. *Frederick Douglass' Paper*, 15 April 1853, 18 May and 10 August 1855; Jane H. Pease and William H. Pease, *They Who Would Be Free: Blacks' Search for Freedom, 1830–1861* (Urbana: University of Illinois Press, 1990), 139–40.

55. Pease and Pease, *They Who Would be Free*, 40.

56. There are no extant copies of the *Herald of Freedom*. Fortunately, *Frederick Douglass' Paper* recorded Clark's comments from the *Herald of Freedom* (*Frederick Douglass' Paper*, 21 September 1855).

57. *Frederick Douglass' Paper*, 5 May 1854, 3 and 10 August 1855, and 21 September 1855.

58. Ibid., 3 August 1855.

59. Ibid.

60. Frederick Douglass to Harriet Beecher Stowe, 8 March 1853.

61. Maria Chapman, quoted in Pease and Pease, *They Who Would Be Free*, 141.

62. The name is derived from the name of a colonial native American settlement in which native peoples and African American and Dutch settlers lived peacefully together (see John Stauffer, *The Black Hearts of Men: Radical Abolitionists and the Transformation of Race* [Cambridge: Harvard University Press, 2001], 186).

63. *Frederick Douglass' Paper*, 10 August 1855.

64. Ibid., 21 September 1855.

65. State Convention of the Colored Freemen of Ohio, *Proceedings of the State Convention of the Colored Freemen of Ohio, Held in Cincinnati January 14–18, 1852* (Cincinnati: Dumas and Lawyer, 1852), 8.

66. *Twenty-Fourth Annual Report of the Trustees and Visitors of Common Schools, to the City Council of Cincinnati, for the School Year Ending June 30, 1853* (Cincinnati: Cincinnati Gazette Co., 1853),17.

67. Ohio General Assembly, An Act to Amend an Act Entitled "An Act to

Amend the Act to Provide for the Maintenance and Better Regulation of Common Schools in the City of Cincinnati" (1856), in Middleton, *Black Laws in the Old Northwest*, 42–43; Matthews, "Black Educational Experience in Nineteenth-Century Cincinnati 1817–1874," 90–91.

68. Cincinnati Colored Public Schools, *Eighth Annual Report of the Board of Trustees for the Colored Public Schools*, 29. John Gaines was reelected to the board, along with Phillip Ferguson, Lovell Flewellen, George Peterson, Wallace Shelton, and Peter Fossett.

69. *Liberator*, 27 April 1860; John Mercer Langston, *From the Virginia Plantation to the National Capitol or The First and Only Representative in Congress from the Old Dominion* (Hartford, CT: American, 1894), 66. On Gaines's life and career, see Taylor, *Frontiers of Freedom*, 164–65; and William Wells Brown, *The Rising Son; or, The Antecedents and Advancement of the Colored Race* (Boston: A. G. Brown, 1876), 450–52.

70. *Liberator*, 27 April 1860.

71. Cincinnati Colored Public Schools, *Eighteenth Annual Report of the Board of Directors for the Colored Public Schools of Cincinnati, for the Year Ending June 30, 1867* (Cincinnati: Moore and McGrew, 1868), 4–5; Colored Schools of Cincinnati, *Nineteenth Annual Report of the Board of Directors for the Colored Public Schools of Cincinnati, for the School Year Ending June 30, 1868* (Cincinnati: Gazette Steam Book and Job Printing, 1968), 18. Turner earned bachelor's and master's degrees from the University of Cincinnati and went on to earn a Ph.D. from the University of Chicago in 1907. He published more than seventy papers in animal behavior and was the first African American to publish in the *Journal of Animal Behavior*.

72. Black teachers earned between twenty-three and thirty-five dollars per month in 1864; principals earned seventy-five dollars per month. Women earned twenty-three dollars per month, while the men earned thirty-five dollars per month (Cincinnati Colored Public Schools, *Fifteenth Annual Report of the Board of Directors for the Colored Public Schools of Cincinnati, for the School Year Ending June 30, 1864* [Cincinnati: A. Moore, Book and Job Printer, 1864], 25).

4. "The Silver Tongued Orator of the West"

Epigraphs: *Cincinnati Daily Commercial*, 5 December 1859; *Cincinnati Daily Times*, 5 December 1859.

1. *Radical Abolitionist*, 2 June 1856 and July 1856.

2. Ibid., August 1856; *Frederick Douglass' Paper*, 20 June 1856; John Stauffer, *The Black Hearts of Men: Radical Abolitionists and the Transformation of Race* (Cambridge: Harvard University Press, 2001), 22–23.

3. The Radical Abolition Party had nearly gone into historical obscurity, hardly ever being mentioned in works on abolitionism until John Stauffer's 2001 book (see Stauffer, *Black Hearts of Men*, 22–23; and *Radical Abolitionist*, July 1856).

4. Stauffer, *Black Hearts of Men,* 16–17.

5. Ibid., 13, 14, 23.

6. *Radical Abolitionist,* July 1856; Stauffer, *Black Hearts of Men,* 9, 13, 23, 25, 42; *Cincinnati Enquirer,* 6 December 1859.

7. *Frederick Douglass' Paper,* 27 June 1856 and 12 September 1856.

8. *New York Daily Times,* 29 May 1856.

9. This is the same reason most African Americans never joined the Radical Abolition Party. For more on that, see Benjamin Quarles, *Black Abolitionists* (New York: Da Capo Press, 1969), 188–89.

10. Clark was not alone in privileging the struggle to raise the status of free African Americans (see Richard Bardolph, *The Negro Vanguard* [New York: Rinehart, 1959], 50).

11. The conventions were called antislavery conventions, although they were essentially abolitionist meetings. Although "antislavery" and "abolitionist" were often interchangeably used as synonyms, there are some measurable differences. The word "antislavery" implies that people were opposed to slavery but were not supportive of immediate and full emancipation, as abolitionists were.

12. Prior to the 1850s, most antislavery conventions had been held on the East Coast. After the publication of Harriet Beecher's Stowe's best-selling *Uncle Tom's Cabin* in 1852, Cincinnati became a popular venue for antislavery conventions. For example, the 1851 antislavery convention held in Cincinnati before the book's publication was relatively small and local; those that followed attracted delegates from away as far as New York and Philadelphia. The 1852 and 1853 conventions, for example, attracted some of the nation's leading abolitionists such as William Lloyd Garrison, editor of the *Liberator;* Wendell Philips; Cassius M. Clay; Lucy Stone; Frederick Douglass; Charles L. Remond, an African American lecturer for the American Anti-Slavery Society; and Henry Bibb, editor of the *Voice of the Fugitive.* Added to those were Ohio's most prominent abolitionists, including Levi Coffin, reputed "president" of Cincinnati's Underground Railroad; John Rankin, one of the most significant Underground Railroad operators in Brown County; and John Mercer Langston. More than two hundred delegates attended the 1852 convention, making it the largest antislavery convention west of the Alleghenies (*Daily Cincinnati Gazette,* 28, 29, and 30 April 1852; *Daily Enquirer,* 20 April 1853; *Anti-Slavery Bugle,* 7 May 1853; William Cheek and Aimee Lee Cheek, *John Mercer Langston and the Fight for Black Freedom 1829–65* [Urbana: University of Illinois Press, 1989], 206–7).

13. *Daily Cincinnati Gazette,* 21 April 1851, 28 April 1852, 20 April 1853, 26 April and 27 April 1855; *Daily Enquirer,* 20 April 1853; *Daily Times,* 20 April and 21 April 1853 and 14 April 1854; *Cincinnati Daily Commercial,* 12 April 1854; *Liberator,* 11 May 1855.

14. *Ripley Bee,* 31 January 1852.

15. Levi Coffin, *Reminiscences of Levi Coffin, The Reputed President of the Underground Railroad* (New York: AMS Press, 1876), 108.

16. Clark served as the orphanage's trustee and treasurer for a number of years after his father's death, and the Coffins managed the place from 1852 to 1855 (Wendell P. Dabney, *Cincinnati's Colored Citizens: Historical, Sociological and Biographical* [Cincinnati: Dabney, 1926], 356–57; *Eleventh Annual Report of the Managers of the Colored Orphan Asylum for 1855–56* [Cincinnati: Henry Watkin, Printer, 1856]; *Twentieth Annual Report of the Board of the Trustees of the Colored Orphan Asylum of Cincinnati, Ohio for 1863–4* [Cincinnati: A. Moore, Book Printer, 1864]; *Twenty-First Annual Report of the Board of the Trustees of the Colored Orphan Asylum of Cincinnati, Ohio for 1864–5* [Cincinnati: A Moore, Book Printer, 1864]; Coffin, *Reminiscences of Levi Coffin,* 245).

17. *Cincinnati Daily Gazette,* 20 September 1877.

18. *Daily Cincinnati Gazette,* 17 August 1853; *Daily Enquirer,* 17 August 1853.

19. *Daily Cincinnati Gazette,* 17 August 1853; *Daily Enquirer,* 17 August 1853; *Cincinnati Daily Commercial,* 18 August 1853; Steven Weisenburger, *Modern Medea: A Family Story of Slavery and Child-Murder from the Old South* (New York: Hill and Wang, 1998), 103.

20. *Provincial Freeman,* 23 June 1855; *New York Freeman,* 3 January 1885; *Cincinnati Daily Commercial,* 12 June 1855; Rev. William J. Simmons, *Men of Mark: Eminent, Progressive and Rising* (New York: Arno Press, 1969), 377.

21. *Cincinnati Daily Commercial,* 19 June 1855.

22. *Frederick Douglass' Paper,* 21 September 1855; *New York Freeman* 3 January 1885.

23. *Frederick Douglass' Paper,* 21 September 1855; *Provincial Freeman,* 3 November 1855; *New York Freeman,* 3 January 1885; Simmons, *Men of Mark,* 377.

24. Unfortunately, there is no 1856 city directory for Rochester, New York.

25. Peter H. Clark, "Biographical Sketch of Peter H. Clark," n.d., William C. Breckenridge Papers, Western Historical Manuscript Collection, Columbia, Missouri.

26. Clark is one of the few African American men who had an amicable relationship with Frederick Douglass. Douglass's contentious relationships with others are documented in Wilson Jeremiah Moses, *Creative Conflict in African American Thought: Frederick Douglass, Booker T. Washington, W. E. B. Du Bois, and Marcus Garvey* (Cambridge: Cambridge University Press, 2004), 54–56.

27. Sadly, Clark never adopted his mentor's commitment to the struggle for women's rights. Not one time in his entire longer political career did Clark ever champion women's rights.

28. *National Era,* 26 June 1856; *Provincial Freeman,* 25 April 1857; *New York Freeman,* 3 January 1885.

29. Along with William James Watkins, Clark spent a great deal of time lecturing and organizing in Ohio. The men held public meetings and circulated petitions in each county. For his abolitionist lecture career, see *New York Freeman,* 3 January 1885; *Frederick Douglass' Paper,* 20 June 1856; and *Cleveland Gazette,* 3 September 1887. There are no known existing copies of *Sore Conscience.*

30. *Provincial Freeman,* 25 April 1857.

31. *Christian Recorder,* 17 August 1867.

32. James Brewer Stewart, *Holy Warrior: The Abolitionists and American Slavery* (New York: Hill and Wang, 1976), 137.

33. August Meier and Elliot Rudwick, "The Role of Blacks in the Abolitionist Movement," in *Blacks in the Abolitionist Movement,* ed. John H. Bracey Jr., Meier, and Rudwick (Belmont, CA: Wadsworth, 1971), 117; Stewart, *Holy Warriors,* 138.

34. August First festivals commemorated the Gradual Emancipation of bondspeople in the British West Indies on August 1, 1834. Specifically, the day allowed "friends of Freedom everywhere, [to] manifest their appreciation of British magnanimity and liberality" (*Frederick Douglass' Paper,* 27 July 1855). Before U.S. Emancipation, August First celebrations served as the representative Emancipation Day celebrations. After U.S. Emancipation in 1865, the date of festivities shifted from August 1 to September 22 to commemorate the day Abraham Lincoln signed the Emancipation Proclamation. In 1872, Cincinnati's community renamed its festival "St. Abraham's Day" and moved the date of commemoration to January 1, in honor of Abraham Lincoln and the Emancipation Proclamation. Some communities did more than change the name and date of their commemorative festivals. Believing the concept "Emancipation Day" too narrow to define their new status, in 1872 the African American community of Zanesville, Ohio, renamed its festival the "Grand Union Celebration" to commemorate "any advancement on the part of our government in the protection of colored citizens" (*Cincinnati Daily Commercial,* 2 January 1872; *Christian Recorder,* 17 August 1872). I will use "Emancipation Day celebration" as an umbrella term for all types of commemorative festivals, including August First celebrations.

35. Mitch Kachun, *Festivals of Freedom: Memory and Meaning in African American Emancipation Celebrations 1808–1915* (Amherst: University of Massachusetts Press, 2003), 68.

36. Patrick Rael, *Black Identity & Black Protest in the Antebellum North* (Chapel Hill: University of North Carolina Press, 2002), 61–63, 77; Kachun, *Festivals of Freedom* 59, 70; Julie Loy Jeffrey, "'No Occurrence in Human History Is More Deserving of Commemoration Than This': Abolitionist Celebrations of Freedom," in *Prophets of Protest: Reconsidering the History of American Abolitionism,* ed. Timothy Patrick McCarthy and John Stauffer (New York: New Press, 2006), 201.

37. *Cincinnati Daily Gazette,* 2 August 1855; *Frederick Douglass' Paper,* 31 August 1855.

38. Rael, *Black Identity & Black Protest in the Antebellum North,* 79.

39. *Cincinnati Daily Commercial,* 31 March 1867; William Wells Brown, *The Rising Son; or, The Antecedents and Advancement of the Colored Race* (Boston: A. G. Brown, 1874), 523–24.

40. *Dayton Ledger,* 24 September 1869; *Christian Recorder,* 17 August 1872; *Dayton Evening Herald,* 22 September 1873; *Cincinnati Commercial,* 23 September 1873.

41. *Frederick Douglass' Paper,* 26 August 1853 and 31 August 1855; *Cincinnati Daily Gazette,* 2 August 1855. Unfortunately neither address was recorded. *Cincinnati Commercial,* 2 January 1872; *Christian Recorder,* 2 September 1880.

42. For more on Emancipation Day celebrations in the Midwest, see Leslie A. Schwalm, *Emancipation's Diaspora: Race and Reconstruction in the Upper Midwest* (Chapel Hill: University of North Carolina Press, 2009), 224–37.

43. *Frederick Douglass' Paper,* 12 September 1856.

44. *Liberator,* February 1856.

45. Ibid. For more on nineteenth-century scientific racism, see Rael, *Black Identity & Black Protest in the Antebellum North,* 242–43.

46. *Liberator,* 3 December 1858.

47. Newspapers reported at least two names of the organization hosting the rally, including the Social Working Men's Association. For news of rally, see *Cincinnati Daily Times,* 5 December 1859; *Cincinnati Enquirer,* 6 December 1859; *Cincinnati Volksfreund,* 6 December 1859; *Cincinnati Daily Commercial,* 5 December 1859; Philip S. Foner and Herbert Shapiro, *Northern Labor and Antislavery: A Documentary History* (Westport, CT: Greenwood Press, 1994), 250–51; and *Cincinnati Daily Commercial,* 6 December 1859.

48. *Cincinnati Daily Commercial,* 5 December 1859; *Cincinnati Enquirer,* 6 December 1859; *Cincinnati Daily Times,* 5 December 1859; *Cincinnati Volksfreund,* 6 December 1859.

49. As Bruce Levine has argued, German immigrants, fearing that the Kansas-Nebraska Act would turn the West into a haven of despotism hostile to free labor, moved from "passive antislavery sentiments" to "overt, organized, and even partisan action" against the institution. German freemen joined the free-soil movement and others joined the Republican Party (see Bruce Levine, *The Spirit of 1848: German Immigrants, Labor Conflict, and the Coming of the Civil War* [Urbana: University of Illinois Press, 1992], 151).

50. *Cincinnati Volksfreund,* 6 December 1859.

51. In that speech, Conway indicts Christian churches for turning a blind eye to slavery. He also praises Brown for having the courage to strike against the institution of slavery: "His deed was stronger than an army" (*Cincinnati Daily Commercial,* 6 December 1859).

52. *Cincinnati Enquirer,* 6 December 1859.

53. Ibid. This comment about "hospitable graves" is a reference to Ohio senator Thomas Corwin's controversial commentary in opposition to the Mexican War—a war that many abolitionists believed had been provoked by the U.S. government in order to seize territory for the spread of slavery. Corwin said: "If I were a Mexican I would tell you, 'Have you not room in your own country to bury your dead men? If you come to mine, we will greet you with bloody hand, and welcome you to hospitable graves.'"

54. Historian Mischa Honeck overstates the case when he asserts that Clark believed "slavery could not be eradicated without bloodshed" (Honeck, *We Are the Revolutionists,* 93). Clark's entire career proves that he used other means to defeat slavery. He was willing to consider violence only after other avenues of mitigation failed.

55. Preston King and Walter Earl Fluker, in *Black Leaders and Ideologies in the South,* argue that there is a distinction between "a legitimate violence of liberation … and an illegitimate violence of aggression." They outline four criteria for the former, including, "(a) the moral objective should be to secure appropriate liberties, (b) these liberties should be due equally to all, (c) the action ought not to be promoted by ulterior motives (as of personal or national gain) and (d) the chances of success should be rather better than even" (Preston King and Walter Earl Fluker, *Black Leaders and Ideologies in the South: Resistance and Nonviolence* [London and New York: Routledge, 2005], 14).

56. For Clark on seizing his rights, see *Liberator,* 3 December 1858.

57. *Anti-Slavery Standard,* 11 January 1862; also reprinted in *Liberator,* 28 February 1862.

58. Clark's definitive abolitionist act after Emancipation was serving as secretary of the local Lincoln Memorial Club. Cincinnati's interracial Lincoln Memorial Club hoped to honor the memory and ideals of the slain president with a legal holiday commemorating his birthday. Members bestowed prominent citizens with honorary memberships, hoping that that sheer political weight of such a list of members might sway Congress to establish a Lincoln holiday. As secretary, Clark's responsibility was writing letters to inform people that they had been selected for membership. The Lincoln Memorial Club, for example, extended an honorary membership to George L. Ruffin, the first African American to graduate from Harvard University Law School and to serve in the Massachusetts legislature (1869–1871). Ruffin also served on the Boston City Council from 1876 to 1878 (see "George L. Ruffin to Peter H. Clark," 7 February 1876, original letter in the hands of Carrie Nelson, private owner). For petition of Lincoln Memorial Club, see "Petition of T. N. C. Liverpool, Peter H. Clark and other Citizens of Ohio," Misc Document No. 148, 43rd Cong., 1st sess.

59. Peter H. Clark, *The Black Brigade of Cincinnati* (New York: Arno Press, 1969), 15. The source indicates that 1,000 men constituted 25 percent of the African American population in 1860, which roughly numbered 3,700.

60. Ibid., 3, 9, 21.

61. National Convention of Colored Men, "Preamble and Constitution of the National Equal Rights League," in *Proceedings of the National Convention of Colored Men Held in the City of Syracuse, New York, October 4,5,6, and 7, 1864 with the Bill of Wrongs and Rights and the Address to American People* (Boston: J. S. Rock and George Ruffin, 1864), 29, 36, 42–43; National Equal Rights League, *Proceedings of the First Annual Meeting of the National Equal Rights League,*

Held in Cleveland, Ohio October 19, 20, and 21, 1865, in *Proceedings of the Black National and State Conventions, 1865–1900,* 64.

62. Ohio State Auxiliary Equal Rights League, "Constitution of the Ohio State Auxiliary Equal Rights League," in *Proceedings of a Convention of the Colored Men of Ohio Held in Xenia on the 10th, 11th, and 12th Days of January 1865 with the Constitution of the Ohio Equal Rights League* (Cincinnati: A. Moore, 1865), 17, 19; *Cincinnati Daily Commercial,* 9 January 1861; *Christian Recorder,* 10 February 1866.

63. Ohio State Auxiliary Equal Rights League, "Resolutions of the Ohio State Auxiliary Equal Rights League," in *Proceedings of a Convention of the Colored Men of Ohio . . . ,* 11–14 passim.

64. Ibid., 14.

65. *Christian Recorder,* 24 August 1867.

5. Voice of Equality

Epigraph: *Cincinnati Daily Enquirer,* 26 August 1873.

1. *Cincinnati Commercial,* 12 April 1870.

2. For more information about how African American women participated in the political process despite not being enfranchised, see Elsa Barkley Brown, "To Catch the Vision of Freedom: Reconstructing Southern Black Women's Political History, 1865–1880," in *African American Women and the Vote, 1837–1965,* ed. Ann D. Gordon, Bettye Collier-Thomas et al. (Amherst: University of Massachusetts Press, 1997): 66–87. Steven Hahn asserts that the black vote was "household and family property" (see Hahn, *A Nation under Our Feet: Black Political Struggles in the Rural South from Slavery to the Great Migration* [Cambridge: Harvard University Press, 2003], 227).

3. *Cincinnati Commercial,* 12 April 1870.

4. Hanes Walton, *Black Republicans: The Politics of the Black and Tans* (Metuchen, NJ: Scarecrow Press, 1975), 4, 5.

5. Ibid., 17.

6. Ibid., 15, 16.

7. Nell Painter, *Exodusters: Black Migration to Kansas after Reconstruction* (New York: Norton, 1976), 35.

8. Andrew Slap, *The Doom of Reconstruction: The Liberal Republicans in the Civil War Era* (New York: Fordham University Press, 2006), 17, 23. According to Slap, the Liberal Republican movement predates the Liberal Republican Party. The movement was organized in New York on 22 November 1870.

9. *Cincinnati Commercial,* 22 March 1871; *Cincinnati Daily Enquirer,* 6 April 1871; Waldo E. Martin, *The Mind of Frederick Douglass* (Chapel Hill: University of North Carolina Press, 1984), 86; Philip S. Foner, *Frederick Douglass: A Biography* (New York: Citadel Press, 1964), 295.

10. Interestingly enough, many of the Liberal Republicans had once been Radical Republicans—some of whom had even been abolitionists and champions of racial equality. One case in point was Massachusetts senator Charles Sumner, who proposed the civil rights bill and became a Liberal Republican out of contempt for the Grant administration. He felt humiliated when the Grant administration removed him from the Foreign Relations Committee. Despite the fact that the Liberal Republican ideology—especially about Reconstruction—contradicted his lifelong principles, Sumner had been sufficiently alienated by the party he had helped to found. He believed he could work within the new political movement to obtain some rights for African Americans. As a Liberal Republican, Sumner worked to combine the issue of amnesty for former Confederates to the protection of African Americans' rights in the same bill because he believed it was the only way to successfully pass any bill protecting African American rights.

11. Heather Cox Richardson, *The Death of Reconstruction: Race, Labor, and Politics in the Post-Civil War North, 1865–1901* (Cambridge: Harvard University Press, 2001), 100–103; Slap, *Doom of Reconstruction,* 207.

12. Charles W. Calhoun, *Conceiving a New Republic: The Republican Party and the Southern Question, 1869–1900* (Lawrence: University Press of Kansas, 2006), 43–44.

13. Lawrence Grossman, *The Democratic Party and the Negro: Northern and National Politics 1868–92* (Urbana: University of Illinois Press, 1976), 30–31.

14. Other speakers included Jacob Cox, former secretary of the interior, and Judge Stanley Matthews, who was destined for the Senate and Supreme Court.

15. *Cincinnati Daily Enquirer,* 6 April 1871; *Cincinnati Commercial,* 26 April 1871.

16. *Cincinnati Commercial,* 16 August 1872.

17. *New National Era and Citizen,* 18 April 1872.

18. Frederick Douglass to Cassius M. Clay, 26 July 1871, in *The Life and Writings of Frederick Douglass,* ed. Philip S. Foner (New York: International, 1955), 4:252; *New National Era,* 10 August 1871, ibid., 4:254–57; Frederick Douglass, "The Republican Party Must Be Maintained in Power: An Address Delivered in New Orleans, Louisiana, on 13 April 1872," in *The Frederick Douglass Papers,* ed. John W. Blassingame and John R. McKivigan (New Haven: Yale University Press, 1991), 298.

19. Foner, *Frederick Douglass: A Biography,* 296–97.

20. *New National Era and Citizen,* 18 April 1872.

21. Ibid., 17 August 1871.

22. *Cincinnati Daily Enquirer,* 14 March 1872; *Cincinnati Commercial,* 13 and 14 March 1872.

23. *Cincinnati Daily Enquirer,* 14 March 1872; *Cincinnati Commercial,* 13 and 14 March 1872.

24. Painter, *Exodusters,* 30; *New National Era,* 16 November 1872.

25. Frederick Douglass, "This Democratic Conversion Should Not Be Trusted: An Address Delivered in New York, New York on 25 September 1872," in *The*

Frederick Douglass Papers, ed. John W. Blassingame and John R. McKivigan (New Haven: Yale University Press, 1991), 336–37 n. 7.

26. *Cincinnati Commercial,* 16 August 1872; *New National Era and Citizen,* 18 December 1873.

27. *Cincinnati Commercial,* 16 August 1872.

28. The bill never went to a vote in May 1870. It was referred to the Judiciary Committee at least twice but never moved beyond that. In December 1871, Sumner attached it to the Amnesty Bill, thinking this would give it a greater chance to pass. He was wrong. In May 1872, a toothless version of the bill passed, but that version omitted schools, churches, and cemeteries as places of protection. In December of that year, the bill was deferred to the Judiciary Committee. Sumner died in March 1874. The bill was finally passed in May 1875 as the Civil Rights Acts of 1875. For the history of the bill, see Ronald B. Jager, "Charles Sumner, the Constitution, and the Civil Rights Act of 1875," *New England Quarterly* 42, no. 3 (September 1969): 362–63.

29. Hahn, *A Nation under Our Feet,* 219.

30. *Cincinnati Commercial,* 23 September 1873.

31. Ibid., 14 April 1873 and 23 September 1873; *Cincinnati Daily Enquirer,* 14 April 1873.

32. Waldo E. Martin Jr., *The Mind of Frederick Douglass* (Chapel Hill: University of North Carolina Press, 1984), 92.

33. There was a preliminary meeting on 30 July 1873 to debate whether the party was genuinely committed to securing equality and full citizenship for them (*New National Era and Citizen,* 11 September 1873).

34. *Cincinnati Commercial,* 23 August 1873; *New National Era and Citizen,* 28 August 1873.

35. *Cincinnati Commercial,* 23 August 1873; *New National Era and Citizen,* 16 October 1873.

36. *Cincinnati Commercial,* 23 August 1873.

37. Ibid.

38. *Cincinnati Daily Enquirer,* 4 August 1873.

39. *Proceedings of a Convention of the Colored Men of Ohio. Held in the City of Cincinnati, on the 23rd, 24th, and 26th Days of November 1854; Liberator,* 3 December 1858.

40. *Cincinnati Commercial,* 23 August 1873; *New National Era and Citizen,* 28 August 1873.

41. *Cincinnati Commercial,* 23 August 1873; *New National Era and Citizen,* 28 August 1873.

42. *New National Era and Citizen,* 11 September 1873.

43. The work of historian Bess Beatty provides the interpretive framework for my analysis of the stages of black independent politics. She identifies several categories of black independents. Some had "continued but critical Republican allegiance," while others had a "disavowal of the Republican Party in non-election months, but support of the party at the polls." Other independents avoided "subser-

vience" to any one party by supporting individual candidates. The final category included those who, through their withdrawal from the Republican Party in a two-party state, became Democrats by default. Although Beatty's interpretation of independents was categorical, my interpretation considers the categories as stages as well. If we examine Clark's entire career, Chillicothe catapulted Clark to the final stage (see Bess Beatty, *A Revolution Gone Backward: The Black Response to National Politics, 1876–1896* [New York: Greenwood Press, 1987], 49).

44. *New National Era and Citizen,* 11 September 1873; *Cincinnati Commercial,* 23 August 1873.

45. *Cincinnati Commercial,* 23 August 1873; *Cincinnati Daily Enquirer,* 23 August 1873; *New National Era and Citizen,* 28 August 1873.

46. *Cincinnati Daily Enquirer,* 13 and 25 August 1873; *Cincinnati Commercial,* 26 August 1873.

47. *Cincinnati Daily Enquirer,* 13 August 1873.

48. *Cincinnati Commercial,* 24 August 1873.

49. Ibid., 26 August 1873; *Cincinnati Daily Enquirer,* 26 August 1873; *Cincinnati Commercial,* 26 October 1876.

50. *Cincinnati Commercial,* 26 August 1873.

51. *Cincinnati Daily Enquirer,* 26 August 1873.

52. Ibid.

53. *New National Era and Citizen,* 11 September 1873. Reverend James Poindexter of Columbus wrote of Clark, "No truer man to the Republican party, no truer man to his own people, and certainly no abler advocate of their cause, lives or has lived in a colored skin" (*New National Era and Citizen,* 16 October 1873).

54. *Cincinnati Commercial,* 17 September 1873.

55. Ibid., 23 September 1873; *Dayton Evening Herald,* 22 September 1873; *New National Era and Citizen,* 2 May 1872.

56. *Cincinnati Commercial,* 23 September 1873.

57. *Dayton Evening Herald,* 22 September 1873. A slight variation of this speech can be found in *Cincinnati Commercial,* 23 September 1873.

58. *New National Era and Citizen,* 18 December 1873; *Cincinnati Commercial,* 23 September 1873.

59. *New National Era and Citizen,* 18 April 1872.

60. Darlene Clark Hine, *The African-American Odyssey,* vol. 1, *To 1877* (Upper Saddle River, NJ: Pearson, 2006), 326.

61. Ibid.; *New York Times,* 8 April 1876.

62. *Cincinnati Commercial,* 24 April 1876.

6. Radical Voice

Epigraph: *Cincinnati Commercial,* 4 March 1881.

1. *Cincinnati Commercial,* 27 November 1875.

2. Ibid., 11 December 1876. George Mack is another of the earliest African

American socialists on record. His name is mentioned in the *Socialist*, 11 January 1879. See also Philip S. Foner, *American Socialism and Black Americans: From the Age of Jackson to World War II* (Westport, CT: Greenwood Press, 1977), 58. However, biographical data about him is difficult to trace.

3. *Emancipator*, 31 March 1877; *Cincinnati Commercial*, 27 March 1877; *Cincinnati Daily Enquirer*, 27 March 1877.

4. Platform of Principle of the National Labor Union, adopted September 26, 1868, in Richard Theodore Ely, *The Labor Movement in America* (New York: Thomas Y. Crowell, 1886), 341. According to W. E. B. Du Bois, the NLU leadership welcomed African American labor "not because they were laborers but because they might be competitors in the market" (see Du Bois, *Black Reconstruction in America 1860–1880* [New York: Atheneum, 1992], 354–55; and John Hope Franklin, *Reconstruction after the Civil War* [Chicago: University of Chicago Press, 1994], 179).

5. Timothy Messer-Kruse, *The Yankee International: Marxism and the American Reform Tradition* (Chapel Hill: University of Chapel Hill Press, 1998), 190, 191; August Meier, *Negro Thought in America 1880–1915: Racial Ideologies in the Age of Booker T. Washington* (Ann Arbor: University of Michigan Press, 1963), 8.

6. Although the actual name of the organization was the Colored National Labor Union, it also has been called the National Colored Labor Union, the National Negro Labor Union, and the black National Labor Union by contemporary press and historians (Manning Marable and Leith Mullings, eds., *Let Nobody Turn Us Around: Voices of Resistance, Reform, and Renewal* [New York: Rowman and Littlefield, 2003], 134; Messer-Kruse, *Yankee International*, 190–94 passim).

7. R. J. M. Blackett, *Beating against the Barriers: The Lives of Six Nineteenth-Century Afro-Americans* (Ithaca: Cornell University Press, 1986), 255; Meier, *Negro Thought in America*, 8–9.

8. *Proceedings of the Colored National Labor Convention Held in Washington, D.C., on December 6, 7, 8, 9, and 10th, 1869* (Washington: Office of the New Era, 1869), 11.

9. Ibid.; Du Bois, *Black Reconstruction*, 361, 366; Meier, *Negro Thought in America*, 8.

10. Foner, *American Socialism and Black Americans*, 47.

11. *Workingman's Advocate*, 27 August 1870, copied in John R. Commons, Ulrich B. Phillips, Eugene Gilmore, Helen L. Sumner, and John B. Andrews, eds., *A Documentary History of Industrial Society* (Cleveland: Arthur H. Clark, 1910), 258–59.

12. James M. Morris, "William Haller: 'The Disturbing Element,'" *Cincinnati Historical Society Bulletin* 28 (Winter 1970): 265; Foner, *American Socialism and Black Americans*, 47; Du Bois, *Black Reconstruction*, 360; Philip S. Foner, *A History of the Labor Movement in the United States: From Colonial Times to the Founding of the American Federation of Labor* (New York: International, 1972), 1:399, 406.

13. *Cincinnati Commercial,* 17 August 1870; Commons, Phillips, Gilmore et al., eds., *A Documentary History of American Industrial Society,* 260–61.

14. Du Bois, *Black Reconstruction,* 361.

15. Eric Foner, *Reconstruction: America's Unfinished Revolution, 1863–1877* (New York: Harper and Row, 1988), 512–13.

16. Morris, "William Haller: 'The Disturbing Element,'" 271.

17. Ibid., 276.

18. *Cincinnati Commercial,* 27 March 1877.

19. See Foner, *American Socialism and Black Americans,* 375–76 n. 12; and Morris, "William Haller: 'The Disturbing Element,'" 259, 265, 278.

20. *New York Times,* 1 February 1874. On the Sovereigns of Industry, see Messer-Kruse, *Yankee International,* 239–41. The Sovereigns of Industry was intended to be an industrial counterpart to the Grange, which was an alliance of farmers established in 1867 to protect their mutual economic and political interests. Grange ideology was rooted in the belief that owners of capital, railroads, merchants, and other middlemen were responsible for oppressing the working classes. The Grange pioneered and perfected the use of cooperatives as a means of reducing the power of the middlemen and empowering farmers.

21. The antebellum forerunners to the cooperative store idea were "Protective Unions," which introduced the working class to socialism through cooperative experiments such as cooperative stores. On Protective Unions, see Mark Lause, *Young America: Land, Labor, and the Republican Community* (Urbana: University of Illinois Press, 2005), 31; and Edwin Charles Rozwenc, *Cooperatives Come to America: The History of the Protective Union Store Movement, 1845–1867* (Philadelphia: Porcupine Press, 1975), chap. 4.

22. *New York Times,* 1 February 1874; Richard Theodore Ely, *The Labor Movement in America* (New York: Thomas Y. Crowell, 1886), 174, 175–76; Foner, *A History of the Labor Movement in the United States,* 476; Philip S. Foner, *American Socialism and Black Americans: From the Age of Jackson to World War II* (Westport, CT: Greenwood Press, 1977), 375–76 n. 12; Solon Justus Buck, *The Granger Movement: A Study of Agricultural Organization and Its Political, Economic and Social Manifestations 1870–1880* (Cambridge: Harvard University Press, 1913), 306.

23. *Cincinnati Commercial,* 27 November 1875.

24. Ibid.

25. According to historian Timothy Messer-Kruse, radicals typically used the word "cooperation" in place of "socialism." It expressed socialists' "anti-capitalistic ideals and a practical tactic for achieving them" (see Messer-Kruse, *Yankee International,* 138, 236).

26. Lause, *Young America,* 31.

27. The Workingmen's Party was alternately called the Workingmen's Society in contemporary sources. It was the first Marxist political party in the United States.

28. In Cincinnati, the Social Democratic Workingmen's Party had been built on the back of the less successful Sovereigns of Industry (Morris, "William Haller: 'The Disturbing Element,'" 278; Philip S. Foner, *The Workingmen's Party of the United States: A History of the First Marxist Party in the Americas* [Minneapolis: MEP, 1984], 33).

29. Foner, *American Socialism and Black Americans*, 43; Morris Hillquit, *History of Socialism in the United States* (New York: Funk and Wagnalls, 1910), 188–89.

30. Foner, *Workingmen's Party of the United States*, 34–35.

31. *Cincinnati Daily Enquirer*, 11 February 1877.

32. Lassalleanism is based on the ideas of Ferdinand Lassalle. For more on them, see Foner, *Workingmen's Party of the United States*, 20.

33. Foner, *Workingmen's Party of the United States*, 37.

34. Historians Philip S. Foner and Winston James assert that Clark "renounced" the Republican Party (see Foner, "Peter H. Clark: Pioneer Black Socialist," *Journal of Ethnic Studies* 5, no. 3 [Fall 1977]:24; Foner, *Workingmen's Party of the United State*, 50; Foner, *American Socialism and Black Americans*, 48; and James, "Being Red and Black in Jim Crow America," 342). That language is too strong and mischaracterizes Clark's sentiment toward the Republican Party. He expressed neither ill-will toward nor condemnation of the Republican Party (*Emancipator*, 31 March 1877). See also *Cincinnati Commercial*, 27 March 1877.

35. In the 22 July 1879 issue of the *Cincinnati Commercial*, Clark claimed he had "always" been attached to the Republican Party.

36. *Cincinnati Commercial*, 17 June 1876 and 26 October 1876.

37. In a 1908 letter, Clark told President William H. Taft that he was "disappointed" that the president's father, Alphonso Taft, had been appointed only as ambassador to Russia because his "great talent and conspicuous service to the Republican Party entitled him to a greater reward." Clark added, "The party owed him more and should have paid the debt." This letter is instructive. It reveals that Clark not only supported the idea of patronage, but believed that supporters ought to be rewarded according to the quality of their political support. This letter not only illuminates that Clark had strong opinions about patronage, but that he harbored resentment for parties that did not award supporters with positions befitting their service (see Peter H. Clark to President William H. Taft, 30 December 1908 in William H. Taft Papers, Library of Congress).

38. *Christian Recorder*, 19 October 1876.

39. Ibid.

40. *Washington Chronicle*, 20 October 1876. The *Christian Recorder*, 1 March 1877, reported that Taft recommended Clark as a man of "great ability, purity of character and shining abilities."

41. *Christian Recorder*, 25 January 1877.

42. John Mercer Langston accused the American Missionary Association and

the First Congregational Church of Washington of misappropriating the school's funds (see Walter Dyson, *Howard University: The Capstone of Negro Education A History: 1867–1940* [Washington, D.C.: Graduate School of Howard University, 1941], 59–60, 62). According to reports, the deficits for the 1874 school year were projected at 38,573.10. In addition, the standing indebtedness amounted to $87,450.

43. Peter H. Clark to Alphonso Taft, 24 October 1876, Library of Congress; *Christian Recorder,* 25 January 1877 and 1 March 1877.

44. Rayford W. Logan, *Howard University: The First Hundred Years, 1867–1967* (New York: New York University Press, 1969), 82–83. Clark received none of the trustees' votes.

45. *Cincinnati Commercial,* 21 July 1877.

46. Ibid.

47. Ibid.

48. Ibid.

49. David A. Gerber, *Black Ohio and the Color Line 1860–1915* (Urbana: University of Illinois Press, 1976), 223.

50. Ibid.

51. *Cincinnati Commercial,* 21 July 1877.

52. Ibid., 11 December 1876; Herbert Gutman, "Peter H. Clark: Pioneer Negro Socialist, 1877," *Journal of Negro Education* 34 (September 1965): 413, 414; Foner, "Peter H. Clark: Pioneer Black Socialist," 23–24.

53. *Cincinnati Commercial,* 27 March 1877; *Emancipator,* 31 March 1877; Foner, "Peter H. Clark: Pioneer Black Socialist," 24.

54. *Cincinnati Commercial,* 27 March 1877, 23 July 1877, and 19 August 1877; *Emancipator,* 31 March 1877.

55. Alfred Anderson to William H. West, 5 August 1877; William H. West to President Rutherford B. Hayes, 8 August 1877. William H. West was a Republican who had served as Ohio's attorney general and a Supreme Court justice in the 1860s and 1870s. For context, see John Hope Franklin, *George Washington Williams: A Biography* (Chicago: University of Chicago Press, 1985), 46–47.

56. William H. West to Rutherford B. Hayes, 8 August 1877; *Cincinnati Commercial,* 21 July 1877; Franklin, *George Washington Williams,* 46.

57. Foner, *Reconstruction, 1863–1877,* 583–84; Foner, "Peter H. Clark: Pioneer Black Socialist," 25–26, 29. Contemporary sources that reported on the strike include the *Cincinnati Daily Enquirer,* 23 July 1877.

58. *Cincinnati Commercial,* 23 July 1877.

59. Ibid.; *Emancipator,* 28 July 1877.

60. *Cincinnati Commercial,* 23 July 1877.

61. Ibid.

62. Ibid.

63. Ibid.

64. Ibid., 23 and 26 July 1877.

65. Ibid., 23 July 1877.

66. Ibid.

67. Ibid.

68. One hundred people died during the strike; more than one thousand were arrested.

69. *Cincinnati Commercial*, 26 July 1877. For a discussion of how elites viewed socialists after the Great Strike, see Heather Cox Richardson, *The Death of Reconstruction: Race, Labor, and Politics in the Post–Civil War North, 1865–1901* (Cambridge: Harvard University Press, 2001), 185.

70. *Cincinnati Daily Enquirer*, 23 July 1877; *Cincinnati Commercial*, 23, 24, and 26 July 1877 and 19 August 1877.

71. *Cincinnati Daily Enquirer*, 7 August 1877.

72. *Emancipator*, 18 August 1877.

73. *Cincinnati Commercial*, 25 August 1877.

74. *Cincinnati Daily Gazette*, 10 October 1877; *Emancipator*, 16 July 1877; Lawrence Grossman, "In His Veins Coursed No Bootlicking Blood: The Career of Peter Clark," *Ohio History* 2 (Spring 1977): 89; Foner, *American Socialism and Black Americans*, 57.

75. William J. Simmons, *Men of Mark: Eminent, Progressive and Rising* (Cleveland: George M. Rewell, 1887), 554, 558; Gerber, *Black Ohio and the Color Line 1860–1915*, 227.

76. *Cincinnati Daily Enquirer*, 10 October, 1878; The SLP's platform demanded that the "resources of life—the means of production, public transportation and communication—(Land Machinery, Railroads, Telegraph Lines, Canals, etc.)— become ... the common property of the whole people, through the Government, [and to] ... abolish the Wages System and substitute in its stead Co-Operative Production.... Among the specific party objectives were an eight-hour work day, the inspection of labor conditions, the compulsory education of all children under 14, and a prohibition on the use of child and convict labor" (see *Socialist*, 31 May 1879).

77. Two different election tallies for Clark are reported in the newspapers. The *Cincinnati Daily Enquirer*, 10 October 1878, reports that he earned 281 votes, while the *Cincinnati Gazette*, 16 October 1878, reports 275. *Socialist*, 9 November 1878.

78. *Socialist*, 19 October 1878 and 26 November 1878.

79. Open positions in the spring of 1879 included mayor, seats on the public works and police boards, city solicitor, city treasurer, judge of the police court, wharfmaster, justice of the peace, and prosecuting attorney (*Cincinnati Daily Enquirer*, 10 October 1878 and 11 April 1879; *Emancipator*, 18 August 1877; *Cincinnati Daily Enquirer*, 16 October 1878; Socialistic Labor Party National Executive Committee, Platform, Constitution, Resolutions, Together with a Condensed Report of the National Convention, Held at Allegheny, PA [April 1880], 10), found at: www .archive.org/details/PlatformConstitutionAndResolutionsTogetherWithACon

densedReportOf. Philip Van Patten, *Report of the NEC to the 2nd National Convention of the Socialist Labor Party of America* (December 26, 1879), 7, found at: www.marxisthistory.org/history/usa/parties/slp/1879/1226-vanpatten-necreport .pdf. Foner, "Peter H. Clark: Pioneer Black Socialist," 29, 30; Foner, *American Socialism and Black Americans,* 57; Morris, "William Haller: 'The Disturbing Element,'" 282, 283; Grossman, "In His Veins Coursed No Bootlicking Blood," 89; James Matthew Morris, "The Road to Trade Unionism: Organized Labor in Cincinnati to 1893" (Ph.D. diss, University of Cincinnati, 1969), 239, 241–42, 244.

80. *Labor Standard,* 24 February 1877 and 25 November 1877; *Socialist,* 12 August 1879; Foner, *Workingmen's Party of the United States,* 60, quoting *Labor Standard,* 25 November 1876; Morris, "Road to Trade Unionism," 243; Morris, "William Haller: 'The Disturbing Element,'" 284, 286.

81. The Cincinnati section brought Haller up on charges of being opposed to party principles. The party placed him on trial, where he was determined to be guilty of the charges (see *Cincinnati Daily Enquirer* 4, 11, 12, 18 July 1879 and 11 and 15 August 1879; Morris, "William Haller: 'The Disturbing Element,'" 283–89 passim; and Morris, "Road to Trade Unionism," 242, 249–52).

82. *Socialist,* 18 January 1879.

83. *Cincinnati Daily Enquirer,* 4 October 1878; *Cincinnati Commercial,* 22 July 1879; *Socialist,* 2 August 1879.

84. Most historians who have written about Clark contend that he was critical of socialism's failure to explicitly address racial issues in labor. Moreover, many also claim that he left the movement because of its failure to confront the unique problems of African Americans. None of the primary source evidence supports that theory, however. For works that erroneously make that claim, see Foner, *American Socialism and Black Americans,* 59; Foner, "Peter H. Clark: Pioneer Black Socialist," 30; Winston James, "Being Red and Black in Jim Crow America," in *Time Longer Than Rope: A Century of African American Activism, 1850–1950,* ed. Charles M. Payne and Adam Green (New York: New York University Press, 2003), 338, 347; and Lawrence Christensen, "Peter Humphries Clark," *Missouri Historical Review* 88, no. 2 (January 1994): 151. The only historians who do not contend that Clark left the party because of its failures to address issues of race are Lawrence Grossman, David Gerber, and Herbert Gutman. Grossman does not speculate as to why Clark moved away from socialism, but he characterizes Clark's involvement as an "idiosyncratic tangent" and, later, an "interlude," perhaps the product of an "iconoclastic mind" (see Grossman, "In His Veins Coursed No Bootlicking Blood," 88, 89). Gerber states that Clark left because he grew "disillusioned by the doctrinaire tendencies within the party" (see Gerber, *Black Ohio and the Color Line, 1860–1915,* 233). Herbert Gutman also states that Clark became disillusioned with socialism but never speculates about why (see Gutman, "Peter H. Clark: Pioneer Negro Socialist, 1877," 415).

85. *Emancipator,* 31 March 1877; *Cincinnati Commercial,* 27 March 1877;

Cincinnati Daily Enquirer, 27 March 1877. Since speeches were recorded by hand, all three papers record the substance of that speech differently. Of the three, the *Emancipator* and the *Cincinnati Daily Enquirer* contain the most details about Clark's comments regarding race.

86. *Cincinnati Commercial,* 22 July 1879.

87. Foner, *American Socialism and Black Americans,* 43.

88. Cedric J. Robinson, *Black Marxism: The Making of the Black Radical Tradition* (Chapel Hill: University of North Carolina Press, 1983), 195–96. Robinson argues that Marx had a Eurocentric view of history. Consequently, his theories about labor and capital emerged from the same core as that historical narrative and thus could never resonate with black radicals.

89. James, "Being Red and Black in Jim Crow America," 338.

7. Voice of Dissent

Epigraph: *AME Church Review* 2 (January 1885).

1. *Cincinnati Commercial,* 26 July 1879.

2. Ibid., 22 October 1879.

3. *Cincinnati Daily Enquirer,* 7 September 1879.

4. *Cincinnati Commercial,* 23 August 1873.

5. Ibid., 24 April 1876.

6. Peter H. Clark to Hon. John Sherman, 10 and 24 April 1881; and John Sherman to Peter H. Clark, 27 April 1881, in "Memorandum Relative to George Washington Williams, Minister to Hayti," Records of the U.S. Treasury Department.

7. Peter H. Clark to William H. Taft, 30 December 1908, William H. Taft Papers, Library of Congress.

8. Then, Garfield had confessed in a private letter to Ohio's governor, Jacob Dolson Cox: "I confess to a strong feeling of repugnance when I think of the negro being made our political equals—and I would be glad if they could be colonized—sent to heaven or got rid of in any decent way it would delight me. But colonization has proven a hopeless failure everywhere." These are jarring words from a man who would later be elected president. One could conjecture that if Garfield had such strong contempt for the idea of political equality in 1865, it is doubtful he would have hired an African American to serve in his administration in 1880, political patronage, or not (see James A. Garfield to Jacob D. Cox, 26 July 1865, Jacob D. Cox Papers, Oberlin College).

9. Both contemporaries and historians conclude that he became a Democrat because he has political ambitions and out of bitterness that Republicans had not appointed him to the Haitian ministry (see A. Gerber, *Black Ohio and the Color Line 1860–1915* [Urbana: University of Illinois Press, 1976], 233.

10. *Cincinnati Daily Enquirer,* 3 October 1882.

11. *New York Freeman,* 27 October 1888; *Cincinnati Daily Enquirer,* 23 October 1883; *Washington Bee,* 14 March 1885; *Index to the Reports of Committees of the*

House of Representatives for the Second Session of the Forty Eighth Congress, 1884–85 (Washington: Government Printing Office, 1885), 576, 583.

12. *New York Freeman*, 27 October 1888; *Cincinnati Daily Enquirer*, 23 October 1883.

13. *New York Freeman*, 27 October 1888; *Cincinnati Daily Enquirer*, 23 October 1883; August Meier, *Negro Thought in America 1880–1915: Radical Ideologies in the Age of Booker T. Washington* (Ann Arbor: University of Michigan Press, 1966), 26–31 passim.

14. Meier, *Negro Thought in America 1880–1915*, 30.

15. Meier, 30–31. For deeper insight into the life of another prominent African American who became a Democrat in the 1880s, see the biography of James Milton Turner by Gary R. Kremer, *James Milton Turner and the Promise of America: The Public Life of a Post–Civil War Black Leader* (Columbia: University of Missouri Press, 1991), 174–93 passim.

16. Lawrence Grossman, *The Democratic Party and the Negro: Northern and National Politics 1868–92* (Urbana: University of Illinois Press, 1976), 82; John Hope Franklin, *George Washington Williams: A Biography* (Chicago: University of Chicago Press, 1985), 86–87; Gerber, *Black Ohio and the Color Line 1860–1915*, 225.

17. Grossman, *Democratic Party and the Negro*, 81.

18. *Cleveland Gazette*, 8 September 1883 and 19 September 1885.

19. While Smith claimed to be purely concerned for the best interest of African Americans, there is some evidence that he used his forum with the *Gazette* for personal gain. Evidence suggests that at some point Republicans purchased Smith's loyalty to the party, whereby he was paid for making the *Cleveland Gazette* a Republican paper. In July 1885, Senator Marcus A. Hanna wrote to Joseph Foraker, advising him that Smith "must either be helped, or his will not be a Republican paper." Hanna stated that he had already sent Smith a check for fifty dollars and encouraged Foraker to "see Mr. Smith and make the best arrangement with him ... to secure his hearty and active support." Hanna advised Foraker to agree to pay Smith not more than from one hundred to three hundred dollars during the entire gubernatorial campaign (see Marcus A. Hanna to Joseph B. Foraker, 2 July 1885, Marcus Alonzo Hanna Papers [Hanna-McCormick Family Papers, Box 2], Library of Congress).

20. *Cleveland Gazette*, 10 May 1884 and 3 October 1885; *Index to the Reports of Committees of the House of Representatives*, 382–84.

21. *Cleveland Gazette*, 3 October 1885.

22. *Index to the Reports of Committees of the House of Representatives*, 373. Meier, *Negro Thought in America 1880–1915*, 29; Frederick Douglass, "I Denounce the So-Called Emancipation as a Stupendous Fraud," 16 April 1888, found at: www.historyisaweapon.com/defcon1/douglassfraud.html.

23. *Cleveland Gazette*, 10 May 1884; Meier, *Negro Thought in America 1880–1915*, 33.

24. *Cleveland Gazette*, 31 May 1884.

25. Ibid., 31 May 1884 and 14 June 1884.

26. Ibid., 29 May 1884; *Index to the Reports of Committees of the House of Representatives*, 589.

27. Contemporaries used the term "mixed" to refer to integrated schools. I use the more modern word to avoid confusion.

28. *Cleveland Gazette*, 8, 15, and 29 March 1884. Surprisingly, Clark, who believed that citizenship rights could only be enforced and protected by state governments, was silent on this issue. He never joined the chorus of condemnation for the weak state civil rights law, proving that he had become more of a partisan than a leader (see *Cincinnati Daily Enquirer*, 23 October 1883).

29. *Cleveland Gazette*, 12 April 1884 and 16 February 1884.

30. Nikki Taylor, *Frontiers of Freedom: Cincinnati's Black Community, 1802–68* (Athens: Ohio University Press, 2005), 161–74 passim.

31. *Cincinnati Commercial*, 23 September 1873.

32. For more on why people supported separate institutions in this era, see August Meier, *Negro Thought in America 1880–1915: Racial Ideologies in the Age of Booker T. Washington* (Ann Arbor: University of Michigan Press, 1963), 13; *Christian Recorder*, 17 April 1884.

33. William M. Banks, *Black Intellectuals: Race and Responsibility in American Life* (New York: Norton, 1996), 25, 26; Meier, *Negro Thought in America 1880–1915*, 48–49.

34. Meier, *Negro Thought in America 1880–1915*, 13.

35. *Christian Recorder*, 17 April 1884.

36. Ibid.

37. In 1864–65, Clark served as president of the Albany Enterprise Academy, which had been established in Athens County, Ohio, to train teachers (see Constitution of the Albany Enterprise Academy Located at Albany, Athens County, Ohio Historical Society).

38. *Cleveland Gazette*, 26 January 1884, 19 and 26 April 1884, and 24 May 1884; *Cincinnati Daily Enquirer*, 11 February 1885; Gerber, *Black Ohio and the Color Line 1860–1915*, 238.

39. *Cleveland Gazette*, 26 January 1884 and 19 April 1884; *Christian Recorder*, 17 April 1884.

40. *Cleveland Gazette*, 12 and 19 April 1884; Gerber, *Black Ohio and the Color Line 1860–1915*, 238.

41. *Christian Recorder*, 17 April 1884; Gerber, *Black Ohio and the Color Line 1860–1915*, 239.

42. *Cleveland Gazette*, 26 April 1884.

43. *Christian Recorder*, quoted in *Cleveland Gazette*, 26 April 1884.

44. *Cleveland Gazette*, 20 September 1884.

45. Ibid., 22 March 1884 and 19 April 1884.

46. *Louisville Bulletin*, quoted in *Cleveland Gazette*, 29 March 1884; *Detroit Plaindealer*, quoted in *Cleveland Gazette*, 6 December 1884.

8. Voice of Betrayal

Epigraph: *Cincinnati Commercial Gazette,* 6 December 1885.

1. *Cincinnati Commercial Gazette,* 31 October 1884.

2. *Cleveland Gazette,* 29 August 1885; *Cincinnati Commercial Gazette,* 2 September 1885.

3. *Cleveland Gazette,* 29 August 1885 and 13 October 1885; *Cincinnati Commercial Gazette,* 16 and 31 October 1884, 2 September 1885, and 30 November 1885. See also Joseph Benson Foraker, *Notes of a Busy Life* (Cincinnati: Stewart and Kidd, 1917), 195–96. Accounts differ about whether 152 or 153 men were arrested that evening.

4. *Cleveland Gazette,* 29 August 1885.

5. According to Wilson Jeremiah Moses, Frederick Douglass was unable to understand machine politics in the Gilded Age (see Moses, *Creative Conflict in African American Thought: Frederick Douglass, Alexander Crummell, Booker T. Washington, W. E. B. Du Bois, and Marcus Garvey* [Cambridge: Cambridge University Press, 2004], 42).

6. Mark Wahlgren Summers, *Party Games: Getting, Keeping, and Using Power in Gilded Age Politics* (Chapel Hill: University of North Carolina Press, 2004), 141.

7. For election schemes, see *Ohio State Journal,* 9 October 1880; *Cincinnati Commercial Gazette,* 19 October 1884, 2 September 1885, and 30 November 1885; *Cincinnati Daily Enquirer,* 19 September 1884 and 1 December 1885; *Afro-American,* 19 September 1885; *Evening Post,* 20 October 1884; *Cleveland Gazette,* 29 August 1885; and Foraker, *Notes of a Busy Life,* 213–14.

8. Zane Miller, *Boss Cox's Cincinnati: Urban Politics in the Progressive Era* (New York: Oxford University Press, 1968), 72.

9. *Cleveland Gazette,* 3 May 1884.

10. For a more in-depth discussion of "bummers," see Miller, *Boss Cox's Cincinnati,* 72; Nikki Taylor, *Frontiers of Freedom: Cincinnati's Black Community, 1802–1868* (Athens: Ohio University Press, 2005), 201, 202; and David Gerber, *Black Ohio and the Color Line 1860–1915* (Urbana: University of Illinois Press, 1976), 225.

11. Summers, *Party Games,* 11, 96.

12. A notorious local boss was George Barnesdale Cox, who tapped into the Cincinnati saloon community to ensure his political ascendancy. He first successfully ran for city council in 1879. By 1884, Cox was a Republican ward boss and a "recognized power in the West End." Boss Cox was a strong manager of James C. Blaine's presidential campaign in Hamilton County in 1884. In the late 1880s and 1890s, he chaired the Hamilton County Republican Committee and later built a reputation as the most powerful city boss in Cincinnati's history (Miller, *Boss Cox's Cincinnati,* 77).

13. Foraker, *Notes of a Busy Life,* 214.

14. Ibid., 214–15.

15. *Ohio State Journal*, 4 November 1884.

16. Ibid., 27 October 1881; *Cincinnati Commercial*, 9 August 1879; *Cincinnati Commercial Gazette*, 13 April 1884.

17. Gerber, *Black Ohio and the Color Line 1860–1915*, 230–31. Estimates of the number of African American voters in Ohio vary. In 1884, the *Cleveland Gazette* estimated there were twenty-five thousand (*Cleveland Gazette*, 29 March 1884).

18. People from around the nation tried to sway the African American vote in Ohio. J. H. Merriwhether, an African American Republican from Washington, D.C., submitted an open letter to the *Cincinnati Commercial Gazette* in which he reminded African Americans that Cleveland was a Democrat and that the party had always acted against them (*Cincinnati Commercial Gazette*, 13 October 1884).

19. *Cincinnati Daily Enquirer*, 17 September 1885; Foraker, *Notes of a Busy Life*, 215.

20. *Cincinnati Daily Enquirer*, 17 September 1885.

21. Foraker, *Notes of a Busy Life*, 217.

22. *Cleveland Gazette*, 29 August 1885; *Cincinnati Commercial Gazette*, 2 September 1885.

23. *Cincinnati Commercial Gazette*, 31 October 1884.

24. *Cincinnati Commercial Gazette*, 21 October 1884; *Evening Post*, 21 October 1884.

25. *Evening Post*, 1 October 1884.

26. *Cincinnati Commercial Gazette*, 2 September 1885; *Cleveland Gazette*, 29 August 1885; *Cincinnati Daily Enquirer*, 1 December 1885.

27. Gerber, *Black Ohio and the Color Line*, 239; *Cincinnati Commercial Gazette*, 30 November 1885.

28. *Cincinnati Commercial Gazette*, 2, 19, and 27 September 1885; *Cleveland Gazette*, 29 August 1885.

29. *Cincinnati Commercial Gazette*, 23 September 1885.

30. Frederick Douglass, in *AME Church Review* 2 (January 1885): 213–14.

31. Timothy Thomas Fortune, in *AME Church Review* 2 (January 1885): 220–21.

32. Peter H. Clark, in *AME Church Review* 2 (January 1885): 235–39 passim.

33. Ibid., 237.

34. Ibid., 237, 238. Clark believed the best way for African Americans to change public sentiment was by ingratiating themselves with white Democrats and cooperating with them to secure civil rights legislation. But this strategy was not born out of accommodationism, as some may think; Clark cannot be considered a forerunner of Booker T. Washington because he never compromised his demand for civil rights or tolerated racism.

35. *Detroit Plaindealer*, quoted in *Cleveland Gazette*, 6 December 1884.

36. Lawrence Grossman, *The Democratic Party and the Negro: Northern and*

National Politics 1868–92 (Urbana: University of Illinois, 1976), 90; *Afro-American,* 19 September 1885; *Cincinnati Commercial Gazette,* 6 December 1885.

37. Gov. George Hoadly to James A. Guy, 2 January 1885, Reel 9, Grover Cleveland Papers, Library of Congress. There is no known extant evidence of what Hoadly may have said to persuade his good friend Clark to reconsider his position, but his letter to Guy is a good indication of his strong feelings on this issue.

38. *Cleveland Gazette,* 10 January 1885.

39. The climate in Cincinnati by then had turned so antagonistic to opponents of the bill that one citizen, Elias Polk, desperately defended his position before an agitated Zion Baptist assembly in February 1885 (*Cleveland Gazette,* 7, 11, and 14 February 1885; *Cincinnati Daily Enquirer,* 11 February 1885).

40. Historian David Gerber concluded that it was destined to fail because it included the issue of intermarriage, along with the school issue. Very few Republican or Democratic legislators were ready to sanction intermarriage in 1885; even those who supported school integration typically opposed intermarriage. The fact that the school issue was tied to the controversial intermarriage issue guaranteed its failure (Gerber, *Black Ohio and the Color Line,* 240).

41. *Cleveland Gazette* editors reasoned that an embittered Clark had aligned himself with the Democrats because had not been appointed to the Cincinnati postmaster position under the Republican administration in 1874. That charge is false, however. He had never even applied for that position; his name is not listed among the official applicants for that position. The *Gazette* also claimed that Clark's son, Herbert, as well as another leading black Democrat from Cincinnati, Samuel Lewis, were upset that they had been fired from federal service. On the names of applicants for the postmaster position in Cincinnati, see *Cincinnati Daily Gazette,* 7, 9, and 17 January 1884; *Cleveland Gazette,* 13 September 1884.

42. *Cleveland Gazette,* 29 March 1884, 3 May 1884, and 19 April 1884.

43. Gov. George Hoadly to Daniel S. Lamont, 28 March 1885, Reel 9, Grover Cleveland Papers, Library of Congress.

44. *Cleveland Gazette,* 29 March 1884 and 5 May 1884.

45. Gov. George Hoadly to Daniel S. Lamont, 28 March 1885, Reel 9, Grover Cleveland Papers, Library of Congress.

46. John Hope Franklin, *George Washington Williams: A Biography* (Chicago: University of Chicago Press, 1985), 149, 154.

47. In 1880, wealthy white residents of the Avondale section of Cincinnati wanted the twelve acres of land near Clinton Avenue, on which the Colored American Cemetery sat. State senator Charles L. Fleischmann, a wealthy yeast and distillery owner, and other Avondale residents schemed to get rid of the cemetery. First, they pulled strings and got the Hamilton County Health Department to declare the cemetery a public nuisance. Senator Fleischmann then enlisted the help of his private legislative secretary, who also happened to be the newly elected black assemblyman George Washington Williams, to introduce a bill to prevent

cemetery trustees from interring any more bodies. Cincinnati's African American community raised strenuous objections to these attempts to deprive them of their only cemetery; but they were even more disgusted that a black legislator had introduced the bill. Clark, whose own father and sister were buried in the cemetery, had many overlapping personal stakes in the issue (*Cincinnati Commercial,* 13 and 16 April 1880; *Cincinnati Daily Enquirer,* 13 January 1880, 13 and 14 April 1880). For the full story, see Franklin, *George Washington Williams,* 88–95.

48. Peter H. Clark to Thomas F. Bayard, n.d., received 17 March 1885, George Washington Williams File, Box 103, Department of State. Other names on that list include Robert Purvis, Dr. J. L. Brotherton, Rev. James Poindexter of Columbus, and Monroe Trotter.

49. William Means to Hon. George Pendleton, 10 March 1885, George Washington Williams File, Box 103, Department of State.

50. Franklin, *George Washington Williams,* 148–63 passim.

51. The Ohio governor stressed that it was necessary to award only a few positions to African Americans; he reasoned that making those few appointments noticeable "was more important than number" (Gov. George Hoadly to Daniel S. Lamont, 28 March 1885, Reel 9, Grover Cleveland Papers, Library of Congress). For a fuller account of Downing's career, see August Meier, *Negro Thought in America 1880–1915: Racial Ideologies in the Age of Booker T. Washington* (Ann Arbor: University of Michigan Press, 1963), 28–29.

52. Gov. George Hoadly to Daniel S. Lamont, 28 March 1885, Reel 9, Grover Cleveland Papers, Library of Congress; Gov. George Hoadly to President Grover Cleveland, 25 April 1885, Reel 11, Grover Cleveland Papers, Library of Congress; Gov. George Hoadly to President Grover Cleveland, 27 October 1885, Reel 22, Grover Cleveland Papers, Library of Congress.

53. Franklin, *George Washington Williams,* 155, 158–59.

54. George Hoadly to Grover Cleveland, 9 September 1885, Reel 19, Grover Cleveland Papers, Library of Congress.

55. *Cleveland Gazette,* 29 August 1885, 5 and 26 September 1885; *Cincinnati Commercial Gazette,* 5, 14, 19, 21, and 27 September 1885.

56. *Ohio State Journal,* 12 October 1882; John Sherman, *John Sherman's Recollections of Forty Years in the House, Senate, and Cabinet: An Autobiography* (Chicago: Werner, 1895), 2:860.

57. Gov. George Hoadly to Daniel S. Lamont, 28 March 1885, Reel 9, Grover Cleveland Papers, Library of Congress.

58. Grossman, *Democratic Party and the Negro,* 82–83; *Cleveland Gazette,* 17 and 24 January 1885.

59. *Ohio State Journal,* 6 October 1883.

60. In his autobiography written in 1917, Foraker reflected that the Mullen case made Ohioans more acutely aware of the efforts to disfranchise African Americans in the South. He also concluded that the case raised his own consciousness about how the right to vote must be protected and guaranteed by

the Constitution. He stated that "every man who has the right to vote must be accorded that right, free from violence, fraud, or intimidation" (Foraker, *Notes of a Busy Life*, 196).

61. *Cincinnati Commercial Gazette,* 30 November 1885.

62. *Cincinnati Daily Enquirer,* 25 September 1885.

63. *Afro-American,* 19 September 1885; *Cincinnati Commercial Gazette,* 30 November 1885.

64. *Cincinnati Commercial Gazette,* 30 November 1885; *Cleveland Gazette,* 5 December 1885.

65. *Cincinnati Commercial Gazette,* 30 November 1885.

66. Ibid., 30 November 1885 and 6 December 1885.

67. *Advance Courier,* cited in *Cleveland Gazette,* 19 December 1885; *Cincinnati Daily Enquirer,* 1 December 1885; *Afro-American,* 19 September 1885.

68. *Cincinnati Commercial,* 31 March 1867.

69. *Cincinnati Commercial Gazette,* 1 December 1885; *Afro-American,* 19 September 1885; *Cleveland Gazette,* 5 December 1885.

70. *Cincinnati Commercial Gazette,* 1 December 1885; *Afro-American,* 19 September 1885; *Cleveland Gazette,* 5 December 1885.

71. *Cincinnati Commercial Gazette,* 6 December 1885.

72. Ibid.

73. *Cleveland Gazette,* 24 September 1887.

9. A Still Voice

Epigraph: Rev. William J. Simmons, *Men of Mark: Eminent, Progressive and Rising* (New York: Arno Press, 1968), 379.

1. "The Black Laws: Speech of Hon. B. W. Arnett of Greene County and Hon. J. A. Brown of Cuyahoga County, in the Ohio House of Representatives, March 10, 1886," in American Memory, "Daniel A. P. Murray Collection, 1818–1907," found at http://memory.loc.gov/cgi-bin/query/r?ammem/murray:@field(DOCID+@lit(lcrbmrpt0d06)):@@@REF.

2. Ibid.

3. There is a discrepancy in the reporting of the final vote. According to "The Black Laws: Speech of Hon. B. W. Arnett of Greene County and Hon. J. A. Brown of Cuyahoga County, in the Ohio House of Representatives, March 10, 1886," the vote was 62 to 28 (see ibid.). The *Cleveland Gazette,* 13 March 1886, reported the vote as 61 to 27.

4. David Gerber, *Black Ohio and the Color Line 1860–1915* (Urbana: University of Illinois Press, 1976), 242–43; *Cleveland Gazette,* 13 March 1886, 9 October 1886, and 19 and 26 February 1887.

5. Rev. William J. Simmons, *Men of Mark: Eminent, Progressive and Rising* (New York: Arno Press, 1968), 884–88; Gerber, *Black Ohio and the Color Line 1860–1915,* 350–51.

6. *Cleveland Gazette*, 5 and 12 March, 1887.

7. *New York Freeman*, 26 March 1887.

8. Ibid.

9. Jack Blocker, *A Little More Freedom: African Americans Enter the Urban Midwest, 1860–1930* (Columbus: Ohio State University Press, 2008), 89; Gerber, *Black Ohio and the Color Line*, 264.

10. *Cincinnati Commercial Gazette*, 12 and 14 April 1886.

11. Ibid., 8 June 1886; Minutes of the Cincinnati Board of Education, vol. 19 (24 May 1886 and 7 June 1886), Cincinnati Public School Administrative Offices; *Times-Star*, 8 June 1886; *New York Freeman*, 19 June 1886; *Cleveland Gazette*, 3 July 1886.

12. *Cleveland Gazette*, 29 May 1886, 26 June 1886, 3 and 24 July 1886; *Cincinnati Commercial Gazette*, 8 June 1886.

13. *New York Freeman*, 19 June 1886.

14. Ibid.; see also *Cleveland Gazette*, 19 and 26 June 1886.

15. *Cleveland Gazette*, 19 June 1886 and 3 July 1886.

16. Ibid., 19 June 1886 and 3 July 1886.

17. Cincinnati Board of Education, *Fifty-Eighth Annual Report of the Public Schools of Cincinnati for the School Year Ending August 31, 1887* (Cincinnati: Ohio Valley Publishing and Manufacturing, 1888), xiv–xv, 65–66, 98–99; *Cleveland Gazette*, 10 September 1887.

18. The *Cincinnati Commercial Gazette* and the *Cleveland Gazette* reported in early April 1886 that Peter Clark had been offered a position as the principal of a ward school and high school in Kansas City—even before he was terminated as the principal of the Colored Schools in Cincinnati. Perhaps he had applied for the Kansas job in anticipation of his termination (see *Cincinnati Commercial Gazette*, 11 April 1886; and *Cleveland Gazette*, 17 April 1886).

19. Harlan, ed. *The Booker T. Washington Papers*, ed. Louis R. Harlan (Urbana: University of Illinois Press, 1972), 2:382. Councill drafted his own biography in Simmons, *Men of Mark*, 390–93. August Meier, *Negro Thought in America 1880–1915: Racial Ideologies in the Age of Booker T. Washington* (Ann Arbor: University of Michigan Press, 1966), 209–10.

20. In 1898, John Temple Graves, a prominent Alabaman, stated that Councill was "the wisest, and most thoughtful, and the most eloquent Negro of his time—as discreet as Washington, a deeper thinker, and a more eloquent man" (Graves quoted in Horace Mann Bond, *Negro Education in Alabama: A Study in Cotton and Steel* [New York: Octagon, 1969], 204). Louis R. Harlan, *Booker T. Washington: The Making of a Black Leader 1856–1901* (New York: Oxford University Press, 1972), 169.

21. Harlan, ed., *Booker T. Washington Papers*, 2:382–83n.

22. *Huntsville Gazette*, 18 April 1885 and 7 May 1887.

23. *Cleveland Gazette*, 20 August 1887 and 10 September 1887; Harlan,

ed., *Booker T. Washington Papers,* 2:382–83; Meier, *Negro Thought in America 1880–1915,* 72, 209; Harlan, *Booker T. Washington,* 170.

24. Common Schools of Cincinnati, *Fifty-Sixth Annual Report for the School Year Ending August 31st 1885* (Cincinnati: Wilstach, Baldwin, 1885), 388, Cincinnati Historical Society; Harlan, ed., *Booker T. Washington Papers* 2:382.

25. *Cleveland Gazette,* 3 December 1887; Record of Proceedings of the Board of Trustees of the Ohio Agricultural and Mechanical College and the Ohio State University May 11, 1870, to June 25, 1890 (Columbus: Board of Trustees of the Ohio State University, n.d.), 352.

26. *Birmingham Era,* reprinted in *Cleveland Gazette,* 10 September 1887 and 4 August 1888; *Cleveland Gazette,* 10 September 1887; William Hooper Council to Booker T. Washington, 3 September 1887, in *Booker T. Washington Papers,* ed. Harlan, 2:382. By the 1890s, Council would routinely seek ex-Confederate officers to serve on the school's board of trustees. Horace Mann Bond, *Negro Education in Alabama: A Study in Cotton and Steel* (New York: Octagon, 1969), 204; Meier, *Negro Thought in America 1880–1915,* 209.

27. *Cleveland Gazette,* 4 August 1888; Meier, *Negro Thought in America 1880–1915,* 209.

28. *Cleveland Gazette,* 10 September 1887; *Birmingham Era,* reprinted in *Cleveland Gazette,* 10 September 1887.

29. Atticus G. Haygood to Rutherford B. Hayes, 5 June 1888, in *Teach the Freeman: The Correspondence of Rutherford B. Hayes and the Slater Fund for Negro Education 1888–1893,* ed. Louis D. Rubin Jr. (Shreveport: Louisiana State University Press, 1959), 2:19; *Birmingham Era,* reprinted in *Cleveland Gazette,* 10 September 1887.

30. *Southern Independent,* quoted in *Cleveland Gazette,* 4 August 1888.

31. Peter H. Clark to Rutherford B. Hayes, 10 September 1887; Peter H. Clark to Booker T. Washington, 16 January 1888, in *Booker T. Washington Papers,* ed. Harlan, 2:408.

32. *Huntsville Mercury,* quoted in *Huntsville Gazette,* 9 June 1888; *Huntsville Gazette,* 5 May 1888; Atticus Haygood to Rutherford B Hayes, 5 June 1888, in *Teach the Freeman,* ed. Rubin, 19; Peter H. Clark to Booker T. Washington, 16 January 1888, in *Booker T. Washington Papers,* ed. Harlan, 2:408; Harlan, *Booker T. Washington,* 170.

33. Randall B. Woods, "C. H. J. Taylor and the Movement for Black Political Independence, 1882–1896," *Journal of Negro History* (Summer 1982): 127.

34. *Cleveland Gazette,* 9 June 1888; Woods, "C. H. J. Taylor and the Movement for Black Political Independence, 1882–1896," 127–28; Bruce L. Mouser, *For Labor, Race, and Liberty: George Edwin Taylor, His Historic Run for the White House, and the Making of Independent Black Politics* (Madison: University of Wisconsin Press, 2011), 67.

35. Gary R. Kremer, *James Milton Turner and the Promise of America: The*

Public Life of a Post–Civil War Black Leader (Columbia: University of Missouri Press, 1991), 149.

36. Ibid., 150.

37. Woods, "C. H. J. Taylor and the Movement for Black Political Independence, 1882–1896," 128; *Indianapolis Freeman,* 25 and 28 July 1888; Kremer, *James Milton Turner and the Promise of America,* 151.

38. Charles H. J. Taylor had been born enslaved in Alabama in 1856 and taught himself to read. After Emancipation, he pursued a formal education, including a bachelor's degree in English from the University of Michigan. After graduating, Taylor spent some time in law school before being admitted to the Indiana Bar in 1877. He migrated to Kansas City, where he built a successful legal practice. Taylor had become a Democrat in 1884 for reasons similar to Clark: disappointment that no patronage position materialized for him after he invested a great deal of time and resources campaigning for the Republican gubernatorial candidate in 1884. Taylor immediately began editing a Democratic journal in Kansas City, *Public Educator.* He fared much better in terms of patronage as a Democrat than he had as a Republican: for example, he was appointed assistant attorney for Kansas City and then received the most enviable and coveted of all patronage plums when Grover Cleveland appointed him U.S. minister to Liberia in 1887. Although Taylor resigned shortly after reaching his post, his appointment confirmed his significance as an African American member of the party. *Indianapolis News,* 26 July 1888; *New York Times,* 27 July 1888; *Cleveland Gazette,* 28 July 1888; www.state.gov/r/pa/ho/po/com/10906.htm. On Taylor's life, see Woods, "C. H. J. Taylor and the Movement for Black Political Independence, 1882–1896," 123–24, 125.

39. *Indianapolis News,* 25 July 1888; *New York Times,* 26 July 1888.

40. *Indianapolis Freeman,* 26 and 28 July 1888; *New York Times,* 26 July 1888; *Cleveland Gazette,* 28 July 1888.

41. *Indianapolis News,* 26 July 1888; *Indianapolis Freeman,* 28 July 1888.

42. *Indianapolis Freeman*, 28 July 1888.

43. *New York Times,* 27 July 1888; *Indianapolis News,* 26 July 1888; *Indianapolis Freeman,* 28 July 1888.

44. Taken collectively, the resolutions were disjointed and lacked the signature clues of having been crafted or influenced by Peter H. Clark (*Indianapolis News,* 26 July 1888).

45. *Cleveland Gazette,* 28 July 1888; Bess Beatty, *A Revolution Gone Backward: The Black Response to National Politics, 1876–1896* (New York: Greenwood Press, 1987), 99.

46. Peter H. Clark to Frederick Douglass, 13 May 1889, Manuscript Division, Library of Congress.

47. G. D. Brantley, ed., *Ninetieth Anniversary Charles Sumner High School Saint Louis, Missouri: A Brief History,* 5–6.

48. Nikki Taylor, *Frontiers of Freedom: Cincinnati's Black Community, 1802–1868* (Athens: Ohio University Press, 2005), 3–4; Julie Winch, ed., *The*

Colored Aristocracy of St. Louis (Columbia: University of Missouri Press, 1999), 5–7 passim.

49. Willard B. Gatewood, *Aristocrats of Color: The Black Elite, 1880–1920* (Fayetteville: University of Arkansas Press, 2000), 119–20.

50. Peter H. Clark to Frederick Douglass, 13 May 1889, Manuscript Division, Library of Congress.

51. Meier, *Negro Thought in America 1880–1915*, 44, 50, 53.

52. Frederick Douglass, "The Nation's Problem," 1889 speech before the Bethel Literary and Historical Society, http://teachingamericanhistory.org/library/index .asp?document=494.

53. Peter H. Clark to Frederick Douglass, 13 May 1889, Manuscript Division, Library of Congress.

54. Meier, *Negro Thought in America 1880–1915*, 55.

55. Francis James Grimké, *The Works of Francis J. Grimké*, ed. Carter G. Woodson (Washington, D.C.: Associated Publishers, 1942), 1:280; *Cleveland Gazette,* 14 May 1892.

56. *Cleveland Gazette,* 14 and 21 May 1892; *Washington Bee,* 28 May 1892; Grimké, *Works of Francis J. Grimké,* 281; Lorenzo J. Greene, Gary Kremer, and Antonio F. Holland, *Missouri's Black Heritage* (Columbia: University of Missouri Press, 1993), 109. According to Greene, Kremer, and Holland, the national Day of Prayer had been initiated by Missouri's prominent African Americans, including James Milton Turner, Peter Clark, George B. Vashon, Walter Farmer, James Burgess, E. T. Cottman, Moses Dickson, and John W. Wheeler.

57. *Cleveland Gazette,* 14 and 21 May 1892; "To the Colored People of the United States and Their Friends," in Grimké, *Works of Francis J. Grimké,* 281.

58. *Cleveland Gazette,* 4 June 1892.

59. *New York Evangelist,* 2 June 1888; also quoted in Grimké, *Works of Francis J. Grimké,* 281–82.

60. Gerber, *Black Ohio and the Color Line, 1860–1915,* 252; Blocker, *A Little More Freedom,* 108–9; *Cleveland Gazette,* 5 May 1900.

61. Woods, "C. H. J. Taylor and the Movement for Black Political Independence, 1882–1896," 130; *Cleveland Gazette,* 3 December 1892.

62. Peter H. Clark to Frederick Douglass, 7 May 1893, Frederick Douglass Papers, Manuscript Division, Library of Congress.

63. Emma Lou Thornborough, *T. Thomas Fortune: Militant Journalist* (Chicago: University of Chicago Press, 1972), 107, 114; Paula J. Giddings, *Ida, A Sword among Lions: Ida B. Wells and the Campaign against Lynching* (New York: Amistad, 2008), 141.

64. Thornborough, *T. Thomas Fortune,* 121–22, 228–34 passim; Meier, *Negro Thought in America 1880–1915,* 173.

65. According to historian Benjamin Justesen, the convention's address to the nation had Washington's "unmistakable imprint" (Justesen, *Broken Brotherhood:*

The Rise and Fall of the National Afro-American Council [Carbondale: Southern Illinois University Press, 2008], 148).

66. *Indianapolis Freeman,* 17 September 1904; *Indianapolis Recorder,* 17 September 1904.

67. *Indianapolis Freeman,* 17 September 1904.

68. Justesen, *Broken Brotherhood,* 129, 148.

69. *St. Louis Globe-Democrat,* 4 February 1899.

70. In fact, Fortune charged that the very platforms of the latter organizations were duplications of the Afro-American League's platform (see Thornborough, *T. Thomas Fortune,* 269–70, 274; and Meier, *Negro Thought in America 1880–1915,* 178).

71. *Afro-American,* 20 July 1907.

72. *Cleveland Gazette,* 2 May 1903.

73. Certificate of Death: Board of Health, Youngstown Ohio; *Commercial Tribune,* 12 August 1902; *St. Louis Argus,* 26 June 1925.

74. *St. Louis Argus,* 26 June 1925.

10. "A Painted Lie"

1. *New York Freeman,* 3 January 1885.

2. His uncle John I. Gaines provided the sketch of Clark's life included in William Wells Brown, *The Rising Son; or, The Antecedents and Advancement of the Colored Race* (Boston: A. G. Brown, 1874), 522–24.

3. *New York Freeman,* 3 January 1885; Peter H. Clark, "Biographical Sketch of Peter H. Clark," n.d., William C. Breckenridge Papers, Western Historical Manuscript Collection, Columbia, Missouri.

4. *New York Freeman,* 3 January 1885.

5. Stephen Hall argues that African American historical writers like William C. Nell "used history to intervene in and contribute to contemporary debates about the failures and future of democracy" (Stephen G. Hall, *Faithful Account of the Race: African American Historical Writing in the Nineteenth-Century* [Chapel Hill: University of North Carolina Press, 2009], 97).

6. For more information on African Americans' role in the Battle of Lake Erie, see www.eriemaritimemuseum.org/maritime_museum/History/battle_of_lake_erie/ African_Americans_in_the_Battle.htm; and www.nps.gov/archive/pevi/html/afro-amer.html.

7. For a list of names of those killed or injured on Lake Erie during the War of 1812, see *American State Papers. Naval Affairs,* 1:566–72. The names are also recorded in Charles B. Galbreath, "The Battle of Lake Erie in Ballad and History," *Ohio Archaeological and Historical Publications* 20 (Columbus: Fred J. Herr, 1921), 440–56. See also www.liverpool.pa.net/pe1812.html; and http://files.usgwarchives .net/pa/perry/military/perry1812.txt. For more on African American service at the

Battle of Lake Erie, see http://www.eriemaritimemuseum.org/maritime_museum/History/battle_of_lake_erie/African_Americans_in_the_Battle.htm.

8. Eva Emery Dye, *The Conquest: The True Story of Lewis and Clark* (Chicago: A. C. McClurg, 1906).

9. Peter Clark to Eva Dye, 26 December 1900, Eva Emery Dye Collection, Oregon Historical Society.

10. Peter H. Clark, "Biographical Sketch of Peter H. Clark," n.d., William C. Breckenridge Papers, Western Historical Manuscript Collection, Columbia, Missouri; http://lewis-clark.org/content/content-article.asp?ArticleID=1890.

11. *New York Freeman,* 3 January 1885; Donald E. Jackson, ed., *Letters of the Lewis and Clark Expedition with Related Documents, 1783–1854* (Urbana: University of Illinois Press, 1962).

12. John Clark, Will probated October 1, 1799; Jefferson County, Kentucky, Court Inventory and Settlement, book 3: 3–14.

13. Brown, *Rising Son,* 522–24; *New York Freeman,* 3 January 1885; *Cleveland Gazette,* 6 March 1886 and 3 September 1887; William J. Simmons, *Men of Mark: Eminent, Progressive and Rising* (Cleveland: George M. Rewell, 1887), 374; Peter H. Clark, "Biographical Sketch of Peter H. Clark," n.d., William C. Breckenridge Papers, Western Historical Manuscript Collection, Columbia, Missouri.

14. Peter H. Clark to Eva Emery Dye, 26 December 1900.

15. Peter H. Clark, "Biographical Sketch of Peter H. Clark," n.d., William C. Breckenridge Papers, Western Historical Manuscript Collection, Columbia, Missouri.

16. Ernestine Garret Lucas, *Wider Windows to the Past: African-American History from a Family Perspective* (Decorah, IA: Anundsen, 1995), 98. For descendants' views, the author refers to unpublished private e-mails between Walter Herz and some of Clark's descendants who now live as whites and wish their relationship to him to remain secret.

17. David W. Blight, ed., *Passages to Freedom: The Underground Railroad in History and Memory* (Washington, D.C.: Smithsonian Books, 2004), 6.

18. Dovie King Clark, "Peter Humphries Clark," *Negro History Bulletin* 5 (May 1942): 176.

19. *St. Louis American,* 22 September 1964. This article compares the life of the pioneer explorer William Clark with that of the pioneer educator Peter H. Clark. Secondary sources that repeat this connection are: Wilhemena S. Robinson, *Historical Negro Biographies* (New York: Association for the Study of Negro Life and History, 1969), 64; Paul McStallsworth, "Peter Humphries Clark," in *Dictionary of American Negro Biography,* ed. Rayford W. Logan and Michael R. Winston (New York: Norton, 1982), 114; David Gerber, "Peter Humphries Clark," in *American National Biography,* ed. John Garraty and Mark Carnes (New York: Oxford University Press, 1999), 943; David Gerber, "Peter Humphries Clark: The Dialogue of Hope and Despair," in *Black Leaders of the Nineteenth Century,* ed.

Leon Litwack and August Meier (Urbana: University of Illinois Press, 1988), 175; William Cheek and Aimee Lee Cheek, *John Mercer Langston and the Fight for Black Freedom 1829–65* (Urbana: University of Illinois Press, 1989), 151; Philip S. Foner and Robert James Branham, *Lift Every Voice: African American Oratory 1787–1900* (Tuscaloosa: University of Alabama Press, 1998), 580; and J. Blaine Hudson, "Slavery in Early Louisville and Jefferson County, Kentucky, 1780–1812," *Filson Club History Quarterly* 73 (July 1999): 277–78.

20. Lucas, *Wider Windows to the Past,* 94, 96.

21. F. A. Sampson to William C. Breckenridge, 4 December 1906, William C. Breckenridge Papers, Western Historical Manuscript Collection, Columbia, Missouri.

22. Gary R. Kremer, *James Milton Turner and the Promise of America: The Public Life of a Post–Civil War Black Leader* (Columbia: University of Missouri Press, 1991), 8–9.

23. Blight, *Passages to Freedom,* 6.

24. Ibid., 4.

Selected Bibliography

Adeleke, Tunde. *UnAfrican Americans: Nineteenth-Century Black Nationalists and the Civilizing Mission.* Lexington: University Press of Kentucky, 1998.

Beatty, Bess. *A Revolution Gone Backward: The Black Response to National Politics, 1876–1896.* New York: Greenwood Press, 1987.

Bond, Horace Mann. *Negro Education in Alabama: A Study in Cotton and Steel.* New York: Octagon, 1969.

Berlin, Ira. *Slaves without Masters: The Free Negro in the Antebellum South.* New York: Vintage, 1974.

Blackett, R. J. M. *Beating against the Barriers: The Lives of Six Nineteenth-Century Afro-Americans.* Ithaca: Cornell University Press, 1986.

Blight, David W., ed. *Passages to Freedom: The Underground Railroad in History and Memory.* Washington, D.C.: Smithsonian Books, 2004.

Bracey, John, August Meier, and Elliot Rudwick, eds. *Blacks in the Abolitionist Movement.* Belmont, CA: Wadsworth, 1971.

Burin, Eric. *Slavery and the Peculiar Solution: A History of the American Colonization Society.* Gainesville: University Press of Florida, 2005.

Calhoun, Charles W. *Conceiving a New Republic: The Republican Party and the Southern Question, 1869–1900.* Lawrence: University Press of Kansas, 2006.

Cheek, William, and Aimee Lee Cheek. *John Mercer Langston and the Fight for Black Freedom 1829–65.* Urbana: University of Illinois Press, 1989.

Christensen, Lawrence O. "Peter Humphries Clark." *Missouri Historical Review* 88 (January 1994): 145–56.

Du Bois, W. E. B. *Black Reconstruction in America 1860–1880.* New York: Atheneum, 1992.

Fishel, Leslie H. "Repercussions of Reconstruction: The Northern Negro, 1870–1883." *Civil War History* 14 (December 1968): 325–45.

Floyd-Thomas, Juan M. *The Origins of Black Humanism in America: Reverend Ethelred Brown and the Unitarian Church.* New York: Palgrave Macmillan, 2008.

Foner, Eric. *Free Soil, Free Labor, Free Men: The Ideology of the Republican Party before the Civil War.* New York: Oxford University Press, 1970.

———. *Reconstruction: America's Unfinished Revolution, 1863–1877.* New York: Harper and Row, 1988.

Foner, Philip S. *American Socialism and Black Americans: From the Age of Jackson to World War II.* Westport, CT: Greenwood Press, 1977.

———. *Frederick Douglass: A Biography.* New York: Citadel Press, 1964.

———. *A History of the Labor Movement in the United States: From Colonial Times to the Founding of the American Federation of Labor.* Vol. 1. New York: International, 1972.

———. "Peter H. Clark: Pioneer Black Socialist." *Journal of Ethnic Studies* 5, no. 3 (Fall 1977): 17–35.

———. *The Workingmen's Party of the United States: A History of the First Marxist Party in the Americas.* Minneapolis: MEP, 1984.

Franklin, John Hope. *George Washington Williams: A Biography.* Chicago: University of Chicago Press, 1985.

———. *Reconstruction after the Civil War.* Chicago: University of Chicago Press, 1994.

Franklin, V. P. *Black Self-Determination: A Cultural History of the Faith of the Fathers.* New York: Lawrence Hill, 1992.

Gerber, David. *Black Ohio and the Color Line, 1860–1915.* Urbana: University of Illinois Press, 1976.

Glasraud, Bruce A. "Beginning the Trek: Douglass, Bruce, Black Conventions, Independent Political Parties." In *African Americans and the Presidency: The Road to the White House,* edited by Bruce A. Glasraud and Cary D. Wintz. New York: Routledge, 2010.

Green, Adam, and Charles M. Payne, eds. *Time Longer Than Rope: A Century of African American Activism, 1850–1950.* New York: New York University Press, 2003.

Grossman, Lawrence. *The Democratic Party and the Negro: Northern and National Politics 1868–92.* Urbana: University of Illinois Press, 1976.

———. "In His Veins Coursed No Bootlicking Blood: The Career of Peter Clark." *Ohio History* 2 (Spring 1977): 79–95.

Gutman, Herbert. "Peter H. Clark: Pioneer Negro Socialist, 1877." *Journal of Negro Education* 34 (September 1965): 413–18.

Hahn, Steven. *A Nation under Our Feet: Black Political Struggles in the Rural South from Slavery to the Great Migration.* Cambridge: Harvard University Press, 2003.

Harding, Vincent. *There Is a River: The Black Struggle for Freedom in America.* San Diego: Harcourt Brace Jovanovich, 1981.

Herz, Walter P. "Influence Transcending Mere Numbers: The Unitarians in Nineteenth-Century Cincinnati." *Queen City Heritage* 51 (Winter 1993): 3–22.

Honeck, Mischa. *German-Speaking Immigrants and American Abolitionists after 1848.* Athens: University of Georgia Press, 2011.

Horton, James Oliver, and Lois E. Horton. *In Hope of Liberty: Culture, Community and Protest among Northern Free Blacks 1700–1860*. New York: Oxford University Press, 1997.

James, Joy. *Transcending the Talented Tenth: Black Leaders and American Intellectuals*. New York: Routledge, 1997.

Justesen, Benjamin R. *Broken Brotherhood: The Rise and Fall of the National Afro-American Council*. Carbondale: Southern Illinois University Press, 2008.

Kachun, Mitch. *Festivals of Freedom: Memory and Meaning in African American Emancipation Celebrations 1808–1915*. Amherst: University of Massachusetts Press, 2003.

Kremer, Gary R. *James Milton Turner and the Promise of America: The Public Life of a Post–Civil War Black Leader*. Columbia: University of Missouri Press, 1991.

Levine, Bruce. *The Spirit of 1848: German Immigrants, Labor Conflict, and the Coming of the Civil War*. Urbana: University of Illinois Press, 1992.

Litwack, Leon. *North of Slavery: The Free Negro in the Free States 1790–1860*. Chicago: University of Chicago, 1961.

Litwack, Leon, and August Meier, eds. *Black Leaders of the Nineteenth Century*. Urbana: University of Illinois Press, 1988.

Lucas, Ernestine Garret. *Wider Windows to the Past: African-American History from a Family Perspective*. Decorah, IA: Anundsen, 1995.

Maizlish, Stephen E. *The Triumph of Sectionalism: The Transformation of Ohio Politics 1844–1856*. Kent, OH: Kent State University Press, 1983.

Marable Manning, and Leith Mullings, eds. *Let Nobody Turn Us Around: Voices of Resistance, Reform, and Renewal*. New York: Rowman and Littlefield, 2003.

Martin, Waldo E. *The Mind of Frederick Douglass*. Chapel Hill: University of North Carolina Press, 1984.

Meier, August. *Negro Thought in America 1880–1915: Racial Ideologies in the Age of Booker T. Washington*. Ann Arbor: University of Michigan Press, 1963.

Messer-Kruse, Timothy. *The Yankee International: Marxism and the American Reform Tradition*. Chapel Hill: University of Chapel Hill Press, 1998.

Miller, Floyd J. *The Search for a Black Nationality: Black Emigration and Colonization 1787–1863*. Urbana: University of Illinois Press, 1975.

Miller, Zane. *Boss Cox's Cincinnati: Urban Politics in the Progressive Era*. New York: Oxford University Press, 1968.

Morris, James M. "William Haller: 'The Disturbing Element.'" *Cincinnati Historical Society Bulletin* 28 (Winter 1970): 259–93.

Moses, Wilson Jeremiah Moses. *Creative Conflict in African American Thought: Frederick Douglass, Alexander Crummell, Booker T. Washington, W. E. B. Du Bois, and Marcus Garvey*. New York: Cambridge University Press, 2004.

———. *The Golden Age of Black Nationalism, 1850–1925*. New York: Oxford University Press, 1978.

Mouser, Bruce L. *For Labor, Race, and Liberty: George Edwin Taylor, His Historic Run for the White House, and the Making of Independent Black Politics.* Madison: University of Wisconsin Press, 2011.

Nelson, Craig. *Thomas Paine: Enlightenment, Revolution, and the Birth of Modern Nations.* New York: Viking, 2006.

Painter, Nell. *Exodusters: Black Migration to Kansas after Reconstruction.* New York: Norton, 1976.

Pease, Jane H., and William H. Pease. *They Who Would Be Free: Blacks' Search for Freedom, 1830–1861.* Urbana: University of Illinois Press, 1990.

Perry, Jeffrey P. *Hubert Harrison: The Voice of Harlem Radicalism, 1883–1918.* New York: Columbia University Press, 2009.

Quarles, Benjamin. *Black Mosaic: Essays in Afro-American History and Historiography.* Amherst: University of Massachusetts Press, 1988.

Quillin, Frank. *The Color Line in Ohio: A History of Race Prejudice in a Typical Northern State.* Ann Arbor: George Wahr, 1913.

Rabinowitz, Howard N., ed. *Southern Black Leaders of the Reconstruction Era.* Urbana: University of Illinois Press, 1982.

Rael, Patrick, ed. *African-American Activism before the Civil War: The Freedom Struggle in the Antebellum North.* New York: Routledge, 2008.

———. *Black Identity & Black Protest in the Antebellum North.* Chapel Hill: University of North Carolina Press, 2002.

Reed, Adolph, and Kenneth W. Warren, eds. *Renewing Black Intellectual History: The Ideological and Material Foundations of African American Thought.* Boulder: Paradigm, 2010.

Richardson, Heather Cox Richardson. *The Death of Reconstruction: Race, Labor, and Politics in the Post-Civil War North, 1865–1901.* Cambridge: Harvard University Press, 2001.

Robinson, Cedric J. *Black Marxism: The Making of the Black Radical Tradition.* Chapel Hill: University of North Carolina Press, 1983.

Said, Edward W. *Representations of the Intellectual.* New York: Vintage, 1994.

Slap, Andrew. *The Doom of Reconstruction: The Liberal Republicans in the Civil War Era.* New York: Fordham University Press, 2006.

Stauffer, John. *The Black Hearts of Men: Radical Abolitionists and the Transformation of Race.* Cambridge: Harvard University Press, 2001.

Stuckey, Sterling. *Slave Culture: Nationalist Theory & the Foundations of Black America.* New York: Oxford University Press, 1987.

Summers, Mark Wahlgren. *Party Games: Getting, Keeping, and Using Power in Gilded Age Politics.* Chapel Hill: University of North Carolina Press, 2004.

Taylor, Nikki. *Frontiers of Freedom: Cincinnati's Black Community 1802–68.* Athens: Ohio University Press, 2005.

Walton, Hanes, Jr. *Black Politics: A Theoretical and Structural Analysis.* Philadelphia: Lippincott, 1972.

————. *Black Republicans: The Politics of the Black and Tans.* Metuchen, NJ: Scarecrow Press, 1975.

————. *The Negro in Third Party Politics.* Philadelphia: Dorrance, 1969.

Walton, Hanes, and Vernon Gray. "Black Politics at the Demographic and Republican Conventions, 1868–1972." *Phylon* 36 (1975): 269–78.

Index

PHC *is an abbreviation of Peter H. Clark.*

CPSIA information can be obtained at www.ICGtesting.com
Printed in the USA
BVOW011632030313

314547BV00002B/6/P

9 780813 140773

did he ever met F. Douglass?